The Encyclopaedia of Midstream and Downstream Oil and Gas

Globe Law and Business

Second Edition

Consulting Editors **Professor Eduardo G Pereira, Professor Kim Talus** and **Reg Fowler**

Consulting editors
Eduardo G Pereira, Kim Talus and Reg Fowler

Managing director
Sian O'Neill

The Encyclopaedia of Midstream and Downstream Oil and Gas, Second Edition
is published by

Globe Law and Business Ltd
3 Mylor Close
Horsell
Woking
Surrey GU21 4DD
United Kingdom
Tel: +44 20 3745 4770
www.globelawandbusiness.com

Printed and bound by CPI Group (UK) Ltd, Croydon CR0 4YY, United Kingdom

The Encyclopaedia of Midstream and Downstream Oil and Gas, Second Edition

ISBN 9781787429406
EPUB ISBN 9781787429413
Adobe PDF ISBN 9781787429420

Table of contents

Introduction

Eduardo G Pereira
Professor of natural resources and energy law
Kim Talus
University of Eastern Finland Law School; Tulane University;
University of Helsinki
Reg Fowler
New Age African Global Energy

The first volume of *The Encyclopaedia of Oil and Gas Law* focused on upstream petroleum – that is, the exploration and production of oil and gas. It thus focused on regulatory and contractual issues connected to oil and gas exploration and production. In addition to purely national regulatory and contractual frameworks, it also covered the relevant international law rules that impact on operations in this area. The relevant agreements and contracts were further examined in detail.

This second volume of *The Encyclopaedia of Oil and Gas Law* focuses on downstream (including midstream) issues. It looks at the central regulatory and contractual issues in downstream energy markets. The regulatory and contractual mechanisms, as well as the underlying policy choices, are profoundly different in upstream and downstream energy. We have discussed this in detail elsewhere.[1] In that context, we used two different expressions to explain the difference:

> *'Energy law and policy' is about markets, security of supply and efficiency. It is about government policies to secure energy sources at least possible costs, including social costs. The modern energy policy typically rests on the markets, at least to some extent, to provide for efficiency and security. Government energy policy is geared to provide constant low-cost supply of energy for the competitiveness of the national economy as a whole.*
>
> *In contrast with this, 'resources law and policy' is about government strategy to maximise revenue and to exercise sovereignty. It is often related to more general development policies of the country. Here, the government policy rests on the idea of maximising resource rent. The objective is to attract as much revenue from the resources before depletion as possible. The revenue is then (ideally, though not always in practice) used to develop the overall economy or other similar objectives. The strategy is not very different in terms of energy resources and other types of resources, say precious metals or similar.*

1 See E Pereira and K Talus, "National Petroleum Supply Reservations: Background and Comparison", *Journal of World Energy Law and Business* 7 (2014) 6.

The difference is striking; and it is also reflected in the content of the two volumes of *The Encyclopaedia of Oil and Gas Law*. Where the first volume focused on issues such as petroleum taxation, government take, production sharing contracts and other granting instruments, national constitutions and petroleum law, health and safety, financing and other issues, the focus of this second volume dealing with downstream energy is very different. Issues covered include regulation of energy storage, purchase and transportation contracts, regulation of access conditions to transmission and distribution networks, unbundling, marketing and trading and other similar issues. Of course, given that the book is written for practitioners rather than academics, certain issues are addressed in both the upstream and downstream volumes. Taxation is one example of this; as is the environment. Regulations in both areas have a direct impact on commercial operations.

The purpose of this new edition is not to provide each detail of every national framework for downstream petroleum. Instead, the main objective is to provide an overview of those areas of downstream oil and gas operations that are central in practice. We consider the key issues that any company or individual that looks at the opportunities presented in downstream oil and gas needs to know. We have edited this book with an eye on the increasing role of liquefied natural gas in the current energy market, as well as small and medium-sized upstream oil and gas companies looking to expand to downstream markets; traders and investors that examine the opportunities in this market segment; and junior practitioners who need to get a full picture of the oil and gas markets and their regulation, as well as contractual frameworks.

The opinions expressed in this book are the authors' and are not necessarily representative of the opinions of their respective employer entities.

Downstream and domestic price subsidies: an overview

Reg Fowler
New Age African Global Energy

---

1. Introduction

The purpose of this chapter is to provide brief insight into the critical issue of petroleum and natural gas subsidies. This is one of the key challenges that must be addressed if society is to remain on target to achieve net zero by 2050.[1] According to some estimates, the real level of petroleum and natural gas price subsidisation, if the economic costs of global warming and local pollution are factored into pricing, reaches $4.2 trillion.[2] Much of those costs are incurred in least developed countries where private and public investment in the clean energy transition is most needed. The last decade – particularly since the Paris Agreement – has seen uneven progress towards moderate price liberalisation and subsidy reform. That progress was not so much disturbed as upended by Russia's invasion of Ukraine in 2022. Present estimates suggest that Organisation for Economic Co-operation and Development (OECD) countries alone are spending upwards of $550 billion on increased and new forms of price subsidy.[3] Natural gas prices are now more expensive in some states than the aggregate of the cost of supply and implicit costs such as global warming and pollution associated with natural gas consumption. Two questions arise: first, will governments find the political will to overcome popular reluctance to pay higher retail prices for transportation and heating fuel, as well as electricity? Second, how will the so-called 'windfall' delivered by remarkable increases in retail gas and electricity prices be distributed between governments and between the public and private sector – and will any of that revenue be redirected to energy transition investments?

---

1 See, for example, Bloomberg NEF, "Climate Policy Factbook: Three Priority Areas for Climate Action", July 2021, www.un.org%2Fsites%2Fun2.un.org%2Ffiles%2F2021%2F07%2Fbp_bnef_climate_policy_factbook_071921_final35.pdf&usg=AOvVaw1PmeZdmPcdUHLf_MuORZrd.

2 Richard Bridle, Shruti Sharma, Mostafa Mostafa and Anna Geddes, "Fossil Fuel to Clean Energy Subsidy Swaps: How to Pay for an Energy Revolution" (IISD 2019), www.iisd.org/articles/fossil-fuel-clean-energy-subsidy-swap; Ian Parry, Simon Black and Nate Vernon "Still not getting energy prices right: a global in country update of fossil fuel subsidies", IMF Working Paper WP/21/236, www.imf.org/en/Publications/WP/Issues/2021/09/23/Still-Not-Getting-Energy-Prices-Right-A-Global-and-Country-Update-of-Fossil-Fuel-Subsidies-466004.

3 International Energy Agency, "World Energy Outlook 2022", www.iea.org/reports/world-energy-outlook-2022.

2. Subsidies and energy markets

The energy supply chain is notoriously complex. One of those complexities arises from the interplay of regulated and deregulated markets in that chain. The crude oil market is famously liquid, and apparently deregulated – although decisions of the Organization of the Petroleum Exporting Countries continue to interfere with ordinary wholesale price fluctuations driven by supply and demand. That price volatility has led to periods of underinvestment in production capacity, which in turn has exacerbated oil price spikes as crude oil demand recovers from slumps. The same lack of capacity can also have a significant effect in the refinery market, which is struggling with new environmental regulations and the switch away from high-sulphur fuel oil. Retail gasoline and diesel prices are, if not regulated, then heavily influenced by a combination of consumption taxation and direct government subsidies. The combination is toxic: when states – particularly developing countries, but increasingly in recent times OECD countries – strive to maintain retail petroleum prices within domestically acceptable boundaries, they expose themselves to uncontrolled budget expenditure for the simple reason that the wholesale prices remain beyond their powers to influence.

The picture with respect to natural gas is different. Liquefied natural gas is fast becoming a globally traded commodity; but again, the cost of the necessary transportation infrastructure will likely limit its contribution to the natural gas supply equation. For those states that are reliant on natural gas for domestic and industrial fuel supply, the market will remain regional, defined by fixed pipeline distribution networks. Where the producer-consumer partnership built around that distribution network breaks down – as has catastrophically been the case with respect to the supply of Russian pipeline gas to Europe – the switch to alternative supply sources is inevitably expensive, driving competition for spot liquefied natural gas (LNG) cargoes in the short term and a rush to invest in LNG infrastructure and indigenous gas supply in the medium to longer term. Russian pipeline gas was purchased by Europe on long-term supply agreements, which were often priced against a basket of commodity prices including crude oil. Such pricing mechanisms might have insulated Europe from the worst of the natural gas price increases; instead, terminating them has increased Europe's exposure to spot market prices.

Europe is a special case where the retail market for natural gas is particularly strong. In Europe and elsewhere, natural gas is a power generation feedstock, competing with coal and renewables. Where regional natural gas prices have spiked, electricity prices have also increased dramatically, yielding a so-called 'windfall' for other power generators not exposed to wholesale natural gas prices.[4]

4 *Financial Times*, "Windfall taxes: good politics, tricky policy", 5 November 2022, www.ft.com/content/bab495e0-ec4d-4026-a13d-1aad9fcc0805.

Some states find themselves obliged to subsidise retail electricity prices to protect consumers and industry,[5] while simultaneously seeking to recover excess profits from such power generators in compensation – and to avoid deterring investment in renewable energy generation.[6]

3. Defining and quantifying subsidies

Defining what constitutes a fossil fuel subsidy is a controversial issue. Explicit subsidies are subsidies which a government intentionally puts in place to achieve a certain domestic price effect.[7] In OECD countries, this might take the form of tax rebates (or what are sometimes termed 'feebates'). In developing countries, state price fixing or price capping is more common, with direct grants also being used. The OECD measures subsidies in terms of a state's forgone revenues, estimating the cost to the state budget of implementing the relevant measure. The International Energy Agency (IEA) has taken a different approach, measuring the difference between the global market price for the subsidised commodity and the local price influenced by subsidisation.[8] The latter approach brings home the real economic cost of subsidisation, but neither approach properly takes into account the human cost of fossil fuel use.

In support of Sustainable Development Goal Indicator 12.C.1, the OECD, the IEA and the International Monetary Fund (IMF) are working together to encourage governments to report their subsidisation policies, and to combine their databases in order to enhance public understanding of the scale and impact of price intervention.[9]

The IMF has published a study which seeks to assess what it terms the 'implicit costs' of fossil fuel subsidisation, estimating the impact of consuming coal, gasoline, road diesel and natural gas in terms of climate change, local air pollution and road congestion costs.[10] Pricing in these externalities has a dramatic effect, leading the authors of the IMF report to conclude that up to $4.3 trillion in implicit and explicit costs could be saved by eliminating the subsidies – a figure equivalent to 3.8% of global gross domestic product (GDP). There is a trade-off – eliminating subsidies will give rise to an efficiency cost of 1% GDP, offset by environmental benefits equivalent to 3.1% of GDP. Such price reform may cause global carbon emissions to be reduced by as much as

---

5 *The Economist*, "As energy prices spike, governments reach for the dirtiest tool in the box", www.economist.com/finance-and-economics/2021/10/30/as-energy-prices-spike-governments-reach-for-the-dirtiest-tool-in-the-box.

6 *Financial Times*, "How to make a mess of an energy windfall tax", 11 October 2022, www.ft.com/content/89fd7fa9-ac2a-48b1-89c3-0db6237bb4b6.

7 This chapter adopts the terminology used by Ian Parry *et al* (n 2).

8 International Institute for Sustainable Development, "Background Note on Fossil Fuel Subsidy Reform, 2022, www.iisd.org%2Fsystem%2Ffiles%2F2022-08%2Fbackground-note-fossil-fuel-subsidy-reform.pdf.

9 International Institute for Sustainable Development "A Guidebook to Reviews of Fossil Fuel Subsidies: from Self-Reports to Peer Learning", 2017, www.iisd.org%2Fsystem%2Ffiles%2Fpublications%2Fguidebook-reviews-fossil-fuels-subsidies.pdf.

10 Parry *et al* (n 2).

36%, as well as delivering significant budget savings, potentially freeing up sufficient revenues to 'plug the gap' between current public investment levels in the energy transition and the level of investment needed to achieve Paris Agreement objectives.

4. A short history of fossil fuel subsidy reform

In its Pittsburgh Leaders' statement, in 2009, the G20 announced that it would commit to: "Rationalize and phase out over the medium term inefficient fossil fuel subsidies that encourage wasteful consumption. As we do that, we recognize the importance of providing those in need with essential energy services, including through the use of targeted cash transfers and other appropriate mechanisms."[11]

Seven years later, the G7 included the following in its Ise Shima Declaration: "We are committed to moving quickly in taking steps to address this issue by enhancing market function, including through coordinated actions that identify and seek to eliminate such subsidies and support ..."[12]

This professed switch away from inefficient and indiscriminate subsidisation to targeted support for vulnerable groups was only partially implemented until 2021 and was then derailed by the onset of the conflict in Ukraine. Inefficient subsidies apparently peaked in 2011, declining progressively over the following five years. In the period before the COVID-19 pandemic, the picture was more nuanced. China reduced its fossil fuel subsidies by 10%, predominantly by removing price support for fuel used by the fishing industry. Countries such as Kazakhstan, Zimbabwe, Libya and Ukraine also reduced subsidy levels.[13] The OECD introduced a series of peer group engagements between OECD and developing economies. Mexico and Indonesia were both supported in their strategy of aligning domestic fuel and electricity prices with the prevailing international marketplace. Mexico's introduction of a floating excise tax turned a budget surplus. Most progress was achieved by 2018 – not so much through political action as because lower wholesale prices for fossil fuels and energy narrowed the gap between efficient prices and subsidised prices.

The peak of recent progress was reached in 2018; in 2019, producer countries introduced subsidies to protect the upstream industry from continued lower prices and revenues.[14] Argentina introduced retail price caps, partly to offset a currency crisis. In the period between 2014 and 2017, Indonesia had made significant efforts to realign domestic prices with international prices, but it reversed its progress on

---

11 www.oecd.org/g20/summits/pittsburgh/G20-Pittsburgh-Leaders-Declaration.pdf.

12 www.consilium.europa.eu/en/press/press-releases/2016/05/27/g7-japan-leaders-declaration/#:~:text=Today%2C%20we%20have%20demonstrated%20our,and%20prosperity%20of%20the%20world.

13 OECD, *OECD Companion to the Inventory of Support Measures for Fossil Fuels 2021*, www.oecd-ilibrary.org/environment/oecd-companion-to-the-inventory-of-support-measures-for-fossil-fuels-2021_e670c620-en.

14 IEA, "Fossil fuel consumption subsidies bounced back strongly in 2018 – Analysis", June 2019, www.iea.org/commentaries/fossil-fuel-consumption-subsidies-bounced-back-strongly-in-2018.

price reform through domestic fuel and electricity price freezes as well as support for the state-owned wholesale sector. India – which had steadily eliminated its support for LPG prices since 2015 – elected to reintroduce a means-tested scheme of price support, increasing the number of supported households by 80 million in 2019. LPG consumption significantly increased as a result.

The onset of COVID-19 destroyed demand in the transportation fuel sector, bringing the wholesale prices of crude oil, aviation fuel, road diesel and gasoline to their lowest points in 30 years. Natural gas consumption was not so significantly affected. The global spend on price support reduced accordingly without any significant policy action from states themselves. It was widely expected and hoped that states would take the opportunity to reduce price support while wholesale prices were low, at levels that might be tolerated domestically. Some countries did follow this course of action – Nigeria announced in June 2020 that it would phase out petrol subsidies and allocate the budget surplus arising to its post-COVID recovery initiatives.[15] While increasing support for LPG consumption, India increased taxes on transportation fuels, as did Costa Rica. Tunisia also set about aligning domestic prices with international prices.

These initiatives come with significant political risk. The *'gilets jaunes'* movement in France was triggered by increases in government-controlled electricity and gas prices.[16] Even before the COVID-19 pandemic, governments in Iran[17] and Ecuador[18] faced civil unrest due to changes to state-controlled energy prices. The removal of liquefied petroleum gas subsidies triggered unrest and appalling levels of loss of life in Kazakhstan in January 2022.[19]

In some cases, maintaining price support has formed a necessary part of COVID-19 recovery packages, particularly in economies where transportation costs absorb significant disposable income. Global economic recovery post-COVID-19 also fed into a sharp recovery in wholesale crude oil and natural gas prices, accentuated by the lack of investment in supply before and during the pandemic. Even before Russia's invasion of Ukraine, producer countries were trying to encourage rapid investment in new supply sources by increasing production subsidies. In 2020 alone, countries such as Argentina, Brazil,

15 E Bala-Gbogbo, "Oil Crash Spurs Nigeria to End Fuel Subsidies, Risk Backlash", Bloomberg, 2020, www.bloomberg.com/news/articles/2020-05-09/oil-crash-spurs-nigeria-toend-fuel-subsidies-risk-backlash.

16 *Financial Times*, "France to block gas and electricity price rises until the spring", 30 September 2021, www.ft.com/content/f11a62dc-1a71-437f-a7a5-493bc4b1dcda.

17 *The Economist*, "Rises in the price of petrol are fuelling unrest in Iran", 23 November 2019, www.economist.com/middle-east-and-africa/2019/11/21/rises-in-the-price-of-petrol-are-fuelling-unrest-in-iran.

18 *The Economist*, "Governments subsidise fossil fuels to the tune of $427bn a year", 14 October 2019, www.economist.com/graphic-detail/2019/10/14/governments-subsidise-fossil-fuels-to-the-tune-of-427bn-a-year.

19 Business and Human Rights Resource Centre, "Kazakhstan: Dramatic price hike for liquefied petroleum gas triggers mass protests", 3 January 2022, www.business-humanrights.org/en/latest-news/kazakhstan-dramatic-price-hike-for-liquefied-petroleum-gas-triggers-mass-protests/.

Indonesia, Mexico and Norway introduced measures costing upwards of $25 billion, including reduction in oil royalties, enhanced capital allowances for fast-track investments and bailout packages for national oil companies.[20] The United Kingdom has since followed Norway's lead in providing capital tax allowances to fresh investment and has recently declared a 33rd bidding round for offshore petroleum licences.[21]

Russia's invasion of Ukraine has effectively put an end to further hope of combining COVID-19 recovery plans with strategic reductions in fossil fuel price support. It has done far more than that: as a result of Russian natural gas supply being decoupled from European markets, natural gas prices in Europe have increased to a point where they far exceed implicit and explicit costs for natural gas consumption as estimated by the IMF. Current retail gasoline prices in Germany and the United Kingdom are nearly three times the combined supply and subsidy cost, as assessed by Parry *et al* in the IMF study. The current situation is the same for natural gas prices in Germany and Japan, where consumers are paying $60 and $30 per gigajoule respectively. In other words, European consumers are now paying a form of penalty for consuming natural gas, well beyond the efficient price; but that benefit is not flowing into energy transition investments or to state budgets, enabling the latter to offset price increases with domestic price support strategies.

This in large measure has justified calls across Europe for new tax measures to extract a share of such windfall profits, to replenish state budgets and finance measures to ease the cost-of-living crisis, particularly with respect to retail energy costs. While politically attractive, the strategy cuts across others. It deters oil and gas companies from investment in fresh supply. It also fails to take into account that Western oil companies earn the bulk of their profits from investments elsewhere in the globe, where their 'windfall' profits have already been taxed.

Renewable energy suppliers are also benefiting from this windfall and – in advanced economies at least – are additionally the beneficiaries of significant levels of subsidisation. In its World Energy Outlook 2022, the IEA states that advanced economies invested more than $1 trillion in renewable energy sources in the period March 2022 to September 2022; the figure for emerging market and developing countries in the same period was less than $100 billion. Advanced economies invested at least $400 billion in short-term retail energy price support in the year to September 2022; the figure for emerging market and developing countries in the same period was more than $200 billion.[22]

Many commentators have argued that the Ukraine crisis presents a renewed

---

20 OECD, *OECD Companion to the Inventory of Support Measures for Fossil Fuels 2021*, Table 1, www.oecd-ilibrary.org/environment/oecd-companion-to-the-inventory-of-support-measures-for-fossil-fuels-2021_e670c620-en.

21 North Sea Transition Authority, "Licensing rounds", www.nstauthority.co.uk/licensing-consents/licensing-rounds/.

22 IEA, "World Energy Outlook 2022", Figure 2.10.

opportunity to accelerate the clean energy transition – and a more compelling one, because indigenous clean energy production also delivers security of supply, when energy supply and energy prices are being weaponised by the protagonists.[23] However, there are at least three problems with this optimism.

First, the economics of clean energy investment and subsidisation are exposed to some of the same complexities that affect domestic petroleum pricing: clean energy sources such as solar and wind feed into national grids which are also supplied by national and international sources of fossil fuel and renewable energy, often at electricity prices fixed by international or regional markets. The future energy supply chain promises to be no less complex than the existing one. Accordingly, the best-laid plans for attracting clean energy investment by subsidies may not survive the first contact with international electricity prices. The complete liberalisation of energy markets may not be possible given the need to blend interruptible renewable sources such as solar and wind with backup non-renewable sources such as nuclear power.

Second, the profits generated by the present energy crisis are not flowing where they are needed to finance the energy transition. As the IEA and others have pointed out,[24] there is an urgent need to redirect public and particularly private finance for green energy to the Global South, where fossil fuel consumption is still climbing because of population increase; and to countries heavily impacted by high energy prices and the food crisis triggered by the disruption of grain exports from the Black Sea. Instead, those profits have flown to renewable energy companies operating in the Global North and enjoying significant fiscal subsidies, or to international and state-run oil and gas companies, at a point in time when they are being incentivised by subsidies to increase production, to plug the hole left by Russian supply. Private investors in both the renewable and oil and gas sectors are unlikely to be encouraged to invest by the ongoing unpredictability of price support strategies.

Lastly, there probably is insufficient supply of key metals to manufacture renewable energy technology at sufficient scale and pace to make a significant impact on present wholesale energy prices. Concerns that there is insufficient metal ore globally for the purpose are overstated, but the mining capacity in place cannot be scaled up fast enough to keep up with price volatility.[25] In that sense, economic history may repeat itself, as electricity price volatility may still be driven in the future by troughs in investment, leaving supply lagging behind demand in periods of economic recovery, following the pattern set by the hydrocarbon era.

---

23 *Financial Times*, "Europe should not be complacent on energy security", 8 November 2022, www.ft.com/content/b2316953-be18-487d-ae28-050e599d958c.

24 IEA, "World Energy Investment 2022", www.iea.org/reports/world-energy-investment-2022.

25 IEA, "The Role of Critical Minerals in Clean Energy Transitions", May 2021, www.iea.org/reports/the-role-of-critical-minerals-in-clean-energy-transitions.

5. Conclusion

Despite the increasing urgency to accelerate the transition to green energy, it is unlikely that democratic and non-democratic governments alike will be able to do better than the objective set out in the 2009 position set out by the G20 quoted above. At best, states may eliminate 'structural' fossil fuel subsidies which have the objective of changing the domestic price for their populations, but will find it necessary to intervene temporarily with targeted subsidies to address the critical needs of vulnerable communities and pacify civilian disquiet. In the immediate future, economic warfare between the North Atlantic Treaty Organization (NATO) bloc and Russia will continue, as NATO countries strive in effect to 'subsidise' Russian natural gas and crude oil prices by forcing them to be sold at a discount to new customers such as India – encouraging incremental fossil fuel consumption and risking entrenching fossil fuel dependency.

The refining industry

David Wood
Sanchez Wood Limited

---

1. Introduction

Refining is almost as old as crude oil production. Today, with the drive to decarbonise the energy industry and electric vehicles (EVs) replacing internal combustion engines (ICEs) using refined products, the industry faces the greatest challenges in its history.

In the conclusion to this chapter, the future of the industry is assessed and some possible solutions and opportunities are discussed.

Crude oil was first produced in Pennsylvania, Venezuela and Azerbaijan around the turn of the 19th century. Early uses were mainly for heating and lighting, such as kerosene lamps. Later in the 20th century fuel oil was found to be the best fuel for large marine engines and power station fuel because it was easier to transport and store than coal.

The largest user of marine fuel oil was the British Royal Navy. At the time, the Royal Navy and Merchant Marine Fleet accounted for more than 50% of global transcontinental shipping.

In 1913, the Anglo Persian Oil Company, which was formed in 1908 to exploit an oil concession in Persia (now Iran), took advantage of the need for marine fuel oil and managed to avoid bankruptcy. This started the development of refining to produce fuel oil. Even today, most of Russia's massive refineries produce mainly fuel oil – as much as 50% of production.

When the Anglo-Persian Oil Company found that it could sell its fuel oil to the British Navy, the first major refined product was created. The lower-cost volatile by-products were discarded, albeit that kerosene was still used for lighting. But in the early 1900s, everything changed when the burgeoning automobile industry created a new product requirement: gasoline. The advent of the gasoline market revolutionised the refining industry. The light fraction by-products which had previously been thought to be of low value suddenly had a greater value than fuel oil. Demand for gasoline and later diesel for heavy-duty vehicles drove up the price of these products, and consequently the price of crude oil.

Soon the price of crude oil exceeded the price that could be obtained for fuel oil. Refining margins were high, but senior executives in the oil companies did not regard this as a reason to avoid producing loss-making fuel oil. So, refineries operated to create a product which was 25% to 30% of production and which sold for 60% of the price of crude oil.

Gasoline production dominated the refining industry until the 1970s, when the market for diesel cars – as opposed to commercial vehicles only – began to boom. This required an increase in diesel production and also a relative decrease in demand for gasoline. The oil companies were slow to react, because in order to produce more diesel and less gasoline, significant investment in hydrocrackers was required in their refineries.

The world economy was changing in several ways: financial markets were becoming more sophisticated and the major oil companies were reacting to many pressures. They began to consider themselves in terms of the total supply chain, placing greater emphasis on exploration, production and marketing and distribution; and refining became the ugly sister.

In the 1980s and 1990s, another parallel change had an impact on the industry. The lending banks and investment analysts chose to focus more on exploration and production (E&P) and marketing and distribution than on refining. The effect of this was to increase the market value of those companies, prioritising these parts of the business at the expense of refining. This hastened the move by the oil majors to downgrade refining in terms of funding and intellectual resources.

There were various reasons for this – not least the accounting decision to use transfer pricing to reduce the profitability of refining. Typically, since the oil majors were international companies, they could choose at which point (and in which country) in the value chain from production to refining to show profit and pay tax, and where to minimise profit and consequently minimise tax.

In the 1980s, certain banks saw the opportunity to refinance the small but consistent cash flow of refining operations and encouraged independent companies to be set up to make leveraged acquisitions buying out the refineries from the oil companies, or for oil companies to spin off their refining business into a subsidiary and refinance it, cashing in on future cash flow. The banks were able to understand and lend to entities with a consistent secure cash flow and, due to transfer pricing, most refineries now fell into this category. The refineries could be leveraged up to the point at which they could repay the debt.

The oil companies focused on seeking the best margins in the entire supply chain from oil well to fuel pump. Therefore, it was advantageous for them if a separate subsidiary owned the refinery. Capital-intensive refineries were thus removed from their balance sheets and they could push inventory into the low-profit refining company. And, of course, by making the refineries simply operating units without purchasing and marketing staff, they reduced the number of employees and the attendant social payments.

For investment analysts, the oil companies were now seen as having a greater return on capital employed because they valued the E&P and market and distribution assets higher than the refining assets.

Many of the oil majors – such as BP, the successor to the British-Persian Oil Company (later the British-Iranian oil Company) – divested their refineries, and significant refining companies such as today's Valero began to emerge.

Because the new refinery companies started life as financial vehicles, they initially concentrated on reducing costs and paid little attention to the marketplace or to improving their products to fit changing market requirements. At first, they obtained their margin by no longer having to pay for corporate overheads, which for companies such as BP, Shell, Chevron, Mobil and Exxon were large.

Another event hit the refineries in the 1980s: after many years of denial by the oil companies, it was shown that the addition of lead in the form of lead tetraethyl (an octane/performance booster) caused serious health problems. There were two consequences of this situation. First, the attempts by the industry to mislead governments and the public, especially in the United States, by producing misinformation showing that lead had no adverse effect on health caused the public to lose faith in the oil companies – a situation which continues to have damaging effects today. Second, environment agencies started to impose even more stringent specifications in relation to refined products. The first environmental requirement was the removal of lead tetraethyl from gasoline. Generally, it was replaced by methyl tert-butyl ether or ethanol/methanol; and/or by increasing the use of high-octane components through the use of refinery processes such as alkylation and isomerisation.

Also in the 1980s came restrictions on emissions of sulphur and nitrogen oxides, which were shown to have damaging effects when emitted into the atmosphere. Sulphur in particular damaged catalytic converters, which had been introduced into automobiles to improve engine exhaust emissions (catalysts are easily damaged by sulphur). Later, there was a call for a reduction in the production of carbon dioxide in the refining process and a general condemnation of any combustion process, because carbon dioxide is a natural product of the combustion of any hydrocarbon.

When the environmental requirements really started to bite, refineries had to look at ways to remove sulphur from their products and reduce nitrogen oxides and sulphur emissions.

At its Pernis refinery in Rotterdam, Shell was the first to look at cutting out products such as fuel oil, which had a selling price lower than crude oil, while at the same time reducing emissions from the refining process. In the production of gasoline and fuel oil, the products are blended in tanks which vent into the atmosphere, emitting noxious fumes. If these products are reduced in quantity or eliminated altogether, emissions are greatly reduced. The Pernis refinery uses solvent deasphalting and gasification to eliminate residues and hence fuel oil. The carbon dioxide produced is captured from the gasifier and used in hydroponic greenhouses to produce tulips, tomatoes and so on.

The environmental legislation on refined products has significantly affected the profitability of refineries and indeed the price of refined products in California, for example, where the price of gasoline is more than twice the price in Texas.

Since the turn of the century, many political events have affected the industry, which is an integral part of the world economy.

The world's largest holder of oil reserves, Venezuela, has fallen foul of US international policy and has been sanctioned, so that few counties can trade with the oil-producing state-owned companies.

Sanctions have also been imposed on Russia and China, with less effect financially; however, the political effects are now becoming clear in light of the conflict in Ukraine and the consequent increases in crude oil and fertiliser prices on the international market.

China and India now buy Russian oil on a bilateral basis at well below the crude oil spot market price and do not pay in US dollars. Also, China now buys crude oil from Iran and Saudi Arabia on a bilateral basis and purchases in Chinese renminbi. This is discussed further below.

Sanctions imposed by the United States on a number of countries have affected the industry in Iran and Russia especially. They are also affecting how crude oil and products are traded. Until recently, before the COVID-19 pandemic, the majority of crude oil and refined products were traded in US dollars; however, to avoid US sanctions and to remove trades from the vagaries of the international spot markets, countries are increasingly entering into long-term bilateral trade deals, which guarantee the refining margin and the real cost of crude oil production.

It will always cost less to transport crude oil than refined products, whether by pipeline or ship; consequently, the move to bilateral deals for crude oil will cause more countries to upgrade their refineries based on a guaranteed cost of crude oil.

Production of refined products in countries from fixed priced crude oil will allow refinery upgrades to be financed without the risk of refining margins eroding.

The profitability of refineries is heavily dependent on logistics and geographical position is thus critical relative to crude oil supply and the market for refined products.

Marketing was not a skill which had been necessary in the refinery subsidiaries of integrated oil companies or in the financial buy-out companies run by accountants and bankers rather than industry businesspeople. Even Shell was driven more by the need to reduce emissions and conform to environmental laws than by the need to improve margins.

Refineries with technology which enables low-cost and adjacent crudes to be processed and requires minimal or no utilities (eg, because water, power and feedstocks either are at the site or are produced from the crude oil with no need for importation of natural gas) will be profitable in almost all economic cycles. However, many existing refineries will need expensive revamps to achieve this; consequently, some are simply in the wrong location.

Today, oil and gas comprise a massive global industry, of which refining is an integral part. But refining has been historically plagued by a lack of management and strategic focus. Refineries were primarily built by oil companies to convert their crude oil into saleable products. Little strategic thought was given to market needs and to optimisation of the logistics of refining; consequently, a lack of investment and focus have resulted in an industry which has many inefficient and low-profit refineries. Unlike in other major industries, little research has been done to analyse the potential market for products and adapt refineries accordingly.

Meanwhile, the changes in how crude oil is traded could reduce the costs of refining; while the need to transition to a low-cost electricity scenario could lead to greater availability of financing for refinery upgrades as venture capitalists which made poorly advised renewables investment switch to real financial returns opportunities. However, if a low-cost electricity environment is created, the move to EVs will accelerate and the market for fossil fuel-based products will decline.

2. Legislation and regulation

This section examines the logistics and locations of refineries and the prevailing conditions in various countries. Regulations and technologies are also discussed.

Refineries are regulated through:

- government authorisation, by granting a licence or authorisation to construct and operate the refinery; and
- environmental legislation, which requires refineries to be built in accordance with product specifications and with strict controls on liquid and gaseous effluents.

In all countries, the oil and gas industry is of major strategic importance and is thus politicised. As a consequence, many governments regulate the industry directly and closely, and this can also apply to the refining sector. This is especially so where the oil industry and thus the refining industry are state owned.

Where there are national oil companies (NOCs), the state through the Ministry of Energy (or the relevant ministry, however named) controls the refining industry and imposes regulations on refineries. Some NOCs do not allow competing companies to own refineries or may allow them to be minority partners only if they bring some essential component (eg, technology).

In general, countries with a large number of refineries have an NOC or control the major refining company. The major exception is the United States.

The European Union has no direct regulation of refineries, except in Italy, France and Poland, where the state owns refineries. Elsewhere in the European Union, regulation is exercised through EU environment laws, which are enforced strictly by the member states.

This means that most refineries in the world are controlled directly by governments – for example, in China, India, Russia, Brazil, Venezuela, Mexico, Iran, Iraq, Indonesia, Saudi Arabia, Thailand, France, Italy and Malaysia, where state-controlled companies dominate the industry.

Other countries with a large number of refineries – such as the United States, Japan, South Korea, Canada and Germany – rely on their environment agencies, which are government organs. All countries have their own environmental legislation and many use the World Bank standards as a guide. The European Union has its own standards, which are stricter than those of the World Bank in some areas. Generally, all countries are adopting EU or World Bank standards, or are bringing their own standards into line with them.

Where refineries are run as businesses independent of the state and are regulated solely by environment agencies, they are more efficient and profitable. This is probably more to do with market efficiencies than with the way they are regulated.

3. Technology

3.1 Upgrading technologies

The technology to improve refining operations and thereby increase margins and reduce emissions has existed for many years – indeed, since long before the switch in market emphasis from fuel oil to gasoline and then to diesel.

However, the lack of investment in refining since the 1970s and 1980s has meant that very few refiners could persuade their budget committees to provide the large amounts of funding required for the necessary improvements. Typically, for an average world-scale refinery, an investment of $1–2 billion could be required to eliminate the production of fuel oil and increase the production of diesel. In addition, refiners had to remove sulphur from all products.

Decision makers in the refinery business tend to focus more on technical issues and less on commercial and economic considerations; therefore, a technology which appears to be elegant and promises high-quality products takes precedence over simpler, more effective or more economical solutions.

There has been massive expenditure on residue upgrading technologies, which rely on fluidised bed catalytic units. Examples include Slovnaft, Slovakia, Neste, Finland KOC and Kuwait. These units are fed refinery residues from the distillation bottoms (ie, the first stage in the refining process) and crack the hydrocarbons to lighter, lower-viscosity components. Unfortunately, however, all of these processes fail to produce the predicted results. There are two reasons for this.

First, residues are tar-like and sticky, so the fluidised catalyst does not stay fluid for long. The catalyst chips clog and the necessary mixing for the process to work ceases. Consequently, the catalyst has to be dug out every few weeks. Typically, these processes account for about 250 days per year of operation, or 68% of onstream time, when more than 90% is required. This level does not provide an acceptable return on capital employed.

Second, catalysts are deactivated by three main residue components:

- sulphur;
- metals; and
- asphaltenes and other high con-carbon materials (heavy tar-like materials).

Residues contain all of the above. The solution is to remove the residues from the feed stream into the upgrading unit, to allow the use of lower-cost fixed-bed catalytic units. The residue which is removed can be used as a fuel or converted to steam and power and the hydrogen required for the hydrocracker and hydrodesulphurisation units. In this way, the refinery becomes an exporter of power and does not require imported natural gas for hydrogen production. This makes the refinery very energy efficient; and since higher-value products are produced, the refinery has dramatically improved margins.

Where the hydrogen produced is in greater quantities than that required by the hydrotreating units, the hydrogen can be an additional product, which is lower cost than electrolysis due to its marginally costed production.

3.2 Residue disposal

In order for the residue product to flow under normal atmospheric conditions, residues were traditionally mixed (or cut) with relatively high-cost gas oil to form fuel oil. However, as fuel oil demand dropped and legislation made the use of high-sulphur fuel oil expensive for power station use, due to the high cost of sulphur removal from the exhaust gases, other ways of utilising the residues were required.

In North and South America, coking has been the preferred solution. This is a thermal cracking process, which releases the higher-value components and leaves behind a solid coke material. However, coking is a poor solution, because the coke produced is friable (ie, it dusts and is an environmental hazard) and low in calorific value; and more importantly, because the coker products are of poor quality because the thermal cracking removes much of the hydrogen from the material as steam. The next step in the refinery process requires material with a high hydrogen content to produce the best results. For example, if the coker products are fed to a hydrocracker, far more hydrogen is needed than with alternative material with a higher hydrogen content. Also, if the next unit in the refinery process is a fluidised catalytic cracker unit (FCCU) used to increase gasoline production, the conversion to gasoline is at least 20% lower if coker products are used as compared to conversion where materials high in hydrogen are used.

Table 1 shows the low yield of distillate and therefore diesel and jet fuel from a coking refinery. Significant fuel oil is also produced.

Table 1. Typical production yield from coking refineries

Product	% yield by mass
Propane/butane	7%
Gasoline	58%
Distillate	28%
Heavy fuel oil and other	15%
Total yield	108%

(Note: natural gas is imported 8%).

3.3 Technology cost

Both residue upgrading units and cokers are very expensive. Moreover, due to their poor margin contribution, it is difficult to justify the investment because the return on capital employed is very low. The reason cokers were utilised was the relatively low price of heavy, high-sulphur crude oil from Venezuela and Mexico. A coker enables such crudes to be processed.

There are solutions which maximise diesel production and provide the necessary upgrading and residue removal. These have lower cost and produce higher value streams for further processing, thus giving very high returns. Shell Pernis was the first step in the use of this technology and Brazil saw the first full utilisation. The production of this technology can be seen in Table 2.

Table 2. Refined product yields

Product	% yield by mass
Propane/butane	5%
Gasoline	0%
Naphtha	18%
Distillate	60%
Hydrocracker lube base oil	7%
Heavy fuel oil and other	0%
Hydrogen, steam and power (~180MW)	10%
Total yield	100%

4. Logistics

The energy industry is in a constant state of flux and this applies especially to the refining industry. Many of the major oil companies are exiting refining; Exxon is the exception. Shell is holding onto only its strategic refineries and is selling or closing others. BP and Chevron are exiting as fast as possible.

The oil industry began by trading particularly in Europe and Asia, but this has now become universal, with gasoline and diesel moving across the Atlantic in opposite directions.

We have seen the change in dynamics which shale oil has caused in the United States and the knock-on effect in the rest of the world. Clearly, oil-exporting countries for which the United States was previously a major market have had to rethink their strategies. One option has been to refine more oil and to sell products where they are needed. This has required more diesel production generally in the expanded or newly built refineries.

Russia and Brazil have declared their intent to refine more and export less of their oil. However, they are struggling both to fund and to manage this objective. Logistics are of major importance, and location and transport will be key for future refineries.

The recent logistical restraints, caused by the COVID-19 pandemic and the sanctions imposed on Russia following its invasion of Ukraine, have changed the dynamics of the industry, as explained in the introduction. These changes may bring about a significant decline in the volume of the international spot market for both crude oil and refined products.

We will need to see how the need to lower the cost of energy and the decline in globalisation will affect the refinery industry. If, as discussed above, there is a trend to improve in-country refining, this will depend on banks and governments approving loans to the industry – an issue which has been a significant restriction over the past 20 years.

Lower-cost crude oil through bilateral trades can provide the basis for in-country investment in refineries to produce higher margins and lower refined product prices.

This trend may delay the move to EVs.

4.1 Refinery location

It is cheaper to ship crude oil to a refinery than to ship all products of the refinery process to their respective markets, so refineries are generally located next to the market and not at the oilfield. Clearly, if the oilfield is near the market, we have a perfect situation.

Many of the largest oil-producing areas are in relatively sparsely populated areas – namely the Middle East and the wastes of Siberia and Canada. This created a need for long-distance transportation of crude oil. The Shell Trading and Shipping Company was initially established to ship crude oil from Baku to Europe. Later, it shipped crude from the Royal Dutch oilfield in Indonesia to Rotterdam, leading to the formation of Royal Dutch/Shell.

(a) United States

Oil and its products have dominated the political and industrial scene in the United States for the past 100 years.

The United States was the world's first major oil producer and a major user of refined products. Until 10 years ago, there had been a steady decline in oil production and a massive increase in demand for refined products in the United States. This trend has recently been reversed: there has been a flattening in demand for products and a large increase in oil production, due to the advent of fracking technology.

Many see a return to the heady days of the 1920s and 1930s, when the United States dominated the oil industry and was the world's major producer. It is unlikely that the United States will become a net exporter of crude oil. Indeed, today, legislation prevents exports of unrefined crude oil. However, lower costs due to transportation savings should be reflected in an increase in investment in US refining.

The United States has seen the most significant restructuring of the industry, first with the emergence of Tosco and then with Valero. Both companies saw the opportunity to develop as refinery companies without any crude oil assets. They used management skills and financial knowledge, coupled with the enthusiasm of US banks for the building of refinery companies.

Valero has grown to become the largest independent refining company. Tosco sold itself to Phillips Petroleum (now ConocoPhillips) in 2001. ConocoPhillips' decision went against the trend of the majors to divest themselves of refining assets. It is probable that ConocoPhillips saw an opportunity to buy refining assets with service stations included at an attractive price at a time when the cost of competing with the other majors for new oil leases was high. This may prove to be attractive for ConocoPhillips as they can act as EV charge stations, which will survive as fossil fuel market share declines.

The increase in lower-cost oil production in the United States could have serious negative consequences for Mexico and Venezuela, as lighter crude oil from fracking improves refining margins and US refiners move away from heavier Mexican and Venezuelan crudes as the price incentive disappears.

(b) Russia

Russia may also make use of fracking eventually, but currently its economy is not growing at a rapid rate and the economic sanctions imposed on Russia since the Ukraine crisis in 2014 have made it difficult for producers to access low-cost finance. The country will be a large net exporter of conventionally produced crude oil for some years to come.

The additional sanctions imposed by the United States and the European Union in 2022 following the extension of the Ukraine conflict have changed the oil, petrochemical and fertiliser industries, with knock-on effects for the refining industry, as explained above.

Russia's oil industry has received a net benefit from the sanctions by selling its crude oil at higher prices, well above the cost of production.

The isolation from Europe which is transpiring should prompt Russia to use the additional income to invest in making its refining industry more efficient and enable the production of lower-cost refined products.

Hitherto, as with the major oil companies, Russian companies have placed a major emphasis on E&P and have neglected refineries. Most refineries produce huge amounts of fuel oil or '*mazut*'. In the harsh winter months, diesel use is limited due to its low freezing point and gasoline is the premier fuel. Russia is a major exporter of high-sulphur gas oil. This gas oil is processed mainly in Europe to low-sulphur diesel and marine gas oil.

This high-sulphur gas oil business will be affected by the latest sanctions and again push Russia to upgrade its refineries.

There has been much talk of upgrades in Russian refineries, but little has been achieved to date. Perhaps recent events will change the situation.

We could see further investment in Russian refineries by Chinese companies so that China will get even lower-cost crude oil.

(c) *China*

China is investing heavily in its refineries but remains a major importer of both diesel and fuel oil. The imported fuel oil is split back into its gas oil and residue components. The gas oil is upgraded to diesel and the residue is burned as fuel for power.

Again, fracking could bring about a massive change in the economics of refining in China. A reliable large local supply would change the industry and would influence many of its current political goals.

China is currently working to develop ties with African countries, which could become suppliers of crude oil. It is also a major importer of refined products. China Sonangol is becoming a major player in Angola and in other places. Meanwhile, Petrochina has also invested in Scotland's large Grangemouth refinery in a joint venture with petrochemical company INEOS, which emerged from the ashes of Imperial Chemical Industries (ICI).[1]

China is also bringing about the greatest challenge to the refining industry: EVs. By concentrating on low-cost coal and nuclear power, the country now has some of the cheapest electricity in the world, which has encouraged it to take the lead in developing EVs. Not only is Tesla manufacturing its high-end cars in Shanghai, but Chinese companies are also leaders in the low and middle-range EV markets.

China's recent bilateral trades in crude oil with Russia have reduced the cost of crude oil and hence refined products; however, the drive to low-cost electricity continues, with practical renewable power developments in addition to thorium fuel fission plants and initial success in fusion plants. This could bring about a shift from ICE fuels to petrochemicals within China's refining industry.

China is a major producer of engineering plastics, such as poly butyl terephthalate, which is lighter and stronger than steel. This material is used in EVs to reduce weight and thereby increase single charge mileage for EVs.

China is the world's largest single market, giving domestic vehicle manufacturers a competitive advantage. The recent purchase of Volvo – with its car, bus and truck market share – puts China firmly in the European and US marketplace for sales of EVs.

Meanwhile, China has more kilometres of electric high-speed train rail network than the rest of the world put together.

---

1 ICI grew rapidly after the Second World War and captured some of the market from continental European chemical companies, especially IG Farben, until successors Hoechst, Bayer and BASF established themselves in the 1960s. The company was predominant in paints, resins and precursors, such as methanol, but began to decline in the 1990s. INEOS absorbed most of ICI's assets. The company also suffered from the state assistance given mainly to its German and French competitors, which became available after the formation of the European Union.

(d) Europe

Europe imports crude oil and diesel, and exports gasoline and fuel oil. Its refineries are in need of modernisation and upgrading, and to date no multi-refinery company comparable to Valero has emerged.

Petroplus – a Dutch company led by Thomas O'Malley (formerly chief executive officer of Tosco) and Marcel van Poecke – tried to set up a Tosco-type operation in Europe but failed to get the necessary support from the banks and ended up relying on the Carlyle Group for funding. This did not work out in the end, because the venture did not provide the investment hurdle rate normally acceptable to Carlyle.

The oil majors are divesting or closing refineries, and generally the industry lacks focus and commitment as well as investment. The two major European companies, Shell and BP, have arguably been politically naive in recent years and have suffered from a poor public image and negative media attention. Their US competitors – Exxon, Chevron and Philips – keep a much lower profile and, with the exception of ESSO (European Exxon), tend to stay out of Europe.

Valero has made one entry into Europe, buying the Pembroke refinery in Wales from Chevron-Texaco. This provided it with Texaco-brand service stations in the United Kingdom. The refinery can also process low-value crude oil.

In Eastern/Central Europe, Russian companies such as LUKOIL have acquired positions, for example, in the former Yugoslavian refineries of Pancevo and Novi Sad in Vojvodina. LUKOIL also purchased Petrotel in Ploesti, Romania and Bulgaria's large Neftochim refinery. There has been much talk of expansion projects for these acquisitions, but progress has been very slow.

MOL in Hungary and Plock in Poland have revamped and expanded their refineries; and OMV in Austria has done likewise, using a cash injection from IPIC of Abu Dhabi. IPIC has moved into CEPSA in Spain and the company has spent considerable sums expanding its refineries. Similarly, Repsol has spent extravagantly on its refineries.

In Portugal, GALP's Sines refinery has been undergoing an expansion, but has been hampered by disagreements between its three owners: Sonangol has the necessary funds, but ENI and the local owners are less ready to meet their commitments.

Shell and BP have been trying to sell their refineries in Sweden and the United Kingdom. Shell sold its ST1 refinery in Sweden in 2010. In 2013, BP closed the UK Corryton refinery, which it inherited following its joint venture with Mobil and Mobil's subsequent acquisition by Exxon. It sold its Grangemouth facility with its integrated petrochemical plant to INEOS in 2005. The refinery is now a joint venture between INEOS and Petrochina.

Exxon (ESSO) remains the main refiner in Europe, together with French company Total, which the French government caused to absorb the other

French oil company, ELF Aquitaine. The three large oil refineries in the port of Antwerp are to be completely modernised. ExxonMobil and Total are investing a total of around €2.3 billion in their plants. US concern ExxonMobil has invested €1.3 billion in a new plant at its existing site in Antwerp to convert heavy crude oil into lighter products such as car fuels. French oil company Total has invested around €1 billion in its refinery for the production of diesel. In May 2020, Russian concern Gunvor closed the refinery in Antwerp that it acquired in 2014, beating Valero at the last minute.

This will safeguard the continued existence of the refineries. Elsewhere in Europe, many refineries have had to close in recent years due to competition from the Far East and the Middle East.

Rotterdam remains the major refining centre in Europe and will benefit from the investments in Antwerp. Crude oil for the Belgian plants is largely imported via Rotterdam and transported by pipeline to Antwerp. In addition, refinery products are exchanged between the port areas by pipeline and inland shipping. Some 100 million tonnes of crude oil a year are shipped to the port of Rotterdam and then pumped to five refineries in Rotterdam, one in Vlissingen, three in Antwerp and two in Germany. Together, these refineries form the biggest petrochemicals cluster in the world. The three refineries in Antwerp process around 35 million tonnes of crude oil a year. In Rotterdam, the Shell, BP, Exxon, Kuwait Petroleum and Koch refineries process roughly 50 million tonnes of crude oil.

Europe has been the most significantly affected by the sanctions imposed on Russia in 2022, which has exacerbated the downturn in economic activity brought about by the COVID-19 restrictions.

The current high price of crude oil is a major issue for refiners; however, due to its poor energy policies – including heavy subsidies on renewables, closure of nuclear plants and over-reliance on Russian gas – Europe has very high electricity prices. This will hamper the move to EVs, which prior to 2020 had been gaining momentum.

Europe has important decisions to make regarding its energy future, which may have a dramatic impact on the refining industry. It could reverse its flawed energy policy and transition to a low-cost electricity environment with the replacement of ICE vehicles with EVs to avoid the consequences of high crude oil and gas prices.

Alternatively, it could invest in its refineries to reduce the cost of refined products and stay with ICE vehicles, with the possible use of hydrogen fuel. Hydrogen can be produced in the refineries at lower cost than alternative production methods.

Either alternative will require a level of planning which the European Union has not engaged in previously.

An outside observer might opine that the answer is simply to remove sanctions and reintegrate with Russia. This would require a political reversal, which many European countries – such as Hungary, Italy and the Balkan states – would approve of, but not the countries that influence EU policy.

Without a clear policy, other than 'wait and see' stagnation, investment in refineries to reduce refining cost or to produce hydrogen is unlikely.

(e) Far East

Until recently, the Far East oil and gas business was dominated by the Japanese *sogo shosha* (trading companies). Today, the oil business is dominated by China; although Japanese concerns such as Mitsui, Mitsubishi, Sumitomo, Itochu and Marubeni still play an important role through importing liquefied natural gas (LNG) and investing in LNG production facilities to secure those imports.

Indonesia's state-owned oil giant, Pertamina, was influential from the 1970s to the early 1990s, but the majors have withdrawn from the refining sector in more recent times. No foreign companies own any refineries in Indonesia.

The 1990s also saw the growth of PTT in Thailand and Petronas in Malaysia, based on their oil and gas discoveries. Major refineries were built or expanded in both countries – especially at Map Ta Phut in Rayong Province in Thailand. This large industrial complex has refineries and petrochemical facilities. Shell had its STAR refinery there but sold its 64% interest to PTT in 2004.

Shell, through its Royal Dutch entity, has a long history in Indonesia and retains a close relationship with Pertamina; likewise, it helped to establish Petronas and keeps closely involved. It owned two refineries in Malaysia, but the small Lutong refinery has closed. Shell has gas interests in Palawan in the Philippines and is a major supplier of gas to Meralco, the major power producer. It also has an extensive service station business in the Philippines and owned a refinery at Batangas on Luzon, the archipelago's largest island and home to the capital, Manila. However, the COVID-19 pandemic caused Shell to close its Batangas refinery; and the remaining refinery in the country – Petron in Bataan – is constantly in the news with threats of closure if government support is withheld.

Shell Eastern Petroleum (Pte) operates the Pulau Bukom I refinery, which is located in Southwest Singapore. This is an integrated refinery owned by Royal Dutch Shell. The refinery, which started operations in 1961, has a Nelson Complexity Index[2] of 8.12. The refinery's capacity is expected to decrease to 304 million barrels per day by 2030. However, because it is integrated with petrochemical production, the refinery may survive; although there is

2 The Nelson Complexity Index seeks to compare the relative costs and complexity of refineries by comparing the added value and cost of secondary conversion facilities at a refinery, compared to a base value of 1.0 for simple crude oil distillation.

speculation that its capacity may be reduced from 500,000 billion barrels per day (Bbls/d) to 250,000 Bbls/day as fuel production is reduced.

Exxon has concentrated on Thailand (Sri Racha), Malaysia and its Singapore refinery. BP's presence in the area is in petrochemicals in Malaysia; and Castrol sells lubricants throughout the region.

(f) *India*

India has been expanding its refining and petrochemical capacity but has overspent in many areas, and time has not been of the essence. The state-owned Indian Oil Company has been unable to bring about the capacity expansions demanded by the pace of the expanding domestic economy; and Reliance's expansion, managed by Bechtel, experienced large cost and schedule overruns.

The Indian refineries also rely on outdated technology and are inefficient, especially when compared to refineries such as Shell Pernis. Efficiency will become increasingly important as pressure from alternative transport options bites into fossil fuel product markets.

Many suggest that, similarly to China, India's entry onto the world stage is inevitable. However, to date, only tentative steps have been taken, in contrast to the Indian steel industry. India is a major importer of crude oil. It remains to be seen what effect the recent bilateral deal with Russia for crude oil will have.

The main reasons for India's absence from the international refining business thus far have been:

- the government's involvement in many areas of the oil and gas business through the Indian Oil Company; and
- a focus on satisfying rapidly growing indigenous demand.

The Indian Oil Company owns and operates 10 of India's 22 refineries with a combined refining capacity of 65.7 million metric tonnes per annum (MMtpa) – that is, approximately 1.30 million barrels per day.

Reliance Industries is the largest publicly traded company in India and the second-largest company after the Indian Oil Company. It started out in textiles and diversified into telecommunications and oil and gas to become the mega-corporation it is today. Its RPL complex claims to be the largest refinery in the world, at 1.24 Bbls per day. Originally commissioned in 1999 as the Jamnagar refinery at 660,000 Bbls/d, it is now part of an industrial complex including aromatics, petrochemicals and infrastructure such as ports and pipelines.

The refinery configuration is heavily US influenced, with a coker and no hydrocracker. It is thus geared to gasoline production and does not focus on diesel and jet fuel, as a modern refinery must do to be competitive on the international market. However, the rapidly growing Indian economy should provide it with an attractive market in which it can be competitive and profitable.

(g) *Africa*

Africa is expected to become a major market for refined products. Oil production has been significant in Nigeria and Angola for some time, but inefficiencies and a lack of organisation and focus have made for slow progress. Both countries are major exporters of crude oil and importers of refined products.

With expanding populations, many African countries will require refined products; but whether successful world-scale refineries will come into play as new builds or revamps remains to be seen. Certainly, with the exception of South Africa, it is hard to find well-run world-scale refineries in the continent. Nigeria has three large refineries, but they barely operate to produce products.

Angola is struggling with the organisation of all of its major investments in both LNG and refining. Revenue and therefore funding are not issues; but Angola has allowed its partners to dictate strategy and schedule, which has not been to its advantage.

Consequently, Nigeria and Angola import products due to a lack of effective refining capacity. China may prove to be a major player not only in Angola, but also in Mozambique.

(h) *Latin America*

Venezuela is one of the original oil-producing countries and a founder member of the Organization of the Petroleum Exporting Countries (OPEC). It initially opened its doors to the oil majors and they set up oil exploration and production and refining and marketing operations. The country benefited and became the richest economy in Latin America.

In the early years, both Shell and Exxon held drilling concessions in Venezuela, which ensured a constant supply of crude oil to the refineries in Aruba and Curaçao. Crude oil production in Venezuela was inexpensive. Integrated companies Shell and Exxon controlled the entire industry, from pumping, transporting and refining to marketing the end product. The refineries in Aruba and Curaçao operated in global markets and were profitable partly because of the margin between the production costs of crude oil and the revenues realised on products. This provided a safety net for losses incurred through inefficiencies or excessive operating costs at the refineries.

In 1915, Royal Dutch Shell decided to establish an oil refinery on Curaçao and the installation was commissioned three years later. There were a number of geographical and political advantages to establishing a refinery on an island off the Venezuelan coast, including:

- predicted market growth in the United States;
- politically troubled oil production in Mexico; and
- an expected increase in traffic through the Panama Canal.

A natural deep-water harbour and a stable political climate made Curaçao the obvious choice.

The companies had to buy oil on the international markets at higher prices. As the Shell refinery on Curaçao was best equipped to process Venezuelan heavy crude, the company was exposed to Venezuelan oil politics when it came to price and supply. Coupled with high operating costs, these difficulties explained why the refinery on Curaçao continually operated at a loss.

The nationalisation of the oil industry in Venezuela in 1975 proved a fatal setback.

Lagoven, Mareven and Corpoven respectively came into being under the umbrella of Petroleos de Venezuela SA (PdVSA). The results were stagnation and decline. Under the premiership of Hugo Chavez, a complete collapse of the economy and the milking of PdVSA to prop up the country in the wake of international isolation brought about a disastrous situation, from which it will be difficult to recover without a radical new approach.

The task ahead for the post-Chavez administration is immense, requiring inward investment and probably privatisation of the oil industry. It remains to be seen whether such change can be made, especially with the country's large oil reserves fuelling nationalistic tendencies.

President Biden's recent approach to Venezuela to supply crude oil and to increase production to bring about a lower crude oil price could potentially mark the start of a rapprochement between the countries. However, this does not appear to be happening and OPEC is distancing itself from cooperating with the United States.

In 1985, after a presence of 70 years, Royal Dutch Shell decided to end its activities on Curaçao and Exxon closed its Aruba refinery. It was later acquired by Valero, but now operates at a lower capacity.

The Venezuelan government wanted to keep the Curaçao refinery open for geopolitical reasons, by involving PdVSA. This resulted in the transfer of all Shell assets to the island territory of Curaçao and a lease of the refinery and terminals to PdVSA in the third quarter of 1985. The settlement with Shell and the lease of the refinery ended a turbulent period in the history of the island – an era which was marked by unrest.

Through Pemex, Mexico has had a similar but far less arduous journey. The country has had its problems but has not lost the support of its big brother to the north. The government decided that regardless of whether it agreed with US foreign policy, it would maintain a flexible relationship so as to avoid damaging its major markets and sources of investment.

Pemex's refineries are in need of modernisation and would benefit from privatisation, but national oil is again increasing in production and newer lighter crudes are being found.

Colombia, Ecuador, Peru, Chile and Bolivia again have state-owned oil and gas companies. Investment is required and new or expanded/modernised refineries are desperately needed. There is distrust of the oil majors – which in many cases is justified – so again, innovative and radical thinking will be needed to grow the refining and general oil business in these countries.

Argentina took a giant step backwards with the nationalisation of Repsol's assets and will remain a pariah in the industry until there is a change in attitude. The country is not a big enough player to be able to dictate to the industry. It is in dire need of inward investment and the oil and gas industry could be a catalyst for this to occur.

Brazil stood apart in Latin America thanks to its vibrant economy, until 10 years ago, when the removal of investment first by the United States and then by China brought growth to a standstill. Over the previous 35 years, the country had evolved into a position where it has both an educated middle class that could support inward investment and a potentially attractive oil and gas industry. It is difficult not to criticise the failure of the government to privatise Petrobras fully and to take the steps necessary to free the industry to capitalise on the vast potential of Brazil's offshore oil and gas reserves and the currently regrowing economy.

Brazil's Ministry of the Economy upgraded its forecast for economic growth in September 2022 to 2.7%, from 2% expected in July, after official data for the second quarter showed brisk activity.[3]

However, overall progress has been extraordinary – even if it could have been greater had sufficient encouragement been given to the private sector and foreign investment.

That said, the Petrobras corruption scandals and controversies surrounding the incumbent President Bolsonaro have hindered economic development and particularly Petrobras, which is trying to sell off its refining division.

It is difficult to see how the refining and marketing business of Petrobras can be profitable while prices are kept down by government policies and gasoline and low-sulphur diesel imported and sold at a loss. Clearly, if Petrobras loses money with this business, foreign investment will be withheld except for export-orientated refineries.

The results of the election in October 2022 could change the economy significantly if the BRICS (Brazil, Russia, India, China and South Africa) initiative attracts renewed investment from China. Further, the increase in the spot oil price has benefited both Petrobras and Brazil.

The federal petroleum regulator and the Ministry of Energy are encouraging foreign investment; but to some extent, without a new approach by the

3 Reuters, "Brazil 2022 GDP growth now forecast at 2.7% up from 2%", 15 September 2022, www.reuters.com/markets/rates-bonds/brazils-economy-ministry-improves-2022-gdp-forecast-27-2022-09-15/.

government, they are fighting an uphill battle. Distrust of Petrobras and the scandals in the press are causing investors to be cautious. Despite this, due to its huge oil reserves, Brazil represents the future of oil and gas in Latin America; and once foreign private (as opposed to foreign government) investment starts to flow into the sector, the refining industry will bloom.

The refinancing and modernisation of Petrobras's refineries and the construction of new refineries will benefit the economy and provide further incentives for foreign investment from Europe, the Middle East and Asia. Angola may be a useful source of investment, since Brazil needs Portuguese-speaking expertise and a way to avoid being dominated by the majors and the United States.

4.2 National oil companies

NOCs are playing an increasingly visible role in the industry, largely at the expense of the oil majors.

Russian companies have made many acquisitions, primarily in the former Council for Mutual Economic Assistance (Comecon) countries and the former Yugoslavia. Most of these refineries are situated on the Druzhba pipeline, which supplies Russian export blend crude oil (REBCO). These companies are not market driven and appear to have changed little in the years since the fall of the Soviet Union. As discussed above, this could be about to change. Refining is a second priority to exploration and production, and little attention is paid to market profile and so on. Much like the oil majors, they are dinosaurs – large and cumbersome. They appear to lack any kind of commercial strategy or focus, other than a drive to increase oil and gas production. As with the oil majors, much of their focus also seems to be on gas and not oil.

Recently, Gazprom (the world's largest oil company) and Rosneft, the world's largest refiner, have been looking into foreign investments and joint ventures. However, their inflexible state ownership has proved to be a serious obstacle; and with the latest sanctions and Russian isolation from the United States and Western Europe, foreign investment other than from China and India is unlikely.

The Middle East companies are also focused on gas and LNG, despite being slow to emerge from the financial crisis of 2008. There has been little change in this regard more recently, except that Saudi Arabia has removed itself from US influence and is making independent policy decisions, driving increased economic growth. The market float of part of Saudi Aramco signalled the start of this policy shift, which has further been emphasised by the recent bilateral crude oil deal with China.

Iran has also shaken off the reins of US sanctions and entered into a 25-year deal with China which will expand its infrastructure in return for supplying low-cost crude oil.

In general (with the exception of Iran, Saudi Arabia and Dubai), the Middle

East has determined that oil and gas are its areas of expertise; and that as reserves decline, today's riches should be used to invest in foreign assets. That said, there does not seem to be a clear plan for achieving this goal. Companies in the region do not have a flexible structure and rely to a large extent on inputs from members of the ruling families. This does not aid speedy reactions when opportunities for acquisitions arise. The one exception is IPIC of Abu Dhabi. IPIC has a controlling interest in OMV, the Austrian former state oil company; and CEPSA, the Spanish oil and petrochemical company.

In the 1980s and 1990s, Saudi Aramco made a number of investments in refineries and oil companies. It acquired a 45% interest in Petron, the state oil company of the Philippines. The government of the Philippines also had a 45% stake in the deal. The transaction involved the large Bataan refinery, which processed Saudi heavy crude oil. A similar deal was done in South Korea with SsangYong and in Japan with Shell and Showa Sekiyu.

Aramco has exited Petron but remains active through the South Korea and Japan deals. It produces two main crude blends: Saudi heavy and Saudi light. These investments were initially aimed at promoting sales of the less attractive Saudi heavy. Aramco has since been largely absent from the international stage and is now rumoured to be considering new acquisitions.

The recent large-scale offering to private investors of shares in Aramco has posed more questions than answers for the future of the Saudi Arabian oil sector.

Downstream, petrochemical arm SABIC has built a successful ethylene derivatives business through multiple acquisitions in Europe, taking over ethylene crackers and building a polymer marketing operation.

4.3 Transportation

The United States was the first country to develop pipeline systems for the transportation of crude oil and products, primarily from Texas to the northeast – the Continental Pipeline.

This system has grown and now covers the continental United States and Canada, linking in Alaska and the Trans-Alaskan Pipeline built by a BP-led consortium to harness the crude oilfields in Arctic northern Alaska.

The crude pipelines provide feedstock to US and Canadian refineries; and the product pipelines deliver product – primarily gasoline – to the large population centres, which were unsuitable for the construction of refineries, being far from the crude oil fields.

Russia built the Druzhba pipeline during the days of the Soviet Union to supply REBCO to Russia and the satellite countries of Comecon, the economic union of countries tied to the Soviet Union.

The pipeline system became the focus for the refining industry of Eastern Europe and the southern Soviet states. It was fed by the giant Tyumen oilfields and serviced refineries in Western Europe, as well as Yugoslavia and the Caucasus states.

All of these refineries were designed to process REBCO or Urals crude oil, as it was also known. Therefore, all of these refineries require upgrading in order to stop producing heavy fuel oil, because REBCO is a heavy crude with medium-level sulphur content. This is the task presented to LukOil in Serbia, Romania and Bulgaria.

These refineries in Poland, Hungary, Slovakia, Romania and Serbia are still closely linked to Russian crude oil and it will be difficult to replace the supply chain infrastructure.

By contrast, Bulgarian refineries and those of Croatia and Gdansk in Poland are coastal and can easily switch to other crude oil supplies, provided that their configuration can be adapted and they can afford the higher-priced crude oil.

Figure 1 shows the extent of the Druzhba system and the consequent problem for refineries in Europe.

Some refiners will ignore EU sanctions and continue to buy Russian crude oil without very large grants to change their infrastructure. Others will simply produce higher-cost refined products or will shut down.

Russian investments in German refineries have been terminated illegally by Germany and the consequences of this are not yet clear.

These refineries are internal to the country and supply chain infrastructure will also be an issue for these refineries.

Figure 1. Druzhba pipeline

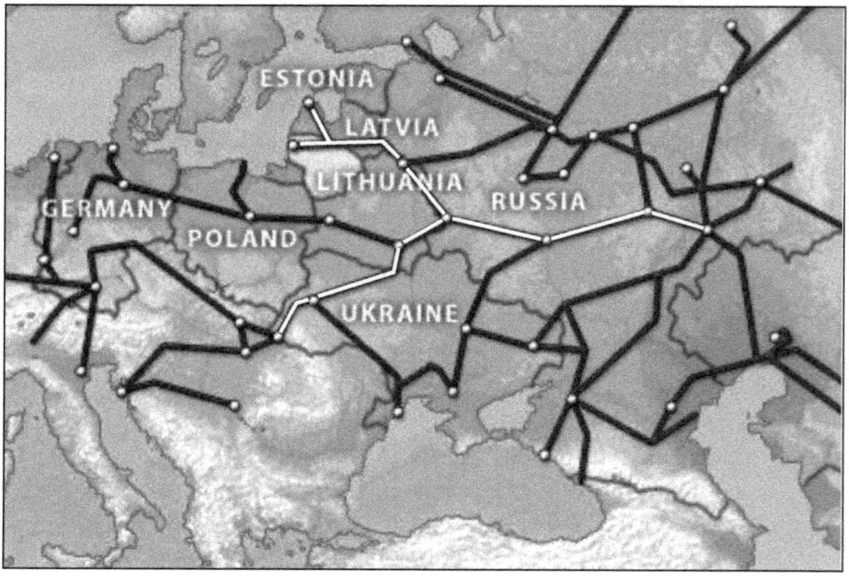

India has a growing pipeline system to supply products from the RPL complex in Jamnagar Gujarat and the existing Indian Oil Company system. The Indian Oil Company's cross-country network of crude oil and product pipelines spans 11,214 kilometres with a capacity of 77.258 MMtpa of crude oil and petroleum products and 10 million metric standard cubic metres of gas per day. This network is the largest in the country. Other large countries have not developed pipeline systems to this extent, because their populations are smaller or either concentrated on the coast (eg, Australia) or in one area of the country (eg, Brazil).

Railways have been used extensively to transport refined products – especially in the United States, India and Russia. Brazil has yet to develop its railways to the degree normally associated with a large country with a growing population and economy. Transportation has traditionally focused on mineral ores rather than oil and refined products. This is likely to change – especially if foreign investment is to come into the oil and gas industry in a significant way.

In Europe, large rivers have been used extensively for the transport of refined products. The Rhine delivers gasoline and diesel from the massive refining centres of Rotterdam and Antwerp. The Danube is also used and is connected to the Rhine by the Rhine/Danube canal. Rhine barges are constantly on the move for this purpose. The vast river systems of the Mississippi in Missouri and Ohio are also used in the United States, albeit to a lesser extent. In Russia, most of the large rivers are frozen for many months of the year and are not used to a great extent. The exceptions are the mighty Volga and Dnieper rivers in the Russian south.

Ocean transportation began with crude oil with Shell Trading and Shipping in Baku and has grown to service the United States from Mexico, Venezuela and the Middle East – especially to bring in crude oil and refined products to the giant Rotterdam trading hub and the refineries of Rotterdam and Antwerp.

Refined products enter:

- New York harbour, serving the northeast United States;
- Baton Rouge and Houston Sea port at Galveston, serving the south; and
- San Diego, serving the most populous US state, California.

These ports provide for the needs of the vast US economy.

The export facilities in the Arabian Gulf serve these shipping lanes, shipping to the above ports and to China and Japan.

Various hubs have grown up to provide transhipment from the mega-ultra large crude carriers – in Rotterdam, Hong Kong and Singapore, for example.

The *shogi shosha* utilise huge fleets of ships to feed the world's third-largest economy, Japan. Currently, China and Japan do not produce (see the discussion on China and shale oil in section 4.1(c))) sufficient crude oil for the needs of the approximately 50 Chinese and 30 Japanese refineries. Both countries will need to revamp/modernise or shelve refineries in order to provide refined products economically in the future. Given the high price of electricity in Japan, cogeneration is essential – especially if there is a real reduction in nuclear power. Most of Japan's nuclear plants have now come back onstream following the shutdowns after the Fukushima incident, as Japan cannot realistically do without nuclear power. In September 2022, Bloomberg reported that Japan was exploring the building of next-generation nuclear power plants, with seven more reactors being eyed for restarts in 2023 or later.[4]

Shipping through the Suez and Panama canals will remain a major factor in crude oil and refined products logistics.

The transoceanic supply of crude oil/products may well shift from the United States to Africa – especially if Latin America, despite its growth, develops its crude reserves efficiently and requires little imported material. For this to happen, an expansion of refining capacity in Latin America is needed.

China and Japan will continue to import from the Middle East, Indonesia, Thailand and Malaysia. If the Philippines develops its potential as an oil producer, its own needs will take up production unless huge fields are discovered.

If we consider the top 20 countries by population, which have little oil production compared to their economy, and exclude Ethiopia and Bangladesh because of their relatively small economies, we have the following main importers of crude oil and refined products: China, Japan, Pakistan, Egypt, Nigeria, the Philippines, Vietnam, Germany, Turkey and France.

Although Nigeria and Vietnam are oil producers, they produce high-grade, light, low-sulphur crude oil and will thus be under pressure to export their oil and not to refine it internally. Should their economies start to grow significantly, they will need to address their refineries urgently. At present, both countries export crude oil and import refined products. Egypt is in a similar position but produces relatively less oil. The other countries will be the major oil importers, assuming that the United States reduces its oil imports as many predict. These countries will require serious reviews of their refineries in order to produce affordable refined products.

Other countries with large populations that wish to refine their own oil (ie, Russia, Brazil, Indonesia, Thailand and Mexico) will need to thoroughly overhaul their downstream refining and marketing/distribution businesses.

History has shown that a combination of privatisation and the use of foreign capital is the most expedient and efficient route to take. For Thailand, this process is ongoing; but it took a step backwards when state-owned PTT took

4 Stephen Stapczynski and David Stringer, "Threats of blackouts drive Japan to embrace nuclear again", Bloomberg News, 24 August 2022, www.bnnbloomberg.ca/threats-of-blackouts-drive-japan-to-embrace-nuclear-again-1.1809614.

over the Shell Star Refinery in Map Ta Phut. Of the other countries, Brazil is best positioned to succeed in creating a modern and efficient well-funded refining and marketing industry; but it needs to privatise Petrobras and commit to developing pipeline and rail infrastructure.

Mexico and Indonesia may struggle to come to terms with foreign investment and privatisation, although both countries are taking initial steps in this direction.

Russia is always the unknown. As long as President Putin remains in power, it is hard to see the state relaxing its grip on the oil and gas industry. Therefore, it is unlikely that sufficient foreign investment from the United States and Europe will be attracted in order to realise the necessary modernisation. However, the overall investment situation may change if China and India invest in Russian refining industry as part of their bilateral crude oil deals.

5. Conclusion

The oil and gas industry is in a constant state of flux, but never more so than today. It has been politically exposed since its inception and wields great power in the United States through its powerful lobby. This is a double-edged sword. In the United States, the industry is regarded as Republican and is therefore a focus for attack by the Democrats. Internationally, it is seen as an arm of the US administration, whether Republican or Democrat.

The industry is part of the political scene in all countries, and consequently purely economic or business decisions will not always be made. Such factors may provide opportunities for NOCs, which are not hampered by political pressures. Indeed, they will continue to benefit from political support. Likewise, opportunities exist for strategically oriented investment funds.

For independent refiners – regardless of whether they are part of an integrated oil company – flexibility will be necessary to be competitive and to achieve sustainable margins. The modern refinery must concentrate on those products demanded by the market and products that will sell at a healthy margin above the crude price.

The move away from fuel production to petrochemicals is also expected to accelerate.

Logistics and crude sourcing will be factors in this business model, but a configuration that maximises margin and that concentrates on low-sulphur diesel and naphtha and aromatics for petrochemicals will provide the greatest security.

Clearly, those refiners located in growing markets with large populations will be the most successful. So, China, the United States, India, Brazil, Indonesia and the Philippines are most likely to host the most profitable refineries. The unknown quantity is Africa. Its success will depend on the stabilisation of governments and probably some privatisation of parts of the industry.

Government ownership can act as a drag on flexibility, and refining and marketing may be better able to operate when in private ownership or in the hands of publicly traded companies, free from government involvement. The United States has reached this point and India and the Philippines are halfway there. The next few years will determine whether the industry will become profitable in China, Russia and Brazil.

The challenges of carbon footprints and EVs must also be addressed.

If governments impose carbon taxes – in whatever form – on refineries, which are already marginally profitable, this will accelerate their closure. Only refineries that can operate in a world with a reduced market for their products can be profitable.

Gasification or partial oxidation of refinery residues, using the configuration introduced into the Shell Pernis Rotterdam refinery, could be a solution for improved margins and carbon capture from the gasifier.

The Shell Pernis refinery in the Netherlands gasifies its residual asphalt, which has been separated from refinery residues through solvent deasphalting, thereby producing all of the hydrogen required for desulphurisation without the need for natural gas to be imported, avoiding increasing the carbon footprint by bringing more carbon to the refinery as natural gas.

The deasphalted oil is an excellent feed for hydrocrackers and FCCUs, thereby increasing margins and eliminating the need for gas oil blending to produce fuel oil from residues.

The gasifier produces less carbon dioxide than would be produced if the hydrocarbons were burned as fuel oil; and the carbon dioxide can be easily captured and used in hydroponic greenhouse production of fruit, vegetables and flowers.

Such refineries can avoid carbon taxes and provide a separate valuable product while being environmentally positive. Also, the gasifiers can be part of hydrogen production centres, where the quantity of hydrogen produced is greater than the quantity required for desulphurisation internally.

A far greater threat is the EV. China will dominate the world in EV production through trains, trucks and buses; however, EV cars are the main threat, as they will replace diesel and gasoline-powered cars once the necessary low-cost electricity and recharging infrastructure are in place. With its huge indigenous market and lower battery costs, China can produce EVs at a lower price than conventional vehicles and market them in Europe and the United States through its Volvo subsidiary. No doubt other similar companies will be acquired.

Battery production cost are also falling and with them the price of EVs, in which battery costs account for up to 40% of the vehicle cost.

The main challenge for countries other than China is the price of electricity. China produces low-cost electricity from nuclear and coal; however, Europe has largely abandoned nuclear and at the time of writing has not yet reached consensus over the use of gas in place of coal. Also, subsidies for wind farms have pushed up the cost of electricity, which will be an issue for Germany's new government.

Subsidies for the wind power industry have proven expensive for Germany, although the cost of the turbines themselves has fallen. Reliance on Russian gas is also a significant issue for both Europe and China. This was turned into an advantage in 2022 by China; while for Germany, the need to diversify from Russian gas has led to the reopening of coal-fired power plants.

Japan is expanding its nuclear power plant industry, and the same trend may well play out in Germany and France – both already have substantial nuclear capacity, but their plants require upgrading and replacement.

New renewable sources of power production from waste coal, industrial and municipal waste and biomass can provide reliable electricity production which is not subject to the weather or the time of day; and refineries can contribute by reinventing themselves as carbon-neutral sources of hydrogen and low-cost electricity.

We are entering a new era of responsible oil refining, with a greatly reduced number of refineries and those remaining able to operate successfully in the post-COVID-19 and post-Russian sanctions world, which has brought about a huge increase in transportation costs, especially shipping costs. This will increase the drive towards refining close to the sources of crude oil and a concentration on local markets for products. Post-pandemic, the centre of gravity of the world economy is shifting eastward and the refining industry must take note and meet the challenges of the new era.

Petroleum storage

Peter Roberts
Cross Keys Energy

1. Introduction

This chapter considers the essential legal and commercial aspects of the business of storing petroleum in its various forms. The principal focus of the chapter is on arrangements for the underground storage of natural gas, but the storage of other forms of petroleum is also considered for completeness.

A number of introductory points will be helpful to note:

- Petroleum: Except where specific references are made, this chapter relates generally to 'petroleum', which is used as a generic term for crude oil, refined oil products, natural gas, associated gas liquids and processed gas forms such as liquefied natural gas (LNG) and liquefied petroleum gas (LPG).
- Fungibility: Petroleum, in whatever form it takes, has one specific characteristic which makes it very different from truly solid and readily divisible goods: once one quantity of petroleum of a particular grade has been mixed with another quantity of petroleum of the same grade, the respective quantities can no longer readily be distinguished. They are rendered molecularly indistinct by the process of commingling. Petroleum is therefore a truly fungible product. 'Fungible' is defined by the *Oxford English Dictionary* as "a thing which precisely or acceptably replaces or is replaced by another". The fungibility of petroleum presents certain challenges when it comes to the storage of commingled stock. It becomes difficult to apply conventional rules relating to the identification of discrete property interests to which title can be held where individual petroleum quantities have become unascertainable through commingling.
- Segregation: Petroleum of a particular grade could be held in segregated storage, with specific identification. The aim of segregated petroleum is to avoid the problems associated with being a part of commingled stock. Segregation is not always an operational possibility, however. In an onshore tankfarm, certain tanks can be set aside for the storage of segregated petroleum quantities. However, in a tank, a pipeline or a ship which is designed for the common transportation of petroleum

belonging to different shippers, segregation is physically and conceptually impossible.

- Facility ownership and access: A distinction can be made between:
  - petroleum storage facilities which are owned, operated and used by a person solely to meet that person's own petroleum storage needs; and
  - facilities which are owned by persons that rent out capacity in those facilities to petroleum owners under a form of services agreement in exchange for a fee.

  It is also necessary to consider the rights at law which non-facility owners might have to compulsorily acquire access to such facilities.

2. Crude and refined oil products strorage

An onshore tankfarm could be constructed for the storage of crude oil or refined oil products. Such a tankfarm could be directly owned and operated by an upstream oil production company or (more likely) by an affiliated company, where the upstream company is part of a vertically integrated undertaking. In the tankfarm, crude oil and/or refined oil products interests would be stored in commingled or segregated tankage.

As an alternative to the notion of the equity ownership of a tankfarm (whether directly by an upstream company or through an affiliated entity), a party requiring the storage of its crude oil or refined oil products could contract with a third party which owns a tankfarm for the provision of storage capacity at that tankfarm, in exchange for the payment of an agreed tariff by the storing party. The resultant storage services agreement which applies between the tankfarm owner and the storing party could go beyond the provision of bare storage, and could also provide for certain processing and/or transportation services to be supplied by the tankfarm owner to the storing party. All of these arrangements would be recited within a combined storage, transportation and processing agreement between the two parties.

As an extension to the conventional business of tankfarm storage of crude oil and refined oil products, where a company will store oil or oil products with a view to immediate physical delivery and sale at the prevailing market price, in storage trading the company will enter into contracts for the future sale and delivery of the stored oil or oil products at a price that is higher than the price which would be realised by an immediate physical delivery. As the intended future date for physical delivery approaches, the existing contracts are closed out, with new contracts entered into for the sale and future delivery of the same oil or oil products. This process is repeated, often with the consequence that the oil or oil products never actually move out of storage.

Trading in this fashion is only properly successful in a contango market – where the price of oil or oil products in the future (the forward price) is higher than the current market prices. Alternatively, the contract could be left in place, with a physical delivery of oil or oil products on the intended delivery date.

The term 'strategic storage' is used to describe a crude oil inventory which is stockpiled by the government of a particular country, providing economic security in the event of an energy crisis. The US Strategic Petroleum Reserve is one of the largest such reserves, with a capacity of approximately 700 million barrels owned by the US federal government and held in underground salt caverns along the coastline of the Gulf of Mexico. A typical target for governments is the retention of a crude oil inventory equivalent to 90 days of net oil imports.

3. LNG, LPG and gas storage

LNG which is unloaded from an LNG ship at an unloading port can go into a purpose-built refrigerated storage tank as LNG, rather than proceed straight to the process of regasification, and can later be released from that storage and regasified when needed. The residence time for such LNG storage is typically relatively short, however, which in part reflects the operational need to keep LNG flowing through an import terminal.

Gas can also be offtaken from a pipeline, liquefied to give LNG and stored as such (with the attendant volume reduction from the gas liquefaction process which allows greater volumetric storage capacity), and then regasified and released back into the pipeline as gas when needed.

LNG storage facilities could be owned and operated directly by the person requiring access to them; or could be owned by a third party and the capacity made available to an LNG owner as a storage customer through a form of storage services agreement.

Natural gas can be stored against future use requirements in specifically constructed steel or concrete surface gas storage tanks (sometimes called gasometers or gas holders). The gas is stored at atmospheric pressure and ambient temperature, and the volume of the storage tank is directly related to the quantity of stored gas, since the storage tank typically has a moveable cap which goes up and down according to the quantity of gas in store. Natural gas held in a pipeline as linepack is also essentially gas in storage; although the principal purpose of a pipeline is the transportation of gas, rather than its storage.

LPG is also stored in specifically manufactured cylindrical surface storage tanks, known variously as pressure tanks or bullets. Such storage tanks could be owned and operated directly by the person requiring access to them; or could be owned by a third party and the capacity made available to a gas owner as a storage customer through a form of storage services agreement.

The conventional view of natural gas sales and transportation arrangements is that gas will be produced, sold, transported and consumed according to the immediacy of the prevailing market demands.

It may be, however, that natural gas (which could be raw gas produced direct from a reservoir or regas delivered from regasified LNG) is not consumed, but instead is injected into a special underground natural gas storage facility (onshore or offshore), to be redelivered at a later date when market demands dictate. This is the essence of gas storage, which is a means of holding a gas inventory for release into an energy market when it is most needed.

The options for storing natural gas and LNG can be expressed by the schematic shown in Figure 1.

Figure 1. Options for storing natural gas and LNG

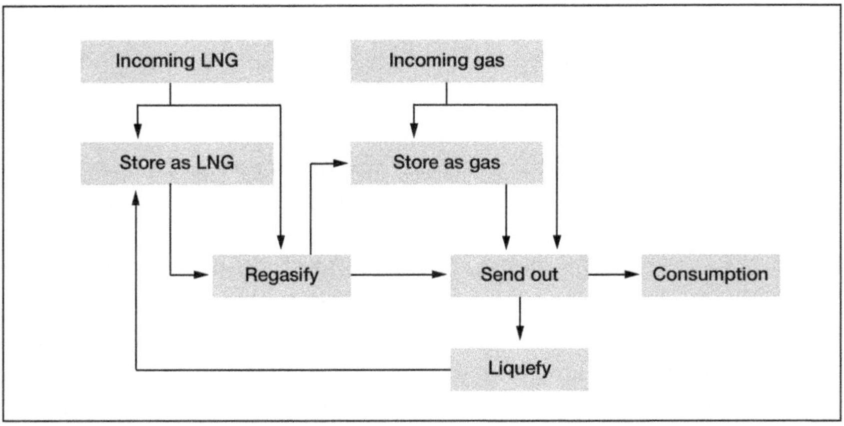

4. Underground gas storage

Underground gas storage is a form of flexible gas supply which supports the ability of a gas supplier to meet gas demand on a daily, weekly, monthly or seasonal basis. It can be invaluable in response to the challenges posed by supply constraints, adverse weather conditions, operational problems or geopolitical issues which might otherwise interrupt the free flow of gas into a market.

Any underground gas storage facility (whether onshore or offshore, and of whatever structure (see below)) is founded on the principle of putting gas in, storing gas and taking gas out when needed, according to the demands of the market. Any such facility will be based on a common set of features:

- Cushion gas and working gas: The facility will contain a permanent gas inventory ('cushion gas', also called 'base gas') which remains in the facility at all times, as an essential operational buffer between the hardware of the facility and those volumes of gas ('working gas') which are put (or injected) into and taken out (or redelivered) from the facility according to the needs of the gas supplier. Cushion gas could be owned or leased by the storage facility owner. The term 'total gas capacity' is used to describe the notional cushion gas and working gas capacity in a facility; the term 'gas in store' accounts for actual working gas (but not cushion gas) in store; and the term 'total gas in store' describes how much cushion gas and working gas actually resides within the facility at any one time.

- Cycling, deliverability and duration: Working gas will be injected into and redelivered from the facility through the process of cycling (also called turnover). The cycle rate represents the number of times in a given period of time that the entirety of a facility's working gas capacity can be so cycled.

  The term 'deliverability' is used to describe the volume of gas which can be redelivered from the facility in a given period of time. This measure of deliverability will vary according to the particular facility, since the rate of deliverability will be at its greatest when the total gas in store is at its highest and will drop off as the facility depletes.

  The term 'duration' is used to describe the time which it takes to redeliver the total working gas capacity from the facility. A larger-volume gas storage project will inevitably have a longer duration, but this is not an absolute measure of performance – as a rule of thumb, doubling the rate of deliverability will halve the duration and halving the rate of redelivery will double the duration.
- Shape: This term is used to define each facility's often unique combination of cushion gas and working gas capacities, cycle rates, rates of deliverability, proximity to market, operating costs and available infrastructure, to give an overall picture of that facility's inherent flexibility and capability. Different gas storage facilities have different shapes, making them suited for different roles, and a gas storage sector participant could have interests in multiple facilities in the interests of building a wide and flexible gas storage portfolio.
- Values: The economic profile of a facility is often defined according to:
  - extrinsic values (ie, by reference to the cycle rate of a facility which can access and arbitrage short-term gas supply and demand variations and price volatility for a profit); and
  - intrinsic values (ie, by reference to the ability of a facility to take advantage of seasonality (see below) and forward gas price differentials over longer-term spreads, without taking extrinsic values into account).

  Intrinsic values, at least notionally, have greater external price visibility than extrinsic values.
- Seasonality and range: A facility might be used to meet seasonal gas demand variations, where gas will be sourced and injected during summer months (where there will be the expectation of lower demand

and lower prices) and redelivered during winter months (where there will be the expectation of greater demand and higher prices), on a single annual cycle. This is 'seasonality'. This principle of seasonality applies where gas is consumed as a fuel for heating in winter months. The opposite cycle of seasonality would apply where gas is consumed as a fuel for air conditioning and district cooling during summer months. It may also be that a particular market demonstrates both seasonal cycles within a single year.

- Gas storage facilities are also sometimes classified as long-range storage (LRS), medium-range storage (MRS) or short-range storage (SRS). What constitutes LRS, MRS and SRS is somewhat opaque, and these definitions are relative rather than absolute. The UK gas regulator, Ofgem, uses the following definitions, based on the length of time taken by a facility to deliver all of its working gas volume at full capacity:
  - SRS – up to five days;
  - MRS – between five and 70 days; and
  - LRS – more than two months.

The only safe thing to say in defining the range of a particular facility is that 'medium' is longer than 'short' and 'long' is longer than 'medium'. LRS, MRS and SRS each operate on the same curve; it is only the amplitude which is different. Typically, LRS facilities are operated to take advantage of seasonality. SRS facilities benefit from much faster cycle times, even including the possibility of within-day flexibility. It is also possible for a single facility to combine LRS, MRS and SRS range characteristics.

Three types of structure can be considered for use as an underground gas storage facility – depleted gas reservoirs, salt caverns and aquifer reservoirs. Each type of facility possesses distinct physical and economic characteristics which determine the suitability of a particular type of facility for a given gas storage application:

- Depleted gas reservoirs: These are onshore or offshore reservoirs from which economically recoverable reserves of gas have been produced (subject to the remainder of any residual native gas). The reservoir is readily capable of storing injected gas and using such a facility is economically attractive because it allows the reuse, with suitable modification, of the extraction and distribution infrastructure remaining from the productive life of the original gas field, which reduces project start-up costs. Depleted gas reservoirs are attractive because of their known porosity and permeability; their geological and physical characteristics have benefited from previous study and so are already understood. Consequently, depleted gas reservoirs are generally the cheapest and easiest to develop, operate and maintain of the various types of underground gas storage facility. In a depleted gas reservoir, the native gas originally in the reservoir could also be kept as cushion gas and the further injection of gas might not be needed, unless gas from the reservoir has been produced beyond the level of the required cushion gas volume.

- Salt caverns: These onshore or offshore facilities are developed from discovered underground salt deposits. Once a suitable salt deposit is discovered and found to be suitable for the development of a gas storage facility, a cavern is created within the salt deposit. This is done by the process of salt leaching, whereby fresh water is pumped down a borehole into the salt deposit. The inherent salt is dissolved, leaving a void, and the salinated water is pumped back to the surface. This resultant void is a cavity which will be used for the storage of gas. Salt caverns are usually smaller than depleted gas reservoirs and consequently salt caverns cannot ordinarily hold the volumes of gas necessary to meet large-volume and/or long-duration gas storage requirements.
- Aquifer reservoirs: These are underground porous and permeable rock formations that act as natural water reservoirs and which, in some cases, can be used for gas storage. The geological and physical characteristics of an aquifer reservoir are not generally known ahead of time; and significant investment is needed to investigate these and evaluate the aquifer reservoir's suitability for gas storage, and to develop topside gas infrastructure, which can make for an expensive and uncertain project.

With salt caverns and aquifer reservoirs, all of the associated sub-surface and surface infrastructure must typically be developed from scratch, increasing the development costs of the project compared to a depleted gas reservoir project. This includes the drilling of wells and the installation of gas injection and redelivery equipment and takeaway pipelines.

5. Underground gas storage project economics

There are two elements to assessing the economics of any underground gas storage project – the costs of developing the project and the revenues which that project then generates. These costs and revenues are key to financial modelling and establishing the overall project value (often as a precursor to making a project investment decision).

Developing underground gas storage facilities is capital intensive. Significant expenses are also incurred during the planning phase and in assessing the location and the nature of potential sites to determine suitability for the construction of a facility.

The level of capital expenditure required to build an underground gas storage facility depends on the physical characteristics of the intended facility.

A salt cavern will generally be more expensive to develop than a depleted gas reservoir, particularly where the associated sub-surface and surface infrastructure must also be developed. Aquifer reservoirs are still a relatively unknown quantity. A relative lack of experience within the industry in developing gas storage projects also means that capital cost estimates can be particularly uncertain.

Another cost component which must be factored into the inception of any project is the cost of the cushion gas. High market gas prices mean high cushion gas prices and can make project economics correspondingly less attractive. The high cost of cushion gas is also what drives the expansion of current facilities versus the development of new facilities, because expansions require relatively little addition to the initial volumes of cushion gas.

Cushion gas could be bought by the underground gas storage facility owner, as an item of capital expenditure. As an alternative, the facility owner could seek to lease the cushion gas from a third party (which could be affiliated to or entirely unconnected with the facility owner) for the duration of the operational lifetime of the facility. In such a leasing arrangement, ownership of the cushion gas would remain with the lessor and the storage facility owner, as the lessee, would make periodic rental payments to the lessor.

The revenue which a gas storage project generates depends on how the project is configured.

In the equity storage model, the facility owner buys and injects gas when the forward gas price spread is low and then redelivers and sells that gas when demand for gas and the forward gas price spread for that gas is higher (according to a variety of time ranges). It is the buy/sell arbitrage between these prices which leads to the generation of revenue from the project. The facility owner typically reserves all of the capacity in the facility to meet its own commercial needs.

In the storage services model, the project generates revenues through the sale of defined storage services to third-party users (which can then conduct their own arbitrage in the manner described above) in exchange for a fee. Storage services can be sold on the basis of a defined, bundled standard storage unit, which is made up of a collection of rights:

- injectability – the right to inject a defined quantity of gas into the facility;
- storage – the right to store a defined quantity of gas in the facility; and
- redeliverablity – the right to withdraw a defined quantity of gas from the facility.

(In each case, the quantity of gas referred to is typically defined by reference to a certain calorific value of the gas.)

Storage capacity which has been bought by a user can be traded on a secondary market for the benefit of other users, where that capacity is not being used by the original user; and the storage facility owner might also be subject to some sort of 'use it or lose it' obligation in respect of unused capacity.

Storage services can be sold to users on any combination of short, medium or long-term contracts. Storage services on offer will also vary according to the nature of the service which is available (eg, in relation to deliverability rates and injection rates), with higher prices payable by users for more flexible access.

The participants within any particular gas storage project might not have the luxury of being able to choose for themselves whether to select an equity storage or a storage services model. Applicable regulatory rules regarding the granting of third-party access rights (see below) could oblige a facility owner to offer storage services to third-party users in certain circumstances, rather than to run the facility solely on an equity basis.

In either the equity storage model or the storage services model, gas storage facilities that operate primarily to take advantage of short-term arbitrage opportunities will have different value drivers from projects that are primarily intended to meet longer-term seasonal supply opportunities. The seasonal valuation of a storage project is evaluated effectively as the difference between long-term price spreads (based on intrinsic values); whereas a high-deliverability, fast-cycle storage facility can respond to variations in demand and price according to shorter time cycles (based on extrinsic values).

From the facility owner's perspective, the principal manner of determining the facility's profitability is by reference to the profits which it generates; but an additional method of looking at the value of the facility is by reference to the savings resulting to the owner from not having to resort to other more expensive gas or other energy supply options in order to meet its obligations under any gas supply commitments.

6. Stored petroleum title issues

In the absence of truly segregated petroleum storage, it is inevitable that the petroleum entitlements of multiple persons will be commingled while that petroleum is being stored. This is an inescapable consequence of petroleum's fungibility (see above).

An underground gas storage facility will contain cushion gas and working gas (and possibly also some native gas). The cushion gas and working gas entitlements could all belong to the same person, in which case it is not necessary to provide for how different title interests are recognised and reconciled. Alternatively, however, the cushion gas could be owned by the facility owner or by a lessor and the working gas could be owned by one or more users, in which case it also becomes necessary to address the issue of how title to the various gas interests is held between the relevant persons.

The options for structuring the ownership of individual petroleum entitlements in a multi-user petroleum storage facility will provoke similar considerations to how the security of title to natural gas or crude oil is structured in a multi-shipper pipeline. Title to all petroleum which is resident in the facility could vest in the facility owner at the point of injection and would transfer back to a user at the point of redelivery; or each user could retain title to its petroleum entitlements in the facility through a form of tenancy in common. In respect of different ownership entitlements of crude oil, refined oil products, natural gas, LNG or LPG, it becomes necessary for a facility owner to maintain a system of stock accounting. Such stock accounting will recognise the entitlement of a user of the facility to a distinct part of the whole volume of petroleum in store, albeit without recognising distinct molecular entitlements.

The concern which a user could have in relation to a structure where the facility owner takes title to all the petroleum at the point of injection is what happens in the event of the insolvency of the facility owner. It could be possible that the user would have to prove its claim for the return of its petroleum entitlement as nothing more than an unsecured creditor, ranking *pari passu* with every other unsecured creditor. To overcome this risk, where title is transferred to the facility owner, some facilities rely on the intervention of an independent security trustee holding title to the stored petroleum on trust for the users.

Commingled petroleum stocks also present difficulties when a user, as an owner of part of the commingled stock, elects to sell its stored petroleum interests to another person. The principal statute to be aware of under English law is the Sale of Goods Act 1979 (as amended). Under this act, where there is a sale of 'unascertained' goods, title to those goods can only transfer to a buyer once the goods have become 'ascertained' (ie, when the goods have become unconditionally appropriated to the contract with the buyer). An effective transfer of title through the sale of a part consignment of petroleum within a commingled stock is not readily achievable. In the event of a dispute relating to title interests in a commingled petroleum stock, the position which applies could be determined by the applicable law of the storage project and also by the laws of the jurisdiction in which the petroleum is physically located.

7. Third-party access rights and wider regulation

Third-party access (TPA) is a simple shorthand for a device which can represent a great deal of complexity for storage facility owners and which can also bestow a fair degree of opportunity on would-be users of storage facility capacity.

The manner of regulation of a particular petroleum sector could apply a presumption in favour of the rights of a facility owner to be able to use that facility solely for its own benefit. Alternatively, that regulation could seek to allow a third party to secure rights of access to any unutilised capacity in that facility, subject to compliance by that third party with certain commercial and financial terms which are promulgated by the facility owner. This is the essence of TPA.

The investment required to build petroleum storage facilities is characterised by significant costs and also by the principle of irreversibility (ie, once a facility has been built and commissioned, it will remain in place until it is eventually decommissioned). A facility owner could develop a facility as it needs it and then keep it for its own exclusive use, but this philosophy of exclusive access suffers from three major deficiencies:

- Proliferation: If every prospective facility owner builds the facility it needs, there is a risk of the proliferation of new infrastructure to the point where the market as a whole is saturated and becomes less efficient than it could be. The proliferation of duplicated infrastructure is generally regarded as undesirable because new infrastructure items could interfere with the rights of other infrastructure owners or users; and because the introduction of uncontrolled amounts of new infrastructure could have a damaging impact on the environment. There is a balance to be struck here, however, because new facilities can enhance competition and can promote greater overall security in the supply of energy.
- Inefficiency: The operational reality is that most facilities will in practice demonstrate a greater level of capacity than was originally envisaged by the facility owner and spare capacity could also become apparent where the level of capacity required by the facility owner drops off over time. Unused capacity makes storage facilities (and also the overall market) relatively inefficient.
- Market exclusion: There may be persons that wish to participate in the petroleum storage market but are unable to realise this ambition because they are unable to develop their own storage facilities (whether for economic, commercial or regulatory reasons). These persons would therefore be excluded from market participation in the absence of a compellable right to access any spare capacity in a facility belonging to another.

Where a right is granted by a facility owner to a third party to utilise spare capacity in a facility, a soft form of TPA exists, where the facility owner voluntarily permits a third party to access spare capacity on an *ad hoc* basis. Moving on from this, however, TPA could become firmer where third-party users start to believe in a sense of entitlement to be allowed to use spare capacity; this will particularly be so where there is some form of regulatory presumption in favour of such an entitlement.

Third-party users might feel that they suffer from an inequality of bargaining power in comparison with existing facility owners, and to this end they could argue the need for clear legal and regulatory support for their positions when negotiating TPA rights. Two requirements are key to note here:

- Negotiated access: In this regime, facility owners and users will negotiate access to the facility according to good-faith negotiations and voluntary commercial agreements based on published conditions of use (negotiated third-party access).
- Regulated access: In this regime, facility owners and users will negotiate access to the facility according to a right of access based on published tariffs and other conditions of use (regulated third-party access).

There is always the potential for some commercial tension between a facility owner and a third party seeking access to that facility, and this tension requires some form of regulation. In terms of facilitating the rights of the third party to secure access to spare capacity in a facility it is necessary to consider two regulatory aspects:

- voluntary codes of practice promulgated by sector participants; and
- the application of English law.

In the United Kingdom, a voluntary, industry-wide code of practice regarding TPA (the Infrastructure Code of Practice) has existed since 1996. The code was revised and reissued in 2004, 2009 and again in 2017, with guidance notes.[1] The code is ultimately a voluntary code, however. If a voluntary agreement cannot be reached between a facility owner and a third party regarding TPA, an aggrieved party can make a reference to government for determination, using statutory powers. TPA rights created by statute in the United Kingdom are now represented principally by Part 2 of the Energy Act 2011. This act establishes a presumption in favour of a third party wishing to access unused capacity in a storage facility, upon application to the facility owner. In certain circumstances the facility owner can apply for an exemption from third-party rights of access. These requirements result from the Third Gas Directive (2009/73) and EU Regulation 715/2009, which were implemented by the United Kingdom when it was an EU member state and which remain in force as domestic law despite the United Kingdom's withdrawal from the European Union (although further change to this regulatory position could always be introduced as a matter of domestic law).

The UK government's regulatory policy – which emphasises the need to maximise economic recovery in the exploitation of the country's petroleum resources[2] – could also require that relevant persons plan, commission and

---

1 Code of Practice on Access to Upstream Oil and Gas Infrastructure on the UK Continental Shelf, August 2017 (available from the UK Oil & Gas Authority).

2 See "The maximising economic recovery strategy for the UK", presented to Parliament pursuant to Section 9G of the Petroleum Act 1998 as amended by the Infrastructure Act 2015; https://assets.publishing.service.gov.uk/government/uploads/system/uploads/attachment_data/file/509000/MER_UK_Strategy_FINAL.pdf.

construct infrastructure in a way that meets the optimum configuration for maximising the value of economically recoverable petroleum that can be recovered from the region in which the infrastructure is to be located, and this obligation could apply to the development of new petroleum storage infrastructure.

Gas sales agreements

Seyram Dzikunu
Bentsi-Enchill, Letsa & Ankomah
Thomas Kojo Stephens
Stobe Law; University of Ghana School of Law

1. Introduction

One of the key commercial agreements for monetising gas projects in the downstream industry is a gas sales agreement (GSA).

A GSA, also known as a gas supply agreement, is basically an agreement for the exchange of gas commodities between the seller and buyer whereby:

- the seller undertakes to make gas available to the buyer for delivery when required; and
- the buyer agrees to pay money to the seller in return for the provision of that gas.

The GSA can be a supply or a depletion contract. Under a supply contract, the seller contracts with the buyer to supply it with agreed quantities of gas for a defined period, without necessarily specifying the source of the gas. A supply contract is thus for a fixed period and there is not necessarily a reservoir dedicated to the supply of the gas. Under a depletion contract, the seller agrees to exclusively provide to the buyer all gas produced from a particular field. Thus, the timeline for supply will be determined by when the field is exhausted as opposed to a specific future date. In other words, there is a defined, dedicated source of supply for the gas and the seller is under no obligation to source gas from anywhere else in order to meet a supply obligation. One can also have a GSA that is a hybrid of the two.

Gas production involves very substantial investments and capital expenditure; to ensure that these costs are recouped, sellers usually insist on long-term contractual commitments from buyers. Thus, a typical GSA has a duration of at least 20 years and has contractual clauses that ensure the buyer is tied in and cannot simply exit the contractual arrangement as and when it deems it convenient so to do.

2. Typical GSA clauses

The typical clauses in a GSA are discussed below.

2.1 Definitions and interpretation

The GSA will set out definitions of key terms in the agreement. The purpose of the definition section is to provide guidance on the interpretation of terms used in the agreement. The definitions of words and phrases in this section will supersede any other interpretation.

2.2 Parties and collateral support

The GSA will specify the precise identity of the parties to the contract. There must be no ambiguity whatsoever as to the entities that are entering into the contractual arrangement. The GSA will identify which entity is the seller and which the buyer.

Further, GSAs are long term in nature, so a key consideration will be the financial wherewithal of the buyer – that is, its ability to perform its contractual obligations. The buyer's principal obligation is to make payments for the product, so its creditworthiness is of paramount importance. If the seller has reservations about the buyer's creditworthiness or its financial strength, it may insist on the provision of collateral support by way of a bank or parent company guarantee, or a letter of credit.[1]

2.3 Sale, purchase and delivery of gas

The GSA will state the primary purpose of entering into the agreement, which is the obligation to sell, deliver, take and pay for gas. It will provide that the seller must deliver gas and the buyer must take and pay for the gas at the agreed contract price.

2.4 Conditions precedent

In *Wickman Machine Tool Sales Ltd v L Schuler*,[2] the court noted that the word 'condition' means "a term the breach of which by one party gives to the other an option either to terminate the contract or to let the contract proceed and, if he so desires, sue for damages for the breach". A 'condition precedent' is defined by *Blacks Law Dictionary* as "an act or event, other than a lapse of time, that must exist or occur before a duty to perform something promised arises".[3]

Conditions precedent deal with matters which must be satisfied before the substantive obligations can crystallise. *Chitty on Contracts* contextualises them as follows: "The parties may enter into an immediate binding contract, but subject to a condition, which suspends all or some of the obligations of one or both parties pending fulfilment of the condition."[4] They enable the parties to the GSA to defer the substantive part thereof – that is, the supply and offtake – until selected matters which are fundamental to performance of the agreement have been satisfied. Thus, as Roberts notes, from an economic perspective, the

1 Daniel O'Neill, *Oil and Gas: A Practical Handbook* (Globe Law and Business, 2009), p139.
2 AG [1974] AC 235, 250H.
3 Bryan Garner, *Black's Law Dictionary*, 8th edition (Thomson West, 2004), p312.
4 *Chitty on Contracts*, 27th edition (Sweet & Maxwell Ltd, 1994), para 12-026.

basic philosophy behind the inclusion of conditions precedent is that the exposure of the parties to legally enforceable performance obligations with corresponding liabilities and the obligation of the parties to embark upon the effort and huge expense of facilities development will be prorogued until it is clear that the GSA is capable of being performed as an operative agreement.[5] If the conditions precedent are not satisfied or waived and the GSA is terminated, the parties will have at least avoided the needless expense of developing the necessary facilities and incurring avoidable costs.[6]

Thus, while the GSA becomes binding upon execution, if the agreement stipulates that it is subject to the satisfaction of conditions precedent, not all rights and obligations will become effective upon signing. As O'Neill aptly notes: "Although the term of the GSA will commence upon signing, if the GSA is expressed as being subject to the satisfaction of conditions precedent, then some but not all of the rights and obligations under the GSA will become binding with effect from signing."[7] These become effective once the conditions precedent are satisfied.

Conditions precedent can include:

- the procurement of all necessary government approvals for the commencement and operation of the project; or
- the entry into or the coming into effect of other key agreements ancillary to the GSA, such as the gas transportation agreement, which could involve:
  - the carrying out of the task by a third party;
  - the securing of financing for a party's commitments; and
  - the completion of an obligation on a party to construct facilities for the operation of the GSA.

If conditions precedent are not satisfied or waived – usually by the party entitled to the protection thereof – the GSA will usually be terminable on notice by the party entitled to the benefit of that condition precedent.[8] Thus, in *Total Trading & Marketing v Arco British Limited*,[9] the court held that a contract to purchase supplies over a long period of time and which contained a condition precedent that a particular facility would be provided was terminable when the facility was not provided.

2.5 Term and effectiveness

A GSA will stipulate the term of the agreement. GSAs are long-term contracts –

5 Peter Roberts, *Gas Sales and Gas Transportation Agreements: Principles and Practice*, 3rd edition (Sweet & Maxwell, 2011), p111.
6 *Ibid.*
7 O'Neill (n 1), p140.
8 Roberts (n 5), p112.
9 [1998] UKHL 22.

usually 20 to 25 years or more. The term may comprise distinct periods during which specified obligations must be met by each party.

2.6 Start date

As noted, although the GSA will become effective on the date of execution, it will also specify a specific date on which certain essential commercial obligations will come into force, such as the date for initial deliveries. At the start date, important rights and obligations – such as the buyer's right to schedule gas for delivery and its take-or-pay commitment – become effective. Setting a start date is important because the whole venture requires careful planning for commercial readiness. The start date is usually determined by a mechanism that seeks to coordinate the date of completion of the facilities in each part of the value chain. If a party is unable to deliver or receive gas on or from the start date ('late start'), and is not excused under the GSA – for instance, due to *force majeure* – that party will be liable for full shortfall gas liabilities, or full take-or-pay liabilities, on and from the start date.

2.7 Facilities

The seller must ensure that it designs, constructs, installs, commissions, operates, maintains, repairs, reinstates and insures its facilities in accordance with the GSA's requirements. Roberts very aptly observes:

> *The reasoning behind such a facilities obligation is that it imposes upon the party responsible to satisfy it an enforceable contractual commitment to ensure that the facilities which are critical to the performance of the gas (or LNG) project will be developed, made available and kept in place as necessary for the performance of the GSA (or SPA) or the GTA.*[10]

He goes on to note: "This obligation will help to better ensure the likelihood of success of the wider gas (or LNG) project because every necessary link in the supply chain will (hopefully) be complete when it needs to be."[11]

(a) Commissioning of facilities

The commissioning of facilities happens before the start date. It basically involves testing to ensure that the facilities are ready for operation, such as ensuring that the gas quality is consistent with the technical specifications of the equipment. The commissioning of the facilities will require the buyer to take gas (commissioning gas). The GSA will prescribe how the coordination and synchronisation will occur at the commissioning of the facility. During the commissioning period, which typically takes place over a number of days or weeks:

---

10 Roberts (n 5), p128.
11 *Ibid.*

- the parties will be obliged either to deliver or to take gas;
- the seller will not be liable for shortfall gas; and
- the buyer will not have take-or-pay liability for failure to take the gas.

The GSA may also provide for performance tests prior to the commissioning period, to test the facilities of each party.

(b) ***Maintenance of facilities***

The GSA will stipulate that the parties will meet at stipulated intervals to discuss when upstream and downstream maintenance will occur, and the parties will be obliged under the GSA to use all reasonable endeavours to coordinate or procure the coordination of planned maintenance. Third parties – for example, the downstream gas transporter or key customers of the buyer, such as a power plant – may influence decisions on the timing of the maintenance. The parties will usually agree in the GSA to provide each other with reasonable information on a regular basis regarding the scheduling of any upstream or downstream maintenance. During periods when maintenance is being performed, the parties will be excused from their supply and offtake obligations.

2.8 Delivery point

The GSA will specify a delivery/sales point at which the obligations of the seller to deliver the gas to the buyer will be effected. The parties will specify that the gas to be delivered will be made available by the seller to the buyer at the delivery point. The 'delivery point' is the point at which the gas is transferred from the buyer to the seller. The delivery point will usually be specified in the GSA as a precise geographical point and is the meeting point between the seller's production facilities and the buyer's receiving facilities. The GSA will further stipulate – unless otherwise agreed – that the seller shall, at its own risk and expense, procure the transportation to the delivery point of all quantities required for the performance of the GSA by the seller.

2.9 Title, risk and warranties

The GSA will stipulate when title to the gas – that is, ownership – passes from the seller to the buyer. This is usually at the delivery point.

The seller will make a number of representations and warranties, including the following:

- It has good title to, and is entitled to tender for delivery and sale at the delivery point, all sales gas to be delivered to the buyer; and the gas is free from all encumbrances.
- All actions, conditions and other obligations required by the law of the host state to be taken, fulfilled and done – including the obtaining of any necessary licences, approvals, authorisations, permissions and

exemptions – have been secured, and all necessary filings, recordings and registrations have been made.

- Anything necessary to be done in order for the seller to enter into and perform its obligations under the GSA will be taken, fulfilled and done at the time anticipated by the GSA.
- It is duly incorporated and validly exists under the host law, and all actions, conditions and requirements under the host state's law to be done in order for the buyer to enter into and perform its obligations under the GSA have been duly fulfilled or will be fulfilled at the time anticipated by the GSA.
- Neither execution nor performance of the buyer's obligations will violate any law or regulation to which the buyer is subject, or any agreement to which the buyer is a party or which is binding on it or any of its assets.

Both the seller and buyer will represent and warrant the following:

- At the start date, they will have full legal title to, and be in possession of, all assets which are necessary to perform their obligations, and there will be no third-party interests in or over such assets.
- They are not party to any litigation or arbitration, or bound by any order, injunction, declaration, award or judgment of any arbitrator, court or other forum, that could adversely affect their ability to perform obligations under the GSA.
- They will use reasonable endeavours to obtain, maintain and comply with the host state's consents, licences or approvals, or anything of such nature necessary to fulfil in all material respects their obligations under the GSA throughout the term thereof.

2.10 Nominations

Nominations can be considered as analogous to a purchase order. They set out the buyer's views on the volumes it will need over the following period. The buyer must notify the seller in advance of its requirement for gas in respect of each nomination period. If the buyer fails to do so, it will be deemed to have made certain nominations, which will constitute valid nominations and will be fixed. The seller will thus have to deliver gas in accordance with these nominations, failing which the seller will be in shortfall. Also, the failure of the buyer to take gas in accordance with its nominations will be the basis for calculating undertake gas.[12]

The buyer will usually want to ensure that the nominations regime has sufficient flexibility to meet its downstream requirements, while the seller will want to ensure that the nominations regime is such that it can be managed within the seller's operational limits. The main rationale for nominations is:

12 Roberts (n 5), pp494–495.

- to enable the buyer to nominate volumes it redelivers into the downstream nomination transportation network; and
- to book the capacity it needs for a continuous flow.

2.11 Quantities

The seller will need to know in advance how much gas is required by the buyer at any particular point in time. In respect of a buyer's nomination regime, it must give the seller a nomination for the quantity of gas that it wishes to have delivered at the delivery point in respect of a given nomination period.[13] The buyer must ensure that its nominations fit with its requirements for gas and its downstream commitments.[14] The seller, on the other hand, must ensure that its nomination timetable is sufficient to give it adequate time to produce the gas and schedule the required gas deliveries in a way that fits with the scheduling requirements of the pipeline or other facilities that the seller may be using to transport the gas to the delivery point.[15]

(a) Contract quantities

The parties to the GSA must agree on the total volume of gas that will be supplied over the term of the GSA by the seller. This total volume is referred to as the 'contract quantity' (CQ). Roberts very aptly notes that: "This can be a difficult matter to estimate in advance and the actual quantities of delivered gas (or LNG) could well be lesser than or greater than the defined contract quantity."[16] The CQ is usually determined based on the volume of gas that the seller will have available over the contract period and the commercial needs of the buyer.

(b) Annual contract quantity

The GSA must provide for the annual contract quantity (ACQ), which is the total amount of gas that the seller is obliged to deliver and the buyer is obliged to take from the seller every year. The ACQ forms a focal point around which a take-or-pay commitment is based. The ACQ is usually provided as an absolute figure in the GSA. It is essential to state the absolute figure so that the parties can determine any shortfalls over the life of the GSA.

(c) Daily contract quantity

The GSA must also specify the daily contract quantity (DCQ), which is the minimum amount of gas that the seller must provide to the buyer every day during the term of the GSA.

---

13 *Ibid*, p136.
14 *Ibid*.
15 *Ibid*.
16 *Ibid*, p122.

(d) *Maximum daily contract quantity*

To provide the buyer with flexibility, most GSAs will permit the buyer to nominate some additional daily quantities of gas above the DCQ. This additional gas enables the buyer to meet any spikes in demand during the day. The additional nomination flexibility provided by the seller is usually a percentage of the DCQ. This additional percentage of DCQ which can be nominated daily plus the DCQ is referred to as the 'maximum DCQ' (MDCQ). The buyer cannot nominate gas above the MDCQ in one day.[17]

(e) *Excess gas*

A GSA will usually provide for the supply of gas above the agreed MDCQ or ACQ. The purpose of this clause is to provide for a situation where the buyer needs more than the contracted volumes to cover a rise in demand. Under the excess gas clause, a seller is not obliged to provide such excess gas, but rather will agree to use reasonable endeavours to provide excess gas if the need arises. Some GSAs may provide for the payment of a premium for excess gas; others may agree to sell excess gas at the agreed contract price; and others, depending on the gas market, may grant the buyer price incentives to take excess gas.[18]

2.12 Undertake gas and overtake gas

Where the supply of gas is through a pipeline, the GSA will make provision for instances where the buyer takes less gas than the buyer nominated for delivery or the buyer takes more gas than the buyer nominated for delivery. Where the buyer takes less gas than it nominated for delivery, this is referred to as 'undertake gas'; and where more gas is taken than was nominated, this is referred to as 'overtake gas'. Since both the undertake and overtake of gas cause problems for the seller and may impact its contracts with other third parties, the GSA will provide disincentives to prevent undertaking and overtaking of gas. The GSA will require a buyer to pay damages in respect of the actual loss suffered by the seller for gas undertake and overtake in respect of any nominated delivery.

2.13 Take-or-pay, take-and-pay

Black's Law Dictionary aptly defines a 'take-or-pay contract' as "a contract requiring the buyer to either purchase and receive a minimum amount of a product ('take') or pay for this minimum without taking immediate delivery ('pay')." It goes on to note that "these contracts are often used in the energy and oil-and-gas businesses".[19]

---

17 *Ibid*, p128.
18 O'Neill (n 1), p146.
19 Garner (n 3), p349.

Some GSAs will include a take-or-pay clause. The purpose of this clause is to ensure that the seller has guaranteed minimum payments coming in from the project, irrespective of whether the buyer takes the gas. As O'Neill puts it: "The purpose of a take-or-pay obligation is to provide the seller with a periodic guaranteed minimum cash flow from the gas commercialisation project irrespective of whether the buyer takes the quantities of gas for which it has contracted."[20] The parties will agree the minimum bill quantity (MBQ) which will be the take-or-pay, and the MBQ is usually adjusted to reflect *force majeure* volumes and make-up.

Under the take-or pay obligation, the buyer is obliged:

- to take the gas and pay for it during prescribed periods; or
- to elect not to take the gas for whatever reason, in which case it will still be obliged to pay for the gas.

The buyer will subsequently have a right to request the gas that it has paid for, but that has not yet been delivered by the seller. The take-or-pay is a financial obligation to pay for the gas and not a financial obligation to take the gas.

On the other hand, under a take-and-pay commitment:

- the seller has a firm obligation to deliver a specified amount of gas; and
- the buyer is also obliged to take that specified quantity and pay for it.

If the buyer refuses to take and pay for the specified delivered gas, the buyer will be liable to pay the seller damages for failure to comply with the terms of the contract. Unlike the take-or-pay obligation – where there is a right to make up for gas paid for and not delivered – there is no such make-up right under a take-and-pay obligation, since any failure for not taking and paying for gas is regarded as damages for breach.[21]

The take-or-pay clause is not a liquidated damages clause, since the buyer has the right to recover for the money paid while in respect of the take-and-pay, the buyer is paying liquidated damages for breach of the contract for not taking the gas agreed.

2.14 Make-up and carry-forward

Where a GSA has take-or-pay obligations, the buyer may take more or less gas in a year than the take-or-pay obligation for that period. Hence, the make-up and carry-forward mechanisms are used to manage the take-or-pay commitment of the buyer. This is to ensure that the take-or-pay obligation does not create a situation where the seller is benefiting financially for gas paid for

20 O'Neill (n 1), p147.
21 Roberts (n 5), p194.

under the take-or-pay commitment but not supplied. Thus, any take-or-pay payments made are credited to a notional make-up account. The buyer is then allowed, during any contract period after it has complied with its take-or-pay commitment for the year, to take additional gas representing the amounts credited to the make-up account. The buyer may not take make-up gas in a contract year to the extent that it exceeds the ACQ for that contract year. In other words, in respect of make-up gas, if in any delivery year the buyer has paid for but not taken any quantity of gas, it will be entitled to take an equal quantity of gas in any subsequent delivery year.

The carry-forward mechanism, on the other hand, is applied in instances where the buyer, in a specific contract year, takes and pays for more gas than the agreed annual take-or-pay contract quantity. In such case, the excess gas taken by the buyer is carried forward into the following year to reduce the take-or-pay commitment for that year.[22]

2.15 Shortfall gas

The GSA will make provision for failure of the seller to supply the required nominated gas to the buyer, which is referred to as 'shortfall gas'. To ensure that the seller is only held responsible for shortfalls arising due to failure to perform its obligations under the GSA, the GSA will provide exclusions for instances where failure to supply will not be regarded as shortfall gas. These might include:

- *force majeure*;
- scheduled maintenance;
- failure of delivery due to the buyer's actions or omissions; or
- non-delivery within the specified tolerance level.

The rationale for this clause is that if the supply falls below the nominated values, this constitutes a breach of the GSA.

Where a shortfall occurs and is not qualified by any of the specified exceptions, the GSA must provide a remedy for the buyer. The remedy is usually a shortfall discount price to cover:

- any losses that the buyer may suffer for failure to provide gas to its resellers or its end users; or
- the cost of the purchase of gas from an alternative source.

If there is a shortfall balance at the end of any delivery year, the quantities of gas made available by the seller to the buyer at the delivery point during the next succeeding delivery year, up to the amount of the shortfall balance, is usually applied to reduce the amount of the shortfall balance. This is paid by

22 *Ibid*, p216.

the buyer at the shortfall gas price and counts towards the ACQ for such delivery year.

2.16 Quality and off-specification gas

The GSA will specify upstream specification requirements of the gas. As such, it will stipulate that during each delivery year, the gas made available by the seller for delivery at the delivery point must comply with stipulated specifications. It will thus state, for instance, that the gas must have:

- a maximum percentage of carbon dioxide by volume;
- a maximum percentage of nitrogen by volume;
- a maximum of total sulphur by volume;
- a maximum volume of hydrogen sulphide by volume;
- a water dew point;
- a maximum water content;
- a minimum specific hydrogen dew point coupled at a specific pressure; and
- a gross heating value within a particular range.

The GSA could also specify that the gas must:

- have a Wobbe index value within a certain range of megajoules per standard cubic metre at standard conditions;
- have a temperature of no more than a degree at the delivery point;
- have a maximum and minimum pressure at the delivery point; and
- at all times be free from dust, sand, gums, oils and impurities.

If gas to be made available fails to conform to the upstream specifications, it is known as 'off-specification gas'. The seller is obliged to notify the buyer promptly once it becomes aware that the gas to be made available at the delivery point fails or is anticipated to fail to conform to the upstream specifications. The buyer must also notify the seller if it becomes aware, prior to receiving notice from the seller, that off-specification gas has been or may be made available by the seller to the buyer at the delivery point.

It is usually agreed that the buyer must use its reasonable endeavours to take off-specification gas that conforms to the downstream specifications if:

- this will not result in physical damage to the buyer's facilities; or
- the gas can be commingled by the buyer with other gas so that it will not result in physical damage to, or have a significant negative health and safety impact at, the buyer's facilities.

The buyer is entitled to reject off-specification gas for a period that is reasonably required for the buyer to determine whether it can accept such gas in accordance with the reasons outlined above.

The buyer can also refuse to take delivery of off-specification gas at the delivery point, provided that it promptly gives notice to the seller and specifies the reasons for the refusal. Any quantity of off-specification gas which the buyer has refused to take delivery of will be deemed not to have been made available by the seller to the buyer at the delivery point. The seller has no liability for any off-specification gas knowingly taken delivery of by the buyer. If the buyer unknowingly takes delivery of off-specification gas, the seller may indemnify the buyer against reasonable loss incurred by the buyer (less any insurance proceeds received by the buyer).

A key cause of controversy is the fact that the gas quality is not measured routinely on a continuous basis and off-specification gas may only be detected hours after the off-specification event commenced.

2.17 Measurement and verification

The seller will usually be responsible for measuring the quality and quantity of gas supplied, and will be obliged to install, operate and maintain measuring and metering equipment at the delivery point. Although the buyer usually has the right of access to the seller's measurement equipment in order to monitor performance, this does not preclude the buyer from having the right to install check meters alongside the seller's equipment to independently monitor the gas quantities and quality. Where the buyer has concerns about the accuracy of the seller's measurement equipment, the GSA can provide a right to seek independent third-party verification.

A typical verification clause will state that a party must give notice of request to the other party to produce such evidence to verify the accuracy of any previous invoice, statement or computation made in respect of such contract year. If any evidence produced reveals any inaccuracy in any previous computation, invoice or statement, then at the option of the party to which payment is owed, an invoice for the necessary adjustment will be prepared by that party and given to the other party for payment.[23]

2.18 Gas price

Another important clause in the GSA is the pricing clause. This will also stipulate the currency in which the gas price is to be determined (usually dollars) per metric million British thermal unit (MMBtu). It will also map out the gas price calculation. The price of the gas is one of the most essential elements of the GSA and one of the most heavily negotiated, as it determines the viability and profitability of the GSA. There is no global price index or assessment for gas – only regional pricing methodologies. In developed gas markets, the gas price may be determined based on reported gas price indices or

23 *Ibid*, p492.

assessments. In less developed gas markets, it will usually be determined by reference to an agreed base price which is periodically indexed by reference to an agreed formula – often a basket of relevant commodity price indices such as crude oil, electricity and/or coal.

(a) *Price review*

It is prudent for the GSA, which is a long-term contract, to provide for a price review clause. This will allow the parties to request a review of the price when market conditions change, making it uneconomical or impractical to continue to sell or buy gas at the initial contract price.[24]

The price review clause must specifically provide for:

- the instances in which a price review can be requested;
- the procedure for the review; and
- what happens when the parties cannot agree on a review.

There is also the option of the price being subject to review at periodic contractually agreed intervals. As such, this latter option – unlike the former – will apply irrespective of any changes in market conditions.

As encapsulated by Roberts:

Alternatively, a price review *provision might be inserted into the GSA (or SPA). Such a provision will provide that the price will be subject to review either at the request of a party which can demonstrate that the resultant price is no longer appropriate in light of prevailing market conditions or by periodic application, wherein the price (by reference to the base price, the choice of indices or the percentage weightings assigned to particular indices) could be revised to something which is agreed (or which is determined) to be more appropriate to prevailing circumstances.*[25]

2.19 Billing/invoicing and payment

In GSAs, the seller usually invoices the buyer on a monthly basis during each delivery year and following termination of the GSA. The seller prepares and delivers to the buyer a statement which shows, in respect of the preceding month or following termination, the information in respect of the amount due and owing. The seller will usually want a regular and quick flow of cash to improve its liquidity; while the buyer will want flexible terms of payment. The GSA will usually also provide for an end-of-year reconciliation statement, which will be scrutinised to determine the accuracy of the prior monthly statements and whether there is a need for set-off by one party to the other.

The monthly statements invoiced to the buyer will include such information as:

---

24 O'Neill (n 1), p155.
25 Roberts (n 5), p189.

- the quantity of gas made available by the seller to the buyer;
- the quantity of gas nominated by the buyer for each day during the invoice month;
- the quantity of gas (expressed in million standard cubic feet and MMBtu) taken by the buyer for each day during the invoice month; and
- the aggregate quantity of gas taken by the buyer during the invoice month.

It will also include:

- any adjustment to the CQ for the purposes of calculating it during the invoice month and the reason for such adjustment;
- the quantities of gas made available by the seller to the buyer at the delivery point at the shortfall gas price;
- the outstanding shortfall balance at the end of the invoice month;
- any quantity of gas provisionally classified as shortfall gas during the invoice month;
- the total quality of off-specification gas made available by a seller to the buyer at the delivery point;
- the total quantity of off-specification gas taken by the buyer during the invoice month;
- the applicable gas price for each separately priced quantity of gas made available during the invoice month and the calculations, if any, used to arrive at each such gas price;
- the monthly take-or-pay payment for the invoice amount;
- the sum due and owing to the seller in respect of the gas made available to the buyer during the invoice month, showing:
  - the relevant price for each separately priced quantity of gas made available;
  - the calculations, if any, used to arrive at such relevant price; and
  - any amount payable by the buyer to the seller; and
- the net amount payable by the buyer to the seller and the net amount due by the seller to the buyer (to be credited in the monthly statement) after taking account of all foregoing matters.

In practice, a buyer may fail to pay an invoice submitted by a seller due to:

- short-term illiquidity;
- a more permanent deterioration of the buyer's creditworthiness; or
- a deliberate decision not to pay.[26]

26 *Ibid*, pp310–311.

There are options open to the seller to protect itself against the risk of non-payment. In respect of illiquidity, the seller could request:

- more frequent invoicing;
- payment by the buyer of pipeline deliveries;
- prepayment for the gas rather than payment in arrears; or
- that the buyer fund and continue to fund a rolling deposit account containing, for example, three months' worth of gas sales proceeds, against which the seller can draw down if the buyer misses a payment.[27]

There are remedies available to the seller if the buyer fails to make payment in full. Under the terms of the GSA, the seller may be entitled to:

- charge interest on late payments;
- call on any guarantee;
- sue the buyer for the debt or under the terms of the GSA;
- suspend the delivery or transportation of gas; or
- terminate the agreement if permitted thereunder.[28]

Usually, the GSA will provide for the apportionment of tax liabilities in respect of the gas sales as well as activities connected therewith. The seller is typically liable for taxes arising from upstream to the delivery point and the buyer for taxes from downstream to the delivery point. Thus, a typical clause, as described by Roberts, would be in respect of the seller's liability: "The Seller shall (subject to Article 10.3 [Goods and Services Tax]) pay or procure the payment of all Taxes arising upstream of the Delivery Point and shall indemnify the Buyer against any liability which the Buyer incurs in respect of such taxes."[29]

And in respect of the buyer's liability: "The Buyer shall pay or procure the payment of all taxes arising at or downstream of the delivery point and shall indemnify the seller against any liability which the seller incurs in respect of such taxes."[30]

All charges for gas under the GSA – including the gas price, the shortfall gas price and the make-up gas price – are exclusive of all taxes. All credits given to the buyer in accordance with the GSA are also exclusive of all taxes where a credit is issued.

2.20 *Force majeure*

Force majeure clauses are very common in GSAs. *Black's Law Dictionary* defines '*force majeure*' as: "a contractual provision allocating the risk if performance

27 *Ibid*, p311.
28 *Ibid*.
29 *Ibid*, p481.
30 *Ibid*.

becomes impossible or impracticable especially as a result of an event or effect that the parties could not have anticipated or controlled."[31] As Roberts notes:

"Force majeure *imports the principle that upon the occurrence of an event or circumstance which is beyond the control of a party which prevents that party from performing some or all of its contractual obligations then that party should be relieved from a liability which might otherwise arise consequent upon a failure of that party to perform those affected obligations.*"[32]

It affords relief from liability to perform an obligation, but does not relieve a party from the requirement of eventual performance of those obligations.

A *force majeure* event is usually any event or circumstances beyond the control of a party, including the following:

- act of war against the host state;
- armed conflict;
- embargo imposed other than by the host state;
- blockade;
- riot;
- insurrection;
- sabotage;
- act of terrorism;
- strike, lockout or other industrial disturbance or labour dispute;
- epidemic, plague or quarantine restrictions;
- fire;
- earthquake;
- flood;
- drought;
- storm;
- navigational or maritime peril;
- some other act of God;
- any breakage, freezing, mechanical breakdown, explosion or other damage or malfunction to the pipelines;
- hindrance of government or failure to act by a competent authority or any of its affiliates; and
- failure of reservoirs or non-recoverability of reserves.

The GSA will sometimes stipulate events which cannot be considered *force majeure*. Usually, the buyer cannot claim *force majeure* in respect of:

- changes in market conditions;
- financial hardship;
- inability of a party to make a profit or receive a satisfactory rate of return;

---

31 Garner (n 3), p673.
32 Roberts (n 5), p351.

- inability to make payment of any money when due; and
- failure to give any required notice under the agreement.

The GSA will usually stipulate that a party claiming *force majeure* must promptly notify the other party of the occurrence of the event. The claiming party must provide details such as:

- the *force majeure* event;
- the affected obligations of the claiming party;
- the date on which the claiming party's performance of relevant obligations was suspended or reduced;
- the steps being taken to mitigate such suspension or reduction;
- the anticipated date on which the claiming party's performance obligations will be resumed; and
- such other information as would be reasonable in the circumstances.

The claiming party must keep the other party reasonably informed of:

- the steps it is taking to overcome the effects of the *force majeure* event; and
- its estimate as to when it will be able to resume full performance of its obligations.

The claiming party must, soon after the commencement of the *force majeure* event, diligently proceed to do all things reasonably practicable at its own reasonable expense to remedy and mitigate the *force majeure* event causing the failure to perform and minimise the interruption of the performance of its affected obligations.

Upon the accepted occurrence of the *force majeure* event by the other party, the claiming party will be relieved of its duty to perform its obligations and of liability for failure to perform its obligations. However, it will be obliged to continue to perform its obligations, to the extent that this is feasible, and take positive steps to bring the *force majeure* to an end.[33] As aptly noted by O'Neill, in negotiating the *force majeure* provisions, each party will seek to limit the circumstances in which the other party can claim *force majeure* relief, while maximising the circumstances in which it can claim such relief itself. As such, the seller will wish to be able to claim relief from its gas supply obligations while conversely, the buyer will seek to claim relief from the take-or-pay.[34] A party that is a government entity will usually be precluded from claiming as *force majeure* changes of law or acts of government within its jurisdiction.[35]

---

33 O'Neill (n 1), p159.
34 *Ibid.*
35 *Ibid.*

2.21 Termination

Apart from the express provision for the term of the GSA, the GSA must provide for other instances in which it can be terminated by the parties. These must include:

- material breach and failure to remedy as specified by the GSA;
- insolvency;
- prolonged *force majeure*;
- contravention of the transfer requirements;
- continuous failure to deliver or pay for gas;
- non-fulfilment of one or more conditions precedent;
- termination of another project agreement critical for the performance of the GSA;
- the date specified in a written agreement signed by the parties terminating the agreement;
- the assignment of rights or obligations in contravention of transfer restrictions under the GSA; and
- a party's engagement in fraud or illegality.

2.22 Insurance

Each party will be obliged to take out insurance for the duration of the GSA, to insure against risks such as damage to facilities and third-party liability. This is necessary to ensure that in the event of any unforeseen calamity, measures have been taken to cover costs arising and operations will not stall due to a lack of funds on hand to deal with the event.

2.23 Liability

Usually, the GSA will provide that the seller will not be liable to the buyer, and vice versa, in respect of any consequential loss. Consequential loss is in respect of any liability may include:

- pure economic loss;
- loss or deferment of profits use;
- opportunity;
- bargain;
- expectation;
- loss, deferment or depletion of revenue, business, goodwill, contract or business opportunity, and anticipated earnings or savings; and
- damage, cost or liability arising from any delay, reduction or loss of ability to produce, store, transport, process or dispose of the gas delivered or to be delivered under the GSA.

Damage, cost or liability associated with business interruption or increased cost of working arising from business interruption, damage, loss, injury or expense caused by the misuse of gas delivered or to be delivered, or any indirect, special, punitive, exemplary or consequential damage or loss of any nature whatsoever, may all fall within the category of consequential loss and a party will not be liable to the other in respect of same.[36] There is also usually a cap on the total aggregate liability of the seller to the buyer with respect to the breach of reasonable endeavours obligations.

Further, the seller:

- is usually responsible for any loss, injury or damage caused by gas while upstream of the delivery point; and
- will agree to indemnify, defend and hold the buyer harmless from and against all losses, damages, costs, fees and expenses arising from claims, except to the extent that such loss, damage or injury is caused by the wilful misconduct of the buyer.

The buyer, on the other hand:

- is usually responsible for any damage, loss or injury caused by gas while at or downstream of the delivery point; and
- will agree to indemnify and hold harmless the seller from all losses, damages, costs, fees and the like arising from claims by any person caused by gas while at or downstream of the delivery point, except to the extent that it is caused by the wilful misconduct of the seller.

2.24 Governing law and dispute resolution

The parties will stipulate which country's law should govern in respect of a dispute and the agreed dispute resolution mechanism. This ensures certainty: in the event of a dispute, these matters will already have been settled and valuable time will not be wasted haggling over them. Although the parties can choose to have different laws govern different aspects of the contract or even oust the rules relating to conflict of laws, it is wise to consider using the governing law applicable to downstream gas in respect of the contract, so that there is some consistency between any decision of the GSA and any other related decision relevant to the downstream sale and/or transportation of the gas.

Disputes might arise in respect of issues such as:

- the performance of obligations;
- the application of *force majeure*;
- the exercise of rights;
- statements and quantities (eg, whether invoices or statements are accurate and whether quantities of gas have been properly classified);
- whether a condition precedent has been satisfied;

36 'Consequential loss' is not a term defined by law; it must be defined by contract and therefore can mean whatever the parties agree it to mean.

- the alleged breach of warranty or representation; or
- price reviews.[37]

Resolution of the dispute will usually commence with both formal and informal dialogue, as the senior management of both parties meet to discuss the matter with a view to resolving it. If the dispute cannot be resolved within a stipulated timeframe, the aggrieved party is free to escalate the matter. Some agreements provide for the parties to jointly agree and appoint an independent expert(s) for the determination of certain matters in dispute – usually technical matters such as invoicing, calculations or measurements.

The parties usually stipulate in the agreement that in the event of a dispute, the matter should be settled by arbitration or in court.[38] O'Neill rightly notes that international arbitration – either institutional (eg, International Chamber of Commerce, London Court of International Arbitration, International Court of Arbitration) or *ad hoc* in accordance with the United Nations Commission on International Trade Law rules – is common in GSAs involving the cross-border sale of gas or international parties.[39]

The dispute resolution method specified in the GSA may be any of the above, or might involve others coming into play in the event that the first port of call fails to resolve the matter.

2.25 Assignment and transfer

The GSA usually provides that no party may assign, transfer, novate or otherwise dispose of all or part of its interests, rights or obligations under the GSA without obtaining the prior written consent of the other party. Where a party has validly transferred all or part of its rights and obligations, the parties must execute a novation agreement to evidence such transfer.

2.26 Confidentiality

The GSA will usually contain a clause requiring that its contents remain confidential during the period of the GSA and often for a stipulated period after termination. This obligation will normally refer to the GSA and all information and data which one party receives from the other party or its affiliates, employees, agents and/or representatives and which concerns the business, assets, dealings, liabilities, transactions, suppliers, customers, processes or affairs of the other party. This will also include:

- geological, geophysical and engineering data;

---

37 Roberts (n 5), pp403–404.
38 *Ibid*, pp406–407.
39 O'Neill (n 1), p162.

- models and interpretations; and
- commercial, contractual and financial information.

A party will be permitted to disclose such confidential information without the other party's written consent to the extent that such information:

- is not in violation of, or otherwise subject to, any obligation of confidentiality to another party or its affiliates;
- is already in the possession of the public; or
- is required to be disclosed by such party by applicable law or by a court of competent jurisdiction, or by the rules of a stock exchange on which the securities of the party or its affiliate are listed.

A party may also disclose such confidential information to an affiliate without the prior written consent of the other party if such disclosure is necessary for the purposes of performing the GSA. In such case, the party disclosing is responsible for ensuring that the affiliate complies with the confidentiality clause as if it is a party to the GSA.

Further, a party may disclose confidential information to:

- employers, officers and directors of the disclosing party, or affiliates or professional advisers, in order to enable them to perform their obligations under the GSA;
- a *bona fide* assignee of a party's rights and obligations under the GSA;
- any lenders or potential lenders providing or proposing to provide loans, insurance, guarantees or other financing; and
- such persons as are required for operational reasons.

2.27 Notices

The GSA will also stipulate the method of giving notice or other communication, which will constitute evidence of effective notice to the other party for the purposes of the GSA. It will usually stipulate that this be:

- provided in writing;
- in a stipulated language;
- signed by or on behalf of the person giving it; and
- delivered:
  - by hand;
  - by recognised international courier; or
  - by email to addresses set out in the GSA.

If notice is provided in the way stipulated in the GSA, it is considered effective and the receiving party is considered duly served.

3. Conclusion

The GSA is a dynamic contract that primarily regulates the long-term relationship between the buyer and the seller. It sets out the legal, technical and commercial framework between the buyer and the seller, and allows for the exchange of gas and money between the buyer and the seller. The gas moves downstream and the money upstream. As the GSA is a long-term contract, it should be drafted in a way that ensures its provisions will work effectively over the term of the contract in order to prevent conflict, protect investments and promote the continuity of business. Further to the typical clauses discussed above, the GSA will also require the boilerplate provisions required for any standard long-term agreement to make it complete.

LNG sales agreements: towards commoditisation?

Ruchdi Maalouf
KOGAS International

This chapter provides an overview of liquefied natural gas (LNG) sales contracts, highlighting the most significant trends in the LNG industry and its evolution towards commoditisation.[1]

What is commoditisation and why is it relevant? In simple terms, the commoditisation of LNG is the process through which LNG becomes a fungible product that has a market value anywhere in the world. This is the case for crude oil and gold, but not LNG. Asian LNG is not the same product as European LNG. Why does this matter? Because a commodity has a global liquid market which facilitates its production and trade. By contrast, if there is no liquid market, a producer must market extensively to offtakers to ensure the viability of its project. In the case of LNG, a project can only raise financing once production has been committed under long-term sales contracts.

1. LNG fundamentals

1.1 Properties of LNG

LNG is natural gas that is cooled for storage and transport in liquid form.[2] LNG is composed of at least 80% methane, longer chain hydrocarbons in small quantities and carbon dioxide, nitrogen, sulphur and mercury. Before natural gas is liquefied, the feed gas is treated in order to remove impurities and some or all of the longer chain hydrocarbons.

Natural gas in liquid form must be contained in special storage tanks. As it slowly evaporates, the boiled-off gas draws heat away from the liquid, which remains refrigerated (a phenomenon known as 'auto-refrigeration'). The boiled-off gas must be extracted from the LNG tank and distributed, reliquefied or, in the worst case, flared or vented.[3] The boil-off process has another notable effect: nitrogen and methane boil first and cause the calorific value to increase

1 For a detailed and comprehensive study of LNG sales and transportation, please refer to Peter Roberts, *Gas and LNG Sales and Transportation Agreements* (Sweet & Maxwell, sixth edition, 2020).

2 When the feed gas is cooled at a temperature of approximately -163 Celsius, its volume is reduced about 600 times and it becomes liquid at atmospheric pressure.

3 Installations are designed to operate without flaring or venting.

gradually. Over time, the specifications of the LNG change. As a result, natural gas can only be contained in LNG form for a limited period, during which its composition changes (which can pose problems – see "Off-spec LNG" in section 2.2(a) below).

The entire process of producing, storing and transporting LNG is time sensitive. LNG infrastructure is costly to build and maintain. These factors differentiate LNG from other hydrocarbons. For a project to succeed, the LNG chain from extraction of the raw gas to distribution of the regasified LNG must be managed competently.

1.2 LNG development projects

The consumption and trade of natural gas are increasing steadily – partly because natural gas is abundant, is relatively cheaper than oil and has lower emissions than oil products and coal. Traditionally, natural gas was considered the poor relation of oil. Oil companies would search for oil and were considered unlucky if they found non-associated natural gas. This situation has since changed dramatically; but even today, the presence or otherwise of hydrocarbons other than methane plays a role in whether a discovery can be economically developed and how profitable it will be.

Once natural gas is liquefied, the LNG must be loaded into special vessels (LNG carriers) and transported to special facilities (LNG receiving terminals) fitted with dedicated jetties, cryogenic pipelines, powerful compressors, storage tanks, regasification and distribution infrastructure. Traditionally, gas was discovered in 'conventional' petroleum reservoirs. In recent years, however, different types of reservoirs have been exploited (eg, shale, coal seams and tight reservoirs), where permeability may require a different production profile. The term 'unconventional gas' covers these sources.

1.3 Project structure

Because of the lack of liquidity in international gas markets, it is difficult to raise financing to develop an LNG project without pre-selling most of the planned production. Traditionally, LNG projects sold their production to final buyers. However, this situation is changing.

(a) Traditional LNG projects

LNG was traditionally a method to monetise stranded gas. If the gas was not stranded, it was sold to the domestic market. In order to monetise a gas discovery, project developers had to find a profitable route to take the gas to market. Distance is one critical factor that determines whether the gas will be piped and shipped, and whether a liquefaction plant will be built onshore or on a barge.

In the early days of the industry, LNG was compared to a 'floating pipeline'.

The success of a project was conditioned on the integrity of the entire chain: from upstream gas production to distribution from the receiving terminal, the LNG chain is only as strong as its weakest link.

Many LNG projects involve upstream production, liquefaction and transportation. A receiving terminal must also be available. Due to the high cost of these projects, debt finance is generally required. Long-term LNG sale and purchase agreements (SPAs) provide the cash flow for the debt service and lenders will be very interested in the credit rating of buyers and the robustness of the entire chain.

Often, a buyer will seek a stake in the upstream production, the LNG plant or both. Sometimes, only certain parties will be involved in parts of the LNG chain – for example:

- the upstream production may be handled by a national oil company (NOC);
- the liquefaction plant may be shared between different projects; or
- the marketing may be handled entirely by an NOC.

LNG shipping is almost always the responsibility of the seller or the buyer, and LNG carriers are often dedicated to a project.

The following factors will influence the structure of traditional LNG projects:

- the regulatory framework – in particular, how the petroleum laws apply to gas operation and sales and the ownership of natural resources and the petroleum infrastructure, as well as the fiscal terms;
- the appetite of various parties for involvement in different parts of the LNG chain – in particular, for buyers to be involved in upstream production, liquefaction and transportation of LNG, motivated by considerations such as energy security, price hedging and knowledge transfer; and
- the lenders' requirements, which will have an impact on things such as the debt-equity ratio in the project, the selection of partners in the development of the project and the acceptability of each buyer.

(b) Alternative structures

The previous decade saw the emergence of a new type of project: instead of monetising stranded gas, these projects sought to monetise gas in a mature market. LNG liquefaction and export projects were developed in the United States, as a result of the abundance of natural gas and the relative ease with which it can be purchased.

Two models exist in this regard. In the first, a merchant LNG company sells LNG at its terminal.[4] The price includes two components:

---

4 There are also significant regulatory hurdles to be overcome in order to obtain the authorisations to build the terminal and export the LNG to countries without a foreign trade agreement with the United States.

- a fixed component corresponding to the fixed infrastructure cost, which is indexed to consumer prices; and
- a variable component corresponding to the feed gas cost, indexed to a Henry Hub price, which is a liquid price marker for the US gas grid.

The buyer is not obliged to purchase any LNG but must pay the fixed infrastructure cost each month.

The second is a tolling structure, whereby the developer of a liquefaction plant (the toller) does not take title to the natural gas feeding the plant or to the LNG. Instead, the toller sells the utilisation of the plant for a fee (the toll). The toller shares neither the risks nor the rewards of upstream production, transportation or marketing. The tolling agreement may offer volume or capacity. If offering volume, the toller may also market any excess capacity. If offering capacity, the toller may allocate excess capacity among users according to rules agreed in the tolling agreements. Payment is usually split between a fixed capacity fee and a variable utilisation fee which is based on the volume of natural gas liquefied. The gas and LNG owners may be final LNG buyers or traders (portfolio players, commodity traders or trading houses). They will be responsible for the transportation of the LNG produced.

(c) New trend: portfolio buyers as project offtakers

While historically new LNG projects sought creditworthy importers to sell their production, in the past 10 years they have increasingly relied on buyers purchasing LNG to resell it. There are two categories of buyers:

- LNG traders (eg, Gunvor, Vitol, Trafigura and Mitsubishi); and
- international oil and gas majors (eg, Total, Shell and Eni).

Some oil and gas majors have developed large portfolios of LNG supplies, which they use for trading and imports in markets where they have a presence. These portfolio players have become the dominant force in today's LNG markets.

This new trend is important because it represents a halfway point between a segmented market in which supply can only fulfil existing demand and a fully commoditised market in which supply balances expected demand. The portfolio players assume the risk of expected demand.

2. LNG sales in general

There are several different types of LNG sales agreements. Traditionally, a distinction was made between LNG SPAs and master sale and purchase agreements (MSPAs). The instruments of choice for short-term trade were cargo-based MSPAs, with each trade based on confirmation notices; while LNG projects used LNG SPAs. MSPAs sell LNG on a cargo basis, while LNG SPAs sell it on the basis of an annual quantity. However, it is no longer useful to distinguish between annual quantities for long-term sales and cargo contracts for short-term sales. More relevant from the point of view of commoditisation is to distinguish between project sales on the one hand and trade sales on the other.

2.1 Types of LNG sales contracts

(a) LNG SPA

An LNG SPA is an LNG sale agreement in which the contract volume is defined as an annual contract quantity, a yearly volume of LNG, as opposed to a set number of cargoes.

The LNG industry distinguishes long-term contracts from short and medium-term contracts. One rule of thumb is that short and medium-term contracts have a duration of less than seven years. Long-term durations typically range from 10 to 20 years, and sometimes up to 25 or 30 years. There are no absolute definitions.

(b) MSPA

An MSPA is a framework agreement between two parties in which the terms and conditions of future LNG sales are agreed first and any sale is concluded later through a separate instrument, generally known as a confirmation notice,[5] incorporating the terms of the MSPA. An MSPA is not an agreement for the sale and purchase of LNG and its parties have no obligation to engage in a transaction.

An MSPA is used for contracts in which the LNG is defined as one or more cargoes to be delivered. It is not an agreement for the sale and purchase of LNG in its own right. An MSPA allows parties with repeat business to save time by agreeing important terms and conditions in advance of agreeing specific trades. MSPAs and confirmation notices are the instruments of choice for cargo-based sales of LNG.

(c) Project SPAs

Project SPAs are LNG SPAs from specific projects with identified upstream and liquefaction facilities. Project SPAs tend to be more complex and often contain specific language on:

- gas reserves;
- conditions precedent;
- the construction and commissioning of the project; and
- adjustments such as price review clauses.

---

5 Other terms are used, such as 'confirmation', 'specific order' or 'confirmation memorandum'.

Greenfield SPAs provide for the sale of LNG from a liquefaction project that has not yet been built. They involve various project risks (including completion, delays and adequacy of reserves) and financing constraints (the debt is typically serviced through the proceeds of the LNG sales). A greenfield SPA requires the inclusion of language on the start-up of deliveries and sometimes the adjustment of quantities in the early years.

Brownfield SPAs provide for sales from an existing project – for example, after an initial greenfield SPA has expired. While a reserve risk may still exist, there is no completion risk or risk of potential delay; and the duration is not constrained by existing debt which has presumably been discharged during the term of the initial greenfield SPA.

Under portfolio SPAs, a seller which has a portfolio of supplies sells LNG to a buyer from various sources. The seller's portfolio normally consists of LNG available under other LNG sales agreements (under which it is the buyer of the LNG). Not all LNG sold under a portfolio SPA need be in the portfolio. The seller may sell LNG that it will procure at a later date in the market.

2.2 Terms common to LNG sales contracts

All LNG sales have common terms and all LNG SPAs have common features derived from the need to convert a contract quantity, defined as an annual volume, into a number of cargo deliveries over a year.

(a) Terms common to all LNG sales (LNG SPAs and MSPAs)

Delivery: Traditionally, LNG is transported by the buyer or the seller and deliveries take place either:

- at the loading terminal (also known as free-on-board (FOB) deliveries); or
- at the receiving terminal (also known as deliveries ex ship (DES)).[6]

In FOB deliveries, the LNG is transferred at a terminal by the seller at the point where the unloading line of the terminal connects with the loading line of the buyer's LNG carrier. In DES deliveries, the LNG is transported by the seller's LNG carrier and delivered at the point where the unloading line of the LNG carrier connects with the loading line of the receiving terminal.

In addition to transportation, custody and transfer, the delivery provisions will include detailed rules on shipping notifications, berthing and loading or unloading. These rules are operationally important and will tie in with the

---

6 The terms FOB and DES are informally used (in the title page of the contracts rather than the body). LNG SPAs should not refer to the International Chamber of Commerce Incoterms. The custody, transportation and transfer of the LNG are governed by the detailed provisions on the LNG SPAs. The 2010 Delivery at Terminal and Delivery at Place Incoterms (which replace DES) have little relevance to the LNG industry.

shipping terms. It may be useful to ensure a smooth operation between the charterparty rules and the shipping rules under an LNG sale agreement.

Facilities: LNG sales agreements identify the seller's and buyer's infrastructure and facilities, including:

- the upstream reservoir (in a project SPA);
- the loading terminal, including the liquefaction plant;
- the LNG carriers; and
- the receiving terminal, including the storage, regasification and distribution facilities.

Quality specifications: An LNG sale agreement will include information on the gas sold, including its allowable chemical composition, calorific value and specific gravity. The calorific value and specific gravity will determine its combustion energy output (known as the Wobbe Index). The quality specifications will determine whether the LNG is acceptable at a particular delivery point.

Credit support: All LNG sales provide for some form of credit support, usually from the buyer. This might take the form of:

- a guarantee (parent company guarantee or bank guarantee);
- a letter of credit; or
- an obligation to maintain a defined credit rating.

Measurement and testing: Measurement of LNG determines the quantity delivered and its composition in order to determine whether it conforms to the specification agreed and to calculate the quantity delivered (and the price to be paid). Measurement is done at the loading and receiving terminal. The LNG carrier will also have some measurement instruments.

***Force majeure*:** *Force majeure* events are common in the LNG industry. Although there is no standard template, *force majeure* clauses usually share the same features.

Buyer's shortfall: Buyer's shortfall will result in a liability that can extend to the whole cargo value in certain circumstances. In project SPAs, a buyer can avoid a shortfall by rescheduling a delivery when the contract allows it. In some cases, the buyer may be liable for payment of the cargo with a right to take it at a later stage ('take or pay').

Seller's shortfall: A seller's shortfall may result in the buyer procuring replacement LNG or natural gas from another source, whether that failure results from the seller's failure to tender enough LNG or from its cancellation of a scheduled cargo. If the replacement LNG or natural gas is more costly than the LNG price, the seller will typically be liable to pay the difference between the replacement cost and the contract price, subject to any cap agreed. Liquidated damages may also be used.

Off-spec LNG: LNG that does not correspond to the contractual quality specifications ('off-spec LNG') may be modified within limits. The calorific value may be decreased by the addition of nitrogen. It can be increased by the addition of longer chain hydrocarbons (eg, liquefied petroleum gas) or over time through boil-off. The specifications of the gas are thus an important element in gas sales and non-conforming gas may be rejected. LNG sale agreements usually contain a reasonable endeavours obligation for the buyer to take off-spec LNG and the seller's liability regime tends to be more onerous when the buyer receives late notice of the LNG's failure to meet the contractual quality specification (and different caps on liability may apply accordingly).

Choice of law and arbitration: Most, but not all, LNG sale agreements are governed by English law. All provide for international arbitration.

(b) Terms common to all LNG SPAs

Annual contract quantity: The contract will provide for an annual contract quantity (ACQ), which will be adjusted to take into account a number of factors, including:

- production profile (project SPAs);
- maintenance; and
- *force majeure*.

The ACQ can also be modified through a defined upward and/or downward quantity tolerance of the buyer.

Annual delivery programme: Each year, the parties will prepare an annual delivery programme (ADP) for the next contract year, including:

- the quantities nominated for each month;
- the date of delivery;
- the cargo size;
- the delivery place;
- the source; and
- the name of the LNG carriers.

The ADP will also take into account such things as maintenance schedules.

Ninety-day schedule: In addition to the ADP, each month the parties will prepare a 90-day schedule, which states the planned deliveries in the next 90 days and essentially is an implementation of the ADP. The schedule is typically a table that specifies:

- the month of scheduling;
- a delivery window;
- an approximate loading date;
- the identity of the LNG carrier;
- the loading or unloading port; and
- the quantity of LNG (volume and calorific value).

Make-up: A make-up right allows the buyer to request and take LNG that was previously paid for and not taken in a contract year where the total LNG taken falls short of the take-or-pay quantity and a take-or-pay payment is due.

Make good: When a buyer is entitled to downward quantity tolerance, it may also be obliged to make good on the LNG not taken.

Excess quantity: Some contracts allow a buyer to take LNG in excess of the annual contract quantity when available.

Carry-forward quantity: When a buyer takes LNG in excess of the annual contract quantity, some contracts provide that the excess quantity will reduce the take-or-pay quantity the following year.

(c) Project SPAs (greenfield SPAs and brownfield SPAs)

Project SPAs are often more than mere LNG sales; by signing one, the buyer becomes a key stakeholder in the project and is not simply buying LNG. In any sale and purchase transaction, the parties are taking a risk regarding the technical and commercial competence of their counterparties. In a project where the core infrastructure does not exist, the risk that it will not ultimately exist or that it will not be fit for purpose at the time of the first deliveries must be added to the risk profile. Delays between execution and commencement of deliveries expose the contract to adverse changes.

Source of LNG: In new projects, a reserve certificate demonstrating there are sufficient proven reserves to supply natural gas for the lifetime of the project will be required. A seller may also reserve the right to deliver LNG or natural gas from an alternative source. This has major advantages: if the start-up date is delayed, the seller may be able to avoid a breach of contract by sourcing LNG from another source.

Duration: Project SPAs differ according to the duration of the delivery period, which can vary from a few years for brownfield SPAs to 15 to 25 years for greenfield SPAs. In greenfield SPAs, the duration is dictated by the requirements of the lenders. In brownfield SPAs, it is for the parties to decide.

Conditions precedent: Term LNG SPAs relating to greenfield projects usually contain conditions precedent reflecting certain project constraints. In some cases, conditions precedent may be first formulated in a binding preliminary agreement and satisfied by the time a definitive SPA is signed. Typical conditions precedent relate to:

- the final investment for the project;
- financing;
- approvals; and
- construction milestones.

Commissioning: Greenfield SPAs include a commissioning period before the commercial term. During commissioning, production is irregular and it is difficult for a seller to commit to firm volumes and a delivery schedule. Commissioning sales are treated differently.

Start-up: The start-up date may be difficult to determine in advance. After a contract is signed, construction must take place and any pending conditions precedent must be satisfied or waived. A common way to deal with the difficulty of predicting the commencement of commercial operations is to include a funnelling mechanism whereby an initial window is notified by the seller to the buyer and, at determined intervals, a shorter window is notified within the preceding window until a commercial start-up is identified.[7]

Destination: DES contracts specify the destination of the cargoes (region, country or port). This is necessary since the seller's costs (which should be included in the price formula) will depend on the shipping distance and the number of LNG carriers required to fulfil its delivery obligations.

Deliveries to destinations that are not pre-agreed are known as diversions. Diversions may be excluded from long-term LNG sales, but they can also be admissible when requested by the buyer and subject to the seller's consent (and to some form of profit sharing). Until the cargo is delivered to a new destination, custody and risk remain with the seller.

---

7 For example, the first window would be a 12-month period ending 48 months after the effective date; the second window would be a six-month period within the first window; the third window would be a three-month period within the second window; and the start-up date would be notified within the third window, 30 days before its commencement.

Take-or-pay: The duration of a term LNG SPA is linked to a take-or-pay clause which secures a regular cash flow for the seller. A take-or-pay clause obliges the buyer to purchase an agreed quantity of LNG (eg, the take-or-pay quantity) in each year for the term of the contract, whether the buyer takes delivery of that LNG during the year or not. That quantity will generally correspond to the ACQ as adjusted under the contract. If LNG has been paid for but not taken, the buyer will be entitled to make-up LNG which can be taken in later years and at the latest during the extended term.

Price review: Price review clauses provide that the parties to a project SPA will review the LNG price at regular time intervals (eg, every five years), subject to defined conditions. Most project SPAs index the LNG price to a commodity other than gas in the destination market (eg, crude oil or gas price in the export market). When that is the case, market changes can significantly affect the contract and it is customary for the parties to make allowance in the contract for a price review.

3. Commoditisation of LNG trade?

3.1 Historical perspective on short-term trade

(a) 1964–1991

The LNG industry started as point-to-point trade – first from Algeria to France and the United Kingdom (in 1964), followed by sales from Libya to Italy and Spain, and from Alaska to Japan (in 1969). By 1980, the LNG industry consisted of nine export terminals in eight countries and 17 import terminals in six countries. Global LNG production amounted to 34 million ton per annum (Mtpa). In 1990, this had grown to 16 export terminals in six countries and 30 import terminals in nine countries, with global production of 52 Mtpa.

The industry grew organically through bilateral relations between producers and importers. All project elements were bespoke. Offtake contracts provided the cash flow to repay the debt to finance the projects. Buyers were experienced gas operators and sellers were upstream operators. The contractual instrument of choice was the long-term LNG SPA. Sales were concluded either as side agreements or through sales agreements for one or more cargoes.

(b) 1992–2004

Up until the end of the 1990s, short-term trading represented only a small percentage of the global LNG trade. In 1992, short-term trading reached the landmark of 1 Mtpa – a little more than one cargo per month. It was only after 2000 that this started to increase, reaching the milestone of 10 Mtpa in 2003. At the time, the short-term market had grown to include 12 exporting countries and 12 importing countries for a total production of 126 Mtpa.

Initially, most short-term trading took place on the margin of long-term trading. Cargo sales developed because some LNG was uncommitted. The industry slowly grew along those lines, as did the number of companies involved. Production was intended to match demand. The instrument of choice remained the LNG SPA and occasionally cargoes were sold outside of the framework of existing contracts. These sales were opportunistic and did not constitute an alternative marketing model, but rather an *ad hoc* optimisation of production which would otherwise be sold through the existing LNG SPAs.

(c) 2005–2013

From 2005 to 2013, the share of short-term traded LNG in the global LNG market grew steadily to reach 27%. The LNG industry gradually moved from a producer/importer model to become a buyer/seller industry where each party can be both a buyer and a seller at the same time.

The contracting methods used thus far (side agreements to long-term LNG SPAs and fully termed contracts for cargo sales) were a significant hurdle to the growth of the LNG trade. In particular, documenting cargo sales in fully termed SPAs added a layer of complexity to the process.

A new contracting method to facilitate cargo sales became widely adopted. Parties with repeat business adopted a two-layer contracting method whereby the parties agreed in advance the terms under which they would transact in one agreement – the MSPA – and purchased and sold LNG cargoes using another agreement, the confirmation notice. MSPAs allowed parties with repeat business to save time by agreeing important terms in advance of their dealings. MSPAs were adopted widely by the LNG industry.

Over time, uncommitted LNG volumes grew in size and an alternative market developed for LNG cargoes. The market saw three types of supplies:

- traditional long-term supplies;
- the occasional cargo that came in excess or failed to be delivered normally (a form of optimisation); and
- volumes resulting from failed long-term LNG SPAs.

New participants such as intermediaries (commodity traders and banks) took part in the trade, buying cargoes from the traditional producers to resell them to the traditional buyers. A new instrument emerged to meet the needs of the new trade: the MSPA, with its confirmation notices. The big buyers also had contracts for supplies from multiple sources and sought to optimise their inventory by buying and selling cargoes when the need arose.

In parallel, sellers that had positions in different parts of the LNG chain developed more sophisticated marketing strategies. Secondary sales developed, initially from a specific source but also with a diversity of sources and source substitution rights for the seller.

(d) *2014 to present*

A turning point for commoditisation occurred when Yamal LNG took its final investment decision and sold the majority of its LNG to companies whose intention was to resell most of the project LNG (Total, Novatek Gas & Power, Gas Natural and Gazprom Marketing & Trading). This was the first time a large LNG project (nameplate production of 16.5 Mtpa) took a final investment decision without selling the bulk of its production to final buyers. As portfolio marketing has become the business model of the largest LNG companies, new projects increasingly rely on companies developing new projects to increase their portfolio LNG.[8] This trend indicates that the LNG market is entering a new stage on its long road to commoditisation. More and more projects are being developed by buyers intending to resell their commitments to secondary buyers.

At the same time, short-term trade has grown from 27% to 40% of the global LNG trade. The growth of portfolio marketing has been instrumental in this evolution.

The evolution has been further supported by the reduced costs of LNG import infrastructure. The costs of regasification terminals were lowered significantly by a new technological solution: the floating storage and regasification unit (FSRU), essentially an LNG carrier with a regasification unit. FRSUs eliminate the need to build onshore terminals and in particular onshore storage tanks. They can also be financed through loans secured by the payment of FSRU hire payments, avoiding the need to borrow large sums to build an onshore terminal. Finally, they allow for the rapid deployment of regasification infrastructure. As a result, new demand has arisen – in particular, in countries without the credit conditions necessary for onshore regasification projects. These new buyers needed gas and could buy large amounts, but they did not have the credit ratings necessary to obtain project finance for new LNG import projects. Many new buyers were unable to take on long-term commitments because of the uncertainty of demand in case the price of LNG increased (typically when the oil price increased for oil-indexed LNG). This caused the secondary LNG market to grow in size supported by portfolio marketing.

3.2 Towards a commodity pricing for LNG?

(a) *The challenges of establishing a global LNG price*

There is no international LNG price index and no international gas price index. LNG pricing thus remains an area where commoditisation is incomplete. Thus far, new projects are still marketing LNG at a price indexed to another commodity – primarily crude oil (Brent and JCC, a Japanese crude oil price index) and natural gas.

8 For example, BP is the sole offtaker of Phase 1 of the GTA project in Senegal/Mauritania.

In the United States (excluding Alaska), there is a liquid gas market for domestic gas production. Feed gas for LNG is priced off the grid and indexed to Henry Hub natural gas futures.[9] The liberalisation of the European gas market has allowed for the emergence of liquid gas indexes (TTF[10] being the most liquid). Gas prices were traditionally indexed to crude oil and oil products, but the use of gas indexes is now replacing oil. For LNG specifically, a significant volume of the trade is done on a short-term basis and local gas indexes make oil indexation a difficult commercial proposition when the competing pipeline gas price is determined by the gas market. Any long-term volumes directed to Europe would need to be priced against the gas market and the gas indexes dominate.

The Asian markets are not currently liberalised and do not benefit from an authoritative gas index. In the past few years, the lack of a credible LNG price index was partially remedied by the progress made by the East Asian JKM price index,[11] an assessment of physical spot prices for cargoes delivered ex-ship to Japan, South Korea, China and Taiwan by price reporting agency Platts. Interestingly, as short-term trade grows, arbitrage between European markets and East Asian markets seems to be increasing, which is an encouraging sign.

(b) LNG derivatives and the path to liquidity

As a result of the low liquidity, an authoritative price for LNG physical cargoes has failed to emerge, despite the efforts of the price reporting agencies. One way to increase liquidity without increasing the number of deliveries is to reduce the size of the units of quantity of LNG traded. This has been achieved in the derivatives market, where quantities as small as 10,000 metric million British thermal units (MMBtu) can be traded.[12]

The JKM comes in two forms:

- Platts' physical assessment; and
- the JKM Futures issued by ICE, a liquid price of a traded derivative contract.

Platts also offers a 'market on close' assessment for LNG derivatives traded in a window in the last 20 minutes of the market trading day, which further enhances the reliability of its price assessment.

A futures contract obliges a buyer to buy, or a seller to sell, an asset at a predetermined future date. For example, a contract where a buyer promises to buy one LNG cargo for delivery in East Asia in July next year at a fixed price with the possibility of closing out the contract by financial settlement would be a futures contract.

---

9 There are other gas indexes, but the price difference generally corresponds to variations in the transportation costs.

10 'Title Transfer Point' in the Netherlands.

11 JKM stands for 'Japan Korea Marker'.

12 A cargo of LNG is typically between 300 and 500 times larger.

Liquidity in the futures market may improve liquidity in a physical market: if the volume and liquidity of the financial instrument exceed a certain level, price manipulation becomes very difficult and the price signal gains in authority.[13] Moreover, the financial markets, if sufficiently liquid, will provide insurance against price volatility on the physical market, known as a 'hedge'. Today, LNG markets are making significant headway in that direction, although the East Asian markets are still far from being commoditised.

Derivative contracts can also be concluded 'over the counter' (OTC), meaning between two parties at arm's length, without the intervention of a futures exchange. For that, counterparties must put in place a special contract which is a master template for OTC derivatives prepared by the International Swaps and Derivatives Association for several products, including commodity derivatives.

4. Trading contracts and commoditisation

Trade sales are effected on either a cargo basis (MSPAs and confirmation notices) or an annual quantity basis (portfolio SPAs). Portfolio sales have grown exponentially in the recent past and these bridge the gap between cargo sales and long-term sales.

4.1 Portfolio SPAs

The portfolio SPA is not a variation of the project SPA. A number of distinctive features are worth highlighting.

(a) The source of LNG

In a portfolio SPA, the source of LNG is not tied to a specific project. The portfolio SPA contains a list of sources which typically belong to the seller's existing LNG portfolio (which consists of a mixture of project SPAs and short-term supplies). The portfolio SPA language on LNG sources contains a list of existing sources that can be amended and a right to substitute cargoes from any source.

The substitution right in the portfolio SPA is not intended as a mitigation mechanism, but rather as an option for the seller to choose the source of the LNG, and thereby optimise its margin on sale. As discussed in the *force majeure* section below, the right to substitute LNG, if absolute, may become an obligation to substitute LNG when, for example, the scheduled delivery is subject to *force majeure*.

(b) Force majeure

For the LNG industry, *force majeure* is not a theoretical risk. Events of *force*

13 The opposite can be the case. The problem with the futures market is that supply and demand can be manufactured virtually, simply by buying or selling futures in a quantity which bears no relationship to physical supply and demand. This enables market manipulators to drive the futures price in one or other direction, particularly if they have a physical position that they want to 'help'.

majeure occur every year for a wide variety of reasons and can last for months or years in the most severe cases. For the portfolio operator, *force majeure* can endanger the profitability of its portfolio if it affects a lucrative contract. For the buyer, *force majeure* will leave a shortfall in its inventory and for as long as the *force majeure* continues, the buyer will be exposed to higher prices on the short-term market and risks of gas shortages. For both buyer and seller, the portfolio SPA provides the ability to spread the *force majeure* risk.

This raises problems because each side will expect the other side to take the risk. For the seller, a *force majeure* event implies a shortfall in its overall supply portfolio which may provide the sources of supply for a portfolio SPA. For the buyer, portfolio procurement provides the portfolio operator with the means to mitigate any event of *force majeure* so that it does not affect the portfolio SPA. To reconcile these positions, a distinction must be made and other contractual mechanisms must be taken into account. While a single cargo failure could be expected to be remedied by the seller, a failure over a significant number would be more difficult to fix.

The expectation that the seller should remedy *force majeure* will need to be considered in light of the seller's freedom to determine and amend the delivery schedule. A portfolio SPA providing the seller with unqualified discretion to determine the source of LNG in the annual delivery programme and the right to modify the source of delivery in any delivery schedule with limited notice to the buyer would be expected to maintain deliveries, even if the *force majeure* affects a scheduled delivery. Indeed, deliveries are scheduled one year ahead and are revised monthly for the 90-day period ahead. As long as the affected delivery is sufficiently remote, the flexibility of sources in the portfolio SPA allows the seller to seek alternative supplies.

(c) Operational clauses in portfolio SPAs

The portfolio SPA may resell LNG purchased under another contract, in which case LNG sold from the portfolio will be subject to terms and conditions from a primary purchase contract. The original purchase can be sourced from equity LNG, long-term contracts, mid-term contracts, other portfolio sales or cargo tenders. It could be FOB or DES. The original sale may take into account the portfolio sale or it may have been agreed previously. Managing this complexity in a profitable way is both the challenge and the opportunity presented by portfolio marketing.

Most of the operational discrepancies need not be included the contract. Areas of discrepancy will include, for example, the shipping terms which may relate to issues such as:

- ship-shore compatibility;[14]
- ship performance;

14 For example, the initial LNG SPA may impose a list of LNG carriers that are deemed accepted, but which the portfolio SPA may not consider compatible with the receiving terminal.

- requirements of the port; and
- the crew.

The seller will need to find a way through the operations management to comply with all contracts along the chain or obtain waivers. Moreover, changes to the delivery programme during the contract year will need the consent of other parties further up the chain. While portfolio SPAs do not refer to other contracts, their wording tends to afford less flexibility to the buyer.

(d) Failure to deliver, failure to take

Traditionally, greenfield SPAs afforded some flexibility to the buyer by entitling it to reduce the annual contract quantity during a contract year and to reschedule cargoes. The underlying realities in portfolio SPAs differ greatly. When an LNG producer agrees to reduce the annual contract quantity, it is free to remarket the cargoes released from the sale or to reduce its production. When a portfolio seller agrees to reduce an annual contract quantity, it may be unable to pass on the change up the chain. Flexibility in a portfolio SPA does not have the same economic value as in a project SPA.

(e) LNG specification in portfolio SPAs

A seemingly difficult question is the LNG specification. One feature of the gas industry is that a wide range of specifications exist and different gas compositions are not compatible with the requirements of all users and downstream transporters. There are no standard LNG composition specifications, pipeline gas grid specifications, gas burner specifications and so on. Therefore, a source of LNG can only be delivered to certain buyers and not to others. A project SPA will define the specifications of LNG within the physical range dictated by the upstream. The portfolio SPA will seek to define the specifications as widely as possible to allow LNG from as many sources as possible to be delivered.

(f) Duration

The duration of the portfolio SPA is freely agreed by the parties without constraints derived by any specific LNG project. A wide range of durations may be observed on the market. Nevertheless, the longer the contract, the greater the risk that the seller will lose an LNG source in its portfolio. Contracts expire and sometimes projects are stopped due to *force majeure* or insufficient reserves. A seller committing LNG on a long-term basis must be able to price the replacement LNG. If it is not available in its portfolio, the risk of sourcing at a cost higher than the portfolio SPA price must be mitigated within the global economic value of the portfolio; otherwise, this will be an uncapped risk.

4.2 MSPAs and confirmation notices

The following describes sales of one or more cargoes based on a master agreement and a confirmation notice. There are two types of cargo sales, depending on the number of cargoes sold:

- the spot contract – a sale of a single cargo for immediate delivery; and
- the strip contract – a sale of several cargoes of LNG. This can also be called a 'multi-cargo sale'.

(a) MSPA

MSPAs contain all the common terms necessary for the sale and purchase of LNG, except those terms that are specific to a sale which will be contained in the confirmation notice.

While project SPAs are not standardised because they contain many elements specific to a project, MSPAs are very similar. Many spot buyers carry out trading activities that involve buying and selling spot cargoes. MSPA terms tend to be generic and minimally tailored. Balanced MSPA terms are in the interests of the buyer and the seller. Unlike long-term contracts, spot and trades have been subject to the development of industry templates, notably by the Association of International Energy Negotiators, Trafigura and BP. Portfolio players tend to use their own in-house templates.

One disadvantage of this method is the requirement for new entrants to spend significant time and resources concluding MSPAs with all desired counterparties. Nevertheless, MSPAs are the methodology adopted by the LNG industry for cargo sales.

(b) Confirmation notice

Although MSPAs were initially conceived for single cargo sales, confirmation notices are widely used for strip contracts. The choice between using an MSPA/confirmation notice or a portfolio SPA will be dictated by the duration of the contract and the volume sold. If deliveries span two contract years or more, a portfolio SPA becomes a more appropriate tool to manage the complexity of the transactions. For durations of less than two years, it is easier to programme a set number of deliveries through a confirmation notice.

Most confirmation notices will structure quantities as a number of cargoes rather than define them as a quantity of energy (in MMBtu). The delivery schedule is normally agreed with the confirmation notice. For strip deals, it will be specified and narrowed down at various points in time (in a similar fashion to term sales).

The concept of take-or-pay does not pertain to MSPAs. Although the expression is sometimes used, it does not have the same meaning as in project SPAs. Failure to take or deliver a cargo will give rise to an obligation to mitigate and to payment (often capped) depending on the loss incurred by the innocent party and the outcome of any mitigation it achieves. There is no concept of paying now for LNG not lifted and making up later.

(c) *Specific terms in the confirmation notice*

The specific terms of a transaction include, among others:

- a contract quantity and number of cargoes sold;
- transportation (DES or FOB);
- a heel and cargo tolerance;
- the identification of the LNG carriers used;
- the loading and unloading ports;
- an approximate schedule of deliveries of each cargo;
- the composition of the LNG;
- a price for each cargo (a single cargo sale can be priced as constant, while a multi-cargo sale usually uses a formula with indexation); and
- any variation to the terms and conditions of the MSPA.

These terms are not the only ones that may need to change from transaction to transaction. The cargoes sold under the confirmation notice are purchased under another contract. Standardising cargo sales does not allow risks contained in non-standard agreements along the chain to be managed. Great care is needed to identify and mitigate those risks; and without careful tailoring of confirmation notices, a party may retain risk exposure to contract discrepancies.

(d) *Methodological limitations to cargo trade*[15]

The MSPA method is a hurdle to tradability. Whether by accident or intention, MSPAs are a barrier to market access. As an MSPA only applies between two parties, each company intending to trade LNG needs to conclude an MSPA with each potential counterparty. As more companies enter the LNG trade, the number of MSPAs required for a fully (or at least optimally) connected market grows exponentially. Instead of simplifying the trade, MSPAs lock the market into a constellation of bilateral relations, outside of which it is virtually impossible to access the LNG market.

The MSPA method also poses risk management problems. Since each MSPA is unique to two companies and each confirmation notice incorporates the terms of the MSPA by reference, a single cargo that is bought and sold several times will be subject to the terms of several MSPAs. Each party between the initial seller and the final buyer will be subject to the terms of the MSPA with its seller, but will also need to manage a divergence with the terms of the MSPAs with each potential buyer. This is highly complex and is likely to slow down any

---

15 For additional background, see R Maalouf, "The Essential Evolution of LNG Trading – Moving to GTCs", (2018) 11(5) *Journal of World Energy Law and Business*, 410–426.

transaction. For each new potential party, the complexity and risk are compounded.

Commoditised markets such as crude oil and oil products, and even natural gas, do not use bilateral contracts but rely instead on general terms and conditions (GTCs). GTCs are standalone contractual terms that contain the conditions of sale and delivery of a given commodity. GTCs function as part of a wider trading contract which includes the element commonly known as 'special conditions' (essentially the same as a confirmation notice *mutatis mutandis*), which are agreed between a buyer and a seller for each transaction. The special conditions incorporate the GTCs by reference to form a binding contract. This is similar to the MSPA and confirmation notice construction, except that GTCs are standalone contractual terms which are not negotiated by the parties (although it is always possible to amend them in the special conditions); whereas the MSPA is negotiated between the parties and is a contract (albeit not a cargo sale). GTCs provide an alternative to MSPAs: instead of each company signing a master agreement with each company, the industry can adopt a set of GTCs which can be used by reference in all trading contracts.

Commoditised markets generally use several GTCs, the point being that successive trades do not need to match all the terms as is the case now. Until that evolution takes place in LNG, the spot trade will remain subject to a hurdle on liquidity.

5. Conclusion

The commoditisation of LNG remains a challenge. There is no global gas or LNG market. Some markets are liberalised and fairly liquid, while others are not. The costs of transportation of natural gas, via pipeline or in the form of LNG, and the costs of storage and containment, present physical and economic hurdles to the commoditisation of LNG. The challenge is to increase liquidity in the LNG trade sufficiently despite the hurdles created by the nature of LNG.

When the short-term market started, it consisted of a little more than one delivery per month. Even today, although the short-term trade represents 40% of the global trade of LNG, that equates to five to six deliveries per day and a large proportion of the sales are not done on a spot basis, which means that price discovery on any day continues to rest on an illiquid number that can be subject to manipulation. The relative success of the Platts price assessment process, including the market on close strategy, does not change this – as evidenced by the fact that market on close is not used and the JKM is avoided when the volatility is too high or when the price difference with the Atlantic basin is too important. Despite a growing and mid-term trade of LNG, liquidity remains relatively limited.

In the past 10 years, short-term LNG trade has grown significantly both in volume and in proportion of global LNG sales. Liquidity has been further improved by the development of LNG futures and the increased use of JKM pricing in the Asian markets. In parallel, project structures have also evolved towards commoditisation: while lenders still expect the production to be fully sold, they no longer require buyers to be the final users of the regasified LNG. Portfolio sellers have emerged as key players in project development and destination flexibility is becoming the norm. This progress is encouraging and it appears that LNG is finally on a path towards commoditisation.

LNG export projects

André Andriw
Assentia Consulting
Gustavo Castro Ribeiro Ferreira Silva
University of São Paulo
Lucas Mota de Lima
University of São Paulo; Energy Platform-EnP
Eduardo G Pereira
Professor of natural resources and energy law

1. Introduction

Liquefied natural gas (LNG) both strongly influences and is influenced by related markets and the changing economic forces that affect them. Global LNG demand has hit record highs each year since 2015, due mostly to surging demand in China and the rest of Asia. Much of this global appetite has been met by steadily rising US LNG exports, which have reached new heights every year since 2016 and look set to continue to increase.[1]

This trend is due to several factors, such as:

- increasing levels of industrialisation and energy demand, mainly in Asia and Africa;
- the transition from coal to gas, mainly in China;
- demand for cleaner fuels due to the International Maritime Organization 2020 regulations; and
- the availability of low-cost gas reserves in North America and the Middle East.

The steady growth of the LNG trade is due to the expansion of liquefaction and regasification technology, and increased demand for cleaner energy sources than oil and diesel. In recent years, some countries have stood out in the production of LNG, such as Australia, Qatar, Mozambique, Nigeria, Russia, Trinidad and Tobago and the United States.

To investigate the LNG market, this chapter:

- analyses how LNG exports are structured;
- identifies the characteristics of the main supplier countries, such as:
  - the market structure;
  - the regulatory environment; and
  - future perspectives; and

1 S Disavino, "US to be world's biggest LNG exporter in 2022", Reuters, 21 December 2021; www.reuters.com/business/energy/us-be-worlds-biggest-lng-exporter-2022-2021-12-21/.

- presents lessons and recommendations for agents in the oil and gas industry.

2. The LNG industry

In this section, the main characteristics of the LNG chain are discussed, starting with the technical characteristics involving the liquefaction process through cryogenics, as well as the details of transport and regasification at processing terminals. Economic issues concerning the market are also presented.

2.1 Technical characteristics

(a) *Cryogenic cycles and liquefaction*

After being produced and treated, natural gas can be subjected to liquefaction through cryogenic processes. LNG is obtained by altering the physical property of molecules which pass from a gaseous to a liquid state, starting at negative temperatures. The composition of natural gas for liquefaction is primarily methane, which on average can reach values of up to 97%; the remainder comprises fractions of ethane, propane and smaller proportions of denser gases.[2]

LNG production takes place through liquefaction plants. The process is complex because of the technical and operational issues involved, as well as economic feasibility factors. Natural gas is liquefied through an interface with a refrigerant fluid; after a cycle, it is subject to expansion and compression processes aimed at removing heat and providing cryogenic cooling at temperatures below -162°C. After liquefaction, the natural gas molecule can be reduced in volume by up to 600 times.[3] The stages of liquefaction, transfer, storage and transport of LNG are carried out at close to atmospheric pressure, with sudden variations achieved only in temperature.

A comparison between the LNG production chains – encompassing the onshore and offshore stages of production, liquefaction, transport and regasification – is presented in Figure 1. The main differences include the development of floating LNG technology, which enables liquefaction on the high seas and is currently being used in several projects in offshore fields.[4]

---

2 HV Araújo, *Análises de sensibilidade e oportunidades de melhoria de diferentes sistemas de refrigeração via critérios termodinâmicos, Universidade Estadual de Campinas*, 2018.

3 LJS Granada, *Logística de transporte de gás natural no Pré-Sal brasileiro: Modelo de otimização. Dissertação (Mestrado em Planejamento de Sistemas Energéticos), Faculdade de Engenharia Mecânica, Universidade Estadual de Campinas.*

4 B Songhurst, *Floating Liquefaction (FLNG): Potential for Wider Deployment*, Oxford Institute for Energy Studies, 2016.

Figure 1. Comparative flowchart between onshore and offshore LNG chains

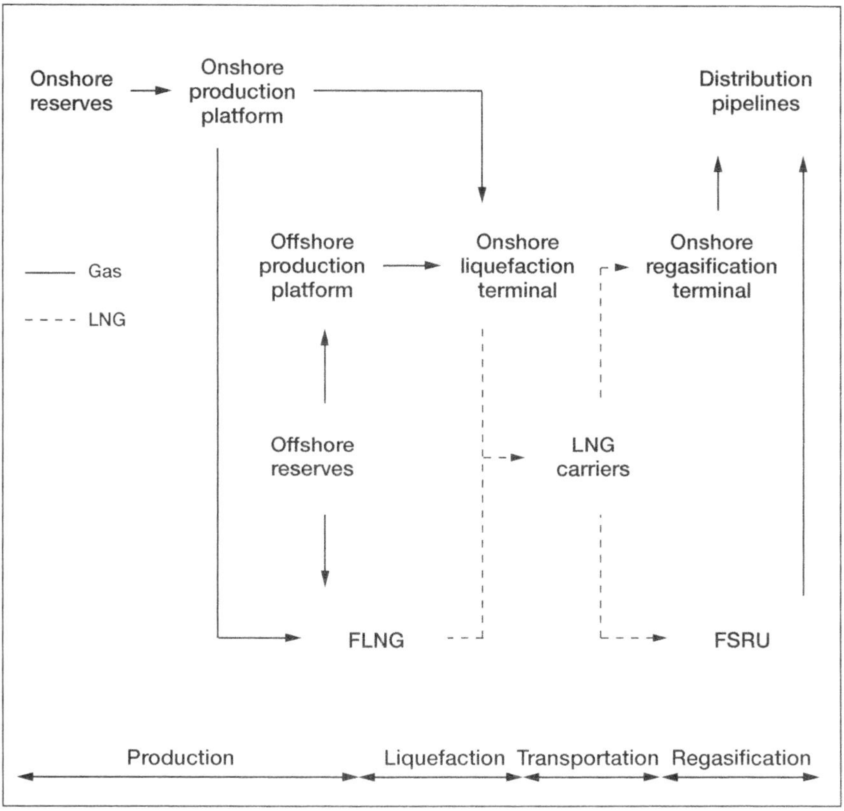

Source: Authors based on data from Won, Lee, Choi and Kwon, 2014 (n 7).

(b) ***Transport and regasification terminals***

Commercial LNG transportation takes place globally through methane tankers, also known as carriers. Once the LNG has been transferred to the carriers, the fleets head to the terminals located on the coast of the importing countries. The ships have, on average, a standard storage capacity that can vary between 30,000 cubic metres (m^3) and 265,000 m^3; LNG is kept in thermally insulated tanks to maintain internal temperature close to -162°C, with spherical, rectangular and even prismatic shapes.[5]

When the carrier docks at the receiving terminals, the transfer for regasification can occur through fixed structures on the quay; however, in most cases, another floating vessel is used. Floating storage and regasification units

5 LJS Granada, *Logística de transporte de gás natural no Pré-Sal brasileiro: Modelo de otimização. Dissertação (Mestrado em Planejamento de Sistemas Energéticos), Faculdade de Engenharia Mecânica, Universidade Estadual de Campinas.*

(FSRUs) can receive, store, regasify and drain natural gas through pipelines to the distribution network or specifically, supplying thermoelectric plants powered by imported natural gas.[6]

Currently, FSRUs receive LNG imports at maritime terminals on a large scale, with several units in operation around the world. FSRUs have regasification plants that use vaporisation processes to increase the temperature through heat exchangers and subsequently transform the physical property of the fluid, returning it to a gaseous state and draining it through the network of pipelines.[7]

2.2 Economic and market characteristics

In recent years, the ratio of proved reserves of natural gas has totalled 197 trillion cubic metres (tcm) globally, with almost 60% of this volume distributed among the territories of Russia, Iran, Qatar and Turkmenistan. In 2019, production averaged 10 billion m^3 per day, with about 39% coming from the United States and Russia.[8]

The International Gas Union has published growth figures and record prices for LNG – mainly due to the recovery in global demand, especially since China has overtaken Japan to become the largest importer in the world. In addition, exports from Australia, Qatar, the United States and Russia remained stable between 2020 and 2021; while countries such as Nigeria and Trinidad and Tobago showed a decline in exported volumes for the same period.[9] A graphical analysis of the largest exporting countries in 2021 is presented in Figure 2.

Figure 2. The largest LNG exporters in 2021

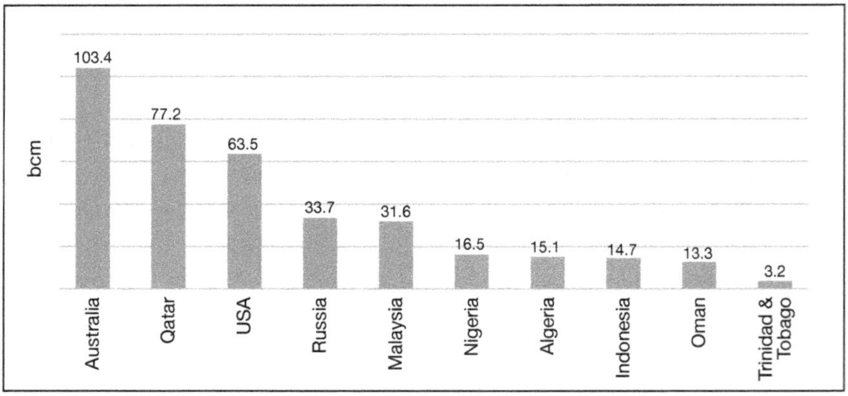

Source: Authors based on data from Rystad.[10]

6 RI Da Silva, *A liquefação como alternativa para monetização do gás natural produzido em pequena e média escala na área do Pré-Sal da região sudeste do Brasil, Universidade de São Paulo*, 2018.

7 W Won, SK Lee, K Choi and Y Kwon, "Current trends for the floating liquefied natural gas (FLNG) technologies", *Korea Journal of Chemical Engineering*, March 2014, pp732–743.

8 Empresa de Pesquisa Energética, 2019, *Boletim de Conjuntura da Indústria do Óleo & Gás.*

9 International Gas Union, *World LNG Report 2022*, www.igu.org/resources/world-lng-report-2022/.

In terms of imports, about half of all natural gas is handled in the form of LNG, according to BP.[11] In recent years, new regasification terminals have been established in Panama and Bangladesh. Data presented in Figure 3 reveals that Asia is the main destination for LNG cargoes.

According to the International Energy Agency (IEA), in the Middle East, an increase of 11% in LNG imports is expected through a new terminal in Kuwait, as well as new terminals which are expected to become operational in 2022 in countries such as Ghana, South Africa and Senegal. Also, according to the IEA, a sharp decline in imports to Central and South America is expected, given that water reservoirs in these regions have been recovering after a drought in 2021, especially in Brazil.[12]

Figure 3. The largest LNG importers in 2021

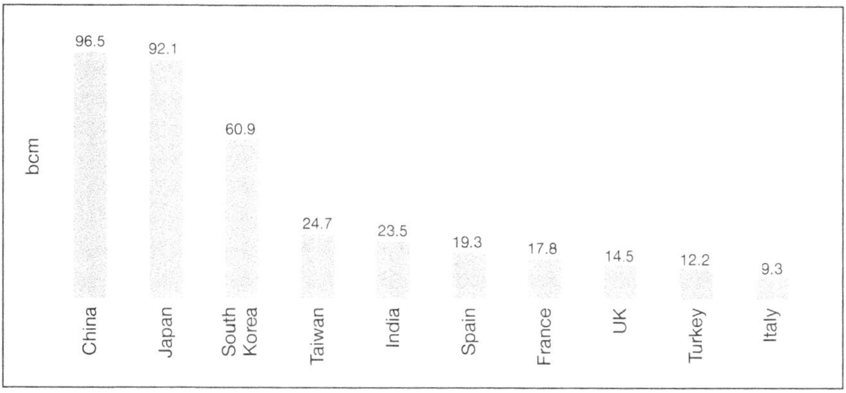

Source: Authors based on data from Rystad.[13]

The natural gas market (including LNG) has fluctuated in recent years, primarily due to decreased demand during the COVID-19 pandemic and uncertainties of supply following Russia's invasion of Ukraine. LNG projects involve large investments in liquefaction, transport and regasification infrastructure. During the pandemic, final investment decisions, as well as the completion of several plants, suffered significant delays in countries such as the United States, Canada, Qatar and Mozambique, creating an environment of insecurity and risk in line with the volatility of international LNG prices.[14]

10 Rystad Energy, *Global Gas Report 2022*, www.snam.it/export/sites/snam-rp/repository/file/gas_naturale/global-gas-report/global_gas_report_2022.pdf.

11 BP, *Statistical Review of World Energy 2021*, www.bp.com/content/dam/bp/business-sites/en/global/corporate/pdfs/energy-economics/statistical-review/bp-stats-review-2021-full-report.pdf.

12 IEA, *Gas Market Report, Q3-2022*, www.iea.org/reports/gas-market-report-q3-2022.

13 Rystad Energy, *Global Gas Report 2022*, www.snam.it/export/sites/snam-rp/repository/file/gas_naturale/global-gas-report/global_gas_report_2022.pdf.

14 International Gas Union, *World LNG Report 2022*, www.igu.org/resources/world-lng-report-2022/.

After the depression caused by the pandemic, a rush for alternative supplies to Russian gas has seen demand for energy soar. With high international prices, there is a trend for new projects and increasing supply for exporting countries.

2.3 Regulatory and policy characteristics

In many countries, various types of deregulation and reforms have been implemented at pace, resulting in more effective legislation and stronger competition in the markets. Table 1 presents the results of reforms and policy initiatives on three different fronts.

Table 1. Major gas market reforms and policy initiatives

Market opening reforms	Security of supply	Decarbonisation/methane
Brazil adopts new Gas Law	Weatherisation of power plants in Texas	European Commission's Hydrogen and Decarbonised Gas Markets package
Nigeria adopts Petroleum Industry Act	EU Toolbox on high energy prices	Global Methane Pledge at COP26
Gas trading takes off in India	Japan revises LNG stock monitoring	Ukraine's biomethane law
Shanghai Exchange launches LNG prices index	Korea increases LNG stock obligations	Japan targets 5% carbon-neutral gas by 2030

Source: Authors based on data from IEA.[15]

In terms of market liberalisation, the Brazilian reforms, the new legislation governing the Nigerian oil industry and recent developments in China and India stand out. Improvements in security of supply are also significant – in particular, steps to ensure safe access to energy sources in the face of weather problems and high prices, as well as the monitoring of inventories in North America, Europe and Asia. Combating greenhouse gas (GHG) emissions through carbon and methane mitigation is also relevant and has featured in European debates. Ukraine stands out for establishing a regulatory model and approving a law to encourage the production and use of biomethane in the energy mix.

15 IEA, *Gas Market Report, Q3-2022*, www.iea.org/reports/gas-market-report-q3-2022.

3. Analysis of the main exporting countries

This section presents comparative national export and import data and a summary of the main regulatory developments in selected countries worldwide.

3.1 Australia

Australia is an important player in the global energy sector. It has extensive mineral reserves combined with fossil and renewable energy potential. In terms of energy balance, coal and oil respectively represent 40% and 34% of the primary energy supply. In recent years, the Australian energy industry has been affected by growing demand from the transport sector, which uses 95% oil derivatives.[16]

Coal still plays an important role in the Australian electricity matrix, as it accounts for 75% of the electricity supply through thermoelectric generation.[17] In a bid to reduce GHG emissions, the Australian state has pursued the gradual adoption of natural gas as a transition fuel. Natural gas is thus seen as a strategic resource to align energy security with sustainable socio-economic development.[18]

According to the Department of Industry, Science, Energy, and Resources, the bulk of Australian natural gas production comes from offshore exploration in the states of Western Australia – responsible for more than 50% of the natural gas supply – and the Northern Territory.[19] Onshore activities are mainly concentrated in the states of Queensland and South Australia through the Cooper Basin, where there are hydrocarbon-bearing formations which are similar to those found in offshore explorations in the state of Victoria.

Figure 4. Australian natural gas production

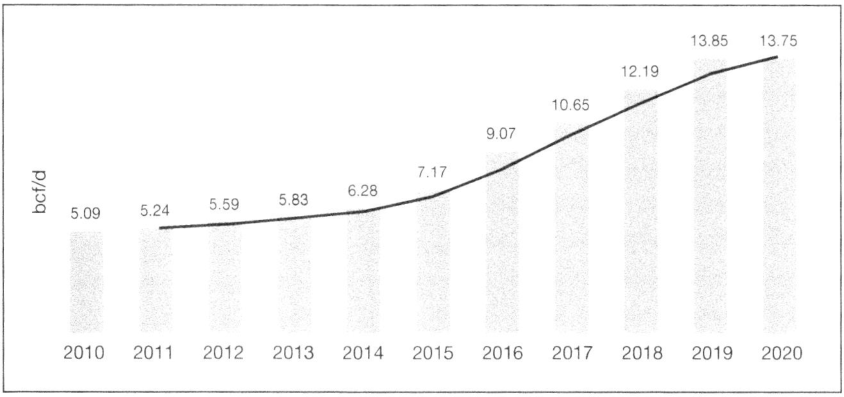

Source: Authors based on data from BP.[20]

16 IEA Asia Pacific, 2022, www.iea.org/regions/asia-pacific.

17 *Ibid.*

18 Australian Department of Industry, Science and Resources, Global Resources Stratement, 3 June 2021, www.industry.gov.au/data-and-publications/australias-global-resources-statement/global-resources-strategy.

19 *Ibid.*

In recent years, Australia has stood out for its extraction of natural gas from coal – that is, coal seam gas (CSG). This unconventional resource is located in both the Bowen/Surat Basin and the Galilee Basin, which together hold 23,925 petajoules in CSG reserves. However, due to technological, environmental and financial limitations, the exploration and production of CSG have been questioned by public authorities and environmentalists, since they incur high economic and environmental costs; as a result, the state of Northern Territory has banned the processing of CSG.[21]

Australian natural gas production increased consistently between 2010 and 2020. In 2010, the production level stood at 5.09 billion cubic feet per day (bcf/d), reaching a peak in 2019 of 13.85 bcf/d and stabilising at 13.75 bcf/d the following year, even during the COVID-19 pandemic.[22] The conditions for this consistent growth were established by major government reforms to the institutional and regulatory framework, aimed at inducing investment in productive capacity for domestic use and the export of LNG. These reforms were accompanied by public policies at the national and subnational levels that boosted the capture of national and international opportunities by the oil and gas industry.[23]

Activity in Australia's oil and gas industry is mainly carried out by national and international private companies, which have extensive international experience in the development of natural gas exploration and production projects. As it is mostly located in Western Australia, the Northern Territory and Queensland, the industry has easy access to transit ports equipped with infrastructure for the storage and transport of LNG.[24]

The main LNG production-export projects are:

- the Northwest Shelf (16.9 million tonnes per annum (mtpa));
- Gorgon (15.6 mtpa);
- Australia Pacific LNG (9 mtpa);
- Wheatstone (8.9 mtpa);
- Ichthys (8.9 mtpa);
- Queensland Curtis LNG (8.5 mtpa);
- Gladstone (7.8 mtpa);
- Pluto (4.9 mtpa);

20 BP, *Statistical Review of World Energy 2021*, www.bp.com/content/dam/bp/business-sites/en/global/corporate/pdfs/energy-economics/statistical-review/bp-stats-review-2021-full-report.pdf.

21 D Ledesma, J Henderson and N Palmer, "The Future of Australian LNG Exports: Will Domestic Challenges Limit the Development of Future LNG Export Capacity?", Oxford Institute for Energy Studies, September 2014.

22 BP, *Statistical Review of World Energy 2021*, www.bp.com/content/dam/bp/business-sites/en/global/corporate/pdfs/energy-economics/statistical-review/bp-stats-review-2021-full-report.pdf.

23 Australian Department of Industry, Science and Resources, Global Resources Strategy Commodity Report, February 2022, www.industry.gov.au/data-and-publications/global-resources-strategy-commodity-report-liquefied-natural-gas/lng-industry-outlook.

24 Appea, "LNG Exports", www.appea.com.au/industry/policy/policy-positions/lng-exports/.

- Darwin (3.7 mtpa); and
- Prelude (3.6 mtpa).

Overall, the Australian production export base has a total capacity of 87.8 mtpa.

Figure 5. Australia's LNG exports

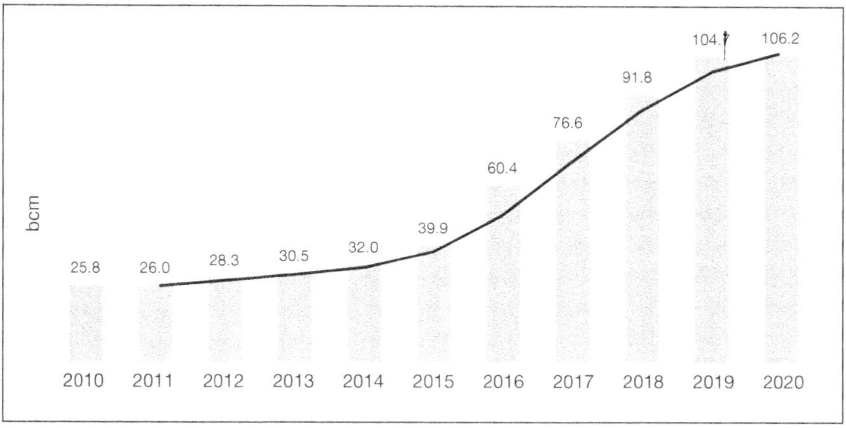

Source: Authors based on data from BP.[25]

In addition to the domestic market, Australian production of natural gas and LNG has been absorbed by the accelerated economic growth of the main Asian economies. China, Japan, South Korea and Taiwan are the main conduits of Australian LNG. Recently, the Australian industry has been prospecting emerging markets that need new supplies for the energy transition, such as Thailand, Vietnam, Indonesia, India, Malaysia, the Philippines and Bangladesh.[26]

Australian LNG exports increased sharply from 2010 to 2020, accumulating 311% growth during that period. A change in this market trend occurred between 2015 and 2016, when exports increased by 51.37% due to growing Australian supply combined with heightened energy demand from China, which – together with other Asian countries – helped drive the evolution of the Australian natural gas industry.[27]

Another important factor is the Australian government's experience in the management of natural resources. Historically, Australia was economically dependent on the extraction and processing of raw materials for export, which

25 BP, *Statistical Review of World Energy 2021*, www.bp.com/content/dam/bp/business-sites/en/global/corporate/pdfs/energy-economics/statistical-review/bp-stats-review-2021-full-report.pdf.

26 Australian Department of Industry, Science and Resources, "Mining, Oil and Gas, 2022", www.industry.gov.au/policies-and-initiatives/supporting-australias-resources-sector.

27 BP, *Statistical Review of World Energy 2021*, www.bp.com/content/dam/bp/business-sites/en/global/corporate/pdfs/energy-economics/statistical-review/bp-stats-review-2021-full-report.pdf.

led to close government interaction with the mining and oil and gas industry to build a robust and favourable institutional and regulatory framework.

In terms of governance, the Commonwealth (federal government):

- regulates offshore industrial operations in Commonwealth waters; and
- determines taxes, rights of indigenous peoples, environmental protection, customs rules and occupational health and safety.

Otherwise, subnational entities – states and provinces – are responsible for regulating activities in their respective territories, which may differ according to the local characteristics of each subnational unit.

The Australian government has a substantial presence beyond the regulatory field through public policies aimed at promoting the development of the industry. Australia's Global Resource Strategy stands out in this regard: its objective is to help the Australian natural gas industry find sufficient and reliable financial, human and regulatory resources to make new investments in the country. The strategy includes the Long-Term Emission Reduction Plan and the Technology Investment Roadmap as auxiliary policies to encourage technological innovation and human resource training.[28]

However, this governance system – which is not always well coordinated among the various authorities – also creates LNG production and export challenges. This is due to the conflict of interest between subnational regulators and companies around environmental preservation, energy security and tax incentives.[29] With the increasing participation of municipalities and state governments in environmental governance, several LNG ventures have been affected both by pro-environment regulations and by the shift of financial and tax incentives from the fossil industry to renewable sources.

'Energy security' refers to the need to guarantee the supply of natural gas at competitive prices in the domestic market.[30] In 2017, in response to the risk of shortages of natural gas for the electricity sector, the Australian government implemented the Australian Domestic Gas Security Mechanism.

This policy grants the Australian state the right to restrict LNG exports to meet domestic demand in a scenario of evident scarcity. The measure is temporary and not a direct price control mechanism.[31] In the Australian

---

28 Australian Department of Industry, Science and Resources, Global Resources Statement, 3 June 2021, www.industry.gov.au/data-and-publications/australias-global-resources-statement/global-resources-strategy.

29 D Ledesma, J Henderson and N Palmer, "The Future of Australian LNG Exports: Will Domestic Challenges Limit the Development of Future LNG Export Capacity?", Oxford Institute for Energy Studies, September 2014.

30 Y Liu, X Shi and J Laurenceson, "Dynamics of Australia's LNG export performance: A modified constant market shares analysis", *Energy Economics*, 89, 104808, https://doi.org/10.1016/j.eneco.2020.104808.

31 Australian Department of Industry, Science and Resources, "Australian Domestic Gas Security Mechanism Review 2019", 1 January 2020, www.industry.gov.au/publications/australian-domestic-gas-security-mechanism-review-2019.

government's view, increasing domestic supply will stimulate competitiveness and relieve pressure on energy prices.

In summary, the Australian natural gas and LNG industrial base has evolved in parallel with Asian demand for resilient fuel at a competitive price. The development of infrastructure projects aimed at domestic supply and export of LNG has thus been fundamental for the industry to remain internationally competitive.

3.2 Qatar

A small monarchical Middle Eastern nation with abundant energy potential, Qatar has a strong competitive advantage on the international stage. This has directly affected its national socioeconomic performance, as 60% of its gross domestic product depends on revenues from the oil and gas industry.[32]

The country is the world's fourteenth-largest oil producer, the third-largest global exporter of natural gas through pipelines and the second-largest exporter of LNG, with 77.1 million tons delivered abroad.[33] Since 2013, Qatar's natural gas production has plateaued, with an average production of 15.87 bcf/d between 2010 and 2020 (see Figure 6).

Figure 6. Qatar's gas production between 2010 and 2020

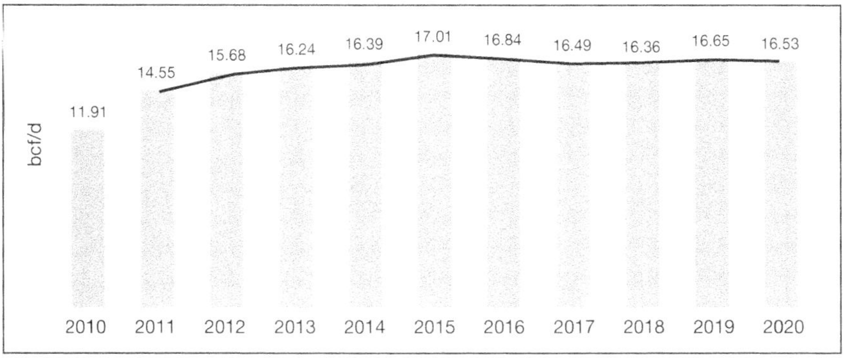

Source: Authors based on data from BP.[34]

The Qatari oil and gas industry is concentrated in the cities of Ras Laffan and Um Said – two industrial bases developed to support companies extracting, producing, transporting and processing oil and natural gas from the North Field and Duffan fields. The organisation of the oil and gas industrial base was

32 E Mahmood, *Oil and Gas Regulation 2020: A Practical Cross-Border Insight into Oil and Gas Regulation Work*, 15th edition, International Comparative Legal Guides.

33 International Gas Union, *World LNG Report 2022*, www.igu.org/resources/world-lng-report-2022/.

34 BP, *Statistical Review of World Energy 2021*, www.bp.com/content/dam/bp/business-sites/en/global/corporate/pdfs/energy-economics/statistical-review/bp-stats-review-2021-full-report.pdf.

facilitated by the country's small territorial space: production sites are interconnected by gas pipelines, oil pipelines and railways, which in turn connect the ports equipped with infrastructure for the storage of oil and its derivatives, as well as LNG.[35]

The structure of the Qatari oil and gas market is deeply concentrated in Qatar Energy (formerly Qatar Petroleum), which has the authority to enter into partnerships with multinational companies. Together with several subsidiaries, the state-owned company operates in the oil and gas, lubricant, fertiliser, petrochemicals and transport sectors. The state-owned company sought to reposition itself in the market after the fall in international oil prices in 2018, which impacted its profit margin.

In a bid to reduce operational costs and direct investments towards sectors with growth potential in the context of the global energy transition, the Qatar government encouraged the merger of Qatar Energy's two subsidiaries in the LNG sector:

- RasGas, which is responsible for producing LNG and transporting it through seven LNG processing plants in the city of Ras Laffan; and
- Qatargas, which operates production plants and LNG storage and transport infrastructure across the country.

The result was the creation of Qatargas in 2018, which invested in the construction of 14 LNG processing terminals, totalling an annual production of 79 million tons (Mt) at the time.[36]

The strong competitiveness of the Qatari oil and gas industry is also due to robust government support through industrial policies that encourage the export of oil products and LNG. Qatar has a long history of promoting economic growth through industrial and urban planning policies, developing and integrating local human resources through industrial cities such as Mesaieed Industrial City and Dukhan Petroleum City.[37]

Since 2011, one economic strategy of the Qatar government has been the establishment of special economic zones, which are managed by state-owned company Manateq. These provide tax and financial incentives aimed at establishing technological, industrial and entrepreneurship hubs. After the Gulf countries imposed an economic blockade on Qatar in 2017, the Qatari government adopted strategies to replace imports of food and raw materials related to the oil and gas sector, as well as to strengthen domestic production.[38]

---

35 HE Alfadala and MM El-Halwagi, "Qatar's chemical industry: Monetizing natural gas" *Chemical Engineering Progress*, February 2017.

36 *Ibid*; Aiswarya Lakshmi, "Qatargas-RasGas Merger" MarineLink, 4 January 2018, www.marinelink.com/news/qatargasrasgas-merger432655.

37 KPMG, *Qatar Industrial Landscape 2.0: Resilient and Stronger*, 2021, https://assets.kpmg/content/dam/kpmg/qa/pdf/2021/04/tl-qatar-industrial-landscape-2.0-resilient-and-stronger-.pdf.

38 *Ibid.*

In 2018, the Qatar government launched the Qatar Manufacturing Strategy (2018–2022), which seeks to accelerate growth and economic diversification in line with the goal of transitioning to a low-carbon economy set out in both the Qatar National Vision 2030 and the National Development Strategy 2. Qatar's industrial strategy has institutional and financial enablers that serve strategic sub-sectors such as polymers, plastics, additive manufacturing, aluminium, pharmaceuticals and environmental resilience services.[39]

In this context, Qatar Energy began to act not only as a generator of revenue for the public coffers, but also as an inducer of investments in technological diversification in the natural gas and oil sectors, in order to increase production of petrochemicals, natural gas, LNG and fertilisers. In 2019, the Qatar government announced an increase in natural gas production from 77 million metric tonnes per annum (MMtpa) to 110 MMtpa by 2024.[40]

In terms of international relations, Qatar continues to position itself as a major player in the international natural gas market. Since 2011, it has maintained a constant 100 billion cubic metres (bcm) of LNG exports, with substantial increases between 2018 and 2020 – the implementation period of the Qatar Manufacturing Strategy 2 (see Figure 7).

Figure 7. Qatar's LNG exports between 2010 and 2020

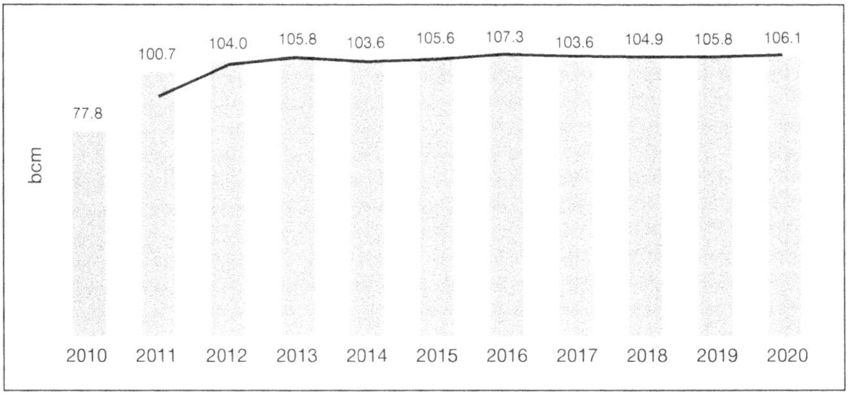

Source: Authors based on data from BP.[41]

39 Qatar Planning and Statistics Authority, Qatar Second National Development Strategy 2018–2022, published 2018.

40 KPMG, *Qatar Industrial Landscape 2.0: Resilient and Stronger*, 2021, https://assets.kpmg/content/dam/kpmg/qa/pdf/2021/04/tl-qatar-industrial-landscape-2.0-resilient-and-stronger-.pdf.

41 BP, *Statistical Review of World Energy 2021*, www.bp.com/content/dam/bp/business-sites/en/global/corporate/pdfs/energy-economics/statistical-review/bp-stats-review-2021-full-report.pdf.

Figure 8. Qatar's LNG top destinations

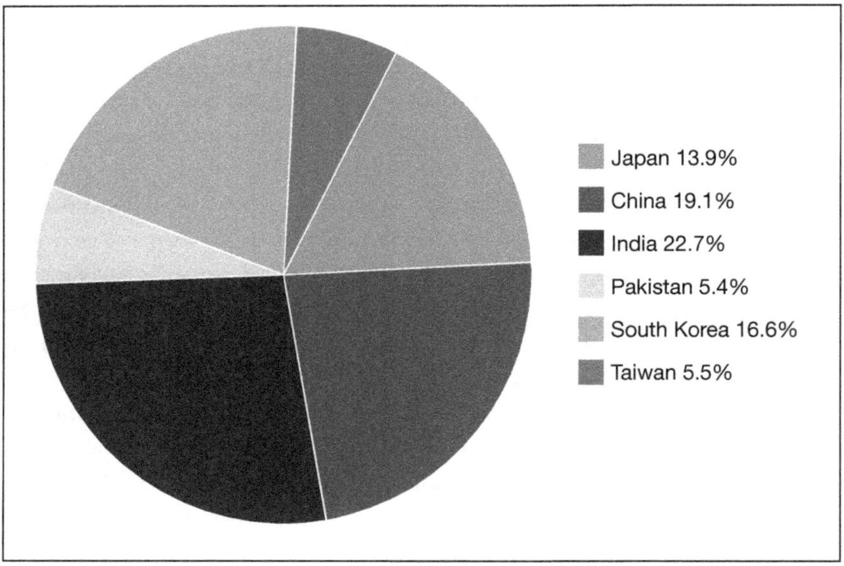

Source: Authors based on OEC data.

Currently, the main importers of Qatari LNG are in Asia, which means that the Qatar LNG industry is disputing clients in the Asian market with Russia, the United States and Australia. India was the main importer in 2020, with 22.7% of exported value; followed by China (19.1%), South Korea (16.6%), Japan (13.9%), Taiwan (5.5%) and Pakistan (5.4%).[42]

Qatar's geographic location – with access to several sea routes in the Middle East – and sophisticated natural gas industry favour the supply of LNG to the Asian market at competitive prices. As a result, attention has focused on the long-distance specialised export of LNG production and transport, to the detriment of the construction of LNG pipelines to supply natural gas to neighbouring countries such as the United Arab Emirates that suffer from shortages of the product to generate electricity.[43]

In summary, Qatar's oil and gas industry was established to meet external energy demand. In this sense, LNG has become an asset for the Qatari people after a long process of maturation of government policies focused on infrastructure and innovation that have allowed market opportunities to be captured, especially in Asia.

42 OEC, Qatar country profile, https://oec.world/en/profile/country/qat.

43 Ali Taha, "The Qatar-UAE Gas Trade: Balancing Geo-Economics with Energy Security", Issam Fares Institute for Public Policy and International Affairs Analysis, August 2021, www.aub.edu.lb/ifi/Documents/publications/Analysis/2021-2022/20210810_qatar_uae_gas_trade_balancing_ geoeconomics _with_energy_security_analysis.pdf.

3.3 United States

Following the successful development of unconventional natural gas reservoirs such as shale gas, the United States became the world's largest gas producer in just a few years. The commercial exploitation of unconventional reservoirs depends on both environmental and technical factors relating to demand, domestic and international.

Since the late 1990s, US gas reserves have increased each year. The exploration of shale gas reservoirs alone increased national reserves by approximately 50% from 2010 to 20%, with a record increase of 30% – 6 trillion cubic feet (tcf) – in 2018 alone.[44] US natural gas production is shown in Figure 9.

Figure 9. US gas production between 2010 and 2020

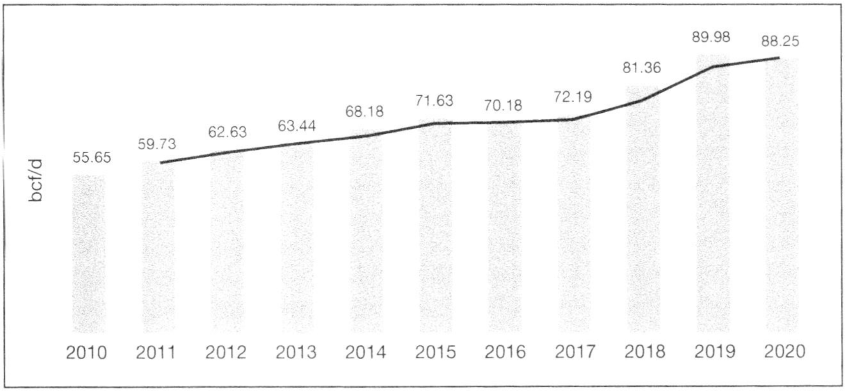

Source: Authors based on data from BP.[45]

Before 2008, analysts predicted that the United States would become increasingly dependent on imported sources of natural gas and significant investments were made in regasification facilities for LNG imports. The focus is currently on LNG liquefaction and export; and since 2015, US export capacity has nearly quintupled. As a result, the United States became a net exporter of natural gas in 2017 for the first time in 60 years.[46]

The first LNG exports took place in 2016. Sabine Pass Liquefaction, in the state of Louisiana, exported the first LNG tanker cargo bound for Brazil.[47] Since then, several regasification terminals initially used for import have been converted into terminals for liquefaction and export. As of 2019, the United

44 R Kurmaev and V Malinin, *Oil and Gas Regulation 2020: A Practical Cross-Border Insight into Oil and Gas Regulation Work*, 15th edition, International Comparative Legal Guides.

45 BP, *Statistical Review of World Energy 2021*, www.bp.com/content/dam/bp/business-sites/en/global/corporate/pdfs/energy-economics/statistical-review/bp-stats-review-2021-full-report.pdf.

46 See n 44.

47 US Department of Energy, *Liquefied Natural Gas (LNG)*, Office of Fossil Energy and Carbon Management, 2022, www.energy.gov/fecm/liquefied-natural-gas-lng.

States had become the world's third-largest LNG exporter, behind Australia and Qatar (see Figure 2).

Figure 10. US LNG export destinations

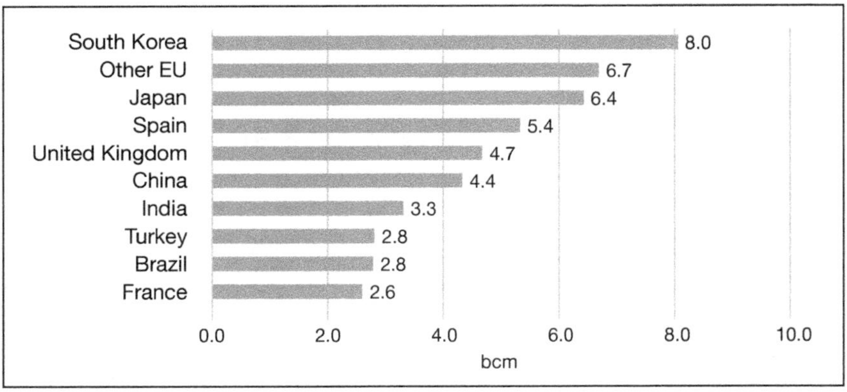

Source: Authors based on data from BP.[48]

Natural gas liquefaction is mainly supplied by onshore fields in states such as Texas, Oklahoma, Wyoming, New Mexico, Louisiana, North Dakota and Colorado, in addition to offshore fields with an important role in the Gulf of Mexico.[49] In 2020, half of the LNG exports were directed to five destinations:[50]

- South Korea (8 bcm);
- the European Union (6.7 bcm);
- Japan (6.4 bcm);
- Spain (5.4 bcm); and
- the United Kingdom (4.7 bcm).

In 2021, the six US LNG export terminals reached 100% nominal capacity, with an average export capacity of 89%.[51]

US LNG exports have already exceeded exports via pipelines; and with the operation of the new liquefaction trains at Sabine Pass and Calcasieu Pass scheduled for 2022, US LNG export capacity will become the largest in the world.[52] US LNG exporters are emerging as the big winners from Europe's supply crisis, as they are exporting record volumes to the European Union. European gas prices have hit all-time highs, just as exporters of LNG in the United States

48 BP, *Statistical Review of World Energy 2021*, www.bp.com/content/dam/bp/business-sites/en/global/corporate/pdfs/energy-economics/statistical-review/bp-stats-review-2021-full-report.pdf.

49 See n 47.

50 *Ibid.*

51 US Energy Information Administration, Natural Gas Weekly Update, week ending 1 December 2021, www.eia.gov/naturalgas/weekly/archivenew_ngwu/2021/12_02/#itn-tabs-1.

52 *Ibid.*

completed projects that had been under development for years to deliver abundant shale gas supplies to international markets.[53]

Figure 11. US LNG exports

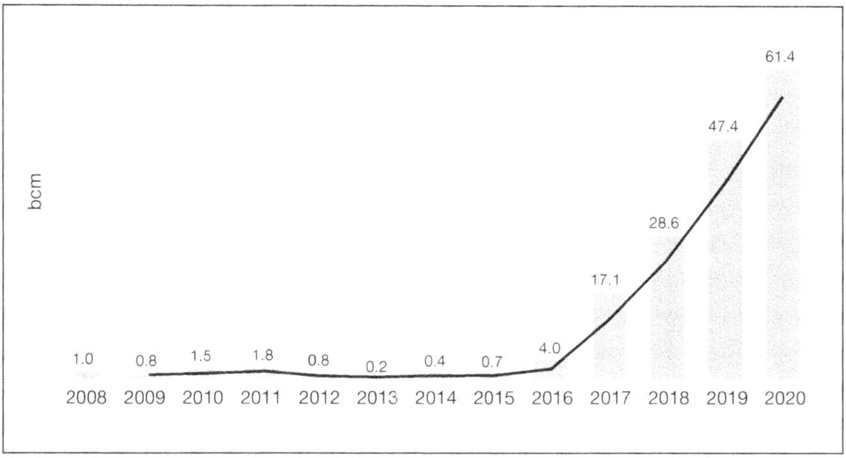

Source: Authors based on data from BP.[54]

LNG projects are subject to various laws and regulations that are administered by:

- federal government agencies such as:
  - the Department of Energy (DOE);
  - the Environmental Protection Agency;
  - the Federal Energy Regulatory Commission (FERC);
  - the US Coast Guard/Maritime Administration; and
  - the US Army Corps of Engineers; and
- the individual states.[55]

The DOE has regulatory responsibilities related to LNG. Companies that wish to export natural gas must obtain authorisation to do so from the DOE's Office of Fossil Energy and Carbon Management (FECM). The Natural Gas Act requires the DOE to make public interest determinations on applications to export LNG to countries with which the United States does not have existing free trade agreements (FTAs). The FECM's natural gas import-export regulatory

53 M Rashad, "US LNG exporters emerge as big winners of Europe natgas crisis", Reuters, 9 March 2022, www.reuters.com/business/energy/us-lng-exporters-emerge-big-winners-europe-natgas-crisis-2022-03-09/.

54 BP, *Statistical Review of World Energy 2021*, www.bp.com/content/dam/bp/business-sites/en/global/corporate/pdfs/energy-economics/statistical-review/bp-stats-review-2021-full-report.pdf.

55 R Kurmaev and V Malinin, *Oil and Gas Regulation 2020: A Practical Cross-Border Insight into Oil and Gas Regulation Work*, 15th edition, International Comparative Legal Guides.

programme is implemented by the Division of Regulation in the Office of Regulation, Analysis and Engagement.[56]

FERC has jurisdiction over the siting, construction and operation of LNG export facilities in the United States. FERC's regulatory authority extends to interstate pipelines as well as onshore LNG import/export terminals, and certain environmental and accounting matters. In these cases, FERC leads the environmental impact assessments of proposed projects consistent with the National Environmental Policy Act; the DOE is typically a cooperating agency as part of these reviews. Obtaining DOE authorisation to export LNG to non-FTA countries is an important step for most projects in their path towards financing and construction.[57]

The DOE also authorises two types of natural gas imports and exports: blanket authorisations and long-term authorisations. Blanket authorisations allow the authorised party to import or export for up to two years. Long-term authorisations are used for natural gas imports or exports that will last longer than two years. Typically, holders of long-term authorisations have, or intend to have, a signed gas purchase or sales agreement in place for more than two years.[58]

3.4 Russia

Russia is a relevant player in the international energy market, as it has the largest reserves of oil, natural gas, coal and other strategic minerals in the world. The country has the largest proven reserves of natural gas, with a total of 38 tcm or 19% of global reserves.[59]

The Russian natural gas sector is complex and well structured, accounting for 25% of the international supply. The industrial base is concentrated in Siberia, with the Yamburg, Urengo and Medvezhye fields generating 40% of production. Natural gas is a strategic industry for Russia, both economically and politically, as much of the fuel produced is shipped to Europe and Asia through extensive pipeline networks.[60]

In terms of LNG market structure, there are three key players in the Russian gas industry: Gazprom, Novatek and Rosneft. Each has developed a strategy compatible with its asset base and previous experience; and as a result, three different approaches to LNG developments in Russia have emerged. The natural gas sector is dominated by state players, most obviously Gazprom. Gazprom is

---

56 US Department of Energy, *Liquefied Natural Gas (LNG)*, Office of Fossil Energy and Carbon Management, 2022, www.energy.gov/fecm/liquefied-natural-gas-lng.

57 *Ibid.*

58 R Kurmaev and V Malinin, *Oil and Gas Regulation 2020: A Practical Cross-Border Insight into Oil and Gas Regulation Work*, 15th edition, International Comparative Legal Guides.

59 BP, *Statistical Review of World Energy 2021*, www.bp.com/content/dam/bp/business-sites/en/global/corporate/pdfs/energy-economics/statistical-review/bp-stats-review-2021-full-report.pdf.

60 J Josefson and A Rotar, "Oil and gas regulation in the Russian Federation: overview", *Thomson Reuters Practical Law*, April 2021, 1–30.

majority owned by the Russian government, boasts more than 70% of the country's proven reserves and is responsible for about 73% of domestic natural gas production.[61]

Most of the domestic gas production comes from onshore fields. The only significant offshore gas operation is the Sakhalin II project. There are only two operating LNG projects:

- Sakhalin II, operated by Sakhalin Energy, in which a Gazprom subsidiary holds a stake of 50% plus one share, with the remaining shares split between subsidiaries of Shell (27.5%), Mitsui (12.5%) and Mitsubishi (10%); and
- the Yamal LNG project, located in the Russian Arctic – a joint venture between Novatek (50.1%), Total (20%), CNPC (20%) and Silk Road Fund (9.9%). The first delivery was made in December 2017 and in March 2018 it shipped 1 million tonnes of LNG. In 2019, the Yamal LNG project officially commissioned its third production line and reached full capacity.

Since the beginning of operationalisation, these two projects have significantly increased Russia's natural gas production. From a foreign policy perspective, the Yamal LNG project has helped to increase Russia's presence in the Asian natural gas market: 4% of the global LNG market is currently supplied by Sakhalin II, which consistently delivers to China, Japan and South Korea.[62]

With EU sanctions closing off access to foreign technology, Novatek will intensify efforts to scale up its Arctic cascade liquefaction process to support the drive to turn Russia into one of the world's biggest LNG exporters. Before Russia's invasion of Ukraine, Novatek repeatedly claimed that it would be able to deliver more than 55 mtpa of LNG to international markets by 2030 from its Yamal LNG, Arctic LNG 1 and Arctic LNG 2 projects. There is growing evidence that sanctions are severely affecting the pace and possibly even the viability of the Novatek-led Arctic LNG 2 project, which is currently the largest of its kind in the country.

In response to this situation, Novatek will soon launch two LNG reloading hubs aimed at cutting transportation costs. The hubs will be built in Kamchatka in the Far East and in the Arctic city of Murmansk. The sites will reduce shipping costs by allowing LNG tankers to transfer cargoes to smaller vessels, saving the expense of sailing tankers to every end user.

Perceptions of the Russian LNG industry have been transformed over the past few years. Henderson and Yermakov predict that Russian LNG production should reach 120–140 mtpa by 2035. This would make Russia one of the world's

---

61 *Ibid.*
62 Shell, Sakhalin-2 – An overview, www.shell.com/about-us/major-projects/sakhalin/sakhalin-an-overview.html.

top three LNG producers and enhance its position as the world's number one natural gas exporter.[63]

LNG is about more than gas exports for Russia. From a geopolitical standpoint, LNG is helping to open up the strategically vital Northern Sea Route in the Arctic, enhancing trading and political relations with Europe and Asia. LNG is also opening up new markets for Russian gas, with commercial and political advantages creating opportunities for a wider range of negotiations and discussions.

It is clear that Russia has set out on an ambitious course of LNG development supported by domestic industrial development; and although it will have to overcome many practical difficulties in achieving its ambition of becoming one of the world's top LNG producers and exporters, it has already taken significant steps forward and appears likely to continue its growth trajectory over the next decade.

Figure 12. Russia LNG export destinations

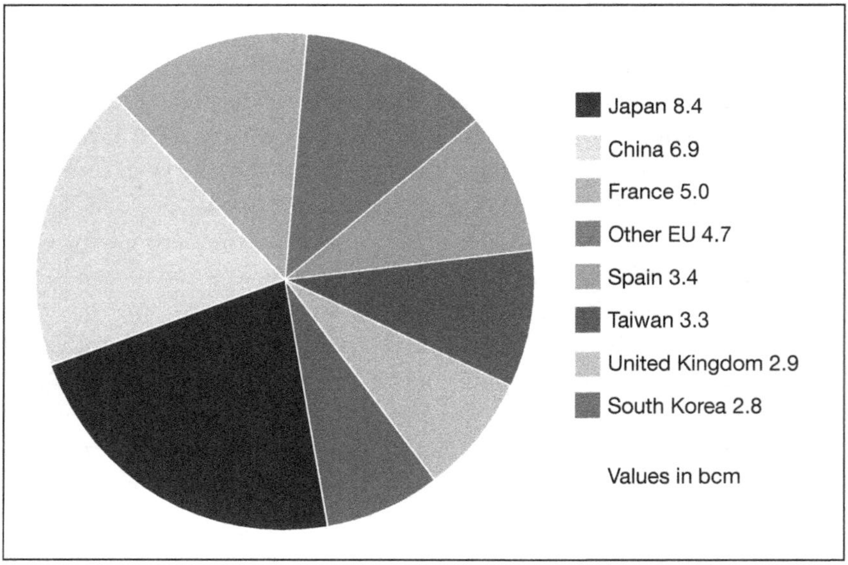

Source: Authors based on data from BP.[64]

Russia exports 40.4 bcm of LNG, corresponding to 8.3% of the entire global market.[65] While the European market has been a traditional and rather stable export destination for Russian natural gas for decades, Russian natural gas exports are already reorienting towards the Asian market.

63 J Henderson and V Yermakov, "Russian LNG: Becoming a Global Force", OIES Paper NG 154, Oxford Institute for Energy Studies, November 2019.

64 BP, *Statistical Review of World Energy 2021*, www.bp.com/content/dam/bp/business-sites/en/global/corporate/pdfs/energy-economics/statistical-review/bp-stats-review-2021-full-report.pdf.

Russia retains its spot as the world's fourth largest exporter, with 29.6 Mt of exports in 2020 and an 8% share of all global exports. The main export markets for Russian LNG are Japan, China, France and Spain.[66] In 2020, Russia's liquefaction capacity and utilisation rate was more than 90%.

Reportedly, most Yamal LNG exports are directed to the Asia-Pacific market, while some cargoes go to Western Europe. All Sakhalin II LNG exports go to the Asia-Pacific region. In 2020, none of the LNG produced in Russia went towards domestic consumption.[67]

Figure 13. Russia's LNG exports between 2010 and 2020

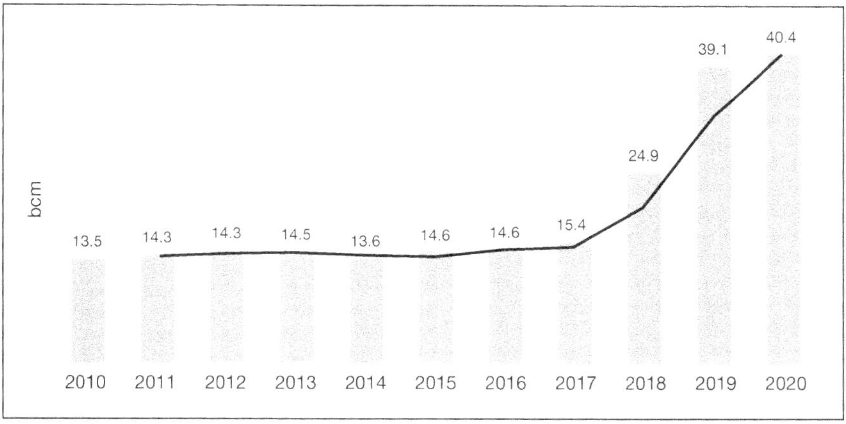

Source: Authors based on data from BP.[68]

State regulation of gas exports is based on the Law on Gas Exports, which considers the need to protect Russia's economic interests. Gas is supplied based on an agreement between the supplier and the purchaser concluded according to the requirements of the Civil Code.[69]

In December 2013 the Law on Gas Exports was amended to allow certain companies to export LNG. In practice, it now applies to Novatek-controlled projects in the Russian Far North. State-controlled companies can also export LNG from gas produced in offshore fields licensed to those companies (or affiliates), but no such LNG project is yet in operation. The amendments did not change the overall scope of the Law on Gas Exports: it continues to cover all

65 *Ibid.*

66 International Gas Union, *World LNG Report 2022*, www.igu.org/resources/world-lng-report-2022/.

67 V Kutcherov, M Morgunova, V Bessel and A Lopatin, "Russian natural gas exports: An analysis of challenges and opportunities", *Energy Strategy Reviews*, July 2020, https://doi.org/10.1016/j.esr.2020.100511.

68 BP, *Statistical Review of World Energy 2021*, www.bp.com/content/dam/bp/business-sites/en/global/corporate/pdfs/energy-economics/statistical-review/bp-stats-review-2021-full-report.pdf.

69 R Kurmaev and V Malinin, *Oil and Gas Regulation 2020: A Practical Cross-Border Insight into Oil and Gas Regulation Work*, 15th edition, International Comparative Legal Guides.

exports of gas – both pipeline and LNG. Two legacy categories of eligible exporters have and retain the right to export gas from Russia:[70]

- Gazprom/Gazprom Export: The owner of the Unified Gas System and its 100%-owned subsidiaries (essentially, Gazprom and Gazprom Export) can export gas (pipeline or LNG) from any source (including any onshore gas fields), whether the licensee of such gas fields is Gazprom or any other producer.
- Grandfathered PSAs: The pre-existing exemption for exports of gas (both pipeline and LNG) produced by grandfathered PSA projects also remains in place.

The licensing regime is administered by the Ministry of Natural Resources and Ecology and the federal agencies under its jurisdiction. Subordinate to that ministry, the Federal Agency for Subsoil Use is primarily responsible for the regulation of oil and gas extraction.[71]

The Ministry of Natural Resources and Environment is responsible for the preparation and subsequent implementation of government policies in the oil and gas sector, as well as the development and regulation of research, use, replacement and protection of natural resources, including subsoil.[72]

The main objective of the Ministry of Natural Resources and Environment is the replacement of reserves, because discoveries are falling as large producing deposits are depleted. The Federal Agency of Subsoil Use – an agency subordinate to the Ministry of Natural Resources and Environment – is the key regulator of oil and gas extraction. With cuts in the supply of Russian LNG to EU countries resulting from the imposition of Western sanctions on Russia, Europe must depend on LNG imports from the United States, given the decline in imports from Africa and its own limited production capacity.

Russia will need to rethink its share of the global LNG market after sanctions targeted the equipment required to expand production. China and India are potential markets that can absorb Russian exports. Russia's key competitors in the global LNG market are the United States, Qatar and Australia.

3.5 Nigeria

The largest oil producer in Africa, Nigeria is one of the world's biggest LNG exporters and one of the top African exporters of LNG. It also has the largest natural gas reserves on the continent. Although Nigeria is the leading crude oil

70 J Henderson and V Yermakov, "Russian LNG: Becoming a Global Force", OIES Paper NG 154, Oxford Institute for Energy Studies, November 2019.

71 J Josefson and A Rotar, "Oil and gas regulation in the Russian Federation: overview", *Thomson Reuters Practical Law*, April 2021, 1–30.

72 N Morozova and R Patterson, "Russia", *The Oil and Gas Law Review*, 1st edition, Law Business Research Ltd, 2013, p202.

producer in Africa, production is affected by sporadic supply disruptions due to political-institutional and macroeconomic destabilisation.[73]

Nigeria is the continent's leading crude producer and has Africa's largest proven gas reserves of about 200 tcf – most of which are unexploited, flared or reinjected into wells. Nigerian LNG is thus strategically designed to utilise the nation's abundant gas resources, which are currently being wasted through decades of flaring.[74]

After the national natural gas market was reformed in 2017, Nigeria saw production increase by 59.5%, reaching 4.77 bcf in 2020 (see Figure 14). Nigerian LNG has contributed significantly to the reduction of gas flaring in Nigeria. It also supplies about 40% of domestic demand for liquefied petroleum gas (LPG).[75]

The sector is vertically integrated – albeit with government involvement in all functional segments as either a policymaker, a regulator or a commercial participant. The regulatory framework is set out in the 1999 Constitution of Nigeria and the Petroleum Act, which vests ownership and control of oil found in the country in the federal government.

The Federal Ministry of Petroleum Resources has primary responsibility for policy direction and exercises supervisory oversight over the industry. Thus, the minister issues regulations, guidelines and directives under the Petroleum Resources Act and other enabling laws. The Department of Petroleum Resources is responsible for the day-to-day monitoring of the petroleum industry and for supervising all petroleum industry operations.[76]

Other important regulatory agencies include:

- the Federal Ministry of the Environment;
- the Nigeria National Petroleum Corporation (NNPC);
- the Nigerian Content Development and Monitoring Board; and
- the National Oil Spill Detection and Response Agency.

The government participates in oil and gas operations through the NNPC by adopting various contractual models for the development of oil and gas resources, such as:

- concession agreements;
- traditional joint venture agreements;
- service contracts;

73 BP, *Statistical Review of World Energy 2021*, www.bp.com/content/dam/bp/business-sites/en/global/corporate/pdfs/energy-economics/statistical-review/bp-stats-review-2021-full-report.pdf.

74 W Clowes, "Nigeria Asks Largest Gas Firm to Up Output in Russia Crisis", Bloomberg, 5 April 2022, www.bloomberg.com/news/articles/2022-04-05/nigeria-asks-largest-gas-firm-to-boost-output-over-russia-crisis.

75 Nigerian Gas Flare Commercialisation Programme, Programme Information Memorandum, 2019.

76 Resolution Law Firm, "Laws regulating oil and gas industry in Nigeria", www.resolutionlawng.com/laws-regulating-oil-and-gas-industry-in-nigeria/.

- production sharing contracts; and
- sole-risk contracts.[77]

Since the first train at Nigeria LNG was commissioned in 1999, the country has built a massive LNG export complex. With six operational LNG processing units, Nigeria's LNG facility can produce 22 mtpa of LNG and 5 mtpa of LPG and condensate. Trains 1, 2 and 3 can each produce 3.33 mtpa of LNG; while Trains 4, 5 and 6 can each produce 4 mtpa of LNG.[78]

Figure 14. Nigeria LNG production between 2010 and 2020

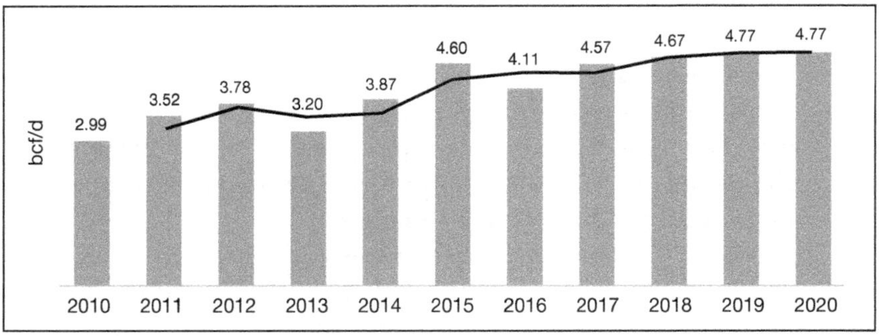

Source: Authors based on data from BP.[79]

Other facilities at the terminal include:

- four 84,200 m^3 LNG storage tanks;
- four 65,000 m^3 refrigerated storage tanks;
- three 36,000 m^3 condensate storage tanks;
- a common LNG processing fractionation plant;
- a common condensate stabilisation plant; and
- 10 gas turbine generators with a combined capacity of more than 320 megawatts.[80]

Further, the facility has:

- two LNG export jetties;
- 23 dedicated LNG ships; and
- a material offloading jetty.

77 *Ibid.*

78 Energy Connects, "After 20 years of exporting LNG, Nigeria wants to boost its consumption at home", 15 March 2022, www.energyconnects.com/opinion/features/2022/march/after-20-years-of-exporting-lng-nigeria-wants-to-boost-its-consumption-at-home/.

79 BP, *Statistical Review of World Energy 2021*, www.bp.com/content/dam/bp/business-sites/en/global/corporate/pdfs/energy-economics/statistical-review/bp-stats-review-2021-full-report.pdf.

80 NS Energy, "Nigeria LNG Plant Expansion, Bonny Island", www.nsenergybusiness.com/projects/nigeria-lng-plant-expansion-bonny-island/.

Figure 15. Nigeria's LNG exports between 2010 and 2020

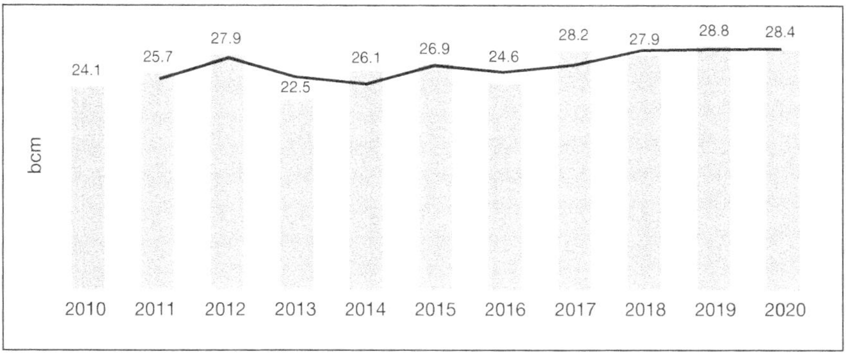

Source: Authors based on data from BP.[81]

Figure 16. Nigeria LNG export destinations

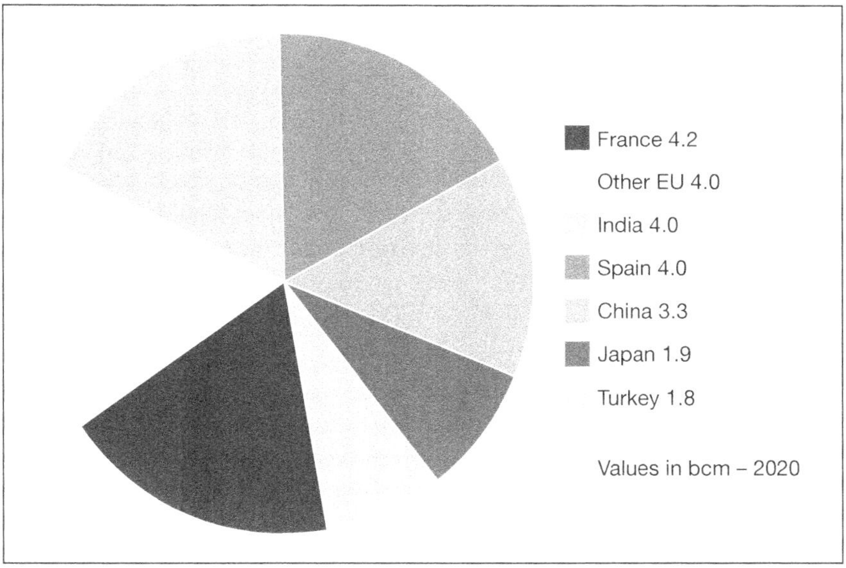

Source: Authors based on data from BP.[82]

An expansion in the Nigeria LNG facility at Bonny Island, owned and operated by Nigeria LNG, is underway, which will add a seventh LNG processing unit and supporting infrastructure to increase total production capacity from 22 mtpa to 30 mtpa. The new liquefaction unit will add approximately 4.2 mtpa

81 BP, *Statistical Review of World Energy 2021*, www.bp.com/content/dam/bp/business-sites/en/global/corporate/pdfs/energy-economics/statistical-review/bp-stats-review-2021-full-report.pdf.

82 *Ibid.*

capacity. The expansion project will also include debottlenecking of the existing six trains, which will increase processing capacity by 3.4 mtpa. The last liquefaction unit at the site is expected to come onstream in 2024.[83]

Nigeria LNG's current output is about 70% of installed capacity at its six-train facility.

Nigeria's net exports of natural gas are expected to increase to 44 bcm by 2030. LNG accounts for most exports and this is expected to rise from 28.8 bcm in 2019 to 41 bcm by 2030.[84]

According to the BP *Statistical Review of World Energy*, the main destination for Nigeria's LNG exports is France (4.1 bcm), which is seeking to increase purchases of the product between 2021 and 2025 to diversify its primary energy sources. Spain, India and other EU member states import 4 bcm from Nigeria; while China, Japan and Turkey are minor markets.[85]

3.6 Trinidad and Tobago

Trinidad and Tobago has a well-established oil and gas industry, highlighting the role of natural gas in the country's socio-economic development. The commercialisation of natural gas began in 1953 and took off in the 1970s following the discovery of large gas reserves off the coast of Trinidad.

Natural gas still plays an important economic role in Trinidad and Tobago today, as 90% of its primary energy supply is made up of natural gas. In 2020, the channelling of fuel for domestic consumption was 1.46 bcf/d, with 55% of this amount destined for the chemical sector, where methanol and ammonia are manufactured for export purposes. In addition, the fuel is used to supply the Point Lisas industrial complex for iron and steel processing, as well as the national electricity sector.[86]

Trinidad and Tobago's oil and gas market structure is essentially comprised of public companies such as the National Gas Company of Trinidad and Tobago Limited, in partnership with international oil companies such as BP, Shell and Atlantic LNG, Group. The institutional framework is headed by the Ministry of Energy and Energy Industries, which collaborates with the Environmental Management Authority to manage the link between industrial activities and the environment.[87]

---

83 *Ibid.*

84 BP, *Statistical Review of World Energy 2021*; International Energy Forum, "Nigeria Focuses on Gas to Drive Future and Lift Economy", 30 March 2021, www.ief.org/news/nigeria-focuses-on-gas-to-drive-future-and-lift-economy.

85 *Ibid.*

86 *Ibid.*

87 Trinidad and Tobago Ministry of Energy and Energy Affairs, *Trinidad & Tobago Gas Master Plan Final Report*, September 2015.

Figure 17. Trinidad and Tobago natural gas production

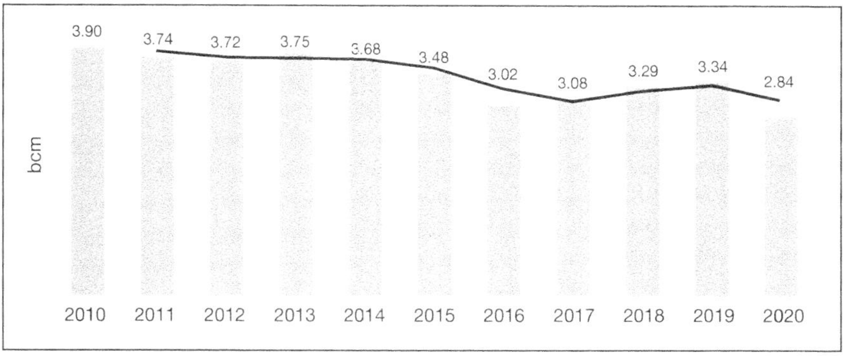

Source: Authors based on data from BP.[88]

The presence of the government of Trinidad and Tobago in the oil and gas industry is further determined by the regulatory instruments that govern private and state activities – especially the Petroleum Act, the Petroleum Tax Act and the Petroleum Production Levy and Subsidy Act. In the natural gas sector, the government participates directly through the receipt of:

- royalties;
- participation contracts;
- dividends (state company shareholders);
- oil profits; and
- LNG import/export fees.[89]

In addition, the government has a strong public policy role within the energy industry. In the field of natural gas, the government has acted to encourage the substitution of gasoline and diesel with vehicular natural gas in the transport sector as part of its sustainable energy transition strategy. Thus, the country is stimulating domestic demand while significantly reducing GHG emissions.[90]

88 BP, *Statistical Review of World Energy 2021*, www.bp.com/content/dam/bp/business-sites/en/global/corporate/pdfs/energy-economics/statistical-review/bp-stats-review-2021-full-report.pdf.

89 See n 87.

Figure 18. Trinidad and Tobago natural gas reserves history

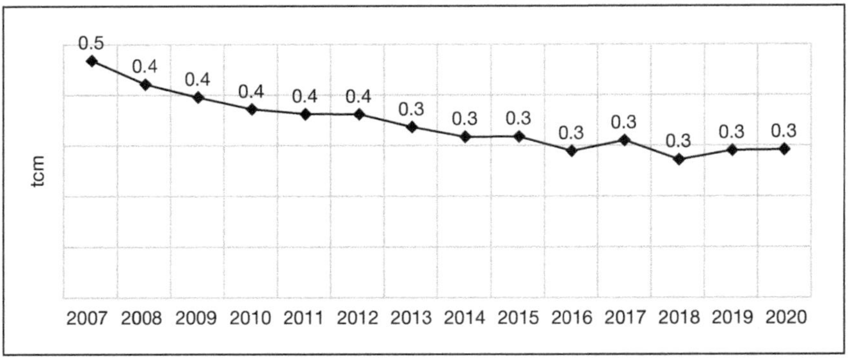

Source: Authors based on data from BP.[91]

Figure 19. Trinidad and Tobago LNG exports between 2010 and 2020

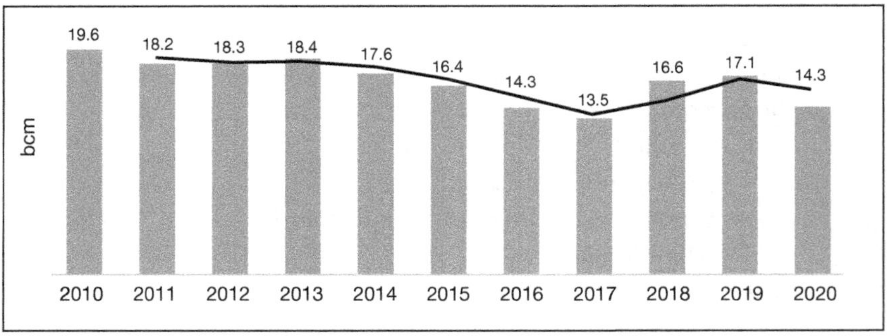

Source: Authors based on data from BP.[92]

However, since 2011, natural gas production has declined substantially, as the sector lost competitiveness following the entry of new producers such as the United States to the international market (see Figure 19). This loss of competitiveness was primarily linked to the maturity of current production fields, which have high production costs as extraction activities progress. There has been a substantial decline in the discovery of new reserves in Trinidad and Tobago; from 2009 to 2020, this represented a drop of -3.1%, as shown in Figure 19.[93]

The lack of new discoveries directly affected the performance of Trinidad and Tobago's LNG exports between 2010 and 2020 (see Figure 19). From 2010

90 See n 87.

91 BP, *Statistical Review of World Energy 2021*, www.bp.com/content/dam/bp/business-sites/en/global/corporate/pdfs/energy-economics/statistical-review/bp-stats-review-2021-full-report.pdf.

92 BP, *Statistical Review of World Energy 2021*, www.bp.com/content/dam/bp/business-sites/en/global/corporate/pdfs/energy-economics/statistical-review/bp-stats-review-2021-full-report.pdf.

93 *Ibid.*

Figure 20. Trinidad and Tobago LNG export destinations

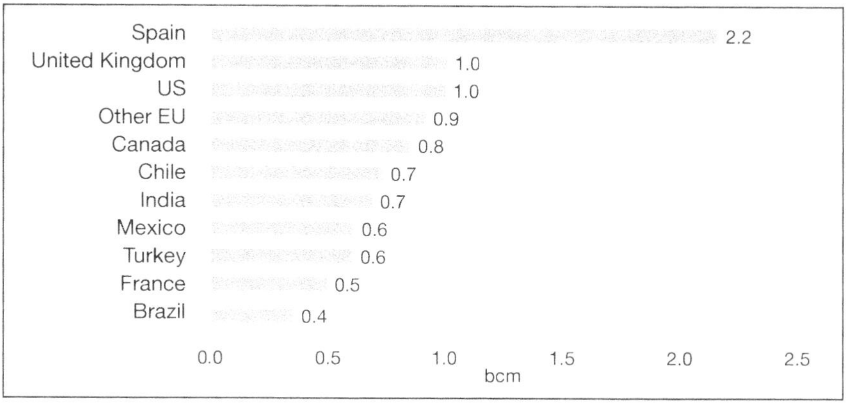

Source: Authors based on data from BP.[94]

to 2017, there was a substantial drop of -31.12%. However, between 2017 and 2019, Trinidad and Tobago saw exports jump by 26.6% after Spain increased its import flows. The following year, exports fell again because of the reduction in economic activities resulting from the COVID-19 pandemic.[95]

In this context, the main importer of LNG from Trinidad and Tobago is Spain (2.2 bcm), followed by the United Kingdom and the United States (1 bcm each). These markets have shown strong demand in recent years – especially the United States and Spain, which have diversified their LNG supply networks. India accounts for 6.1% of demand, reflecting the Indian strategy of diversifying its suppliers, which are primarily concentrated in Asia and thus exposed to Asian price shocks.[96]

The importance of the oil and gas industry to the socio-economic development of Trinidad and Tobago is clearly apparent. The government has played a key role by establishing a system of partnerships between public and private companies to invest in oil and gas exploration and production. However, the sector's loss of competitiveness has become a major challenge that must be overcome if Trinidad and Tobago is to maintain its vibrant economy.

4. Lessons learned and recommendations

The analysis of LNG structured markets presented in this chapter allows us to identify common themes that have favoured their rise. It is thus possible to present recommendations for potential producers of LNG wishing to enter the international market, such as Brazil, Mozambique, Argentina and Norway.

94 *Ibid.*
95 *Ibid*; and OEC, Trinidad & Tobago country profile, https://oec.world/en/profile/country/tto.
96 *Ibid.*

The first lesson to be learned concerns the need for efficient coordination between the state and the natural gas industry to identify opportunities and challenges in the domestic and international markets. The use of natural gas as an energy transition fuel in the coming years is a clear opportunity, as it should help drive a relative decrease in GHG emissions by 2050.[97]

In parallel with this, it is evident that current natural gas producers have benefited from geographical proximity to tie the supply of LNG to the demand of countries with rapid economic growth and energy transition needs. In Europe, Germany and Italy saw natural gas from Russia as a low-cost opportunity to transition to a cleaner energy mix. In Asia, China, India, South Korea, Taiwan and Japan have been driving the development of the Australian, North American, Qatari and Russian natural gas industries.[98]

In this context, the relationship between the state and industry becomes fundamental in developing solutions to facilitate exports. Policies that encourage investment in natural gas processing, storage and (re)gasification terminals – as well as transport infrastructure such as ports for maritime transport (LNG carriers) and even gas pipelines interconnected with the storage system – are essential.

Efficient regulation is undoubtedly the differentiator in attracting foreign investment to the natural gas industry. As an example, institutional and regulatory reforms in Australia and Qatar facilitated the entry of capital into the LNG sector, especially through joint projects between national and international companies. Reductions in the taxation of exports have further promoted the adoption of LNG at competitive prices in the international market.

In terms of challenges, the analysis in this chapter demonstrates that the natural gas and LNG sectors are not immune from geopolitical interference and domestic macroeconomic destabilisation. This is evident from the regional embargo on Qatar and the political and economic sanctions imposed on Russia following its invasion of Ukraine, which have destabilised international markets and fuelled inflation in national energy and food systems.

While the impacts of these sanctions are being felt all over the world, this scenario also favours the entry of new players – such as the United States and Norway – to the market, which should increase gas exports to countries that currently depend on Russian gas. Argentina, Mozambique and Brazil are other potential suppliers; but they still lack the necessary regulatory systems and infrastructure to monetise their gas reserves.[99]

---

97 International Gas Union, *World LNG Report 2022*, www.igu.org/resources/world-lng-report-2022/.

98 BP, *Statistical Review of World Energy 2021*, www.bp.com/content/dam/bp/business-sites/en/global/corporate/pdfs/energy-economics/statistical-review/bp-stats-review-2021-full-report.pdf; and OEC, 2022, "The best place to explore trade data", https://oec.world/en.

99 EPE, *Boletim de Conjuntura da Indústria do Óleo & Gás*, 2019, www.epe.gov.br/sites-pt/publicacoes-dados-abertos/publicacoes/PublicacoesArquivos/publicacao-226/topico-508/7%20Boletim%20de%20Conjuntura%20da%20Ind%C3%BAstria%20do%20%C3%93leo%20e%20G%C3%A1s.pdf.

In Brazil, new FSRU ships for large-scale natural gas liquefaction could be an innovative gas solution to monetise the country's growing natural gas production on the international market – as borne out by the success of recent offshore liquefaction projects in Mozambique. In Argentina, ramping up exploration of unconventional gas from shale reservoirs could make the country a key player in global supply. However, both Brazil and Argentina will need to make the natural gas sector a policy priority, as it has received little attention from government thus far.

With new investments in liquefaction, transport and gasification infrastructure forecast in the billions of dollars, the data indicates that the total supply of LNG could grow by 67% by 2030, as the United States consolidates its position as one of the world's leading exporters and demand in Europe increases. However, investments should be reduced from 2024 onwards due to the growth of new low carbon projects, such as renewable energies, green hydrogen and biofuels.[100]

The sanctions on Russia have severely impacted LNG operators, preventing them from importing essential equipment and project know-how from foreign players. As a result, the domestic industry is finding it difficult to keep up with the technologies and standards of internationally competitive manufacturing. This could prevent Russia from becoming a major supplier of LNG to international markets by 2030.

Meanwhile, Nigeria and Trinidad and Tobago have lost competitiveness due to the exhaustion of productive resources and political difficulties that have hindered the development of public policies to promote the natural gas industry and its complementary activities.[101]

As a result, the main economic and energy indicators of natural gas and LNG suppliers should be continually monitored in order to help importers to anticipate risk. In addition, reconciling energy security with the use of energy at competitive prices has become a challenge due to the uncertainties in the LNG segment – that is, few suppliers, technologies under development and high payback times on investment. Therefore, diversifying suppliers, markets and sources is a vital risk mitigation strategy to consider.

5. Conclusion

This chapter has analysed the structure of LNG exports, identifying the characteristics of the main suppliers to derive lessons and recommendations for players in the oil and gas industry. As has been demonstrated, specific technical and infrastructure requirements apply to the processing of natural gas, making investment in transport, storage and (re)gasification technologies imperative.

---

100 epbr, *Investimentos em GNL caminham para patamares recordes*, 2022, https://epbr.com.br/investimentos-em-gnl-caminham-para-patamares-recordes/.

101 Nigerian Gas Flare Commercialisation Programme, Programme Information Memorandum, 2019.

In this case, investment in the LNG segment is justified based on the identification of domestic or international demand, considering issues of geographical proximity to production and consumption centres. This relationship, together with the production costs incurred by the companies involved, should determine the competitiveness of prices at both the national and international levels. Our analysis of supplier countries allows us to highlight the following key points:

- There is a need to develop strategies for the natural gas industry in order to identify opportunities and challenges.
- The LNG segment is not immune from domestic geopolitical and macroeconomic interference.
- Public policies are necessary to support exports and increase the generation of value for society.

In conclusion, the development of LNG exports results from a combination of factors, including the state's willingness to support the local natural gas industry in exploring opportunities on the international markets. This requires robust regulations that can guarantee the satisfaction not only of domestic demand, but also of international demand. The growing desire for cheap, less carbon-intensive fuel compared to coal and oil should assist countries in their economic expansion.

Therefore, new interdisciplinary studies are needed to further the establishment of an institutional and regulatory framework that is favourable to the development of the natural gas and LNG industry.

LNG shipping

Chantal Carriere
Latham & Watkins LLP
Carlos Diaz
White & Case LLP
Igor Tostes
Equinor Brasil

1. Introduction

The shipment of liquid natural gas (LNG) – that is, natural gas that has been cooled to a liquid state, reducing its volume to some 1/600th of its gaseous state[1] – has evolved from a niche facet of certain regional energy markets to a headline-grabbing international issue. And interest continues to grow as LNG accounts for an increasing share of global energy needs, due in large part to the ability to ship LNG more readily and the increasing prominence of LNG within energy portfolios in key markets. As a consequence of this trend, global geopolitics have a complex relationship with LNG shipping. For instance, the desire to prevent energy disruption in Europe following the Russian invasion of Ukraine has resulted in multiple countries competing for LNG shipments, to the point that "Europe's LNG needs are expected to outpace supply capacity additions in 2022, and to account for more than 60% of the net growth in global LNG trade through 2025".[2]

Even with record price increases, these market conditions are unlikely to ease. Depressed gas prices throughout the 2010s curtailed investment in additional global LNG export capacity; and while numerous projects are set to come online, labour shortages during the COVID-19 pandemic have led to construction delays.[3] The immediate energy crisis is also playing out as the world continues to grapple with the consequences of climate change and the need to invest in the energy transition, including the role that LNG will play in the energy supply chain going forward (including accounting for emissions from the shipping value chain itself).

Interestingly, countries that are reliant on shipments of LNG in certain regions, such as the European Union, also have strict carbon emission regulations. These European countries are attempting to phase out gas sourced from conflict areas such Russia, while delaying or attempting to delay restarting

1 US Energy Information Administration, "Natural gas explained", www.eia.gov/energyexplained/natural-gas/liquefied-natural-gas.php.
2 International Energy Agency (IEA), *Gas Market Report, Q3-2022,* https://iea.blob.core.windows.net/assets/c7e74868-30fd-440c-a616-488215894356/GasMarketReport%2CQ3-2022.pdf at 8.
3 *Ibid.*

some of the old coal power plants which were shut down when natural gas was plentiful. At a global level, the European Union is far from alone in its growing demand for LNG. In 2022, the global LNG market remained robust. Nineteen countries exported LNG to 44 countries, with China overtaking Japan as the world's largest importer and Australia and Qatar remaining as the world's largest exporters – although there was a major ramp-up of US LNG production as five major liquefaction projects came online (Cameron LNG Trains 2 and 3; Corpus Christi LNG Train 3; Freeport LNG Trains 2 and 3).[4] Demand in Asia – in particular, China and Korea – was spurred by economic recovery and the transition from coal to natural gas to fire power plants.[5]

With this context in mind, the role that LNG shipping plays is complex and multifaceted. Understanding it more deeply, as we outline in this chapter, involves three key prongs:

- a general understanding of the LNG industry and value chain;
- an introduction to the fundamentals of LNG shipping, including the key contracts that underpin the value chain; and
- attention to nascent developments in both the LNG markets and the shipping industry response to climate change and the energy transition.

2. Shipping logistics

2.1 How is LNG shipped?

LNG can be transported by ship, truck or rail, thereby overcoming the geographical limitations of the natural gas market (it is challenging to transport natural gas across long distances, oceans, mountainous regions or regions experiencing conflict).

The first major LNG cargo was originally transported from Lake Charles, Louisiana to Canvey Island, United Kingdom in 1959 using a converted World War II freighter called the *Methane Pioneer*.[6] Since 1959, the fleet of LNG tankers has proliferated: as of the end of 2021, there were approximately 650 LNG vessels capable of transoceanic transportation of LNG in operation.[7]

Less frequently, LNG is shipped by truck or railcar to serve markets in the same geographic plane. LNG has been shipped in the United States by truck for decades.[8] LNG is loaded in specialised isocontainers that are then loaded onto

4 International Group of Liquefied Natural Gas Importers (GIIGNL), *GIIGNL Annual Report 2022,* https://giignl.org/wp-content/uploads/2022/05/GIIGNL2022_Annual_Report_May24.pdf at 6.

5 *Ibid.*

6 Energy KnowledgeBase, "LNG history", www.energyknowledgebase.com/topics/lng-history.asp. The Canvey Island website also has a detailed history of the *Methane Pioneer* including photos of the vessel; www.canveyisland.org/history-2/workplaces-clubs/workplaces/gas/gas-terminal-1956-2008.

7 GIIGNL, *GIIGNL Annual Report 2022,* https://giignl.org/wp-content/uploads/2022/05/GIIGNL2022_Annual_Report_May24.pdf at 22.

8 Natural Gas Intelligence, "U.S. AGs call for 'Prompt Suspension of LNG Transport by Rail Rules", 4 January 2022, www.naturalgasintel.com/u-s-ags-call-for-prompt-suspension-of-lng-transport-by-rail-rules/.

the truck. Shipment by truck is increasingly appealing as a domestic natural gas transportation option, given the challenges associated with building new pipeline infrastructure.[9] Interest in rail transport, however, is new. The Trump administration authorised the transport of LNG in specialised railcars in 2020, but the rule was suspended by the Biden administration.[10]

2.2 Types of ships used for LNG transport

Shipping vessels for LNG include LNG tankers, floating liquefied natural gas facilities (FLNGs) and floating storage regasification units (FSRUs). Tankers and FLNGs are distinguished by the type of tank (or containment system), which keeps the LNG in its liquid state. Generally, LNG tanks are classified as either moss or membrane. Moss-type LNG carriers typically have recognisable dome shaped structures atop the main deck of the ship. Each of these spherical tanks is independent from the hull of the ship, making it easier to control the quality of the LNG. Membrane-type LNG carriers have a membrane structure built into the hull of the ship. This wrinkled stainless-steel membrane helps the ship to maintain a lower temperature by absorbing the expansion of the natural gas.[11] Self-support prismatic shape tanks have heat insulation on the exterior and have the benefit of being easy to fit into and install on a hull.[12] As of 2021, there were 517 membrane-type vessels and 122 moss-type vessels in operation.

While vessel type and related logistics are interesting from a technical standpoint, ultimately the complexities on the legal side of LNG shipment arise from the overlapping jurisdictions that result from the interplay between vessels and ports. International law provides a governance framework for understanding maritime cooperation, including state jurisdiction, but international law must be implemented through state regulation.[13] For a vessel, jurisdiction is dictated by the flag of the vessel (ie, the national registry where the ship is registered); while for ports, jurisdiction is based on where they are located. States may, as a general principle of international law, regulate the extraterritorial conduct of their nationals through the exercise of extraterritorial jurisdiction. Typically, states grant nationality to a vessel through registration with a registry, after which the vessel flies under the flag of such state. Flag states are important because the laws of the flag state determine the applicable employment laws for the crew. The flag state is also responsible for ensuring,

9 US Energy Information Administration, "Natural gas explained", www.eia.gov/energyexplained/natural-gas/liquefied-natural-gas.php.

10 Congressional Research Service, "Rail Transportation of Liquefied Natural Gas: Safety and Regulation", 28 July 2020, https://sgp.fas.org/crs/misc/R46414.pdf at 1.

11 This distinction appears in LNG sale and purchase agreements – LNG ships are required to arrive in compliance with an 'arrival temperature' which typically distinguishes between the temperature required for a moss versus membrane vessel.

12 Mitsui OSK Lines, "Energy Transport [LNG Carriers]", www.mol.co.jp/en/iroiro_fune_e/ships/03_lng.html.

13 For example, the Convention on the Law of the Sea.

through inspections and surveys, that ships flying under the flag comply with minimum requirements for the construction, equipment and operation of ships set out in the International Convention for the Safety of Life at Sea 1974.

In addition to exercising control over ships flying under their flag, states may exercise jurisdiction over vessels that call at their ports through the exercise of territorial jurisdiction, called 'port state control'. Port states can inspect foreign ships to ensure compliance with international regulation to the extent that the port state has an agreement with the flag state.

To add to the complexities, vessels must be insured. In order to be insured, a vessel must be 'classed' – that is, certified by a classification society which confirms that the vessel has been built and maintained in accordance with the standards of the applicable society at the time of periodic inspection. There are 12 internationally recognised classification societies, which are all members of the International Association of Classification Societies. These classification societies also play an important role in ensuring maritime safety and pollution prevention, including facilitation of the administration of the aims of the International Convention on the Law of the Sea and the International Convention for the Safety of Life at Sea. For example, typically, one the requirements for a state to accept a ship registered in another country in its ports is that the vessel have structural integrity and maintain pollution and accident control, which may be covered by the class rules of a classification society.[14]

Insurance is administered by a protection and indemnity (P&I) club, which insures vessels based on the applicable club rules. Typical shipowner insurance policies include hull and machinery, protection and indemnity, loss of hire and war risks; and cover open-ended risks such as war, damage during carriage and environmental pollution. The main 13 P&I clubs belong to the International Group of P&I Clubs (IGP&I), which provides insurance for large claim events; together, these clubs provide marine liability cover for approximately 90% of the world's ocean-going tonnage, according to the IGP&I.[15] Each club is an independent, not-for-profit mutual insurance association owned by the member-charters and shipowners that provides insurance coverage to members for third-party liabilities arising from the use and operation of ships.[16] While each club provides insurance to shipowners, the IGP&I handles claims sharing (or 'pooling') and collective reinsurance. The IGP&I is bound by the terms of the pooling agreement, which enables claims sharing – under the pooling agreement, each club pays a pre-determined contribution of any claim in the

14 International Association of Classification Societies, "Classification societies – what, why and how?", https://iacs.org.uk/media/8871/classification-what-why-how.pdf.

15 IGP&I, "About the International Group", www.igpandi.org/about/. Gard, a Norwegian club and a member of the IGP&I, has also issued a helpful history of P&I coverage at www.gard.no/web/publications/document/chapter?p_subdoc_id=20747884&p_document_id=2074788.

16 IGP&I, "About the International Group", www.igpandi.org/about/.

pool.[17] Participating clubs share claims which are in excess of the club's individual retention up to the pool limit. The pool itself is divided into two tiers, with the upper tier subject to reinsurance by a captive insurance company. For claims above the pool, the IGP&I purchases reinsurance on a per-event basis, with different caps for oil pollution, passenger and crew liabilities, and passenger liabilities. Above these caps is an 'overspill'.[18] Looking across the jurisdictional overlap, insurance requirements and the bifurcation of major regional markets help to underscore the nuances at play in dealing with LNG shipping internationally. As a consequence, a deeper overview of the LNG markets themselves is necessary before examining the legal aspects that shape the long-term nature of deals for sale and purchase in the sections below.

3. LNG markets

Undergirding the shipment of LNG is, of course, the LNG market itself. A few common core fundamentals outlined below provide an introduction to the subject, beginning with the value chain (production, loading and unloading) and common shipment methods.

3.1 How is LNG produced and unloaded?

In order to create LNG, natural gas is first transported from upstream fields to a processing plant, where all impurities (eg, butane, mercury, carbon dioxide and other natural gas liquids) are removed from the gas (and sold off as condensate).[19] The resulting methane is moved into cryogenic chambers which hypercool the LNG using liquefaction process technology. The liquefaction process may be undertaken on land, in so-called 'LNG trains'; or offshore, in an FLNG. Most LNG production facilities are on land and range in size from 2 million tonnes per annum (MTPA) of production capacity to 27 MTPA.[20] Offshore FLNG projects range in size, from the 1.2 MTPA of Petronas' PFLNG SATU[21] to a planned 13 MTPA for Delfin LNG.[22] Global production capacity in 2021 amounted to 462 MTPA.[23]

---

17 Britannia, "Bulletin", 21 June 2016, https://britanniapandi.com/wp-content/uploads/2017/09/PandIcover-LNGterminalconditionsofuseCOU-06-2016.pdf.

18 *Ibid*. There are also international agreements that cover catastrophic oil spills, such as the 1969 International Convention on Civil Liability for Oil Pollution Damage and the 1971 International Convention on the Establishment of an International Fund for Compensation for Oil Pollution, as well as local laws (in the United States, the Oil Pollution Act of 1990).

19 US Department of Energy, "Global LNG Fundamentals", www.energy.gov/sites/default/files/2018/03/f49/Global%20LNG%20Fundamentals%2C%20Updated%203.15.18.pdf at 20.

20 Christopher Caswell and Douglas Attaway, "Does (Train) Size Really Matter?", GTI Energy, www.gti.energy/wp-content/uploads/2019/10/199-LNG19-05April2019-Caswell-Christopher-paper.pdf.

21 Petronas, "Liquefied Natural Gas (LNG)", www.petronas.com/progressing-energy/liquefied-natural-gas#JbopTabs2.

22 *Offshore*, "Delfin Midstream, Devon Energy enter into LNG export partnership", 8 September 2022, www.offshore-mag.com/regional-reports/us-gulf-of-mexico/article/14282490/delfin-midstream-devon-energy-enter-into-lng-export-partnership.

23 GIIGNL, *GIIGNL Annual Report 2022*, https://giignl.org/wp-content/uploads/2022/05/GIIGNL2022_Annual_Report_May24.pdf at 44.

Once LNG has been delivered, it is offloaded at a regasification terminal, where it is transported as natural gas to the next customer in the value chain. Regasification terminals may be onshore or offshore (through floating storage units and/or regasification units – noting that these functions may or may not be combined in a single vessel). At the end of 2021, global regasification capacity reached 993 MTPA.[24]

As indicated above, FSRUs are vessels built or retrofitted for the purpose of receiving LNG from other LNG tankers, storing the LNG and then regasifying such LNG. The natural gas resulting from the regasified LNG is then used as fuel or feed gas for power projects or other natural gas-intensive projects. Although regasification terminals may be built onshore, the ability to conduct these activities onboard a vessel affords both the owner of the vessel and the owner of the project greater flexibility, in that the vessel is mobile and can be shipped to different locations.

By contrast to FSRUs, FLNGs act as offshore liquefaction capacity. FLNGs are typically used in locations with little to no access to pipelines due to infrastructure conditions in the host country, where there are above-ground challenges to infrastructure development, or in locations where the natural gas basin is geographically remote. FLNGs have thus played a critical role in unlocking natural gas resources.

FLNGs have the unique advantage of being able to produce, treat, liquefy, store and transfer LNG to an offshore carrier, thereby enabling monetisation of offshore gas resources. The FLNG then liquefies and stores the LNG until a ship moors alongside the FLNG and loads LNG before sailing onwards to its next destination. The first FLNG facility was Petronas' PFLNG SATU moored offshore in Malaysia in 2017. PFLNG SATU was developed for the Kanowit offshore gas field.[25] The FRSUs and FLNGs used around the world are of various different designs, types and sizes; many have project-specific characteristics and/or are designed to take in natural gas with the specifications of the location where the FSRU or FLNG will be moored.

Although nascent, small-scale LNG is also increasingly garnering attention. 'Small-scale LNG' refers to using LNG in its liquid form, rather than regasifying it. Small-scale production is typically developed for a specific market and has a production capacity of 0.5 MTPA or less (by contrast to onshore facilities, which may have up to 16 MTPA). As examples, small-scale LNG can be used for marine fuel, fuel for heavy road transport and power generation for off-grid markets, such as small island nations.[26]

---

24 GIIGNL, *GIIGNL Annual Report 2022,* https://giignl.org/wp-content/uploads/2022/05/GIIGNL2022_Annual_Report_May24.pdf at 52.

25 US Department of Energy, "Offshore LNG Technologies and Facilities", www.energy.gov/fecm/downloads/offshore-lng-technologies-facilities.

26 Strategy&, "Small going big: Why small-scale LNG may be the next big wave", www.strategyand.pwc.com/gx/en/insights/2017/small-going-big.html.

3.2 What price is payable for LNG?

Generally, a buyer of LNG will pay the market price for LNG in the market into which the LNG is being delivered, based on the price of a substitute fuel. In the United States, LNG is priced on Henry Hub, which is a physical distribution hub for natural gas located in Louisiana. In Europe, LNG is priced based on natural gas traded virtually at the Dutch Title Transfer Facility. In the UK, LNG is priced based on natural gas traded virtually at the National Balancing Point. In Asia, while LNG may still be indexed to oil, the Platts Japan-Korea Marker (which represents the daily price of physical LNG spot cargoes delivered ex-ship into Northeast Asia) is increasingly popular.[27, 28, 29]

In addition to the index price, the price payable for LNG depends on numerous factors, including:

- the source of LNG;
- the destination market;
- the terms of the contract and the quantity to be delivered thereunder; and
- the contractual terms applicable to the index.

While a full overview of the LNG pricing is beyond the scope of this chapter, understanding how LNG pricing has developed over time is helpful to understand LNG transactions.

3.3 How have LNG markets developed?

While LNG now factors into energy portfolios globally in some of the largest economies in the world, at this point the natural gas markets remain largely regional. Historically, the two distinct LNG trade regions comprise the Asia-Pacific region and the Atlantic Basin region (including North America, South America and most of Europe). These markets developed in relative isolation from each other, primarily due to the high cost of natural gas transportation. Buyers in these regions seeking LNG were typically required to enter into long-term take-or-pay contracts with the production facility. LNG in these contracts would be priced based on a substitute commodity – for example, in Japan, LNG was priced based on the Japan Customs-Cleared Crude, an oil-based index. As a consequence, the market was illiquid.

However, as more LNG production facilities have come online, the market

27 SPGlobal, "Platts JKM (Japan Korea Marker) LNG Price Assessment", www.spglobal.com/commodityinsights/en/our-methodology/price-assessments/lng/jkm-japan-korea-marker-gas-price-assessments.

28 DLA Piper, "What is the future of LNG pricing?" 20 August 2019, www.dlapiper.com/en/us/insights/publications/2019/08/energy-infrastructure-and-projects-global-insight-issue-2/what-is-the-future-of-lng-pricing/.

29 SPGlobal, "Platts JKM (Japan Korea Marker) LNG Price Assessment", www.spglobal.com/commodity insights/en/our-methodology/price-assessments/lng/jkm-japan-korea-marker-gas-price-assessments.

for LNG has become increasingly liquid, with LNG competing with pipeline gas. As projects have matured, additional capacity has facilitated additional short-term trade, leading to the emergence of reference prices and futures market. At present, there are North American, European and Asian markets, each with typical price indexes (as noted below). Greater market certainty is also facilitating alternative project structuring and financing. Integrated LNG projects required the price of LNG to factor in the cost of capital. There are now more tolling projects, whereby the customer pays a tolling fee that prices in the cost of capital and, in the United States, source gas at the Henry Hub at market prices, permitting the customer to on-sell LNG to downstream customers at a mark-up to the Henry Hub price.[30] Moreover, as a result of these step-changes in market conditions, contracting terms have become increasingly flexible. For example, contracts for LNG shipped into Asia historically included destination restrictions which prevented the buyer from diverting the cargo to a terminal other than that specified in the contract to take advantage of higher pricing therein. With the shift away from destination restrictions, differences in market prices led to regional arbitrage opportunities and the ability for LNG traders to maximise their portfolio of assets by taking advantage of such opportunities. Regional differences in price are becoming less pronounced.

As a consequence of advancements in the production of LNG, as well as the ability to ship more readily, LNG has become an increasingly liquid commodity – and will likely become more so as the futures markets for LNG deepen and the LNG and natural gas markets become increasingly connected.[31] Taken together, these market shifts foretell of the increased commoditisation of LNG.[32]

4. Commercial agreements

With the nature of the LNG markets and the shipping industry in mind, numerous commercial contracts are required in an LNG purchase and sale transaction.

First, the buyer and seller must enter into an SPA for the LNG. The party responsible for delivering (or taking delivery, as the case may be) of the LNG must then arrange for transportation; ship chartering arrangements are discussed below, noting that contracting for railcars or trucks will be required in the event of such transportation.

The vessel will then need to enter into a marine terminal liability agreement with the terminal to be able to berth at the port. The vessel will also need to contract with service providers at the port in order to navigate the vessel

30 Australian Competition and Consumer Commission, *LNG Netback Price Services Review – Issues Paper 1* at 23.

31 *Ibid* at 30.

32 Oxford Institute for Energy Studies, "LNG Portfolio Optimization: Challenge, Opportunity and Necessity", October 2020, www.oxfordenergy.org/wpcms/wp-content/uploads/2020/10/Insight-74-LNG-Portfolio-Optimization.pdf at 1-2.

through the shipping channel and berth or moor alongside another vessel for loading/unloading, as applicable. Finally, the vessel and the owner of the LNG will sign commercial papers in connection with the transport of the LNG. Note that although tolling agreements are briefly mentioned above, they are beyond the scope of this chapter.

4.1 SPAs

LNG is typically bought and sold through sale and purchase agreements (SPAs) – either long-term contracts or one-off cargoes or strips of cargoes traded pursuant to standard terms and conditions. Today, many LNG SPAs share common features and there are generally standard forms that LNG market players tend to be familiar with. For long-term transactions, the Association of International Energy Negotiators has published a long-form model LNG SPA. For spot transactions or strips of cargoes, Trafigura has published a form of master SPA, as has BP. Moreover, many executed LNG SPAs offtaking from US Gulf Coast LNG terminals are publicly available.

The key shipping provisions in an LNG SPA pertain to the movement of the vessel and transit to the destination. Principally, this distinction depends on which party is responsible for shipping (commonly denoted by Incoterms).[33] If the buyer is responsible for shipping, the LNG is sold 'free on board' (FOB); and if the seller is responsible, the LNG is sold 'delivered at place' (DAP). These Incoterm definitions are largely the inverse of each other, except with respect to:

- costs (ie, the costs of transportation will be factored into the price of LNG if the LNG is being shipped DAP); and
- transfer of title (for FOB sales, title transfers when the LNG passes into the vessel; for DAP, title transfers when the LNG passes out of the vessel).

For ease of reference, FOB delivery is discussed below in general terms, in the sequence of events from pre-arrival through arrival to loading and departure.

(a) Vessel

In an FOB transaction, the buyer is responsible for procuring a vessel that satisfies certain requirements, as set forth in the contract.

Typically, a vessel must:

- be compatible with applicable law;
- have received certain approvals;
- meet international standards;

---

33 'Incoterms' are periodically published by the International Chamber of Commerce, which sets out standard abbreviations and rules and guidelines for trade. https://iccwbo.org/resources-for-business/incoterms-rules/incoterms-2020/.

- maintain on board valid documentation;
- comply with:
  - the International Safety Management Code for the Safe Operation of Ships and Pollution Prevention, effective 1 July 1998; and
  - the International Code for the Construction and Equipment of Ships Carrying Liquefied Gases in Bulk;
- be in class (as discussed above); and
- maintain adequate insurance.

The vessel must also comply with the specifications of the loading terminal as well as any modifications thereto. The LNG SPA also sets forth the responsibility for the allocation of costs of any modifications to the vessel if such modifications are required in order to be compatible with the specific technical characteristics of the terminal. Typically, the seller also has inspection rights with respect to the vessel. The consequence for the buyer, in the event that the vessel does not meet the requirements set forth in the applicable agreement, is that the seller may reject the vessel.

(b) Port charges

The buyer is typically responsible for all port charges, which are broadly defined as all charges connected with the vessel entering or leaving the loading port at which the terminal is located.

(c) Port liability agreement

Although port liability agreements are discussed below, the LNG SPA will also typically include an obligation on the buyer to cause the transporter or the master of the vessel that is calling at the terminal to enter into a port liability agreement, which must be signed before the vessel's arrival at the terminal. It is common for a form of port liability agreement to be appended to the LNG SPA.

The purpose of the port liability agreement is to apportion liability in the event of any losses incurred or damages sustained during the berthing of the vessel. Typically, under the LNG SPA, the buyer indemnifies the seller for losses in the event that the transporter does not enter into the port liability agreement – although the scope of the indemnity is negotiated on a transaction-by-transaction basis. This indemnity is typically accompanied by a mutual release of liability between buyer and seller in the event that the port liability agreement is signed. Alternatively, the LNG SPA may provide that the seller has the right, or the obligation, to refuse to berth a vessel that has not executed a port liability agreement.

Moreover, the LNG SPA will contain restrictions on modifications to the port liability agreement. For example, the buyer may have a right to approve modifications to the extent that they may affect its ability to obtain indemnity coverage from its P&I club or if the modification would prevent the buyer from performing its obligations under the LNG SPA. However, the rights of the buyer typically should not fetter the ability of the terminal to amend its form of port liability agreement in response to operational changes or other developments.

(d) *Arrival*

The buyer is typically afforded a certain window – a 'delivery window' – during which the vessel must arrive at the terminal to load LNG. In order to facilitate this process, under the LNG SPA, the vessel provides a series of notices when it departs for the terminal, including an estimated time of arrival.

Once the vessel arrives in the waters of the terminal, it may be required to undergo a series of inspections and administrative procedures before it can proceed to the berth, including clearing customs. Once the vessel is ready to proceed to the berth, it tenders a notice of readiness (NOR). The LNG SPA will then contain procedures determining when the NOR is effective. In some cases, effectiveness depends on whether the NOR is tendered before, during or after a delivery window. The NOR triggers the seller's obligation to berth the vessel and load LNG, as well as the period during which the seller must carry out these obligations. From this point, the seller has a fixed amount of time – typically called 'allotted laytime' – during which it must complete berthing and loading operations. The amount of time that the seller actually takes to complete berthing and loading operations is called typically called 'actual laytime'; it starts on the effectiveness of the NOR and ends when the vessel has loaded the LNG, has all necessary cargo documents onboard and is cleared for departure. If actual laytime exceeds allotted laytime, the seller is responsible for paying the buyer an amount of liquidated damages, called 'demurrage'. The seller may also be responsible for paying excess boil-off. Further, if the buyer is delayed in loading, the seller may be required to pay the buyer compensation for LNG that boils off during such delay. Allotted laytime may typically be extended for enumerated reasons, which are typically outside the control of buyer.

The buyer is also responsible for loading expeditiously. The buyer must load LNG and depart within a fixed period of time (the 'allotted laytime'); if there is an unexcused delay and the buyer fails to depart on time and thereby causes another vessel to be delayed in berthing and loading LNG, the buyer must compensate the seller for costs incurred by the seller for such other vessels. The seller also typically has the right to require the buyer to vacate the berth.

The allotted laytime and allowed laytime are typically extended outside the control of the seller and buyer, respectively.

Note that for a DAP contract, the responsibilities of the buyer noted above shift to the seller and the responsibilities of the seller to the buyer.

4.2 Charterparty agreements

A charterparty agreement, in its simplest form, involves the lease of a vessel or naval object for the purpose of transporting, storing or transforming goods and services, or performing other activities which require specialised equipment, whereby one party (the vessel owner) leases such vessel to the other party (the charterer) for a determined period of time or until a specific activity has been completed. As time has progressed, charterparties have become more complex. The parties may agree on different types of indemnities, liabilities and uses for the vessel or naval object. The most typical form of indemnity is a 'knock-for-knock indemnity', in which a party is responsible for all damages to its property and injuries to its personnel, regardless of cause or fault. This provides certainty to the parties, which are no longer required to quantify and/or allocate losses or risks among one another when considering the infinite scenarios in which the vessel might find itself during the charter.

There are several types of charterparty agreements. The most common is a bareboat charterparty, under which the owner of the vessel leases such vessel to the charterer in exchange for a fee; the vessel is effectively transferred to the charterer in all but title for such period and the charterer bears all responsibility for procuring the crew and maintaining the vessel, subject to certain rights retained by the vessel owner (eg, flagging, registration, mortgages over the vessel and removal proceedings). There are several forms available for this type of agreement, the most common of which is the BIMCO form. This form was drafted based on the English tradition of shipping, given that this has one of the oldest records for such agreements in the world.[34] The other two types of charterparty are the voyage charterparty and the time charterparty. In a voyage charterparty, the shipowner agrees to transport cargo between two ports for an agreed fee ('freight'), which is based on the tonnage of the cargo loaded. Freight includes the costs incurred by the vessel owner, including the bunkers and crew costs. The International Group of Liquefied Natural Gas Importers (GIIGNL) published a form of voyage charterparty in 2012; and in 2016 Bimco and GIIGNL published LNGVOY. Finally, for a time charterparty, the charterer pays a lump sum on a period basis (typically daily, called 'hire') for use of a ship in accordance with the terms of the contract, plus incidentals as agreed between the parties, such as specialised crew, spare parts, maintenance and general upkeep. Hire starts when the ship is delivered and ends when the ship is returned, but may be interrupted for events enumerated in the agreement (eg, the vessel not performing the activity for which it was chartered for reasons not attributable to the charterer). The time charterparty also typically includes geographic restrictions on use of the vessel and prescribes the parameters of redelivery. In both the voyage and time charterparty, the shipowner operates

34 BIMCO, "BIMCO Contracts", www.bimco.org/contracts-and-clauses/bimco-contracts.

the vessel and must maintain seaworthiness, and is responsible for providing the crew and procuring insurance. One of the more common forms of time charter is ShellLNGTime1.

Historically, time charters were used for LNG trading, but increases in the spot market for LNG have dovetailed with the increased use of voyage charters (and indeed, the GIIGNL published its voyage charterparty in response to the growing number of spot trades).[35] Time charterparty agreements are now mainly used in stationary arrangements, such as FSRU and FLNG facilities. Charterparties for LNG are complex, in part because of the on-board complexities of an LNG vessel. The UK Defence Club has identified three main areas for claims resulting from charterparties: underperformance, breakdowns and terminal compatibility.[36]

With respect to performance claims, typically claims focus on whether there are cargo shortages or overages. However, LNG is both a fuel and a cargo on an LNG ship – while LNG is loaded as a cargo, it may be consumed by the ship as excess boil-off. If LNG is consumed in excess, there may be a performance claim against warranties set out in the charterparty. Charterparties typically address these issued by setting forth a specific conversion between fuel oil and LNG (a 'fuel oil equivalent'), setting out maximum allowable consumption and maximum permitted boil-off.

With respect to breakdown claims, the types of claims are myriad, reflecting the complexity of the ship. Typical charterparty protection comes through maintenance obligations. Typically, the owner is obliged to use 'due diligence' to maintain the vessel; failure to do so may result in deductions to hire payable or, for a voyage charter, there may be the ability to place the ship off-hire.

Finally, it is important that the vessel be technically compatible with the terminal. Typically, there is an owner warranty of compatibility, but the scope of this obligation varies across standard forms.

4.3 Port liability agreements

The vessel and the terminal will enter into a port liability agreement when the vessel calls at the loading (or unloading) port. As noted above, port liability agreements allocate ship-shore liability.[37]

In the United States, port liability agreements counteract the effect of the Limitation of Liability Act, 46 USC §§ 181 *et seq*. The act limits a vessel owner's

35 A related concern is the impact of charter rates on LNG shipping. For a discussion of this issue, see Oxford Institute for Energy Studies, "The LNG Shipping Forecast: costs rebounding, outlook uncertain", March 2018, www.oxfordenergy.org/wpcms/wp-content/uploads/2018/02/The-LNG-Shipping-Forecast-costs-rebounding-outlook-uncertain-Insight-27.pdf.

36 UK Defence Club, "LNG Charters Common Issues", July 2021, www.ukdefence.com/insights/july-2021-lng-charters-common-issues-155989/.

37 For an excellent overview of port liability agreements, see Monica Huang, "Allocation of ship-shore liability: use of port liability agreements to provide protection and mitigate uncertainty for US LNG project participants", Lexology, 3 December 2012.

liability in a marine casualty event to the value of the vessel and cargo determined at the end of the voyage during which the event occurred. This limitation of liability can lead to perverse outcomes in cases where the damage results in a total loss of the vessel and cargo, as the vessel owner would consequently be able to limit liability to third parties to zero.

A port liability agreement, by contrast, typically sets out a clear fault-based liability regime subject to a mutual cap which must be covered by the vessel's P&I club; the vessel owner waives the right to limit liability pursuant to the act. Moreover, port liability agreements clearly set out the indemnified and indemnifying parties. The terminal group typically includes persons involved in offloading/loading LNG and the vessel and its group members. The vessel group typically includes the vessel owner and persons involved in the ownership/operation of the vessel.

Port liability agreements also clearly identify the scope of damage and the cause of damage covered by the indemnity. For example, typically liability is apportioned for a 'marine incident', which may include:

- losses or damage to the vessel or the marine terminal;
- losses or damage caused by or contributed to by the vessel; and
- obstructions or dangers to the operation of the marine terminal.

The key consideration for a port liability agreement is that it must be 'poolable' according to the rules of the vessel's P&I club, in order to ensure that the club will insure the risks associated with calling at the port. In order to be poolable and thus benefit from claims pooling, the port liability agreement must comply with the terms of the pooling agreement. Given the interaction with the insurance requirements for LNG shipping, we set out additional guidance below.

The pooling agreement for the IGP&I establishes criteria that liabilities under a contract must satisfy in order to be poolable. First, certain risks are excluded entirely and are consequently not poolable, including nuclear and war risks. The general principle is that an insured owner should not assume responsibility, under contract or otherwise, for liability or loss arising from an act or omission for which, under applicable law, the insured owner would have otherwise been entitled to exclude or limit liability – such liabilities and losses are not poolable. However, a knock-for-knock indemnity may be poolable as long as the insured owner does not waive any rights of limitation available under applicable law. There is also an exception to the general rule for contracts for services to an insured vessel – liabilities arising under a contract for services to a vessel may be poolable provided that the shipowner can demonstrate 'best endeavours' to ensure that the contract complied with the requirements.[38]

38 www.westpandi.com/getattachment/d5cbe5c8-71bc-4379-98ae-071ae873ba76/woe5504-lng-publication_web_aw4.pdf.

Generally, indemnities for LNG are excluded from pooling, unless specific criteria are satisfied.[39] Usually, the club can only provide full cover if the terminal is liable for its sole negligence and there is an acceptable limitation of liability. Specifically, under the pooling agreement, the port liability agreement must be subject to the applicable statutory limitation (ie, the Convention on Limitation of Liability for Maritime Claims 1976 (LLMC) or any protocols or amendments thereto);[40] or, if the limit has been waived or if there is no such limit, a contractually agreed limit of either $150 million or an amount equivalent to the limit specified under the LLMC or any protocols or amendments thereto. Where this limit is created contractually:

- it cannot be conditioned on the performance of insurance or other obligations which cannot be reasonably expected or an owner when complying with its terms and conditions of entry with its P&I club; and
- the limitation must apply to all liabilities under the conditions of use arising from one event.

Liability for crew members or for wreck removal that does not comply with the foregoing two requirements may still be poolable if the P&I club determines that best endeavours were used to ensure that the port liability agreement was compliant. Moreover, any indemnity given by a vessel owner must exclude any liability arising from the sole negligence of the terminal or port (the only exception is a knock-for-knock indemnity). Liability for personal injury/death of vessel crew/employees and wreck removal that does not comport with the foregoing may nonetheless be eligible for pooling where the shipowner has used best endeavours to negotiate the offending provisions to be eligible for pooling.[41]

Port liability agreements for different geographic regions tend to have similar features; and in instances where a port does not have a port liability agreement, liability is typically allocated according to local law. In some cases, the port and the terminal will each require the vessel owner to enter into a condition of use.

39 In 2018 the IGP&I established a working group to review whether there is justification to continue differentiated treatment of LNG indemnities and other conditions of use indemnities where 'best endeavours' provisions apply. Standard Club, "Pooling Agreement, Specialist Ops & contracting", www.standard-club.com/fileadmin/uploads/standardclub/Documents/Import/events/2018-events-/2734848-pooling.pdf.

40 The LLMC limits liability to two types of claims: personal injury/death and property. Limits are set based on the tonnage of the ship and are expressed in special drawing rights, the value of which is posted daily on the International Monetary Fund website. www.imo.org/en/About/Conventions/Pages/Convention-on-Limitation-of-Liability-for-Maritime-Claims-(LLMC).aspx.

41 The Britannia Steam Ship Insurance Association, Bulletin, 21 June 2016, https://britanniapandi.com/wp-content/uploads/2017/09/PandIcover-LNGterminalconditionsofuseCOU-06-2016.pdf.

4.4 Port services and tug agreements

Typically, the buyer is responsible for entering into a host of contracts for services at the port – including tug services contracts.

5. Energy transition and green LNG

Because LNG is no longer a niche element in the energy portfolio and has now become a major feature of global energy markets, it is increasingly subject to political and social pressures in destination markets. Legal and contractual pressures – including from consumers and investors – are leading to increased awareness of the carbon footprint of LNG. In the context of reaching net zero, and in response to concerns from investors and regulators on what is needed to meet the goal of the 2015 Paris Agreement,[42] energy companies and governments in a variety of destination markets for LNG are seeking a broad range of alternatives to offset their carbon emissions. While natural gas is seen as a bridge fuel from carbon-intensive energy to other sources of renewable energy, the LNG also has a transitional function and will play a prominent role in the reshaping of the energy mix.

Since 2020, 'carbon-neutral' LNG cargoes have represented a slim but growing proportion of the global LNG traded worldwide.[43] Considering that the first shipment of LNG occurred only six decades ago, the change has been modest but marked. In 2019, there were three 'carbon-neutral' cargoes. In 2020, there were seven.[44]

Carbon-neutral initiatives take various forms – from project financing, implementation and credit issuance/registration to leakage reduction and the employment of less carbon-intensive liquefaction technology, as well as alternatives to offsetting remaining emissions through the procurement and retirement of high-quality carbon credits.

With regard to green LNG, the mitigation or neutralisation of carbon footprints usually occurs by offsetting pollution from crude oil cargoes by reducing, avoiding or removing a certain amount of metric tonnes of carbon dioxide (tCO2e) or an equivalent amount of other greenhouse gases (GHGs) in the supply chain. Offsets are registered in a voluntary market certified by independent standards bodies and verified by third parties in conformance with rigorous, published offset protocols.

---

42 R Black, K Cullen, B Fay, T Hale, J Lang, S Mahmood and SM Smith, *Taking Stock: A Global Assessment of Net Zero Targets*, Energy & Climate Intelligence Unit and Oxford Net Zero, 2021.

43 Erin Blanton and Samer Mosis, *The Carbon-Neutral LNG Market: Creating a Framework for Real Emissions Reductions*, Columbia Center on Global Energy Policy, July 2021.

44 Erin M Blanton and Samer Mosis, "The carbon-neutral LNG market: Creating a framework for real emissions reductions", Columbia School of International and Public Affairs Center on Global Energy Policy, 8 July 2021, www.energypolicy.columbia.edu/research/commentary/carbon-neutral-lng-market-creating-framework-real-emissions-reductions.

5.1 Defining a 'carbon-neutral' LNG cargo

There is still uncertainty as to what constitutes a 'carbon-neutral' LNG cargo. Some traders not only consider emissions that are offset in the value chain of the LNG, but also capture emissions in the exploration and production segment. Players that operate upstream use the emissions across the whole value chain to classify a cargo as 'carbon neutral'; while other companies account for emissions in the transportation, liquefaction operations, shipping and regasification segments; and some traders only cover direct emissions from final consumption – which raises the question of whether carbon-neutral LNG is really neutral from a lifecycle perspective.

The carbon intensity of the LNG supply chain and how emissions are divided between segments:

Figure 1: Breakdown of emissions[45]

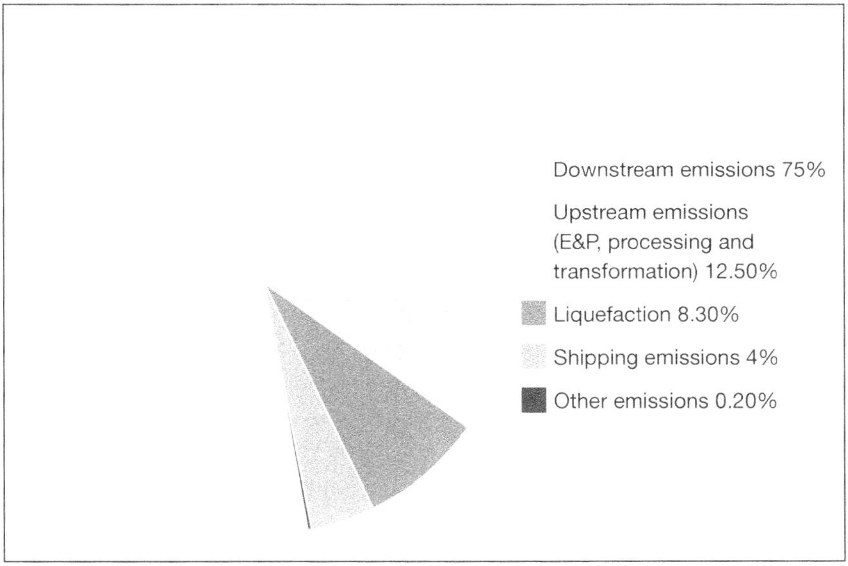

Given that 25% of emissions from an LNG cargo can be associated with non-downstream emissions, and in light of the significant variations in the methodologies used, it is important that the market establishes a default criterion for 'carbon-neutral' LNG cargo which, once agreed, can be certified by

45 Based on information from Sphera, "GHG Intensity of Natural Gas Transport", 8 July 2020, http://sphera.com/research/ghg-intensity-of-natural-gas-transport; UK Department for Environment, Food and Rural Affairs, "Greenhouse gas reporting: conversion factors 2020", 17 July 2020, www.gov.uk/government/publications/greenhouse-gas-reporting-conversion-factors-2020; and Center on Global Energy Policy, "The Carbon-Neutral LNG Market: Creating a Framework for Real Emissions Reductions", 8 July 2021, www.energypolicy.columbia.edu/research/commentary/carbon-neutral-lng-market-creating-framework-real-emissions-reductions.

an independent third party, in order to prevent agents from using green LNG as a 'greenwashing' tool.

Addressing the above, Erin Blanton and Samer Mosi summarised the issue in a publication for Columbia's Center on Global Energy Policy involving carbon-neutral LNG:[46]

> *Serious questions remain about scaling the carbon-neutral LNG trade, including which emissions are accounted for, what methodology is employed in the emissions measurement and verification, and how the emissions are priced – either through a carbon credit or a carbon tax. If these questions are sufficiently addressed, natural gas and LNG may align better with global policy direction and emissions requirements. That is to say, GHG verification and mitigation will be critical to the sustainability of LNG in the decarbonising global energy stack in the coming decade, with knock-on impacts on long-term LNG contract structure, trade flows, and market pricing.*

Regardless of how the carbon intensity of LNG is mitigated across the supply chain of a lower-carbon LNG transaction, the monitoring, reporting and verification (MRV) of GHG emissions will play a major role in the structuring of such transactions.

While historically there has not been an internationalised methodology to account for emissions along the LNG value chain, the GIIGNL recently published a Monitoring, Reporting and Verification and GHG Neutral Framework which will help to promote 'GHG-neutral' LNG, with full disclosure of verified emissions based on GHG account criteria. The framework is intended for use by any entity that must report GHG emissions.[47]

5.2 Structuring carbon-neutral LNG transactions

The issue is thus how to structure lower-carbon and carbon-neutral LNG transactions within a more commoditised LNG market.

In addition to the type of transaction (ie, spot sale or term sale) that will shape a carbon-neutral LNG transaction, the terms and conditions of the LNG sales agreement will dictate how the carbon footprint will be mitigated or neutralised by removing a certain amount of tCO2e or an equivalent amount of other GHGs.

In a transaction where the buyer is paying a premium[48] for a certain quantity of lower-carbon LNG cargo, the seller will need a well-established MRV

46 Erin M Blanton and Samer Mosis, "The carbon-neutral LNG market: Creating a framework for real emissions reductions", Columbia School of International and Public Affairs Center on Global Energy Policy, 8 July 2021, www.energypolicy.columbia.edu/research/commentary/carbon-neutral-lng-market-creating-framework-real-emissions-reductions.

47 GIIGNL, "Driving transparency on emissions and GHG neutral LNG cargoes", https://giignl.org/framework/.

48 Which may arise, for instance, from operating costs, capital costs, natural gas (upstream) costs associated with the LNG cargo and the transaction costs of purchasing the carbon offset credits.

procedure to evidence compliance with the carbon reduction associated with that cargo, as well as with the associated targets and caps. Thus, the LNG SPA should provide for warranties, covenants and undertakings from the seller in connection with these reductions and the seller's ability to keep emissions below the defined cap.

Other important provisions to be negotiated under an LNG SPA include the buyer's rights and remedies if the seller fails to keep its GHG emissions commitment and the carbon intensity of the LNG cargo thus exceeds the agreed footprint. Similar to the contractual mechanics of 'out-of-spec' clauses under gas sale agreements, the parties should agree on:

- the buyer's ability to refuse delivery of the LNG cargo and the scope of damages owed where the seller breaches the warranties given; and
- the extent of losses to which the buyer is entitled due to an 'out-of-spec' LNG cargo.

On the other hand, if the LNG transaction is backed up with offsetting carbon credits, the seller will need to structure the MRV to:

- calculate the amount of offsetting carbon credits that will be transferred by the seller to the buyer as a result of the sale; and
- establish the terms and conditions for the transfer of the carbon credits that will offset all or part of the GHG emissions associated with the relevant LNG cargo.

While many of these provisions could be incorporated into the LNG SPA, it is also becoming customary for the buyer and seller to enter into a separate agreement with respect to GHG emissions.

5.3 Other economic benefits of carbon-neutral LNG

Finally, while LNG is an increasingly reliable option for offsetting carbon emissions and meeting commitments towards the energy transition, from the buyer's perspective, there are other benefits of engaging in lower-carbon LNG transactions. Some jurisdictions impose carbon taxes or regulatory commitments that can be reduced through emissions trading. Insofar as governments and authorities tax carbon and charge prices for each tonne of GHG emitted, investments in environmental projects allow companies to reduce their emissions and offset these carbon taxes.

As part of the European Green Deal introduced by the European Commission,[49] 19 European countries have implemented carbon taxes, which vary from less than €1 (eg, Poland and Ukraine) to €100 (eg, Sweden) per metric

49 European Commission, "A European Green Deal", https://ec.europa.eu/info/strategy/priorities-2019-2024/european-green-deal_en.

ton of carbon emissions.[50] In a political scenario where the marketing of gas in Europe has intensified, low-carbon LNG is a clean alternative that can meet demand while reducing emissions and avoiding carbon taxation.

As another economic benefit of low-carbon LNG, the buyer can enjoy positive reputational impact and public perceptions while still operating in other hydrocarbons markets and jurisdictions. Some companies have long-term financial commitments in other jurisdictions (eg, investments in fossil fuel resources and the upstream oil and gas value chain) which cannot easily be unplugged. Carbon-neutral LNG may allow international oil/energy companies to maintain their strategic position by compensating for emissions in the downstream segment and within the trading/shipping market.

Furthermore, access to capital from certain sources is increasingly being made conditional on the reduction of GHG emissions and financial arrangements commonly require borrowers to meet emissions obligations under various commitments for decarbonised solutions. Buyers should also take advantage of carbon-neutral LNG to comply with these obligations.

As a final point, and perhaps most pertinent to this chapter, is the increasing move towards decarbonising shipping, including LNG shipping, Numerous initiatives are underway in the shipping industry to combat climate change. For example, the International Maritime Organization (IMO) has adopted an initial GHG strategy with a goal of reducing carbon emissions on average across international shipping by at least 40% by 2030 and 70% by 2050, as compared to 2008. In 2011, the IMO adopted mandatory measures, through amendments to the Convention for the Prevention of Pollution from Ships Annex VI, to measure efficiency for international ships. The Energy Efficiency Design Index applies to new ships and requires a minimum energy efficiency level per capacity mile based on ship type and size. All ships must comply with the Ship Energy Efficiency Management Plan (SEEMP), which establishes a mechanism to improve efficiency.[51] In June 2021, the IMO adopted additional short-term measures, through amendments to the Convention for the Prevention of Pollution from Ships Annex VI, to reduce the carbon intensity of ships through improvements to efficiency. All ships must calculate their efficiency, based on their technical design, using the Energy Efficiency Existing Ship Index; ships will then be classified based on a new Carbon Intensity Indicators Index (A–E, where A is best), which is recorded in the SEEMP and reported annually.[52] Ships that attain a D for three years or E for one year must submit a corrective action plan. Ratings can be improved through energy efficiency measures, operational

50 A breakdown of the latest carbon taxes across Europe is available at https://taxfoundation.org/carbon-taxes-in-europe-2022/.

51 IMO, "Initial IMO GHG Strategy", www.imo.org/en/MediaCentre/HotTopics/Pages/Reducing-greenhouse-gas-emissions-from-ships.aspx.

52 IMO, "Rules on ship carbon intensity and rating system enter into force", 1 November 2022, www.imo.org/en/MediaCentre/PressBriefings/pages/CII-and-EEXI-entry-into-force.aspx.

efficiency measures and the use of greener fuels. These amendments entered into force on 1 November 2022, with the obligations effective 1 January 2023.

Although shipping only accounts for 4% of the emissions associated with an LNG cargo, LNG can both facilitate and benefit from GHG reductions in the shipping value chain – given that LNG itself is a fuel, it can help to reduce the carbon footprint of shipping more generally.[53] The use of LNG as a fuel is one potential solution – along with renewable fuels such as green hydrogen and renewable ammonia, and technological innovations – to reduce the overall carbon footprint of the LNG shipping industry.

6. Conclusion

Fundamentally, the shipment of LNG is bound up with the LNG lifecycle and requires a detailed understanding of the ongoing development of the LNG markets and the impact of geopolitics and global pressures on energy demand. More importantly, LNG shipment involves not just complex legal issues, but a wholly formed and integrated set of technical, political and economic considerations. At present, pressures to reduce carbon footprints across the entire value chain of LNG – despite markedly increased demand in those same markets – are putting LNG shipment at the heart of an uneasy marriage between the desire for diversification and energy security on the one hand, and the creation of a more sustainable and reliable energy supply on the other.

53 The World Bank has produced three reports discussing the decarbonisation of shipping: *The potential of zero-carbon bunker fuels in developing countries*, *Charting a course for decarbonizing maritime transport* and *The role of LNG in the transition toward low- and zero-carbon shipping*. All three are available at https://documents.worldbank.org/en/publication/documents-reports/documentlist?qterm= P168079. The International Renewable Energy Agency has also published a report charting a pathway to decarbonising the shipping sector: "A Pathway to Decarbonise the Shipping Sector by 2050", October 2021, www.irena.org/publications/2021/Oct/A-Pathway-to-Decarbonise-the-Shipping-Sector-by-2050.

LNG import projects/ LNG to power

Jose L Valera
Mayer Brown LLP

1. LNG import projects

A liquefied natural gas (LNG) import facility or terminal is purpose built at a port to receive LNG from carrier ships and store and regasify the LNG.[1] The four basic components of the import terminal are:

- the berthing facilities for the arriving LNG carrier ship;
- storage tanks for the LNG unloaded from the carrier ship;
- vaporiser units to regasify the LNG; and
- facilities to send out the regasified LNG (ie, gas) by injecting it into a pipeline for subsequent delivery to one or more offtakers within the local gas market.

At some terminals, some of the LNG received is not regasified, but loaded onto trucks for surface transportation and subsequent regasification at other locations or reloaded onto other carrier ships.

1.1 Berthing of LNG carrier ships

The LNG carrier ship arriving at the terminal needs to berth at a specified location in the port so that its hose lines for the unloading of LNG can connect with the loading hose lines of the terminal.

The LNG terminal may be land based or floating. On a land-based terminal, the storage tanks and vaporiser units are onshore and the LNG carrier ship is given berth at the dock. A floating terminal consists mainly of a floating storage and regasification unit (FSRU), which is a vessel purpose built (or converted from an LNG carrier ship) to receive the LNG from the carrier ship and subsequently store it and regasify it on board. The FSRU then sends out the regasified LNG through a pipeline connecting the FSRU with land-based gas receiving facilities. The FSRU is moored in a fixed location that can vary from a few hundred feet to half a mile from shore. The LNG carrier ship is given berth alongside the FSRU and the LNG is transferred ship to ship through the

1 Various countries have small onshore facilities for the production of LNG for surface transportation (by truck or rail) and regasification at an industrial operation. The specifics of these regasification terminals are not covered in this chapter.

interconnected unloading and loading hose lines of each vessel. In some terminals, the LNG carrier ship is given berth at a jetty across the FSRU. A hybrid terminal uses a floating storage unit (FSU) simply to receive the LNG from the carrier ship and store it. The FSU then sends the LNG by a cryogenic pipeline to shore, where the vaporiser units are located. Much like an FSRU, the FSU is moored in a fixed location and the LNG carrier ship is given berth alongside the FSU or at a jetty across the FSU.

1.2 LNG storage tanks

The LNG storage tanks are necessary to facilitate the receipt of a full cargo of LNG from the carrier ship in a process that typically takes between 12 and 22 hours. The LNG can then be regasified at varying rates while a carrier ship is discharging into the tank and/or in the period after the ship has discharged and left the berth, depending on the level of demand for gas.

Most modern LNG carrier ships have an LNG carrying capacity of between 125,000 cubic metres (m^3) and 175,000m^3. However, some ships have a carrying capacity of up to 267,000m^3 and others as little as 1,000m^3. LNG storage tanks on land terminals may hold from just 10,000m^3 to more than 200,000m^3. These are aboveground, double-walled concrete tanks lined with specialised metal to withstand the extremely cold temperature of the LNG. An advantage of land-based terminals is that there is usually space to build more than one LNG storage tank. Overall storage capacity in the terminal is sized according to the expected carrying capacity of the fleet of carriers serving the terminal and the expected gas throughput. Efficient and reliable storage at regasification terminals helps to ensure uninterrupted LNG supply and delivery of gas to consumers. Spare storage capacity may also be added for strategic reasons, as LNG availability, delays in delivery or downtime during operation may have a direct impact on the ability to meet gas demand. Aside from spare operational storage capacity, terminal developers do not normally build excess storage capacity simply for the purpose of offering short-term services during periods of high demand. Terminal developers seek long-term contracts to support their capital investments (see further discussion of this topic in section 2.2).

The storage capacity at floating terminals is limited to the storage capacity of the tanks within the FSRU or FSU being used. This capacity is typically between 145,000m^3 and 180,000m^3 in order to accommodate a full cargo unloaded by most modern LNG carrier ships.

1.3 LNG regasification

The regasification of LNG involves converting the LNG back into natural gas by increasing its temperature. This is most commonly done using a heat exchanger with sea water as the medium to increase the heat of the natural gas and change it from a liquid to a gaseous state. In some terminals, the LNG is heated by burning natural gas. Aggregate regasification capacity at a land-based terminal can be sized as a function of expected throughput. Regasification units on an FSRU are located on deck and the overall regasification capacity is limited to deck space.

1.4 Advantages and disadvantages of land-based terminals versus floating terminals

A land-based regasification terminal generally demands a larger upfront capital investment by the terminal owner than a floating terminal. Since the revenue is mostly derived from gas throughput (regasification services) at rates that cannot render the total cost of the gas non-competitive, the upfront capital investment is amortised over a long term. This requires a corresponding long-term gas demand. By definition, land-based terminals require the use of land for their entire footprint and this typically attracts more environmental and local scrutiny. An FSRU or FSU, on the other hand, can be chartered by the terminal owner for a certain period of years, such cost typically being treated as an operational or lease expense rather than a capital expense over the same period of years. The capital expense for the FSRU or FSU is borne by the vessel owner. Floating terminals also normally require shorter lead times to put into operation, even if the FSRU or FSU is newly built.

(a) Land-based terminals

The advantages of land-based terminals include their expandable flexibility, allowing them to have more than one berth for LNG carrier ships and more than one storage tank. They also require less downtime for scheduled maintenance and therefore have higher levels of operational availability. Concrete land storage tanks have greater insulation efficiency than the tanks in an FSRU, thus minimising boil-off rates (boil-off is the natural regasification of LNG due to the exposure of the tanks to ambient temperatures – no insulation is perfect). Despite higher upfront capital requirements than a floating terminal, land-based terminals are also more economical than floating terminals over the long term due to their relatively lower operating costs.

The disadvantages include the large upfront capital investments required and normally more stringent environmental permitting requirements.

(b) Floating terminals

The advantages of floating terminals include the following:

- They have less visual impact;
- The vessel, as the main component, can be leased instead of being held as a capital asset;
- The facilities have a smaller footprint; and

- They can be located flexibly closer to final points of consumption, assuming that the necessary port infrastructure is available.

They are generally more profitable than a land-based terminal in the short to medium term, due to lower upfront capital investment by the terminal owner. In the longer term, the economics reverse in favour of the land-based terminal due to the latter's lower operating costs.

The disadvantages are as follows:

- They have inherent limitations in storage and regasification capacity;
- They have higher operating and maintenance costs; and
- They have lower LNG insulation efficiency, due to the nature of the materials that can be used to build a tank on a vessel.

2. LNG to power

The increasing use of LNG helps to reduce emissions and improve air quality by displacing coal and other more-polluting fossil fuels in a variety of sectors, including power generation, heavy industry and heating. Gas-fired power generation also supports the introduction of intermittent renewable energies by reinforcing grid stability. Imported LNG can complement domestic gas production and replace depleting local supply sources. For some countries, imported LNG is their only source of natural gas.

Most nations have traditionally relied to some extent on coal as a source for generating electricity due to its relatively lower cost. In many countries – especially in Asia-Pacific and the Indian subcontinent – coal has been the primary source for power generation.

The increasing use of LNG around the world is due to a series of factors, including:

- global economic growth, with a general increase in the demand of gas for power generation, industry and heating;
- demand growth in emerging economies, where industrialisation from a lower base translates into incremental gas demand for power generation and industrial uses at rates exceeding gross domestic product growth rates;
- environmental policies, which incentivise the use of renewables and cleaner-burning fossil fuels;
- local and regional market reforms, which open the business of power generation to the private sector and bring more capital to the development of infrastructure;
- fuel switching by users;
- domestic gas production capability in excess of domestic requirements (eg, the effect of the shale gas revolution in the United States); and
- limited international gas pipeline supply for geographic and economic reasons.

Some LNG import terminals serve the gas requirements of large gas and/or power utilities (eg, Tokyo Electric in Japan and Kogas in Korea). Given the relative constant and predictable large aggregate gas demand profiles of multiple end users, those offtakers can support long-term LNG supply arrangement with fixed large volumes and rateable deliveries during the year. On the other hand, LNG-to-power projects, where the terminal is developed and the LNG imported solely or primarily to provide fuel gas to a power generation project, present very complex issues.

Depending on the market in which the power plant operates, it will often have variable fuel requirements both over the course of a year and from year to year. This is due to several factors, including:

- the seasonal availability of water for hydroelectric generation and the impact of increasing generation with renewable resources;[2] and
- competing thermal technologies, including nuclear.

Variable dispatch for generation results in variable needs for fuel gas.

An LNG-to-power project has five discrete components in its value chain:

- feed gas production and transportation to the liquefaction facility;
- LNG production and shipping;
- LNG receipt, storage and regasification;
- pipeline transport from the terminal to the power plant; and
- power generation and power sales.

Each component presents specific risks relating to its development and operation, requiring significant capital expenditure and a long development time. The successful operation of each component also depends on the successful operation of the other components in the chain.

Below is a brief discussion of the costs and risks faced by LNG-to-power projects derived from LNG supply arrangements and the structure of regasification services at the LNG import terminal. This discussion relates to LNG supply and terminal regasification arrangements for the benefit of direct gas offtakers operating facilities that consume natural gas (eg, a power plant). There are other terminal services under which the LNG is regasified and gas delivered in bulk at daily rates dictated by the operational needs of the terminal (to maximise throughput), and not as a function of specific gas requirements of the offtaker. Terminals that provide services in this manner operate in regions with a large downstream gas transmission network and a large and diversified

2 Hydroelectric and other renewable energy generation plants are normally dispatched before thermal plants in interconnected electric markets where aggregate electric demand is served by the different generation units in ascending order of operating costs. All other things being equal, the more renewable electric generation available, the less need for gas-fuelled power. This dynamic may play out at different seasons during a year or within a single day.

set of final offtakers, often associated with gas storage facilities; the terminal gives the terminal customer a pre-set number of days and daily rates to receive the gas. It is the customer's responsibility to receive the gas at such rates and to transport and market it downstream of the delivery point. Likewise, this discussion excludes commercial arrangements whereby a customer has the right to store LNG at the terminal for discretionary periods. This can be done in single-customer terminals; but (as discussed in sections 2.4 and 2.5 below) in most cases, it is not commercially feasible in multi-customer terminals where at least one of the customers requires daily throughput.

2.1 LNG supply arrangements

In the early days of the LNG industry, purchase and sale arrangements were structured as long-term contracts (15 to 25 years), with fixed take-or-pay quantities and year-ahead scheduling to justify, on the part of the seller, billions of dollars in the development of otherwise-stranded gas fields and associated liquefaction facilities; and to ensure, on the part of the buyer, security of supply. This was fine for traditional destinations such as Japan and Korea that wanted to diversify from oil and could manage this LNG supply profile because they had large, stable and diversified baseload gas demand.

But the number of purchasers with more variable and/or smaller needs has increased over time (to a great extent because there is more LNG to be had).

An LNG-to-power project derives its revenues from the sale of power – whether under one or more power purchase and sale agreements or under a series of spot transactions in the wholesale power market in which it participates. These revenues have limited elasticity, meaning that the power project may be unable to pass through or recover through power sales any and all costs associated with LNG procurement and regasification services.[3] At best, a power purchase and sale agreement may allow for a pass-through of the actual cost of the gas used as fuel; but other potential costs unrelated to fuel used may not be recoverable under the purchase and sale agreement, including the costs that may be incurred under the LNG supply agreement when gas is otherwise not obtained (eg, LNG take-or-pay payments, cargo rescheduling or cancellation fees) and costs that may be incurred under the regasification services agreement irrespective of actual usage (see discussion in section 2.5 below). To mitigate such potential costs, the power project must thus have flexibility under the terms of LNG sale and purchase agreements, including with respect to scheduled annual volumes, cargo sizes and cargo delivery times.

The challenge to avoid commitments to purchase LNG in excess of actual requirements under inflexible take-or-pay arrangements may be aggravated by:

---

3 Other project costs and risks which are also common to other infrastructure projects, such as construction and financing costs and permitting, completion and counterparty risks, are not discussed.

- limited LNG storage capacity;
- the lack of local gas storage facilities for excess contracted volumes;
- an illiquid domestic gas market to resell excess contracted volumes;
- the expectations of LNG sellers;
- unique issues under LNG regasification agreements; and
- unpredictable variations in fuel gas demand.

An effort to avoid over-contracting LNG volumes may result in contracting less LNG than actually required. This may put the power project in the position of having to purchase spot cargoes in the open market at unpredictable prices to make up the necessary volumes.

An electric generator in a competitive power market sourcing its fuel gas from LNG requires:

- security of LNG supply in order to avoid contractual or regulatory penalties for lack of generation availability;
- flexibility in the quantities of LNG that it may schedule in any year under the supply contract in order to manage expected fuel requirements that may vary from year to year;
- flexibility in cargo delivery times during a year in order to respond to seasonal variations in thermal power demand; and
- competitive LNG pricing in relation to the fuel costs of other competing generators.

This flexibility may be achieved in part through:

- the right of the power project to nominate in any given year within the term of the contract LNG deliveries anywhere between 75% and 125% of the base annual contracted quantity;
- the scheduling of the delivery of LNG cargoes during a year following the project's expectation of seasonal variations in fuel demand;
- the sizing of cargoes to reflect the power project's available LNG storage capacity at the terminal and actual fuel requirements;
- the right of the project to cancel scheduled cargoes (usually in consideration for the payment of a cancellation fee) to manage situations in which it may find itself over-contracted;
- the seller's undertaking to use reasonable commercial efforts to reschedule a cargo at the request of the project in order to manage unexpected variations in fuel demand during a year; and
- the seller undertaking to use reasonable commercial efforts to supply unscheduled cargoes that the project may need to buy on short notice during the year.

Competitive pricing may be achieved by:

- matching the index used for the determination of the LGN price to the index for fuel adjustment costs that may be used in the power purchase and sale agreement; and
- providing in the supply agreement that the LNG price will be reduced at the request of the power project if the plant is not dispatched due to its relatively high fuel costs.

The tenor of the LNG supply agreement is also an important factor. Given the increased availability of LNG in the global market, a relatively short contract term (less than 10 years) will give the power project the opportunity during the lifetime of the power plant to reset from time to time all its LNG procurement contract terms to reflect the prevailing market conditions.

With additional LNG volumes to sell, sellers are having to adapt to the requirements of new, smaller purchasers such as LNG-to-power projects. Increasing liquefaction sources result in a movement from long-term 'country-to-country' supply arrangements (eg, early Indonesia to Japan trade), and have brought in relatively more flexible supply by portfolio players (typically large oil and gas companies) and trading houses (eg, Trafigura, Gunvor, Vitol and Glencore). These market participants make or purchase LNG from different liquefaction sources to subsequently distribute it through their own marketing channels. With substantial balance sheets, portfolio players and trading houses are in a position to provide liquidity and flexibility to the market – often committing to offtake from a liquefaction project on a long-term basis irrespective of the structure of their resale contracts. Portfolio sellers and trading houses usually have more room to manage the supply flexibility required by smaller buyers.

2.2 LNG regasification arrangements

Regasification of the LNG at the import terminal is carried out under a regasification services agreement (also often called a terminal use agreement) entered into between the terminal owner/operator and the customer that brings in the LNG to be stored and regasified. The services to be provided by the terminal operator to the customer under the agreement include the following:

- berthing of LNG carrier ships bringing the LNG in;
- unloading and receipt of the LNG from LNG carrier ships;
- storage of the customer's LNG inventory in the terminal's tank(s);
- regasification of the LNG held in storage upon nomination by the customer; and
- delivery of the gas (regasified LNG) to the customer at the agreed delivery point, which normally is the point of interconnection of the terminal's send-out pipeline and the local pipeline network (or dedicated pipeline to a power plant).

The structure of the LNG regasification services between the terminal and the power project may also have a significant effect on the costs and risks to be incurred by the power project.

The storage tanks(s) of the import terminal must have a certain minimum capacity in order to receive the LNG in full cargo lots. The purchase of LNG in a quantity that only partially fills the carrier ship increases the relative unit cost of the LNG and may make it uncompetitive. Most LNG carrier ships have a capacity of between 125,000m^3 and 175,000m^3. Because the import terminal should be large enough to receive a full cargo lot from the delivery ship, the cargo size of the largest delivery ship that the terminal is designed to unload dictates the minimum size of the import terminal. Thus, a terminal is typically designed to store at least 145,000 to 180,000m^3 (if it has only one storage tank) or more (if it has two or more storage tanks). A terminal designed to store 145,000 to 180,000m^3 of LNG will be able to receive a full cargo lot from most LNG carrier ships.

A key consideration in the decision to develop an LNG import terminal is the demand for regasification services. If there is only one potential initial customer for the terminal – the power project which will use the imported LNG for power generation – it is important to determine whether the power project will demand gas in a quantity sufficient to support the minimum size that the terminal should have. If there are two or more initial customers, the terminal will be sized to accommodate the aggregate requirements of the customers.

The cost to a customer to receive regasification services has two basic components:

- a fixed fee to repay the capital invested by the terminal owner and provide a return on such capital; and
- a variable fee that pays for operation and maintenance expenses.

This cost, when coupled with the cost to acquire the LNG itself, forms the bulk of the 'fuel cost' for a power project. This fuel cost can be significant and, together with the expected cost of building and maintaining the power plant, forms one of the key economic considerations of whether to develop the power project at all.

A terminal is rarely sized with excess capacity to serve other natural gas markets that do not exist at the time but may develop in the future. This will depend on whether there is a significant cost to building the import terminal (or chartering the FSRU) with excess initial capacity, since the related excess cost must be borne by someone: it is either absorbed by the terminal owner or is borne by the power project as increased fees, which may result in the initial customer subsidising the development of a wider natural gas market at a later time from which it may not benefit. More commonly, terminals are expanded as additional demand for regasification services materialises. Obviously, this is more practical for land-based terminals. While an FSRU can expand its regasification capacity within the constraints of deck space, it cannot expand its storage capacity. To expand the storage capacity of a floating terminal, it would be necessary to bring in a larger replacement FSRU.

2.3 The effect of terminal services design

In a single-user terminal, the customer has access to the entire storage and daily regasification capacity of the terminal and can use that capacity as it sees fit subject to the operational limits of the terminal. This is an optimal position for an LNG-to-power project, but the project must pay for the entire capacity of the terminal. In the case of a multi-customer terminal, the storage and daily regasification capacity must be shared between customers. Sharing capacity in a terminal allows customers to tailor the terminal fees to be paid to their actual gas requirements. In many instances, for economic reasons an LNG-to-power project shares capacity in a terminal with other customer(s).

It is in the context of a multi-customer terminal that an LNG-to-power project expecting to nominate gas only as a function of its actual fuel requirements faces significant additional risks and costs relative to being the single customer of the terminal. Unless the storage capacity of an LNG terminal is large enough for all customers to be able to store their own full cargo lots of LNG simultaneously (very unlikely due to cost considerations), the principal considerations that must be faced by any customer of a multiple-user LNG import terminal are operational and arise from:

- the impact that limited storage and regasification capacity has on scheduling LNG supply to and gas send-out from the terminal; and
- the need to balance available LNG in storage with the gas nominations of the terminal's customers.

These considerations exist for all terminals, but are magnified when the terminal is an FSRU whose storage capacity does not significantly exceed the size of the cargoes that will be delivered to it one at a time. Where each customer is responsible for procuring its own LNG supply, the scheduling of LNG deliveries to and gas deliveries from the terminal makes it harder to accommodate users such as the operators of peaking or mid-merit power plants, which have gas requirements that fluctuate and cannot be readily estimated in advance.

2.4 LNG scheduling and gas balancing

Scheduling LNG deliveries to and gas deliveries from an LNG import terminal is always complex – in large part because LNG is delivered to the terminal in cargo lots which are generally scheduled a year in advance and gas is delivered from the terminal in a continuous flow nominated on a day-ahead or intra-day basis. One of the principal tasks of the terminal operator is to work with the terminal's customers to develop the annual LNG delivery and gas nomination programme, and then to ensure that the actual LNG deliveries and gas nominations during the year are in accordance with the programme. This should be done in a way which gives the terminal sufficient available storage space to accept LNG deliveries when they are scheduled and does not allow the inventory of LNG in the terminal to fall below certain levels to ensure continued gas send-out as required by the customers before the next LNG cargo is delivered.

Development of the annual delivery programme starts with each customer providing the terminal operator with a schedule of daily gas nominations within its contracted regasification rights and a schedule of proposed LNG cargo delivery dates and quantities. The terminal operator combines the terminal customers' individual schedules into a terminal-wide schedule. In order that each customer has available LNG in storage to support its gas nominations, the aggregate planned daily gas nominations of a customer in the year must not exceed or be lower than, on a British thermal unit (BTU) basis, the aggregate LNG deliveries by such customer during the year. Put another way, a customer may not deliver to the terminal more or less LNG in a year than the equivalent quantities of gas on a BTU basis to be withdrawn by such customer from the terminal in the year. The terminal-wide schedule should balance periodic LNG deliveries with daily gas nominations.

In a single user terminal, the ability of the terminal's customer to react to changes in gas demand depends on the delivery flexibility that the customer's LNG supplier is willing to offer. The historic LNG market – which relied on take-or-pay contracts with little or no intra-year volume flexibility – did not really accommodate peaking and mid-merit power plant customers which are unable to predict their daily and annual gas demand a year in advance. The current LNG market offers much greater flexibility, which makes LNG a viable fuel for power plants with varying fuel requirements.

Although intra-year variations from the annual LNG delivery programme of a single terminal customer can frequently be accommodated in today's market, the ripple effects from a single customer making intra-year changes to its annual LNG delivery and gas nomination schedule in a multiple customer terminal are much more difficult to accommodate. Changes in the LNG deliveries and gas nominations by one customer affect the LNG delivery schedule of other terminal customers, which may not have the contractual right to change the delivery schedule agreed with their LNG suppliers without paying a substantial penalty, and the ability of such other terminal customers to satisfy their own gas requirements.

For example, if a mid-merit power plant (Customer A) is not dispatched as frequently as was anticipated when the annual LNG delivery and gas nomination programme for the terminal as a whole was developed, the failure to nominate gas may mean that there will not be sufficient storage capacity to accommodate the next scheduled cargo, which may be scheduled for delivery to a different customer (Customer B). Forced deliveries of natural gas to Customer A may not be practical in the absence of gas storage facilities or a liquid gas market. Flaring gas for the account of Customer A in order to make storage space for the next cargo may be prohibited by environmental regulations. In order for Customer B to avoid LNG failure-to-take penalties, Customer B would have had to build flexibility into its LNG delivery schedule to accommodate Customer A's variable gas demand. That flexibility may come at a price – which, in the absence of an agreement to the contrary, will be paid for by Customer B and not Customer A, whose variable gas demand created the need for the flexibility in the first place. If rescheduling the next cargo is not possible, Customer B may be forced to cancel the delivery of the cargo, with the attendant liquidated damages payable to its seller. On first impression, Customer A contracted to receive services in consideration for a fee payable to the terminal operator; but, due to the nature of a multi-user LNG terminal, it may end up being liable for indemnification payments to Customer B arising from its variable gas demand.

2.5 Terms of terminal use

For the scheduling process described above to operate properly, the terms of use of a terminal should include provisions that allow the terminal operator and all customers to enforce the annual LNG delivery and gas nomination programme. In practice, this has several aspects, as discussed below.

(a) Minimum daily gas nominations

In order to free up storage space to accommodate each scheduled LNG cargo when it is due to be delivered, the terms of use of a terminal should require each customer to nominate a minimum quantity of gas for delivery each day. The daily minimum nomination is determined as part of the development of the annual terminal-wide programme. In other words, in the period inter-cargoes, a customer should be required to nominate deliveries of gas in the quantity it said it was going to require during that period at the time of the preparation of the annual programme. The required minimum daily gas nomination grows higher as the delivery date of the next cargo approaches if the customer is falling behind in nominations. This circumstance presents real practical and commercial problems for a peaking or mid-merit power plant customer, because the customer cannot accurately predict its gas demand in advance and may be unable to utilise a minimum quantity of gas each day. (The need to dispose of gas that is not taken by a terminal customer presents even greater difficulties where the terminal is connected only to a power plant which may not be operating and there is no gas pipeline grid or market into which to sell gas that cannot be taken by the power plant.)

(b) ***Maximum daily gas nominations***

Because the daily regasification capacity of a terminal is limited, limitations must be placed on the quantity of gas that can be nominated by each customer on any day so that the aggregate nominations of all the customers do not exceed the terminal's daily regasification capacity. These limitations are usually dictated by the maximum regasification capacity contracted by each customer. Additionally, a particular customer may not be permitted to nominate gas in a manner that is materially different from its nomination schedule in the annual programme even though the requested nominations are within the customer's contracted maximum limit. For example, in the period inter-cargoes, a customer may not nominate gas in excess of the LNG attributable to such customer under the programme from the last cargo (see borrowing and lending discussion in section 2.5(c) below). The customer is given an LNG 'quota' from each cargo delivery to match its projected gas nominations during the period inter-cargoes. This excess nomination would deprive other customers of LNG inventory against which to make their own nominations. Of course, limitations of this kind are problematic for peaking or mid-merit power plants which must run when they are dispatched.

(c) ***Borrowing and lending of LNG***

Even with the imposition of maximum and minimum limits on daily gas nominations, customers of a multiple customer terminal which contract for their own LNG supply will constantly be in a position where they are borrowing LNG from each other. The reason why this is the case is best illustrated by the example of a 165,000m^3 FSRU with two customers, each of which has approximately the same daily gas demand. In order for the customers to be able to procure LNG in full cargo lots, they must alternate cargo deliveries. This means that when Customer A's cargo is in storage, the daily gas deliveries to Customer B are actually loans of LNG by Customer A from 'its' cargo to Customer B. When Customer A's cargo is used up and Customer B's cargo is delivered, these loans are repaid by Customer B through the terminal making daily gas deliveries to Customer A from Customer B's cargo of LNG. The quantity of LNG that a customer may borrow is determined by the quantity of gas such customer included in the annual programme as its gas requirements for the relevant period. The terms of use of a regasification terminal in these circumstances should make the borrowing and lending of LNG mandatory; otherwise, one customer could not nominate gas deliveries against LNG belonging to another customer and thus on an ongoing basis both customers would be unable to nominate gas deliveries at the same time. This mandatory borrowing and lending regime has several important implications that must be dealt with in the terminal terms of use.

One effect of the mandatory borrowing and lending is that each terminal customer either is a lender to or is a borrower from each other customer on a rotating cycle for the quantity of LNG loaned or borrowed. Where all of the terminal users have similar credit capacities, this may not be too significant of an issue. However, where that is not the case, the terms of use may require that a customer whose credit capacity falls below an agreed common level must provide credit support in favour of all of the other customers. Even where inter-customer credit support is not required, the terms of use may impose a maximum credit exposure (eg, an LNG borrowing cap) that a customer may not exceed. Credit support under the terminal services agreement may reduce the credit capacity of an LNG-to-power project seeking to finance the construction of the power plant on a non-recourse basis.

The mandatory borrowing and lending regime increases the importance of adherence to advance schedules. If an LNG cargo is late or is not delivered at all, the problem is not a problem only for the customer whose cargo was delayed or cancelled; rather, the likely result is that no customer will be able to receive gas. The customer that loaned LNG to the customer whose cargo is not delivered did so with the expectation that the borrowing customer would deliver LNG to the terminal in time to allow the lending customer to nominate gas deliveries after its LNG cargo has been used up. Although the LNG loaned to the borrowing customer can be settled financially, financial settlement does not always put the lending customer back to where it expected to be. Any penalties payable under a power purchase and sale agreement due to lack of generation capacity availability or electric energy shortfalls may not be covered fully by the financial compensation due to be received under the terminal use agreement. This illustrates how an LNG-to-power project sharing a terminal with another customer may have increased liabilities resulting solely from this circumstance and potential fuel disruptions due to events not attributable to the power project. These risks and potential liabilities may also affect the ability to obtain financing for the power project.

The terminal terms of use should distinguish between a failure to deliver LNG by a customer that is caused by *force majeure* and a failure to deliver LNG that is not the result of *force majeure*. However, even the equities in the case of *force majeure* are not always straightforward. Although all customers may have accepted the risk of *force majeure* affecting the operation of the terminal, the same may not be true in the case of the *force majeure* risk embedded in each terminal customer's LNG procurement strategy.

An often-cited benefit of LNG-to-power projects is that the LNG regasification and gas send-out infrastructure can be a subsequent springboard for the development of a broader natural gas market. The sale of natural gas to other industrial users and final consumers requires a gas distribution system that can be built and connected to the initial infrastructure for the power project. While a power project may have the economic wherewithal to purchase

LNG (which must be done in cargo lots that may cost tens of millions of dollars each), not all potential gas consumers may do so given their far-smaller requirements on an individual basis. On an aggregate basis, however, the demand can be significant. By contracting to use the regasification infrastructure, some market participants may fill the role of aggregating gas demand from small customers and purchasing LNG to supply to them under separate contracts. The new capital investments would be limited to expanding the import terminal, if necessary, and building the gas distribution system downstream from the terminal.

3. Recommendations and conclusion

The liquefaction and regasification projects that are increasingly being developed throughout the world reinforce each other in support of the growth of the industry and will eventually make LNG a global commodity. Unlike crude oil, however, which is purchased by refiners under fairly standard terms and conditions and not directly by fuel consumers, LNG is bought by a great diversity of purchasers for different purposes. This requires, on the part of LNG industry participants, a disposition to enter into bespoke agreements and a tolerance for varying commercials risks. In order to support the growth in global demand, LNG must be offered with as much embedded flexibility as possible in relation to contract duration, committed quantities and times of delivery.

Fortunately, large portfolio players and trading houses are contributing to market liquidity and enabling the larger adoption of natural gas for a cleaner transition to a world with net-zero emissions. But some rigidity remains, primarily due to financing requirements for liquefaction projects. In order to obtain limited recourse financing on a long-term basis, liquefaction project sponsors must enter into long-term sale agreements and thus ensure a stable revenue commensurate with the tenor of the loans to limit the risk of lenders. This should ease over time as liquefaction projects expand and more flexible financing is available. This lessened dependency on long-term contracts by LNG sellers bodes well for the proliferation of dedicated regasification projects, which in many cases cannot predict on a year-ahead basis how much LNG then are going to need.

Downstream distribution network

Laura Huomo
Bird & Bird
Cea Mittler
Legal counsel

The principal focus of this chapter is on the downstream distribution of gas. Gas is distributed through transmission pipelines and distribution pipelines. This chapter discusses gas distribution operations in the European Union, the United States, Asia and Russia – mainly from a regulatory perspective.

1. Introduction

The natural gas value chain is typically illustrated through a trichotomy of streams: production, transmission and distribution, also referred to as 'upstream', 'midstream' and 'downstream' respectively. These terms indicate the location of the activities taking place: the closer to the end user a function is, the further downstream it is said to be. The distribution of natural gas is the last step in the natural gas value chain and occurs after the processing and purification of raw natural gas. Natural gas is distributed through distribution pipelines, which are narrower and have lower pressure than transmission pipelines. In other words, the closer the gas gets to the end user, the narrower the pipelines get. In practical terms, the types of pipelines used in the gas industry vary according to many factors, such as:

- the product to be transported;
- the delivery stage; and
- whether the activity is taking place in the upstream, midstream or downstream sector.

The EU Third Gas Directive (as defined below) defines 'distribution' as "the transport of natural gas through local or regional pipeline networks with a view to its delivery to customers, but not including supply".

The characteristics of the natural gas markets in the United States, Europe, Russia and Asia differ quite significantly. Natural gas markets in the United States and in Russia are more developed than those in Europe and Asia.

In the United States, the natural gas distribution network is vast and covers almost all 50 states. Local gas utilities are generally awarded exclusive rights (although in some states/regions, there is competition) to distribute natural gas within a specified geographic area and to perform services such as billing, conducting safety inspections and providing natural gas connections for new customers. As with interstate pipelines, natural gas utilities have historically been viewed as natural monopolies, which has led to regulation to ensure that the utilities do not misuse their position. In some states, commercial customers/industrial customers can choose their provider. State public utility commissions oversee and regulate investor-owned local natural gas utilities. Local government-owned utilities are usually regulated by local government agencies. State regulators oversee the construction of new distribution networks, including approving installation sites and proposed additions to the network.

The Russian gas industry is dominated by OAO Gazprom, which is a publicly listed company. In 2019, the Russian Federation held a 50.23% stake in Gazprom. Gazprom is also considered a monopolist on the distribution side, because it owns close to 75% of low-pressure distribution networks in Russia. According to Russian competition law, the gas transportation market (exports) is considered to be a natural monopoly.[1] As such, since Gazprom operates in this market, it can be viewed as a monopolist. However, this is not a single market comprising the entire territory of Russia, but rather a number of smaller markets in which Gazprom operates through its numerous subsidiaries, which are considered to be monopolistic. In terms of gas distribution, there is no monopoly in Russia.

In Europe, there is a noticeable difference between different countries (competitiveness, size and geographical coverage) as regards the penetration of the natural gas distribution network to industry and households. Usually, the countries that are most densely populated have the most developed natural gas distribution networks.

In certain Asian countries, natural gas distribution has historically been reserved to the public sector. This means that the monopolistic nature of distribution networks prohibits competition. The lack of downstream regulation in the market also slows downstream development. Vertically integrated companies may take advantage of their market position. Currently, there are initiatives aimed at improving market efficiency, increasing competition and putting downward pressure on prices. Liberalisation of gas distribution is one of the current trends.

---

1 In particular, Federal Law 147-FZ of 17 August 1995 on Natural Monopolies.

2. Regulatory regimes

2.1 Europe

(a) Gas directives

On 22 June 1998, the European Parliament and the Council issued Directive 98/39/EC concerning common rules for the internal market in natural gas ('the First Gas Directive'), which entered into force on 10 August 1998.

On 26 June 2003, the European Parliament and the Council issued Directive 2003/55/EC concerning common rules for the internal market in natural gas and repealing Directive 98/30/EC ('the Second Gas Directive'), which entered into force on 4 August 2003.

Then, in 2009, the European Parliament and the Council issued Directive 2009/73/EC concerning common rules for the internal market in natural gas and repealing Directive 2003/55/EC ('the Third Gas Directive'), which entered into force on 3 September 2009.

The First Gas Directive was the first step towards the creation of an internal, integrated, fully liberalised market for gas. The Second Gas Directive focused on completing the internal gas market by regulating non-discriminatory access (eg, to the networks of distribution system operators (DSOs)). It therefore helped to create an internal gas market within the European Union. The Third Energy Market Directive was also an attempt to ensure that the roles and responsibilities of DSOs were defined, in order to facilitate well-functioning and transparent retail natural gas markets. It focused on:

- contractual arrangements;
- rules of settlement;
- customer commitments;
- data exchange;
- data ownership; and
- metering responsibility.

The European Green Deal, published in December 2019, framed the European Union's plans for decarbonisation and its ambition to become carbon neutral by 2050. As the region's flagship climate and energy policy, it provided the basis for all strategies which have followed, such as the Energy System Integration and Hydrogen strategies of July 2020, which identified actions to facilitate the gas sector's contribution to decarbonisation. In September 2020, the European Commission announced that a new EU regulatory framework for competitive decarbonised gas markets would be developed in 2021. The "Fit for 55" package announced by the European Commission in July 2021 contains legislative proposals to revise the entire EU 2030 climate and energy framework, including legislation on the decarbonisation of gas markets. The European

Commission presented most of its proposals under the "Fit for 55" package on 14 July 2021. However, the proposals on a revision of the Third Energy Package for gas to regulate competitive decarbonised gas markets and legislation to reduce methane emissions from the energy sector were put forth in the fourth quarter of 2021. At this stage, the package is just a proposal that will be submitted to the European Parliament for formal debate – which will last at least a few years.

(b) ***DSOs and TSOs***

The Third Gas Directive defines a 'distribution system operator' as:

> *a natural or legal person who carries out the function of distribution and is responsible for operating, ensuring the maintenance of, and, if necessary, developing the distribution system in a given area and, where applicable, its interconnections with other systems, and for ensuring the long-term ability of the system to meet reasonable demands for the distribution of gas.*

In contrast, a 'transmission system operator' (TSO) is an entity entrusted at a national or regional level with the transportation of energy in the form of natural gas or electricity through fixed infrastructure. The Third Gas Directive provides the following definition:

> *A natural or legal person who carries out the function of transmission and is responsible for operating, ensuring the maintenance of, and, if necessary, developing the transmission system in a given area and, where applicable, its interconnections with other systems, and for ensuring the long-term ability of the system to meet reasonable demands for the transport of gas.*

Just as a TSO is responsible for the natural gas transmission network within a member state, a DSO is responsible for the distribution network. Member states must designate, or require undertakings which own or are responsible for distribution systems to designate, one or more distribution system operators. Member states must ascertain that DSOs:

- meet the tasks assigned to them in the Third Gas Directive (Article 25);
- fulfil the unbundling requirements (Article 26); and
- meet their confidentiality obligations (Article 27).

The non-discriminatory nature of the rules also applies to the terms and conditions, including rules and tariffs, and the provision of such services by DSOs. The tariffs must be cost reflective. Operators must publish the rules and tariffs used in their distribution network. (See further section 2.1(f) and also the possible exemptions for closed distribution networks in section 2.1(c) below.)

(c) ***Closed distribution networks***

The Third Gas Directive also provides regulations for a closed distribution network. In practice, this means that certain specialised operations – such as industrial, commercial or shared services sites (eg, airports, train station buildings, hospitals or chemical industry sites) – can include closed distribution systems.

Recital 28 of the Third Gas Directive provides that:

where a closed distribution system is used to ensure the optimal efficiency of an integrated energy supply requiring specific operational standards, or a closed distribution system is maintained primarily for the use of the owner of the system, the Member States may exempt the distribution system operator from obligations which would constitute an unnecessary administrative burden because of the particular nature of the relationship between the distribution system operator and the users of the system.

In practice, this means that they receive an exemption (eg, from *ex ante* approval by the national regulatory authorities of tariffs and/or calculation methodology).

(d) Third-party access

In addition to non-discriminatory access to transmission pipelines, non-discriminatory access to distribution pipelines is a prerequisite for competition. This is because natural gas distribution pipelines are natural monopolies. Distribution pipelines act as 'entry gates' to retail markets in most countries and have an important influence on the level of competition alongside transmission pipelines.

For as long as the gas distribution networks are owned by a vertically integrated company, the national legislature must ascertain that the regulatory system guarantees third-party access. A national energy market authority must ensure that third-party access is also possible in practice.

Article 32 of the Third Gas Directive sets out the obligations for member states to create a system that allows third-party access to distribution pipelines: "Member States shall ensure the implementation of a system of third party access to the ... distribution system ... based on published tariffs, applicable to all eligible customers ... and applied objectively and without discrimination between system users."

Operators of distribution infrastructures must grant third parties non-discriminatory access and earn a regulated return on their investment for such assets.

However, as provided for in Article 35 of the Third Gas Directive, natural gas undertakings may, having regard to certain criteria and procedures, refuse access to the system on the basis of lack of capacity or where access to the system would prevent them from carrying out the public service obligations which are assigned to them or on the basis of serious economic and financial difficulties with take-or-pay contracts. This cannot be a permanent exception because the pipeline owners are under an obligation to build up capacity in the event of demand. Member states may take the measures necessary to ensure that a natural gas undertaking that refuses access to the system on the basis of lack of capacity or a lack of connection makes the necessary enhancements insofar as it is economic to do so or when a potential customer is willing to pay for them.

Further exceptions to third-party access are included in Article 36 of the Third Gas Directive, which allows major new gas infrastructure (ie, interconnectors, liquefied natural gas (LNG) and storage facilities), upon request, to be exempted for a defined period from the provisions of Articles 9, 32, 33 and 34 and Article 41(6), (8) and (10) under strict conditions. The European Commission will verify that these conditions are met in each case. If the commission finds that some or all of the conditions are not met, it may ask the national authority to amend or to withdraw its decision.

Although the Third Gas Directive is an attempt to ensure third-party access to distribution pipelines, there are still barriers to competition within the internal market in natural gas in the European Union.

(e) ***Unbundling***

The Third Gas Directive introduced a structural separation between DSO activities (staff) and generation, production and supply activities. The goal of these network unbundling provisions is to avoid conflicts of interest and ensure that DSOs take their decisions independently, ensuring transparency and non-discrimination towards all network users – especially domestic customers and small non-domestic customers. The regulations aim to prevent DSOs from taking competitive advantage of their vertical integration on the market. The unbundling regime as regards distribution seeks to ensure the proper functioning of the internal gas market and security of supply for consumers, and is key in the further development of retail competition.

The Third Gas Directive includes unbundling provisions imposed on TSOs and DSOs. The unbundling obligations are much stricter at the TSO level. At the DSO level, functional and legal unbundling rules are considered adequate. Also, in order to shield small DSOs from undue financial or administrative burdens, member states may exempt such companies from legal unbundling rules.

The rules on DSO ownership unbundling are set out in Article 26 of the Third Gas Directive. Article 26 provides that "when a distribution system operator is part of a vertically integrated undertaking, it shall be independent at least in terms of its legal form, organisation and decision-making from other activities not relating to distribution". Those rules, however, do not require the ownership of the assets of the distribution system to be separated from the vertically integrated undertaking. The distribution function must be clearly branded to make clear its separation from the other functions included in the gas delivery chain.

Article 26 sets out qualification requirements for those persons who are responsible for the management of the DSO. The DSO must also have sufficient human resources to carry out the unbundling successfully. Further, Article 26 focuses on effective decision-making rights which are independent from the integrated natural gas undertaking, with respect to assets necessary to operate, maintain or develop the network. The DSO must closely monitor its decision making and establish a compliance programme. This programme must set out the measures that must be complied with in the decision-making process so as to avoid discriminatory conduct. Finally, compliance with the programme must be monitored and a yearly report must be submitted by a compliance officer to the national regulator. One difficult aspect of the unbundling is the separation of information flows.

Member states must ensure that the activities of the DSO are monitored by regulatory authorities or other competent bodies if the DSO is part of a vertically integrated undertaking.

If a member state's integrated natural gas undertakings serve fewer than 100,000 connected customers, the member state may choose not to apply the above rule.

In addition to allowing third-party access to transmission pipelines, member states must ensure that the third-party access regime also applies to the distribution system and is based on published tariffs which are applied objectively to all eligible customers, and without discrimination between system users. Therefore, regulated tariffs are the cornerstone of regulated third-party access.

(f) Tariffs

According to Article 32(1) of the Third Gas Directive, access to distribution systems must be "based on published tariffs, applicable to all eligible customers, including supply undertakings and applied objectively and without discrimination between system users". In addition, national regulatory authorities must, sufficiently far in advance, fix or approve their methodologies for calculating or establishing the terms and conditions for connection and access to national networks, including distribution tariffs. Natural gas distribution tariffs should be non-discriminatory and cost reflective. If necessary, the national regulatory authorities have the authority to require DSOs to modify their tariffs and methodologies to ensure that they are proportionate and applied in a non-discriminatory manner.

2.2 United States

(a) Regulation

US natural gas markets are competitive and effective. In 1985, the Federal Energy Regulatory Commission (FERC) enacted Order 436, which allowed distribution companies to exit long-term supply contracts with interstate pipeline companies and purchase natural gas directly from natural gas producers. This was the first step towards competitive gas markets.

The second important regulation as regards competitive markets came into force in 1992, when FERC enacted Order 636. This order stipulated that the sale, transportation and distribution of natural gas must be functionally separated in interstate sales that triggered competitive natural gas markets. This introduced an obligation to unbundle gas trading from pipeline operation activities and set up separate transportation and trading affiliates.

The following laws regulate natural gas markets in the United States:

- the Natural Gas Act of 1938;
- the Natural Gas Policy Act of 1978 (regulation of the transportation of natural gas as authorised by the Natural Gas Policy Act);
- the Natural Gas Wellhead Decontrol Act of 1989; and
- the Energy Policy Act of 1992.

In addition, the Outer Continental Shelf Lands Act of 1953 governs offshore oil and gas activities.

(b) Third-party access

Order 436 instituted an open access regime for interstate pipeline transportation. The rules apply only to interstate pipelines which are long-distance, wide-diameter and high-capacity transmission lines and not distribution lines. Third-party access to distribution pipelines is regulated at the state level.

(c) Unbundling

As mentioned above, unbundling became a compulsory requirement in 1992 with the enactment of FERC Order 636 for interstate pipelines. The requirement was to separate the pricing of natural gas sales and natural gas transportation. The idea behind this functional unbundling was to ensure non-discriminatory transportation services for third-party gas and the pipeline company's own gas. Functional unbundling had the desired result, increasing competition between various gas sellers and mitigating the market power of pipeline companies. It also aimed to ensure the maintenance of adequate and reliable services. Even though Order 636 was aimed only at interstate natural gas pipelines, it has also had an influence on certain intrastate distribution pipelines.

(d) Tariffs

In the United States, tariff regulation is twofold and varies from the European model. FERC sets prices and conditions of service for interstate transportation pipelines and the state regulators set prices for end-use customers, intrastate pipelines and local distribution. Tariff regulation in general is based on the idea that the transportation of natural gas is a monopoly because a licence is required to build a pipeline and because usually there is only one pipeline that can transport natural gas from point A to point B. Production and wholesale supply of natural gas are not price regulated at either the federal or state level. In practice, since smaller end customers typically purchase a bundled product, an argument has been presented that the price is regulated for household customers. Generally, there is only one local distribution company in each geographical area, and that company usually owns the distribution pipelines.

2.3 Asia

(a) China

China has adopted an integrated oil and gas legislative model. In recent years, China's oil and gas industry has been moving towards more market-based pricing schemes, promoting competition among energy enterprises and greater market access for smaller companies.

Legislative reform: Historically, China's natural gas prices have been highly regulated, with the goal of protecting consumers. However, the previous government pricing regimes did not provide enough incentives for natural gas suppliers. Therefore, in 2014 China launched a reform of its gas system. The reform affected the entire industry chain, including upstream, midstream and downstream; the basic idea was to "control the middle and liberalise the two ends". The 'middle' here refers to the pipeline network transmission link. The reform of the 'middle' aimed to make the pipeline independent and promote the fair opening of pipeline transmission. After years of continuous efforts, the reform of China's gas system has made great progress.

On 9 December 2019, China National Petroleum Corporation (CNPC) announced the establishment of the China Oil & Gas Piping Network Corporation. Its establishment marked a key step in the reform of China's natural gas pipeline network operation mechanism, with the gradual establishment of a negotiated third-party access system and the gradual implementation of a 'permitted cost plus reasonable revenue' pricing model for pipeline services.

In March 2020, the National Development and Reform Commission (NDRC) removed gas prices from the Catalogue of Pricing by the Central Government, marking the end of the historical mission of government-set gate prices.

Third-party access: The main instruments covering third-party access are:

- the Measures for the Supervision and Administration of Fair Opening of Oil and Gas Pipelines Network Facilities (for Trial Implementation) (3 February 2014);
- the Notice on the Disclosure of Information Relating to the Opening of Oil and Gas Pipeline Network Facilities (2 September 2016);
- the Measures for the Administration of Natural Gas Pipeline Transportation Prices (for Trial Implementation) and the Measures for the Supervision and Review of Natural Gas Pipeline Transportation Pricing Costs (for Trial Implementation) (9 October 2016);
- the Measures for the Supervision and Administration of Fair Opening of Oil and Gas Pipelines Network Facilities (24 May 2019); and
- the Measures for the Administration of Natural Gas Pipeline Transportation Prices and the Measures for the Supervision and Review of Natural Gas Pipeline Transportation Pricing Costs (7 June 2021).

Currently, entities subject to these statutes are limited to:

- gas storage facilities;
- pipelines;
- LNG receiving stations; and
- related ancillary facilities.

Although China has opened the pipeline network in accordance with the principle of fairness, this does not mean that any third party can enter the market in an uncontrolled and unconditional manner; the relevant laws and administrative regulations will impose the necessary restrictions and limitations on them.

In order to expedite the application process, two types of applications are adopted: decentralised and centralised applications. Applicants can select the optimal type of application based on their specific circumstances. China has also adopted a contract management regime in relation to third-party access and the relevant legislation clearly stipulates the service model, standard contract terms and liability for failure of performance. The key to the regime is contract management and each participating party protecting its own rights and interests according to the relevant contracts.

Tariffs/price: Since 2015, the NDRC has introduced a series of policies and measures aimed at improving the management of natural gas gate prices and increasing the degree of marketisation of natural gas prices. In November 2015, the NDRC issued the Notice on Reducing the Gate Price of Non-Residential Natural Gas and Further Promoting Price Market Reform, which changed the management of non-residential gas from the highest gate price to the 'base price plus floating range' model in one year. In November 2016, the Notice on Matters Related to Natural Gas Gate Pricing Policy in Fujian Province was issued, implementing a pilot market-oriented reform of natural gas gate prices in Fujian Province. In May 2018, the Notice on the Rationalisation of the Sales Price of Residential Gas Gate Stations was issued, stating that the benchmark prices of residential gas and non-residential gas would be aligned starting on 10 June 2018.

At present, the natural gas pricing schemes in China are as follows:

- For those that need to access long-distance pipelines for the shipment of gas unconnected with a gas sales transaction (ie, enterprises with integrated pipeline transportation and sales), a unified gate price is implemented.
- For coal-bed methane, coal gas, shale gas factory gate prices and LNG, gas prices are liberalised, determined by mutual agreement between supply and demand.
- For those that need to access long-distance pipelines for shipment of gas unconnected with a gas sales transaction, the price of the gas source will be negotiated between the supply and demand sides, and the transport costs will be paid to the pipeline transport enterprises according to the pipeline transport prices stipulated by China.
- The city gas supply terminal sales price is still under local management and the degree of marketisation is relatively low.

Transportation pricing: Pipeline transportation prices are also regulated by the government, pursuant to the Interim Measures for the Administration of Natural Gas Pipeline Transportation Prices issued by the NDRC on 9 October 2016. The interim measures have authorised the Pricing Authority of the State Council to determine the pipeline transportation prices for natural gas in accordance with the 'permitted cost plus reasonable revenue' model. The pipeline transportation prices are determined for each natural gas transportation enterprise based on factors such as the enterprise's permitted costs, permitted revenue and tax burdens. Based on their own calculation, natural gas transportation enterprises may also submit their proposed prices to the Pricing Authority for approval.

(b) Philippines

In the Philippines, pipelines require a legislative franchise, meaning that any private person or entity wishing to build a pipeline for downstream distribution must have permission from the Congress of the Philippines. If natural gas is sold for electricity production, the gas sales are not regulated. However, the electricity tariff is regulated where electricity is sold to distribution utilities that are regulated entities. There is no third-party access regime in the Philippines.

There is presently no legislation covering the downstream gas sector. However, under the previous administration legislation governing the natural gas sector was proposed, including provisions on the third-party access regime; this now needs to be refiled after elections that took place in May 2022.

(c) Indonesia

Indonesia's oil and gas sector is governed by the Oil and Gas Law (22/2001) and its implementing regulation, Government Regulation 36/2004 on Downstream Oil and Gas Business Activities, most recently amended by Government Regulation 30/2009.

Downstream activities are controlled by the regulatory agency (*Badan Pengatur Hilir Minyak dan Gas Bumi* ('BPH Migas')). BPH Migas supervises all downstream activities, including refining, storage, transportation, distribution and commercial activities of petroleum and petroleum products. Downstream businesses must operate through a company incorporated in Indonesia. The company must obtain a business licence issued by the government under the Ministry of Energy and Mineral Resources (MEMR) with input from BPH Migas.

With the issuance of the Job Creation Law (11/2021) and its implementing regulation, Government Regulation 5/2021, business licences in all business sectors in Indonesia – including the oil and gas sector – are issued based on risk-based categories: low, medium or high risk. Only those businesses that fall within the high-risk category require a business licence and a business identification number (NIB). Businesses that fall within the medium-risk category require not only an NIB, but also a standard certificate. Meanwhile, businesses that fall within the low-risk category need only obtain an NIB. According to Government Regulation 5/2021, the oil and gas sector – and specifically downstream business activities – is categorised as a business with a high level of risk. Therefore, the requisite business licences for downstream activities consist of an NIB and a licence.

Business actors must obtain an NIB and the licence through the Online Single Submission (OSS) system managed by the central government. The use of the OSS system is a fundamental change, given that prior to the Job Creation Law, the licensing of oil and gas businesses was managed directly by the MEMR.

Regarding distribution, the MEMR has the authority to determine and set technical standards relating to gas and minimum technical standards for distribution and facilities.

Gas transportation by pipelines via a transmission segment or a distribution network area is permitted only after the business entity has obtained an oil and gas transportation business licence and a special right in transmission sections from BPH Migas. The 'special right' here is the right to operate pipes in certain transmission sections and/or distribution network areas in the context of business activities involving the transportation of natural gas by pipeline. In order to obtain the special right, the business entity must engage in an auction process organised by BPH Migas.

Those business entities that hold a licence for transporting natural gas by pipelines and that have privileges in a transmission section and/or distribution network area are prohibited from conducting natural gas trading activities through a pipeline at the natural gas transportation facility that the business entity owns and/or controls. This is to encourage fair and healthy competition and improve efficiency in utilising infrastructure and quality of service.

(d) *India*

Under the Constitution of India, the regulation and development of oilfields, mineral oil resources, petroleum and petroleum products (which includes the construction of oil and gas pipelines) fall within the jurisdiction of the Indian Parliament. Under these constitutional powers, the Indian Parliament has passed the Petroleum and Natural Gas Regulatory Board (PNGRB) Act 2006, which became effective as from 1 October 2007 (ie, the appointed date).

Downstream gas activities – including, storage, transportation (including pipeline construction), distribution, marketing and sale of natural gas (excluding exploration and production natural gas) – are regulated by the PNGRB, which was established under the terms of the PNGRB Act.

In the exercise of its powers under the PNGRB Act, the PNGRB has framed regulations on various downstream activities. These regulations fall under three main categories based on the nature of the pipelines and the products transported:

- natural gas pipelines;
- petroleum and petroleum product pipelines; and
- city or local natural gas distribution networks (including domestic piped natural gas and compressed natural gas).

Among other things, these regulations seek to regulate:

- the grant of authorisation to entities to lay, build, operate or expand the relevant pipeline network;
- the natural gas pipeline transportation tariff;
- common carrier principles, access codes for common carrier or contract carrier natural gas pipelines and city or local natural gas distribution, and affiliate codes of conduct for entities involved in the marketing of natural gas and the construction of pipelines; and
- health, safety and environment issues.

As stated above, in addition to the abovementioned laws, there are several other legislative instruments and policies that apply to specific downstream activities.

Tariffs: In India, tariffs/prices for the distribution of natural gas through pipelines, the distribution of natural gas through city gas distribution networks and petroleum/petroleum products are determined and regulated differently. While the pipeline transportation tariffs for natural gas, petroleum and petroleum products are determined by the PNGRB as per the principles laid down under the respective regulations, retail tariffs for the city gas distribution network and compression charges for compressed natural gas are not regulated. As per the recently amended tariff regulations, even natural gas pipeline tariffs will differ depending on whether the pipeline falls within or outside the national gas grid. A unified tariff will apply to pipelines falling within the national gas grid, determined for transportation either:

- within 300 kilometres of the entry point; or
- throughout the remaining length of the national gas grid.

The petroleum pipeline tariff is benchmarked against the goods tariff for railways.

(e) ***Russia***

Gazprom – a state-controlled company – owns the world's largest gas transmission system, most of which forms part of Russia's Unified Gas Supply System (UGSS). The UGSS encompasses gas production, processing, transmission, storage and distribution facilities in European Russia and Western Siberia. In addition, a number of gas trunk pipelines are controlled by other entities – for example, JSC Sakhatransneftegaz operates trunk and distribution pipelines in Yakutia. Hence, there is not a single gas transportation market comprising the entire territory of Russia, but rather a number of smaller markets in which these subsidiaries are deemed monopolists. Gazprom, a financially vertically integrated company, holds a monopoly on transport through its wholly owned subsidiary, Transgaz. Transgaz is not a single legal entity, but comprises several subsidiaries operating in different territories. Certain regional companies own regional pipeline networks, such as the abovementioned JSC Sakhatransneftegaz, of which 85.47% of the share capital is owned by Yakutia. All of these are obliged to grant access to third parties in exchange for a fee (tariff) set by the state.

Downstream gas is regulated by the following instruments:

- Federal Law 147-FZ of 17 August 1995 (as amended) on Natural Monopolies;
- Federal Law 69-FZ of 31 March 1999 (as amended) on Gas Supply in the Russian Federation;
- Government Resolution 858 of 14 July 1997 (as amended) on Ensuring Access of Independent Organisations to the Gas Transportation System of OJSC Gazprom;

- Government Resolution 1370 of 24 November 1998 (as amended) on Adoption of Regulations on Ensuring Access of Organisations to Local Gas Distribution Networks; and
- Government Resolution 1021 of 29 December 2000 (as amended) on State Regulation of Prices for Gas, Tariffs on Services of Its Transportation and Fees for the Technological Joining of Gas-Using Equipment to Gas Distribution Networks on the Territory of Russia, together with the Main Provisions of Forming of State Regulation of Prices for Gas, Tariffs on Services of Its Transportation and the Fee for Technological Joining of Gas-Using Equipment to Gas Distribution Networks on the Territory of Russia (as amended).

3. Contractual provisions

3.1 Access agreements

Natural gas distribution access agreements include the terms and conditions according to which natural gas consumers obtain access to the distribution system. The terms covered by the agreement usually include:

- connection to the distribution system;
- the installation site for the metering system;
- the consumer's gas installation;
- service and distribution pipelines;
- access to the gas supply system and gas installation;
- ownership of the distribution system and ownership of the natural gas;
- takeover/occupancy;
- metering;
- settlement basis;
- invoicing;
- prices and settlement principles;
- vacation/termination of metering sites;
- operational disruptions;
- *force majeure*;
- liability; and
- disputes.

3.2 Distribution access service agreements

Natural gas distribution access service agreements include the terms and conditions according to which natural gas consumers obtain service in the distribution pipelines. Entering into a service agreement must be preceded by an access agreement to the distribution pipeline. The terms covered by the agreement usually include:

- the contents of the service and the option to change the service;

- invoicing;
- interruption of service;
- termination; and
- liability.

3.3 Natural gas purchase agreements

The terms of natural gas purchase agreements between a gas company and a consumer are quite simple. The agreement mostly covers:

- the term of the agreement;
- pricing and invoicing (and possible collateral);
- termination;
- the delivery point; and
- title to the delivered gas.

4. Conclusion

This chapter has discussed gas distribution in the European Union, the United States, Asia (China, India, the Philippines, Indonesia, India) and Russia. The chapter has outlined the different regulatory regimes, pricing methodologies and contractual provisions in these countries and regions. It serves as an overview and introduction to the different regulatory and policy set-ups, with some insight as to how market developments affect the development of regulation.

The chapter has intentionally not shed light on the current geopolitical tensions and the energy crisis and risks relating to dependence on an autocracy; nor has it evaluated the role of gas DSOs and distribution networks in the context of the energy transition (ie, the decarbonisation of the gas sector). Current global affairs and the pressing climate crisis are contributing to the reinvention of the energy market, which is seeking to strike the right balance between efficiency and security. Addressing the impact of these circumstances at the distribution network level from a legal perspective would require, for instance, an evaluation of existing national and supranational frameworks and the identification of barriers and cracks that may prevent the injection of new gas sources at the distribution level. This analysis would need to be followed by an assessment of the need for new market rules at a regional level, such as network planning and operation, storage and flexibility, as well as interoperability issues that arise from the blending of gaseous fuels and the injection of gases of varying specifications at the distribution level. When it comes to operating in a new environment and building futureproof and functioning markets, the role of the gas DSO and the gas distribution network should also be re-evaluated. Here the focal question is: what does the role of gas DSOs and gas distribution networks look like in the new energy reality that is being shaped by the emergence of biogas, hydrogen, power to gas technologies and system integration?

Storage projects

André Andriw
Assentia Consulting
Gustavo Castro Ribeiro Ferreira Silva
University of São Paulo
Lucas Mota de Lima
University of São Paulo
Cosmos Nike Nwedu
Federal University, Ndufu-Alike Ikwo
Eduardo G Pereira
Professor of natural resources and energy law

1. Introduction

Increased worldwide demand for liquefied natural gas (LNG) has fuelled the development of significant LNG storage tank facilities for LNG exporters and importers. These massive storage tanks are essential in order to receive and safely store liquid gas. LNG is usually converted to a liquefied state through a special cooling process which lowers the temperature to approximately -162°C. LNG occupies 600 times less space than natural gas in its gaseous state, making it practical to ship by ocean tanker. It is also stable and safe, because even when compressed in volume, the liquid remains at normal atmospheric pressure. On land, LNG is stored in specially engineered and constructed double-walled storage tanks. At these temperatures, the requirements for the containment structures are very stringent and post-tensioned concrete tanks are ideally suited to the task. These large concrete tanks are extremely robust, with significant amounts of pre-stressing required; design and installation are subject to tightly controlled quality conditions, with hardware requiring special certifications. The design and construction techniques have been specially formulated for LNG tank construction. This chapter outlines the key features of LNG storage, as employed in various projects around the world.

Natural gas is a vital component of national energy supplies, and underground gas storage plays an important role in ensuring that natural gas can be delivered to end users on a consistent basis to meet expected demand. In an underground gas storage facility, the aim is to inject gas underground, where it will remain in place until such time as it needs to be withdrawn. There are three principal types of underground natural gas storage fields, with different geological characteristics and capabilities that govern their suitability for storage:

- depleted hydrocarbon reservoirs;

- aquifer reservoirs; and
- solution-mined salt caverns.

In the United States, there are more than 400 active storage facilities containing 4 trillion cubic feet (tcf) of natural gas that can be stored and withdrawn for consumer use. Most existing natural gas storage in the United States is in depleted natural gas or oil fields that are close to consumption centres.

This chapter presents economic and regulatory information on the natural gas and LNG storage market, as well as the context and recent highlights in the United States, Europe and Asia.

2. The storage market

2.1 Economic and market characteristics

Over the years, LNG has become a crucial multi-purpose element of the international energy market. Its main feature is the flexibility it affords to consistently meet the diverse needs of the industrial, transport, heat and electricity generation sectors.[1]

With the development of gas-to-liquid conversion technology, the transport of gas to markets that were previously inaccessible by pipeline became viable, favouring the adoption of natural gas as a useful energy source for many countries. The transportation solution that LNG offers is one reason why developing countries are increasingly engaging in the LNG market. In addition, LNG is less polluting than oil and coal derivatives, making natural gas and LNG a key driver of the energy transition for many countries and regions, such as the United States, the European Union, China, Australia and Japan.[2]

These characteristics have driven the development of LNG flow management and control to meet the demands of multiple consumers. Storage, for example, has become an important strategy for maintaining gas distribution in markets with limited infrastructure. It also helps to mitigate geopolitical risks, which often disrupt the international market by limiting the supply of oil and gas.[3]

---

1 Drielli Peyerl et al (2002), "Applying Small-Scale Liquefied Natural Gas Supply Chain by Fluvial Transport in the Isolated Systems: The Case Study of Amazonas, Brazil", 68 *Energy for Sustainable Development* 192.

2 International Energy Agency (IEA), *Southeast Asia Energy Outlook 2022*, www.iea.org/reports/southeast-asia-energy-outlook-2022, license: CC BY 4.0.

3 IEA, *Southeast Asia Energy Outlook 2022*, www.iea.org/reports/southeast-asia-energy-outlook-2022, License: CC BY 4.0; International Gas Union (IGU), *World LNG Report 2022*, www.igu.org/resources/world-lng-report-2022/.

Figure 1. Storage tank capacity for LNG worldwide in 2021

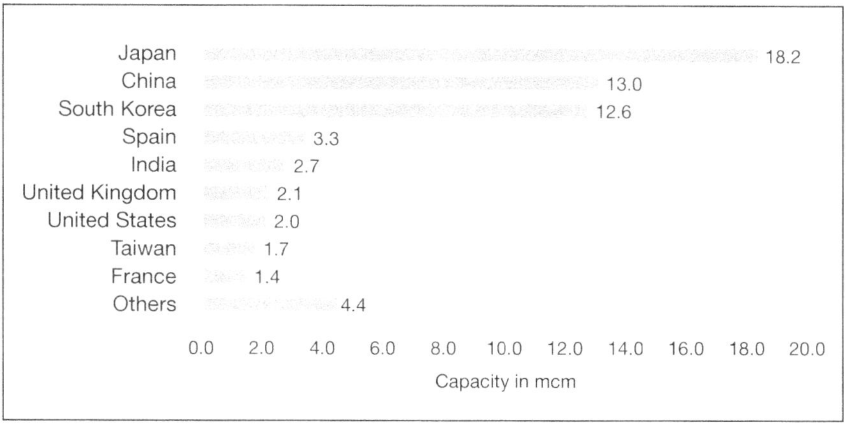

Source: Authors based on data from Statista.[4]

According to international consultancy Statista, Japan, China and South Korea together account for 60% of global LNG storage capacity. Japan alone has 18.2 million cubic metres (mcm) in storage, followed by China (13 mcm) and South Korea (12.6 mcm). In the West, Spain is the main storage hub, with 3.3 mcm; the country also serves as a re-export warehouse for cargo arriving in Europe from Latin America and North America.[5]

The LNG storage sector can be sub-divided into the onshore segment and the offshore segment. Onshore, companies build large concrete tanks to store LNG near the processing (receiving and regasification) terminals, where it will ultimately be directed to the distribution network. In addition, large companies often stock LNG near major maritime routes, creating a distribution hub to facilitate the export or re-export of the fuel.[6]

This dynamic is mainly evident in the European Union and Asia. The European Union has receiving terminals in the Netherlands, Belgium, France, Spain and more recently Croatia, favouring the re-export of LNG throughout the European territory. Meanwhile, Asia's storage and distribution hubs are based in Singapore, China, Indonesia and Japan.[7]

In the offshore segment, one key business model combines transport, loading and unloading – either on land or on ship. In this scenario, the floating

4 Statista, "LNG Storage Tank Capacity for Liquefied Natural Gas Worldwide in 2021", www.statista.com/statistics/723079/lng-global-storage-tank-capacity-by-country/.

5 *Ibid.*

6 Michelle Michot Foss, "An overview on liquefied natural gas (LNG), its properties, the LNG industry, and safety considerations", Center for Energy Economics, 2012, https://docplayer.net/21534709-Introduction-to-lng-an-overview-on-liquefied-natural-gas-lng-its-properties-the-lng-industry-and-safety-considerations.html; International Gas Unions (IGU), *World LNG Report 2022*, www.igu.org/resources/world-lng-report-2022/.

7 IGU, World LNG Report 2022, www.igu.org/resources/world-lng-report-2022/.

storage unit (FSRU) plays a key role in the commercialisation of LNG. The FSRU is characterised by its versatility in integrating the production of natural gas at sea to receiving terminals, either by unloading directly at the port or by operating in conjunction with a floating storage unit (FSU).

Another business model that has developed in the offshore segment is vessel bunkering. According to the International Gas Union (IGU), companies have begun to specialise in this niche area due to growing demand from the maritime sector for less polluting fuels, which has positioned LNG as a resilient and more sustainable source for heavy transport and long shipments. The new International Maritime Organization (IMO) 2020 regulation on the production, distribution, storage, processing and use of marine fuel will further promote this technological niche.

Vessel bunkering involves the use of units with LNG tanks to supply cargo ships or exploration ships at sea. According to the IGU, there are now 30 LNG bunkering units in operation worldwide. The model is expanding because it allows for the conversion of ships with diesel engines to LNG.

2.2 Regulatory and policy characteristics

(a) Contract construction

The design, construction, installation and use of LNG storage tank systems are important aspects of the LNG infrastructure, which is highly engineered. Essentially, these activities involve specific legal obligations and working conditions, making the LNG storage contract construction vital to the industrial project as a whole. Typically, the contractor will fulfil certain standards, while the purchaser will adhere to specific conditions of use.

There are three different types of LNG storage tanks: single, double and full containment. Deciding on the choice of tank and its containment configuration is one of the initial steps in the design and engineering process. Therefore, a construction contract and applicable conditions will depend on the specification and the type of storage tank required. This notwithstanding, quality assurance remains a guiding standard in the contract between the parties.

(b) Quality regulation policies

The engineering of LNG storage tanks is a core health, safety and environmental issue, requiring a holistic risk evaluation and a diligent environmental impact assessment. Thus, global standards and best practices are a key requirement for the safe design, construction, installation and use of LNG storage tanks. In the 1960s, the American Petroleum Institute developed standards for storage tank design, construction and materials. These standards help to ensure industry quality and safety, and are continually updated to reflect new industry developments and best practices. There is also an EU standard for installation and equipment for LNG – European standard EN 1473 – which is an interlocking document for the design, building and operation of onshore LNG facilities.[8] Local regulatory policies for LNG storage tanks may also exist, depending on jurisdiction and use. And various regulatory agencies may additionally play a role – for example, in jurisdictions with a federal system of government.

Ensuring that contracts for the construction of LNG storage tanks comply with industry standards and best practices is one way to support energy security, as non-compliant tanks will result in exposure to risks and undermine resilience capacities.[9] Evidence has shown that the overall safety record of LNG storage tank systems is good. However, one LNG tank failure with a severe safety impact was recorded in Cleveland, Ohio in 1994. This incident has proved central to energy security concerns.[10]

3. Analysis of the main storage regions

3.1 United States

Natural gas is the most diversified fuel in the United States. This domestic fuel is used to cook food, fuel vehicles and generate electricity, and as a raw material for products such as fertilisers and plastics. One of the most important uses of natural gas is to heat buildings and homes: about half of all US homes use natural gas as their main heating source.[11]

This use results in significant seasonal variations, with natural gas consumption highest during the wintertime and lowest during mild-weather months. On the highest-demand days, storage delivers about half of the natural gas consumed. Natural gas storage enables supply to match demand on any given day throughout the year by adjusting to daily and seasonal fluctuations in demand while natural gas production remains relatively constant year-round.[12]

The underground storage of natural gas is a critical component of the natural gas supply system in the United States. When natural gas production is higher than natural gas consumption (typically April to October), it can be placed into storage. When natural gas production is lower than consumption (typically November to March), it can be withdrawn from storage to meet

---

8 GMS Consult, "What is an LNG storage tank and what is it used for?", 15 October 2021, www.gmsthailand.com/blog/what-is-lng-storage-tank/.

9 A Cherp and J Jewell, "The concept of energy security: Beyond the four As", 75 *Energy Policy* 415, December 2014.

10 C Collins, D Patel and J Tarlowski, "Development in LNG Storage: Overview of LNG Storage Tanks", LNG Conference, London, 2000.

11 American Petroleum Institute, "Underground Natural Gas Storage", https://energyinfrastructure.org/energy-101/natural-gas-storage.

12 *Ibid.*

demand. About 20% of all natural gas consumed in the United States each winter comes from underground storage.[13]

The underground storage of natural gas is an integral component of the US energy system. Natural gas storage enables companies to adjust for daily and seasonal fluctuations in demand throughout the year while natural gas production remains relatively constant year-round. Without storage, customers – including power generators, transportation operators and residential users – would face potential supply shortages and highly variable prices.[14] The flexibility and resilience provided by storage are key to maintaining reliable and responsive natural gas delivery.

Natural gas is stored in several different ways. It is mostly held in inventory underground under pressure in three types of facilities:

- depleted reservoirs in oil and/or natural gas fields;
- aquifers; and
- salt cavern formations.

Natural gas may also be stored above ground in refrigerated tanks as LNG.

Each storage type has its own physical characteristics (porosity, permeability, retention capability) and economics (site preparation and maintenance costs, deliverability rates and cycling capability), which govern its suitability for applications.[15] Two important characteristics of an underground storage reservoir are:

- its capacity to hold natural gas for future use; and
- the rate at which gas inventory can be withdrawn – called its 'deliverability rate'.

Most natural gas storage in the United States is in depleted natural gas or oil fields that are close to consumption centres. Conversion of a field from production to storage duty takes advantage of existing wells, gathering systems and pipeline connections. Depleted oil and natural gas reservoirs are the most commonly used underground storage sites because of their wide availability.

Approximately 400 active storage facilities in 48 states – in the form of depleted natural gas or oil fields (80%), depleted aquifers (10%) and salt caverns (10%), and comprised of almost 17,500 storage wells – are in service today. Approximately 60% of the facilities span state boundaries and 40% are intrastate.[16]

Over 300 cities, towns and other populated areas are located near a natural

13 *Ibid.*

14 *Ibid.*

15 US Energy Information Administration, "The Basics of Underground Natural Gas Storage", 16 November 2015, www.eia.gov/naturalgas/storage/basics/.

16 American Petroleum Institute, "Underground Natural Gas Storage", https://energyinfrastructure.org/energy-101/natural-gas-storage.

gas storage site. Operators often locate natural gas storage sites near major population centres or large gas pipelines to improve their ability to deliver natural gas when needed.[17]

The total design capacity in the United States (based on the physical characteristics of the reservoir, installed equipment and operating procedures on site, which often must be certified by federal or state regulators) in 2020 was 4.715 tcf, with a demonstrated peak capacity of 4.253 tcf. Southcentral is the region with the largest capacity (1.54 tcf), followed by the Midwest (1.221 tcf) and the East (1.065 tcf).[18]

Facilities identified as interstate represented 63% of total storage capacity and 65% of working gas capacity.[19] This capacity is enough to meet an average state's residential natural gas consumption for more than 20 years.[20]

The regulation of underground natural gas storage facilities is currently divided between federal and state regulatory jurisdictions. Storage facilities associated with interstate commerce are regulated by the Federal Energy Regulatory Commission (FERC) and the Pipeline and Hazardous Materials Safety Administration (PHMSA).[21] FERC is responsible for issuing permits to underground gas storage facilities; while the PHMSA – a branch of the US Department of Transportation – has primary authority over the operation of interstate gas storage facilities. Storage facilities associated solely with intrastate commerce are regulated by the state in which they are located. The states' oil and gas agencies regulate operations associated with wells and reservoirs; while the states' public utility commissions regulate aboveground pipelines and facilities.

The principal owners/operators of underground storage facilities are:

- interstate pipeline companies;
- intrastate pipeline companies;
- local distribution companies (LDCs); and
- independent storage service providers.

About 120 entities currently operate the nearly 400 underground storage facilities operational in the United States, approximately half of which are

17 US Government Accountability Office, "Natural Gas Storage: Department of Transportation Could Take Additional Steps to Improve Safety Enforcement Planning", 22 November 2017, www.gao.gov/products/gao-18-89.

18 US Energy Information Administration, "Underground Natural Gas Working Storage Capacity," Natural Gas Reports, 30 April 2021, www.eia.gov/naturalgas/storagecapacity/archive/2021/index.php.

19 Pipeline and Hazardous Materials Safety Administration, Department of Transportation, "Pipeline Safety: Safety of Underground Natural Gas Storage Facilities", 2 December 2020, www.federalregister.gov/documents/2020/02/12/2020-00565/pipeline-safety-safety-of-underground-natural-gas-storage-facilities#footnote-8-p8106.

20 American Petroleum Institute, "Underground Natural Gas Storage", https://energyinfrastructure.org/energy-101/natural-gas-storage.

21 ALL Consulting LLC, "Underground Natural Gas Storage in the US", June 2016, https://iogcc.ok.gov/sites/g/files/gmc836/f/documents/2021/statesfirst_gas_storage_report.all_consulting.pdf.

interstate and half intrastate.[22] Interstate serves interstate facilities, such as providing storage for interstate gas transmission pipelines.[23] These types of storage facilities commonly receive surplus gas from interstate pipelines during warmer months and then send it back into the product stream during colder winter months. If a storage facility serves interstate commerce, it is subject to the jurisdiction of FERC; otherwise, it is state regulated.

Historically, natural gas storage facilities were used as a buffer between the near-constant supply and variable demand. Under this framework, storage was included with transmission and distribution as a bundled commodity that was sold by the pipelines to distribution utilities. In 1992 FERC issued regulations to the effect that interstate transmission companies were required to unbundle their services (transmission, storage and distribution). By unbundling transmission, storage and distribution services, the capacity in each was opened up to non-discriminatory and non-preferential contracts.[24] When this restriction was removed, anyone could use the available storage capacity for commercial or operational uses, giving rise to the first natural gas marketers.

This deregulation encouraged the construction of additional storage capacity and increased competition for the various parts of the downstream natural gas industry (transmission, storage and distribution), with a common goal of keeping prices low and reducing volatility.

As a reflection of this unbundling, the number of salt cavern storage sites developed has also grown steadily – principally because of their unique capabilities and high cycling rate (inventory turnover).[25] Nevertheless, conventional storage facilities are still very important to the industry.

The owners/operators of storage facilities are not necessarily the owners of the natural gas held in storage. Most working gas held in storage facilities is held under lease with shippers, LDCs or end users that own the gas. The type of entity that owns or operates the facility will determine to some extent how its storage capacity is utilised.

Interstate pipeline companies are required to operate their storage facilities on an open-access basis – that is, the major portion of working gas capacity (beyond what may be reserved by the pipeline/operator to maintain system integrity and for load balancing) at each site must be made available for lease to

22 US Energy Information Administration, "The Basics of Underground Natural Gas Storage", 16 November 2015, www.eia.gov/naturalgas/storage/basics/.

23 Pipeline and Hazardous Materials Safety Administration, Department of Transportation, "Pipeline Safety: Safety of Underground Natural Gas Storage Facilities", 2 December 2020, www.federalregister.gov/documents/2020/02/12/2020-00565/pipeline-safety-safety-of-underground-natural-gas-storage-facilities#footnote-8-p8106.

24 ALL Consulting LLC, "Underground Natural Gas Storage in the US", June 2016, https://iogcc.ok.gov/sites/g/files/gmc836/f/documents/2021/statesfirst_gas_storage_report.all_consulting.pdf.

25 Paul Metro, "Regulatory Framework for Natural Gas Storage in Pennsylvania and Tariff Development for Natural Gas Storage", Pennsylvania Public Utility Commission, https://pubs.naruc.org/pub.cfm?id=538938E5-2354-D714-51B7-7FCDF9266AFB.

third parties on a non-discriminatory basis.[26] In addition to interstate storage sites, many storage facilities owned or operated by large LDCs, intrastate pipelines and independent operators operate on an open-access basis – especially those sites affiliated with natural gas market centres. Open access has allowed storage to be used other than simply as backup inventory or as a supplemental seasonal supply source.

3.2 Europe

With strong demand for natural gas, Europe is home to several large consumer countries, most of which are highly dependent on the international market through imports via pipelines and LNG. Table 1 presents a ranking of the top European countries in terms of volume consumed in 2021. According to data from Rystad Energy,[27] storage levels in Europe remain low, with a volume 30% lower than the average for the last five years, equivalent to two months for the gas supply to meet next winter's demand.

This situation has placed market analysts and government bodies on high alert, making the region particularly vulnerable to market movements – as seen in the record high natural gas prices quoted at the Dutch Title Transfer Facility in 2022.[28] Catalysed by Russia's invasion of Ukraine, the European Commission has been outlining new planning and policies to reduce dependence on Russian natural gas imports and establish viable alternatives.[29]

Table 1. Consumption of natural gas in 2021 in billion cubic metres

Germany	90.5	Netherlands	35.1
United Kingdom	76.9	Spain	33.9
Italy	72.5	Ukraine	26.1
Turkey	57.3	Poland	23.2
France	43.0	Belgium	17.0

Source: Authors based on data from BP.[30]

26 US Energy Information Administration, "The Basics of Underground Natural Gas Storage", 16 November 2015, www.eia.gov/naturalgas/storage/basics/.

27 See *Oil & Gas Journal*, "Rystad: Russia-Ukraine tensions could jeopardize 30% of European gas demand", www.ogj.com/general-interest/economics-markets/article/14233531/rystad-russiaukraine-tensions-could-jeopardize-30-of-european-gas-demand.

28 *Ibid.*

29 M Fulwood, J Sharples and M Ouki, "Quarterly Gas Review: Short- and Medium-Term Outlook for Gas Markets", Oxford Institute for Energy Studies, May 2022, https://a9w7k6q9.stackpathcdn.com/wpcms/wp-content/uploads/2022/05/Gas-Quarterly-Review-Issue-17.pdf.

With a possible energy crisis in sight, the energy security debate is evolving among EU policymakers – especially in relation to the search for a source of gas supply as an alternative to dependence on Russian exports. In the short term, the conflict in Ukraine has triggered a debate on the insecurity of Russian supply in the second half of 2022, as the winter period in the northern hemisphere approached.

As highlighted by the IGU, in addition to the conflict in Eastern Europe, more extreme temperatures in recent winters – especially in 2020 – consumed substantial volumes of European stocks, contributing to the possibility of a large-scale crisis for the first time in the recent history of the global natural gas market. In seeking strategies to safely solve the problem of supply, the European Commission has mainly invested in options to increase and guarantee the natural gas storage capacity of member states.[31]

As an advantage, in the medium term, a good storage strategy can compensate for interruptions in the import chain by establishing minimum stock to use only in a crisis and encouraging policies for the rational use of energy by the population. To expand inventories through an alternative supply to Russian gas, one option that is increasingly being used is the installation of new LNG terminals – already, a total of 14 FSRU regasification vessel projects have been built in 11 European countries.[32]

To further address these risks, the European Union has adopted a new regulation to ensure that the storage capacity of member states – whether in FSRUs or underground structures – is filled to at least 80% of capacity before Winter 2022 and 90% before the following winter.[33]

However, according to the International Energy Agency (IEA), the reduction of supply through the Nord Stream pipeline could impact gas storage plans in Winter 2022.[34] Furthermore, Germany has come under threat from Russia, which has reduced natural gas flows through the pipelines of Ukraine and the Wysokoje region between Belarus and Poland. This situation could have severe repercussions for the European economy, as German industry is heavily dependent on natural gas imports.[35]

To meet the target set by the European Commission for Winter 2022, Fulwood *et al*[36] state that it will be necessary to inject about 38 billion cubic metres (bcm) of natural gas into storage infrastructure between mid-May and

---

30 BP, *Statistical Review of World Energy* 2021, www.bp.com/content/dam/bp/business-sites/en/global/corporate/pdfs/energy-economics/statistical-review/bp-stats-review-2021-full-report.pdf.

31 IGU, *World LNG Report 2022*, www.igu.org/resources/world-lng-report-2022/.

32 *Ibid.*

33 IEA, *Gas Market Report*, Q3-2022, July 2022, www.iea.org/reports/gas-market-report-q3-2022.

34 *Ibid.*

35 M Fulwood, J Sharples and M Ouki, "Quarterly Gas Review: Short- and Medium-Term Outlook for Gas Markets", Oxford Institute for Energy Studies, May 2022, https://a9w7k6q9.stackpathcdn.com/wpcms/wp-content/uploads/2022/05/Gas-Quarterly-Review-Issue-17.pdf.

36 *Ibid.*

October. This volume is slightly lower than what was injected during the same period in the previous year.

Planning to increase gas storage capacity, whether in a gaseous or liquefied state, will give European countries greater control and power to manage consumption at different times. The IGU data highlights that the world's gas storage is still unevenly distributed, concentrated between the United States, Russia and Europe; Europe has a total storage capacity of 33%. Figure 2 depicts the main countries with storage capacity.[37]

To this end, the European Commission has announced the REPowerEU plan, under which underground storage throughout the European Union would be filled to at least 90% of its capacity in October each year, preceding the winter period.[38]

In addition to greater investment in expanding storage and new FSRU projects, other policies debated by European governments are strongly linked to the reactivation of coal-fired thermal plants as an alternative to preserving natural gas stocks, as in Italy and Germany.[39]

Figure 2: Gas storage capacity in Europe

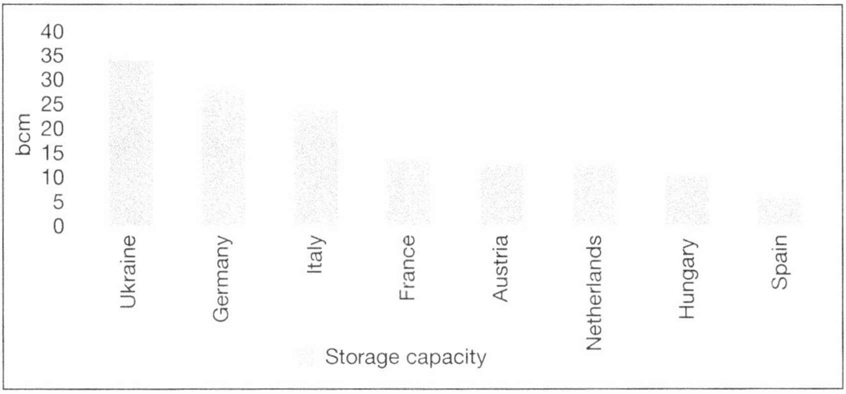

Source: Authors based on data from IGU.[40]

3.3 Asia-Pacific

Asia and the Pacific are two regions that, from an energy point of view, are interdependent. The LNG market is no different: 73.2% of LNG imports are directed to Asia, according to data from the International Group of Liquefied

37 IGU, *World LNG Report 2022*, www.igu.org/resources/world-lng-report-2022/.
38 *Ibid.*
39 M Fulwood, J Sharples and M Ouki, "Quarterly Gas Review: Short- and Medium-Term Outlook for Gas Markets", Oxford Institute for Energy Studies, May 2022, https://a9w7k6q9.stackpathcdn.com/wpcms/wp-content/uploads/2022/05/Gas-Quarterly-Review-Issue-17.pdf.
40 IGU, *World LNG Report 2022*, www.igu.org/resources/world-lng-report-2022/.

Natural Gas Imports (GIIGNL).[41] Both Australia and Qatar have positioned themselves as major exporters of LNG to the productive centres of China, Japan and South Korea.[42]

In China, LNG imports grew by 15% – or 10.4 million tons – in 2021. During that same period, China imported a total of 79.3 million tons of LNG, which was used to energise its economic recovery after the COVID-19 pandemic.[43] This trend was driven by the Chinese state strategy of not only replacing coal-fired thermoelectric plants with natural gas, but also using the demand for fuel in the international market to induce improvements in the local production chain, requiring investments in research and development (R&D) in the engineering and storage of natural gas.

In December 2021, the China National Offshore Oil Corporation (CNOOC) – China's largest LNG importer – signed a long-term LNG import contract with US company Venture Global LNG in order to purchase 3.5 million tonnes per annum (mtpa) of LNG from the Plaquemines and Calcasieu Pass terminals. Furthermore, the state-owned company is seeking to consolidate minority positions in Australian LNG production through partnerships with local companies.[44]

In the storage sector, CNOOC has excelled with large-scale projects to keep up with domestic demand for LNG. According to Maritime Executive , CNOOC has commenced the construction of the world's largest onshore LNG storage plant, with capacity at 9 mtpa; and it is seeking to double the infrastructure at the Yancheng terminal through the construction of six additional 270,000-cubic-metre tanks.[45]

Japan is another prominent market for the storage segment. Historically, the Japanese are major consumers of natural gas, especially in heavy industry. Following the Fukushima nuclear disaster in 2011, the flow of gas was expanded to generate electricity, as the country began to reduce its dependence on nuclear plants in the energy matrix.[46]

To this end, the import of LNG has become vital to the functioning of the Japanese economy. As a result, Japanese companies are increasingly participating in natural gas production projects abroad to supply the domestic

41 GIIGNL, *Annual Report 2022*, https://giignl.org/wp-content/uploads/2022/05/GIIGNL2022_Annual_Report_May24.pdf.

42 IGU, *World LNG Report 2022*, www.igu.org/resources/world-lng-report-2022/.

43 GIIGNL, *Annual Report 2022*, https://giignl.org/wp-content/uploads/2022/05/GIIGNL2022_Annual_Report_May24.pdf.

44 *Maritime Executive*, "China's CNOOC is building the World's Largest LNG Storage Tanks", 22 February 2022, https://maritime-executive.com/article/china-s-cnooc-is-building-the-world-s-largest-lng-storage-tanks.

45 *Ibid.*

46 Satoru Hashimoto (2020), "A New Idea for LNG Trade: Enhancing Market Competition through a Tanker-Based Trading System", *Journal of Asian Energy Studies* 4 (1): 9–19. https://doi.org/10.24112/jaes.040002.

market. In 2021, Japan imported 166.21 mcm of LNG, accounting for 20% of global demand for the fuel.[47]

Storage is thus a strategic component to ensure Japanese energy security. Japan's tank system is designed to facilitate flexibility in supply, which guarantees price stabilisation and expands the negotiation margin for contracts in the short term (spot market), medium term and long term. However, there are many practical difficulties, as the distribution system for large consumer centres is not fully integrated with LNG terminals.[48]

Another Asian country that is a key player in LNG storage is South Korea. As the country is a major gas importer, Korean companies were encouraged by the government to specialise in transport engineering, tanking and maintenance services for natural gas terminals. Korea Gas Corporation (KOGAS) holds 90% of Korean LNG imports, making the market extremely concentrated.[49]

KOGAS's business model is to import LNG to generate electricity and heat for homes, commerce and industry through a portfolio of subsidiary companies. Storage and maintenance activities are conducted through KOGAS-Tech, a subsidiary specialising in engineering and R&D in the natural gas area. KOGAS-Tech is one of the few companies with expertise in the design, construction and maintenance of cryogenic tanks for LNG storage and other utilities for the natural gas industry.

South Korea also stands out for its advanced shipping industry, which has a close relationship with the LNG storage market due to its specialisation in the construction of LNG, FSRU and FSU carriers. According to GIIGNL, Hyundai Heavy Industries, Daewoo Shipbuilding and Marine Engineering and Samsung Heavy Industries received the main orders for LNG, FSRU and FSU carrier tanks between 2020 and 2021.[50]

In addition, with the economic growth of Southeast Asian countries, demand for LNG has increased sharply due to the gradual reduction of traditional biomass *vis-à-vis* fossil-fuel-based energy intensification to power the industrialisation of emerging economies. According to the IEA, between 2000 and 2020 natural gas in Southeast Asia's energy mix increased by 83.8%, with a slight drop in 2020 due to the outbreak of the COVID-19 pandemic.[51]

The IEA has primarily identified energy intensification in the economies of Malaysia, Indonesia, Thailand, Vietnam and Myanmar. LNG is in significant demand in these markets due to the lack of interregional gas pipelines; this

47 GIIGNL, *Annual Report 2022*, https://giignl.org/wp-content/uploads/2022/05/GIIGNL2022_Annual_Report_May24.pdf.

48 Satoru Hashimoto (2020), "A New Idea for LNG Trade: Enhancing Market Competition through a Tanker-Based Trading System", *Journal of Asian Energy Studies* 4 (1): 9–19. https://doi.org/10.24112/jaes.040002.

49 KOGAS, "Natural Gas Information", www.kogas.or.kr/site/eng/1040201000000.

50 GIIGNL, *Annual Report 2022*, https://giignl.org/wp-content/uploads/2022/05/GIIGNL2022_Annual_Report_May24.pdf.

51 IEA, *Southeast Asia Energy Outlook 2022*, www.iea.org/reports/southeast-asia-energy-outlook-2022.

Figure 3. Energy supply by fuel in Southeast Asia[52]

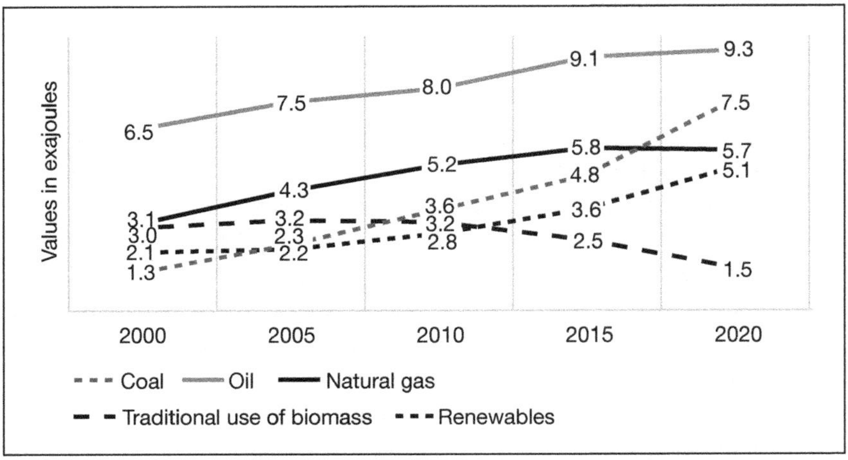

Source: Authors based on data from IEA.[53]

requires the movement of fuel by sea, which is facilitated by the construction of receiving, storage and regasification terminals. Thus, natural gas is a strategic resource for these countries due to the security that it affords for industrialisation, while also contributing to emissions reductions, since natural gas is less polluting than coal and oil.[54]

The use of natural gas in these markets has also driven an increase in LNG re-exports throughout the region, as oil and gas multinationals and LNG exporting companies respond more quickly to LNG-dependent markets such as Japan, China, South Korea and Taiwan. In this business model, the construction of storage hubs with easy access to commercial maritime routes has reduced the costs associated with long sea voyages, while also ensuring the supply of fuel at competitive prices in Asia through short and medium-term contracts.

LNG re-export hubs are mostly concentrated in Singapore (10%), but are also present in Thailand (2%), and Indonesia (3%). They primarily serve the Chinese (18%), Indian (13%), Japanese (7%) and South Korean (5%) markets.[55] The inauguration of LNG exports from Papua New Guinea in 2014 has further diversified the sources of supply in Asia-Pacific, which guarantees the flexibility needed for importers to acquire LNG at competitive prices.[56]

52 Note that an exajoule (EJ) is equivalent to 1 quintillion joules.
53 IEA, *Southeast Asia Energy Outlook 2022*, www.iea.org/reports/southeast-asia-energy-outlook-2022.
54 *Ibid.*
55 GIIGNL, *Annual Report 2022*, https://giignl.org/wp-content/uploads/2022/05/GIIGNL2022_Annual_Report_May24.pdf.
56 IGU, *World LNG Report 2022*, www.igu.org/resources/world-lng-report-2022/.

4. Conclusion

In the United States, the increase in domestic production of natural gas through shale gas reservoirs is expected to continue, strengthening the country's position as an LNG exporting power. However, given the economic recovery in Asia and the energy crisis in Europe, sound planning will be required so that, in addition to exporting LNG loads and advancing the national economy, the United States can maintain its storage levels in a strategic way.

Under average conditions, and from a nationwide perspective, gas storage has historically appeared adequate to meet seasonal demand and plays a critical role in ensuring the energy independence and reliability of the US energy supply. It has also reduced the need for larger transmission pipelines and allowed for a continuous supply of natural gas in the event of supply interruptions. Gas storage may be the best way to manage gas commodity prices, so the long-term adequacy of storage investment will depend on how much price volatility customers consider acceptable. Ongoing commodity price volatility further indicates that more storage may be appropriate.

Over the past 10 years, natural gas storage in the United States has increased by 16% – prompted, in part, by significant growth in domestic shale gas production. Underground gas storage will continue to be carried out in a manner that ensures the reliable delivery of natural gas to the nation for the foreseeable future.

Across the Atlantic, with the recent crisis triggered by the war in Ukraine and the potential risk of shortages in the coming years, the European market has seen significant changes, such as reduced industrial demand and energy generation, and high projections for injections into the storage network and shipping of LNG. However, as highlighted by Fulwood *et al*,[57] the main powers in the bloc will remain dependent on physical flows from Russian gas pipelines for a long time to come. As a result, bodies such as the European Commission are in a state of high alert and have recognised the difficulty of achieving their stipulated goals. The REPowerEU strategy seeks to reduce this dependency on Russian gas by two-thirds in the short term.

The availability of LNG in Europe also depends on the levels of demand and supply between producing and consuming countries. Asia could play an increased demand-side role in this regard, given the significance of Russian supply to geopolitical issues. In supply terms, while Asia may be threatened by possible European competition for global LNG supplies, it should also benefit from the diversion of Russian natural gas flows, as countries such as China and India have strong trade relations with Russia.

57 M Fulwood, J Sharples and M Ouki, "Quarterly Gas Review: Short- and Medium-Term Outlook for Gas Markets", Oxford Institute for Energy Studies, May 2022, https://a9w7k6q9.stackpathcdn.com/wpcms/wp-content/uploads/2022/05/Gas-Quarterly-Review-Issue-17.pdf.

The current energy crisis in Europe demonstrates that, while still a long way off, independence from Russian gas supplies is not impossible to achieve. By maximising storage strategies and seeking supply solutions through LNG, the continent is taking a late but vital step towards future independence. Measures such as planned consumption, both industrial and residential, are important to maintain the level of storage in the short term – especially given the uncertainties of supply and gas flows coming from Ukraine. Investment in new energy sources, diversification of use and research into both new renewable technologies and fossil sources should help mitigate the effects of the crisis and enhance energy security.

Natural gas storage operators have consistently provided safe and reliable natural gas storage around the world. Because of the critical role that storage plays in national energy portfolios, natural gas storage operators are continually searching for new equipment, processes and methodologies to improve safety and reliability.

The legal aspects of cross-border pipelines

Chowdhury Ishrak Ahmed Siddiky
University of Asia Pacific

1. Introduction

The legal framework governing cross-border pipelines is rather complicated, as there is no single overarching regime that applies worldwide. This chapter outlines the various types of cross-border pipelines and the international agreements and conventions that govern their construction and operation. Geopolitics also play a crucial role in determining the success or failure of cross-border pipeline projects.

2. Different types of cross-border pipelines

There are two types of cross-border pipelines. First, domestic pipelines are governed by the national laws of the country through which the pipeline passes. As such pipelines may pass through several different countries,[1] the pipeline chain may have several operators or owners at the same time. Further, "the regulation of transnational pipeline issues is based on contracts between owners or operators of national sections, or by agreements with respective governments".[2] Although a sound legal framework can help to reduce the risk of disputes between various contractual parties in the transnational pipeline chain, "the most durable would be bilateral and multilateral treaties that provide the legal foundation on which commercial agreements relating to cross-border pipelines would be based".[3]

The second type is the international model, whereby the entire pipeline chain is considered as a single integrated entity. Such pipelines are generally governed by various intergovernmental agreements and commercial contracts between the parties involved in the pipeline project. These kinds of projects are "protected by intergovernmental agreements proscribing unwarranted disruption of the flow and undue burdens of excessive transit fees or taxes".[4] They are typically found in politically volatile areas, where active participation by the relevant governments is needed to ensure the smooth operation of the project.

1 In each country the pipeline will fall under that country's domestic laws.
2 S Vinogradov, *Cross-border Oil and Gas Pipelines: International Legal and Regulatory Regimes*, AIPN study, 2001.
3 World Bank, *Russian Oil Transport and Export Study, Strategic Export Expansion Options and Legal, Contractual and Regulatory Framework*, 1997.
4 R Lagoni, "Pipelines", in *Encyclopedia of Public International Law*, 3, 1997.

3. Legal framework

International legal agreements such as the Energy Charter Treaty (ECT), the World Trade Organization (WTO) agreements and the 1921 Barcelona Convention are also relevant to cross-border pipelines. However, their objectives are different[5] and are not aligned with the needs of such projects.[6] A distinction may be drawn here between offshore and onshore pipelines. Offshore pipelines are governed by international law in the form of the 1982 United Nations Convention on the Law of the Sea (UNCLOS).[7] UNCLOS sets out a clear framework on the construction, operation and protection of offshore pipelines.[8]

Onshore pipelines have no status under international law; instead, they are governed by bilateral or multilateral agreements between the various parties involved in the pipeline project. Although international treaties do not specifically regulate cross-border pipelines, they do set out certain principles and rules on the various means of transport and communication. The principles of freedom of transit, non-interference, non-discrimination and equal treatment are vital for cross-border pipeline projects.[9]

4. International legal arrangements

4.1 UNCLOS

UNCLOS is the most complicated, comprehensive and multifaceted treaty ever adopted to control and protect the rights and interests of both coastal states and other states. It has been ratified and acceded to by more than 160 states.[10] The most relevant provisions of UNCLOS in relation to cross-border pipelines are as follows:

- Article 56 concerns the rights, jurisdictions and duties of coastal states in exclusive economic zones;[11]
- Article 58 concerns the rights and duties of other states in exclusive economic zones;[12]
- Articles 79 and 182 concern the laying of submarine cables and pipelines in the sea;[13]
- Article 114 concerns damage caused by the owners of a submarine cable or pipeline to another submarine cable or pipeline; and

5 That is, they are more geared towards investment and trade and not specifically directed towards pipelines or their problems.
6 *Supra*, n 2, pp20–28.
7 *Ibid*, pp29–35.
8 *Ibid*.
9 CIA Siddiky, *Cross-border Pipelines Arrangements: What Would a Single Regulatory Framework Look Like?* Kluwer Law International, 2011.
10 See www.un.org/depts/los/convention_agreements/texts/unclos/UNCLOS-TOC.htm.
11 *Ibid*.
12 *Ibid*.
13 *Ibid*.

- Article 115 concerns the indemnity for loss incurred in avoiding injury to a submarine pipeline.[14]

The legal status of submarine pipelines is determined by the legal regime governing different maritime zones, such as:

- territorial seas;
- archipelagic seas;
- exclusive economic zones;
- continental shelves; and
- the high seas.[15]

The nature of the pipeline is an important criterion in determining whether the pipeline falls under a coastal state's national regulations or under international regulations. A distinction may be drawn between pipelines that constitute an integral part of offshore installations and operations and long-distance oil or gas transmission pipelines.[16] Further, according to Article 79(4) of UNCLOS, "nothing in this part affects the coastal state's jurisdiction over cables and pipelines constructed or used in connection with the exploration of its continental shelf or exploitation of its resources or the operations of artificial islands, installations and structures under its jurisdictions".[17]

The territorial sea is part of a coastal state's territory and as such, a coastal state may decide on the status of submarine pipelines in its territorial seas. Thus, pipelines can be constructed and installed only with the permission of the coastal state. UNCLOS gives the coastal state the right to formulate its own rules and regulations on the construction of any submarine pipelines or installations within its territorial waters.

The high seas, by contrast, are not exclusive to any one particular country; all states are free to use them. According to Article 87 of UNCLOS: "The high seas are open to all States, whether coastal or landlocked. Freedom of the high seas ... comprises inter alia, both for coastal and landlocked states: freedom to lay submarine cables and pipelines, subject to Part VI."[18] However, there are certain limitations on the general freedom of the high seas, which includes the laying of submarine pipelines. Submarine pipelines must be laid in the general interests of multiple states rather than just one single state. Further, due regard must be paid to activities in the deep seabed area. Article 79(5) provides that: "States require to pay due regard to cables and pipelines already in position."[19]

When it comes to exclusive economic zones and continental shelves, the

14 *Ibid.*
15 *Ibid.*
16 *Ibid.*
17 See *supra* n 9, p35.
18 See *supra* n 9, p39.
19 *Supra*, n 9, p40.

interests of coastal states and other states must be balanced. Article 56(2) of UNCLOS provides that: "in exercising its rights in the EEZ, the coastal state shall have due regard to the rights and duties of other states and shall act in a manner compatible with the provisions of this Convention."[20] The freedom to lay submarine pipelines in exclusive economic zones comes with certain limitations, in that due regard must be given to the rights and duties of the coastal state. Therefore, a state or any other entity must comply with the rules and regulations adopted by the coastal state in accordance with UNCLOS and other instruments of international law. Moreover, Article 79(1) of UNCLOS states that: "all states are entitled to lay submarine cables and pipelines on the continental shelf, in accordance with the provisions of this article."[21] Article 79(2) provides that entities and states must ensure that pipelines do not cause pollution.[22] Further, Article 235 provides that states are responsible for the fulfilment of their international obligations and must ensure that recourse is available in accordance with their legal systems for prompt and adequate compensation.[23]

Part XV of UNCLOS provides for dispute resolution between state parties, including through international adjudication, arbitration and special arbitration.

4.2 Covenant of the League of Nations, 1919

According to this treaty: "the members of the League would make provision to secure and maintain freedom of Communications and of transit and equitable treatment for the commence of all Members of the League."[24] The covenant was the first of its kind, ensuring that countries could freely transfer good and services without discrimination. Equal treatment and freedom of transit are two principles enshrined by the covenant.

4.3 1965 Convention on Transit Trade of Land-Locked States

This treaty was the first of its kind dealing with the issues faced by land-locked states. It does not include any specific provisions on pipelines; however, signatory states may include these should the need arise. Its key provisions include the following:

- Article 1 concerns freedom of transit;
- Article 2 concerns non-discrimination;
- Article 3 concerns non-interruption of good and services in transit;[25] and

---

20 *Supra,* n 11.
21 http://treaties.un.org/pages/ViewDetails.aspx?src=TREATY&mtdsg_no=X-3&chapter=10&lang=en.
22 *Ibid.*
23 *Ibid.*
24 Article 23(e) of the convention states this.
25 *Supra,* n 21.

- Articles 11 and 12 provide for certain exceptions to the convention, including protection of a contracting party's essential security interests.[26]

The main problem with this convention is that it is based on reciprocity between states. If one contracting state decides not to cooperate with another, none of the contracting parties can force it to act and a separate agreement might be required between the countries in respect to non-interruption of goods and services.

4.4 1921 Barcelona Convention and Statute on Freedom of Transit

This convention was signed just after the Covenant of the League of Nations in 1919, giving a more political justification to the principle of freedom of transit. Its main objective was to "proclaim the right of free transit and to make regulations thereon as being one of the best means of developing cooperation between states".[27] Important aspects of the convention include the following:

- State parties must facilitate free transit by rail or waterways on convenient routes for international transit (Article 2);[28]
- States cannot impose special dues in respect of transit, save for those which are levied solely to defray the costs of supervision and administration (Article 3); and[29]
- States can take reasonable precautionary measures to ensure the safety of routes, means of communications and other related interests (Article 5).[30]

Although the Barcelona Convention is not directly relevant to cross-border pipelines, it enshrines important principles such as freedom of transit and non-interruption of good and services, which are vital to the proper functioning of cross-border pipelines. Further, some of its principles have acquired the status of customary international law, which applies to any transit-related activities.[31]

5. Energy Charter Treaty

The ECT was first proposed during the 1990s by former Dutch Prime Minister Ruud Lubbers, who thought that the breakdown of the Soviet Union would cause problems for the Eastern European countries that were previously dependent on it. At a ministerial meeting in The Hague in 1991, 49 countries signed the European Energy Charter, which subsequently led to the signing of the ECT in 1994.[32]

---

26 *Ibid.*
27 See http://treaties.un.org/Pages/LONViewDetails.aspx?src=LON&id=554&lang=en.
28 *Ibid.*
29 *Ibid.*
30 *Supra*, n 9, p54.
31 *Supra*, n 9, p55.
32 *The Energy Charter Treaty: The Reader's Guide*, www.encharter.org.

The ECT was intended to help both the Eastern European countries and the newly independent countries of the Caspian region, which needed a legal and investment framework to attract investments from big multinationals. It also aimed to:

- promote energy-related investment and trade;
- alleviate transportation and political risk; and
- protect the investments of multinationals that invested in these regions.[33]

The ECT regarded investment protection, trade and transit as the most important goals of the European Union and sought to ensure that the newly independent Caspian countries and the Eastern European countries pursued the liberal ideas of the European Union. By focusing on these three areas, the ECT sought to help these states to achieve the goal of economic and political stability.

The ECT's investment protection regime protects investors from expropriation and other legal and political risks. It provides the stability that big companies need to make long-term investments in these countries. The ECT expects all signatory states to align themselves with the provisions of the General Agreement on Tariffs and Trade (GATT), which advocates for free trade all over the world.[34]

Transit is another important issue that is covered under the ECT. One of the main objectives and goals of the ECT was to facilitate the transportation of energy products without hindrance or discrimination. This is extremely important because many countries are either landlocked or dependent on other countries for their energy supply; strong and fair transit facilities thus help to mitigate some of the problems that these countries may face. Article 7(10) defines the concept of 'energy transit' as follows:

(i) the carriage through area of a contracting party, or to or from port facilities in its area for loading or unloading, of energy materials and products originating in the area of another state or (ii) the carriage through the area of a contracting party of energy materials and products originating in the area of another contracting party and destined for the area of that other contracting party…[35]

The ECT allows countries and companies to invest in energy transit and to obtain necessary supplies of energy. The interests of all parties in relation to energy transit are dealt with under Article 7 of the ECT. The transit issue is extremely complex because it requires significant long-term capital and

33 TW Walde, *The Energy Charter Treaty: An East West Gateway for Investment and Trade*, Kluwer Law International, 1996.

34 W Shan, "Towards a Common European Community Policy on Investment Issues", 2 *Journal of World Investment*, 2001.

35 The Energy Charter Treaty at www.energychartertreaty.org.

technological investment. There are also many different parties involved and it is quite difficult to fulfil all of their demands. As one expert pointed out:

> *carriage of energy materials, petroleum and especially gas, requires costly investments, sometimes as costly as or costlier than the investments needed for production. This requires a stable legal framework because it is a long term approach and this is precisely what the ECT seeks to achieve by providing a sectoral international legal regime for energy.*[36]

Article 7 of the ECT deals with access to transit, non-discrimination and conditions of transit. Important provisions include:

- Article 7(1), which states that the contracting parties must take measures to facilitate the transit of energy materials without discrimination as to origin and without unreasonable delay;[37] and
- Article 7(2), which concerns the modernisation of infrastructure.[38]

The interests of exporting, importing and transit countries vary significantly. Exporting countries will seek to export energy as cheaply as possible and will thus choose a transportation route which will keep costs low and increase their income. They will also want to export their resources as quickly as possible – especially if their economy is heavily reliant on energy exports. Importing countries will want to import energy at an affordable price and obtain a stable and secure supply. The role of transit countries is limited to the transportation of energy across their territories. They can earn a substantial amount of revenue for letting energy resources pass through their territories and may also enjoy access to hydrocarbon resources at a preferential rate. However, if the transit country is also an exporting or importing country, this might cause problems because its interests may then diverge.[39]

One of the main roles of the ECT concerns the resolution of transit disputes. This is undertaken under Articles 7(6) and (7), 26 and 27.[40] Article 7(6) deals with the non-interruption of transit in case of a dispute.[41] Article 7(6) states that even if there is a dispute between the parties, they cannot disrupt the flow of any resources due to the conflict until and unless the dispute is settled.

Article 7(7) describes the various mechanisms available to parties to resolve their disputes. Article 7(7) states that "it shall apply to a dispute over any matter arising from an existing transit".[42] If there is a dispute between the parties, they must first inform the secretary general of the Charter Conference Secretariat of

---

36 *Ibid.*
37 *Ibid.*
38 *Ibid.*
39 *Ibid*
40 *Ibid.*
41 J Dore and R De Bauw, *The Energy Charter Treaty – Origins, Aims and Prospects*, Royal Institute of International Affairs, 1995.
42 The Energy Charter Treaty at www.energychartertreaty.org.

the dispute. The secretariat will then consider whether the parties have fulfilled their obligations and whether they have taken advantage of all mechanisms available to them. Once it is satisfied that all mechanisms have been exhausted by the parties, the secretariat will then give the parties time to prepare for the procedure. During this time, all signatory countries will also be informed of the dispute. After consultation with all parties involved, the secretary general will appoint a conciliator within 30 days. The conciliator's main role is to resolve the differences between the two sides and help them reach agreement.[43]

If the conflicting parties fail to reach agreement within 90 days of the conciliator's appointment, the conciliator can pass an interim order regarding the tariffs and other matters in dispute in under Article 7(7)(c). Both parties are bound to follow that decision for a year. If the parties reach agreement, they will be bound by that agreement and the conciliator need not adjudicate on the matter. The ECT also has a conciliation mechanism aimed at helping disputing parties before they resort to the national courts for relief.

After the expiry of one year, if the parties still have not reached an agreement, they can proceed to arbitration under Articles 26 and 27 of the ECT. According to Article 26, "disputes arising from any sort of investment can be addressed under this article".[44] Transit in this case is considered as an investment under Article 1(6) of the ECT.[45] If there is any dispute regarding the interpretation of the treaty, Article 27 deals with this issue.[46]

5.1 The Draft Energy Charter Protocol on Transit

Negotiations on the draft protocol on the ECT on transit started in 2000 and as yet the parties have not fully agreed on the various terms and conditions of the protocol.[47] There is an emphasis on the definition of available capacity and the establishment of the principles governing transit tariffs.[48] It is widely acknowledged that successful implementation of the transit protocol would:

- reduce the risks involved in transit;
- improve the financing of projects related to transit;
- improve the competitiveness of supplies; and
- provide greater energy security.[49]

At the Energy Charter conference in 2002, all 51 members agreed on the initial draft of the protocol but there are still countries that have problems with

---

43 *Supra*, n 40.
44 KP Waern, "Transit Provisions of the Energy Charter Treaty and the Energy Charter Protocol on Transit", 20 *Journal of Energy and Natural Resources Law*, 2002, pp172–183.
45 *Ibid*.
46 *Ibid*.
47 A Konoplyanik, "Gas Transit in Eurasia: Transit Issues between Russia and the European Union and the Role of Energy Charter", *Journal of Energy and Natural Resources Law*, pp445–486.
48 *Ibid*, p454.
49 *Supra*, n 47, p481.

the protocol and have thus not signed up to it.[50] The features of the new protocol include the following:

- an obligation to observe transit agreements;[51]
- a prohibition on the unauthorised taking of energy materials and products in transit;[52]
- a definition of available capacity in energy transport facilities;[53]
- negotiated third-party access to available capacity;[54]
- a duty to facilitate the construction, expansion or operation of energy transport facilities used for transit;[55]
- coordination in the event of accidental interruption, reduction or stoppage of transit;[56] and
- a requirement that transit tariffs be:
  - non-discriminatory, objective, reasonable and transparent;
  - not affected by market distortions; and
  - cost based.

6. General Agreement on Trade and Transit and World Trade Organization agreements

Although the GATT and WTO principles are geared towards international trade, they also have implications for energy trade. Article 1 of GATT deals with most-favoured nation treatment (MFN). MFN means that "WTO members are obliged to extend any advantage, favour or privilege or immunity granted to any product originating in or destined for any country to like product originating in or destined for the territories of all other WTO members".[57] The MFN clause ensures that no country will enjoy an unfair advantage over another. This relates to levies such as customs duties and charges that are imposed on the international export or import of international transfer payments.[58]

In the case of energy, if a WTO member imposes a border tax, regulations or other internal measures on an energy product from a particular country, it must apply similar conditions or measures to energy products coming from other countries.

Article III of GATT deals with the national treatment of imported goods. Article III provides that "with respect to internal taxation and domestic laws, regulations and requirements, imported products shall be accorded treatment

50 The Energy Charter Treaty Protocol at www.energychartertreaty.org.
51 *Ibid.*
52 *Ibid.*
53 *Ibid.*
54 *Ibid.*
55 *Ibid.*
56 *Ibid.*
57 Y Selivanova, *The WTO and Energy: WTO Rules and Agreements of Relevance to the Energy Sector*, Energy Charter Secretariat, ICTSD, Issue Paper 1, August 2007.
58 *Ibid.*

no less favourable than that accorded to domestic products".[59] The national treatment clause differs from the MFN clause in that it takes effect once the goods enter the domestic market. MFN applies to both exports and imports of goods; whereas national treatment applies only to imports and not exports.[60] In the case of energy trade, imported energy products must be dealt with in the same way as domestic products, and no extra charges or customs duties can be imposed which might afford domestic providers an unfair advantage. However, this relates only to 'like' products, meaning that a government cannot impose taxes or charges on imported products which are similar to domestic energy products produced at home. This means that governments can impose taxes and charges on imported products which are not 'like' the domestic products.[61]

Quantitative restrictions are another aspect of the WTO rules which can have an impact on energy trade. Article XI on quantitative restrictions states that "protection should be carried out through tariffs and not through measures directly affecting the volumes".[62] This protection of exports and imports is also relevant to energy trade, because it reduces the amount of imports or exports that can be effected by any country. For example, if imported goods are cheaper than domestic goods, such a restriction will not allow them to compete effectively in the domestic market. Similarly, exports may not be competitive due to higher prices. An energy exporting or importing country can invoke the right to introduce temporary quantitative restrictions under this article if there is a serious shortfall of energy products in its country. In that case, a short-term ban or restriction on energy exports and imports may help to overcome the problem.

Market access is another aspect of the WTO rules. However, energy products do not suffer from problems with market access because of their nature. During the Uruguay Round of negotiations, the tariffs for hydrocarbons were reduced.[63] Hydrocarbon exports normally face high tariffs because of the prices set by exporters. However, it is in exporters' interest not to overcharge because this might make them less competitive. Importing countries are interested in obtaining energy supplies at a low price. However, the export duties imposed on these resources must be made on an MFN basis.[64,65]

The role of state trading enterprises is also covered in the WTO agreements and has caused some concerns among energy trading countries. In the energy sector, state companies play an active role in the transportation, production and management of energy resources. Since these enterprises are actively involved

---

59 The GATT Agreement at www.wto.org.
60 *Ibid.*
61 *Supra,* n 57.
62 *Supra,* n 59.
63 *Supra,* n 60.
64 J Pauwelyn, *Trade in Energy: WTO Rules Applying under the Energy Charter Treat,* ECS, 2001.
65 Pipelines are specifically excluded from this.

in the export and import of energy, questions have been asked about their role under the WTO rules.

According to Article XVII of GATT, "GATT members undertake to ensure that state trading enterprises act in a manner consistent with the general principles of non-discrimination prescribed under GATT".[66] Although this article clearly imposes obligations on states in relation to their state enterprises, most of these state enterprises are involved in the transportation of energy resources and in turn give access to third parties. A problem arises as to whether this article obliges state enterprises that control transportation infrastructure to act in a non-discriminatory manner in relation to other companies or competitors.[67]

It is difficult to interpret this article in line with energy trade, especially when it comes to transportation infrastructure. In most countries, energy companies have been privatised, raising the question of whether they have the same obligations as the state or state-run enterprises. According to some experts, private companies might also fall under this provision, as Article XVII "applies to any enterprises that possess exclusive or special privileges granted by the state".[68] This is quite ambiguous and lacks precision, which will further increase the risk of conflicts between energy trading countries.

Transit is another issue that is addressed in the WTO rules.[69] Article V states that "there shall be freedom of transit through the territory of each member, via the routes most convenient for international transit, for traffic in transit to or from the territory of other members".[70] The rules also state that any form of transit must not be subject to delays or any other restrictions.[71] They also advocate for an exemption from transit duties and any other charges. This means that WTO members involved in transit cannot charge customs duties or tariffs for hydrocarbon resources that pass through their country.[72] However, they can charge for administrative, transportation and other expenses relating to transit.[73] These expenses must be in line with Article V.

However, this aspect of the WTO rules is not followed within the energy trade in practice, as transit countries can charge excessive fees depending on their bargaining power. Good examples are Ukraine and Belarus, which sought to increase the transit tariff despite there being an agreed tariff structure between the two countries and Russia.[74] Moreover, all forms of transit are based

66 *Supra*, n 59.
67 *Supra*, n 64.
68 *Supra*, n 59.
69 Again, with the exception of pipelines.
70 *Supra*, n 59.
71 *Ibid.*
72 The reason why this is not a solution to the transit problems associated with pipelines is because Article V does not take into account the geopolitical aspects of these projects.
73 UNCTAD, *Trade Agreements, Petroleum and Energy Policies*, UNCTAD/ITCD/TSB/9. United Nations, 2000.
74 A Belyi *et al*, "A New Energy Charter: Myth or Reality?", *Oil, Gas and Energy Law*, 2009.

on negotiation between the actors involved in the project. There are instances where a producing country is also a transit country. Some hydrocarbon-rich countries are landlocked and in those instances bilateral negotiations rather than WTO rules and regulations play an important role. The WTO Dispute Settlement Body (DSB) has not yet dealt with a single case involving transit problems, which further puts this body in a difficult situation.[75]

In order for Article V to take effect, all parties to the dispute must be members of GATT or the WTO. For example, if the exporting country and the importing country are members of WTO but the transit country is not, the transit country will not be bound by the obligations laid down in Article V. This kind of scenario raises problems in relation to the transport of energy, especially via pipelines. However, Article V(2) of GATT states that nothing in the article limits a WTO member's scope to raise concerns if a dispute arises. Article V will apply if:

- there is a transit through the territory of a WTO member;
- either the exporting or importing country is a WTO member; and
- the country which is alleging that the right to freedom of transit, as stipulated in Article V of the GATT, has been violated has access to the WTO DSB (ie, it is a WTO member).[76]

The WTO DSB may not be the appropriate forum for energy-related claims, because the WTO rules do not specifically deal with energy-related problems – although they are not excluded from its rules. Some of the WTO rules – such as Article XI on quantitative restrictions and Article I on MFN treatment – are relevant to energy, but they are not always ideal for dealing with the energy trade. There are several reasons for this, including:

- the uniqueness of the energy trade;
- the fact that resources are not always distributed evenly and there are thus vital economic and social issues for countries that are dependent on these resources;
- the natural monopolies dominant in the sector; and
- the different interests of exporting and importing countries, which make it quite challenging to reach a consensus among the different parties.[77]

All these factors militate against some of the key ideals of the WTO rules, making it difficult for the WTO DSB to assess the conflicts brought before it.

The WTO rules also deal more with import barriers than with export

75 This is because the countries involved in the conflict might be of the opinion that the DSB is incapable of handling transit disputes or lacks credibility due to its lack of experience in solving transit disputes.

76 *Supra*, n 74.

77 T Walde and A Gunst, *International Energy Trade and Access to Competing Networks* in *Energy and Environmental Services: Negotiating Objectives and Development Priorities*, UNCTAD, United Nations, 2003.

barriers, which is also problematic for energy exporting countries. Energy exporting countries would like to see greater access to markets and fewer hindrances to exports. This is especially the case for countries that are heavily reliant on energy exports: any import barriers or higher taxes would reduce their revenues, which is not ideal. Therefore, the WTO rules might not always be suitable for them. There are also many countries involved in the energy trade that are not members of the WTO because they are sceptical of its rules and regulations.[78] In fact, non-WTO members make up 50% of world trade in energy products.[79] However, as these countries have grown more powerful over the years, it has become imperative for the WTO to try to bring them into the fold. Any conflict between a WTO member and a non-member cannot be brought before the WTO DSB because one of the parties is not a member of the organisation.[80] This further hinders the effectiveness of the WTO DSB in energy disputes.

Transit is an extremely important issue in the energy trade. Although the WTO rules indirectly deal with this factor, they are not ideal for actors involved in the energy business. Article V of GATT highlights the issue of freedom of transit, calling for an exemption from transit duties and a uniform way of calculating costs and services. In reality, however, transit countries can negotiate for a higher rent from exporting or importing countries, depending on their bargaining power. If the exporting or importing country is landlocked, the demands of the transit country might be even greater. Accordingly, no case regarding transit has yet been brought before the DSB and most of the problems regarding transit have arisen from the WTO DSB framework.

Some of these states (eg, Iran, Iraq, Algeria, Kazakhstan and Azerbaijan) are not members of the WTO. Transit problems in the energy trade do not always involve these states, but rather powerful and influential energy companies which are part of the consortiums that own the pipelines. Article V of GATT "does not provide any effective obligation on the members of the WTO to ensure that the companies owning the pipelines abide by the transit obligation enshrined in Article V".[81] This further highlights the lack of relevance of the WTO DSB in dealing with energy disputes.

While the WTO rules and its DSB are innovative and flexible in dealing with trade disputes, they could also help in dealing with energy-related conflicts. By being members of the WTO, energy trading countries could benefit by bringing claims before the WTO DSB relating to issues such as:

- the discriminatory aspects of energy-related environmental regulations;
- border tax problems;

---

78 *Ibid.*
79 *Ibid.*
80 *Ibid.*
81 *Supra*, n 59.

- energy efficiency standards;
- inspection and regulation; and
- access to markets.[82]

The WTO DSB provides such a platform for energy trading countries. However, it is a less attractive option for those countries that rely on energy imports for their economic development, due to factors such as:

- the problems relating to restrictive practices within energy exporting countries;
- the monopolistic nature of the companies involved in the energy trade, and their special privileges and rights; and
- transit problems.[83]

Most energy-related agreements are bilateral or regional in nature. Therefore, a multilateral framework such as the WTO, which lacks any specific provisions on energy, might not be beneficial for energy exporting, importing and transit countries. The energy trade is a unique and niche area which requires technical knowledge and a customised approach.[84] The WTO DSB does not seem to provide this.

The WTO DSB also does not address the problems faced by participants involved in the pipeline regime. Although the WTO has a mechanism to address economic disputes after they have arisen, it does not provide any kind of safety net for the other actors involved in the pipeline regime when there is intervention from the government or other actors due to economic, geopolitical or legal reasons.[85]

Additionally, pipeline disputes generally require quick resolution by experts who are familiar with these sorts of problems. The WTO DSB does not have the necessary expertise to deal with these problems quickly and any issues brought before it take a long time to be resolved.

The WTO DSB further does not serve a regulatory function and can only become involved once the parties have approached it with a problem. This might not be suitable for cross-border pipeline disputes; a more proactive and regulatory approach is thus needed to protect the interests of all actors in a regime when there is intervention from other players or from external bodies for geopolitical, legal or economic reasons.

The WTO DSB thus might not be the appropriate forum for dealing with problems relating to cross-border pipelines. The WTO rules and regulations are

---

82 See S Zarilli, *International Energy Trade and Access to Competing Networks* in *Energy and Environmental Services: Negotiating Objectives and Development Priorities,* UNCTAD, United Nations 2003.

83 *Ibid.*

84 *Ibid.*

85 See K Talus, "WTO Panel Report in the EU – Energy Package Dispute and the European Commission Proposal to amend the 2009 Gas Market Directive", *Journal of Energy and Natural Resources Law,* 2018.

not geared towards these kinds of disputes, and the WTO DSB does not have the necessary expertise to deal with the various conflicts affecting cross-border pipeline projects. It does not consider the economic, legal and geopolitical implications of such disputes, which are all important factors at play. Cross-border pipeline disputes also require the enforcement of various rules and regulations between the various stakeholders involved, which the WTO DSB does not provide for.[86] The WTO DSB is further viewed as protecting the interests of governments.

While the WTO rules include some basic provisions on energy transport and transit, these are incomplete and have rarely been tested in practice. Further, as only governments can access the WTO DSB, the WTO rules fall shorter than the ECT, bilateral investment treaties and even some preferential trade agreements.[87]

Hence, in the event of a pipeline dispute involving governments, it might not be possible to protect the interests of other pipeline regime members – especially more vulnerable governments or weaker participants. Many countries involved in the energy trade are not comfortable with the idea of mixing energy trade with other forms of trade, given that energy is a strategic resource.[88] All of these factors make the WTO DSB unsuitable for cross-border pipeline conflicts.

7. Conclusion

The problem with cross-border pipelines is that there is no overarching legal framework that governs these projects. A pipeline may pass through various jurisdictions, with their own individual rules and regulations; but some sort of consistency must be maintained in order to ensure the smooth functioning of the pipeline.[89] Further problems arise in regard to the acquisition of land and other third-party rights. Although many bilateral and multilateral agreements are signed between the parties to pipeline projects, there is no overarching legal regime that regulates these sorts of contracts.[90] As a result, in case of a dispute between the various parties, the weaker parties may be held hostage by the stronger and more dominant actors during the negotiations.

Although some international legal instruments are relevant to cross-border pipelines, countries tend to negotiate themselves rather than adopting these international legal instruments, for the reasons outlined in this chapter; if these international legal instruments are used at all, it is generally only as a stop-gap measure.[91] The very nature of cross-border pipelines also makes it difficult to

---

86 M Wustenburg, and K Talus, "WTO law perspectives on EU–Russia energy trade: worlds apart or minor differences?" *Journal of World Energy Law and Business*, OUP, 2018.

87 See M Cossy, "Energy Transport and Transit in the WTO", in *Global Challenges at the Intersection of Energy, Trade and Environment*, Centre for Trade and Economic Integration, 2010, pp113–121.

88 *Ibid.*

89 *Supra*, n 2, 45.

90 *Ibid.*

91 *Supra*, n 9, p65.

keep pace with all of the international legal instruments that may potentially be relevant to them. As a result, each pipeline has its own unique set of rules and regulations which are followed by the players involved in the pipeline project.

ESG considerations for midstream and downstream oil and gas

Elena I Athwal
Damilola S Olawuyi
Hamad Bin Khalifa University

Oil and gas processing and distribution worldwide have been linked to a wide range of adverse environmental, social and human rights outcomes, particularly when governance and institutional quality are low. To address these adverse environmental, social and governance (ESG) concerns, international law has consistently advocated the need for business enterprises, operators and stakeholders across the entire petroleum sector value chain to anticipate, measure and address cumulative ESG risks in operational activities and planning.

This chapter examines the ESG risk points that are commonly encountered in midstream and downstream oil and gas investments. First, it discusses the drivers and contours of the growing recognition of ESG risk management in oil and gas operations. It then puts forward the following ESG risk management strategies, which can enable midstream and downstream operators to unlock efficient, safe, orderly and environmentally responsible development of oil and gas resources:

- a step-by-step approach that focuses on operational material risk identification;
- the appointment of a focal point for enterprise-wide risk control;
- timely and transparent information dissemination; and
- ESG risk monitoring.

Each of these strategies will bolster responsible business management standards and ESG compliance across the entire business value chain.

1. Introduction

Oil and gas processing and distribution worldwide have been linked to a wide range of adverse environmental, social and human rights outcomes, particularly when governance and institutional quality are low.[1] Chief among these is the

1 Damilola Olawuyi, "Corporate Accountability for the Natural Environment and Climate Change", in Ilias Bantekas and MA Stein (eds), *Cambridge Companion to Business and Human Rights* (Cambridge University Press, 2021) pp234–258.

concern that the transportation and storage of oil, natural gas products and by-products (midstream operations), as well as the refining, marketing and distribution of oil, natural gas and by-products to final end users (downstream operations), directly generate significant adverse environmental, social and human rights outcomes in local communities.[2] For example, the adverse environmental impacts of midstream and downstream operations in the Niger Delta area of Nigeria have been documented in several studies, including a 2011 report of the United Nations.[3] In many other resource-rich countries, thousands of sites and cities have been contaminated by:

- oil spillages (from pipelines, barges, cargo ships, oil tankers and trucks);[4]
- the emission of pollutants from stationary or mobile sources; and
- the unsustainable discharge of effluents and heavy metals associated with midstream and downstream operations.[5]

Large-scale environmental problems resulting from oil and gas processing and distribution activities – such as climate change, water pollution, air pollution, loss of biodiversity and land degradation – accentuate the need for greater corporate accountability for environmental harm.[6] Meanwhile, a number of studies have documented how the siting and location of midstream and downstream infrastructure have increasingly been linked with land grabs, forced displacements, marginalisation, exclusions, governmental repression and other social and human rights impacts in local communities – especially in developing countries.[7] The ESG impacts of midstream and downstream operations on human rights and the environment raise fundamental questions of policy and practice.[8]

These concerns have accentuated calls for operators, planners, financial institutions and other stakeholders in midstream and downstream operations to anticipate, minimise and address ESG risks across the entire value chain of their

2 *Ibid.*

3 According to the report, it could take 25 to 30 years to reverse many of the environmental and social consequences of oil spillage in the Niger Delta. United Nations Environment Programme (UNEP), *Environmental Assessment of Ogoniland* (United Nations Environment Programme, 2011) https://wedocs.unep.org/bitstream/handle/20.500.11822/25282/ogoniland_chapter1_UNEP_OEA.pdf?sequence=1&isAllowed=y.

4 For example, there is a long history of fatal accidents involving oil trains. Over 31 train accidents including oil trains were recorded in the United States and Canada between 2013 and 2015. For instance, on 5 July 2013, a train that had been left unattended derailed, spilling oil and catching fire inside the town of Lac-Megantic in Quebec. About 1.6 million gallons of oil were spilled, with 47 people killed and 30 buildings burned down. See Associated Press, "A timeline of recent oil trains crashes in the US and Canada", www.apnews.com/84b1e8273d854697b34af57bc60badc2.

5 See DS Olawuyi, *Extractives Industry Law in Africa* (Springer, 2018) pp78–80.

6 *Ibid;* also Olawuyi (n 1).

7 K Taylor, "Improving Substantive and Procedural Protections for Indigenous Rights in REDD+ Projects: Possible Lessons from Brazil", 5 *Afe Babalola University Journal of Sustainable Development Law and Policy* (2015) 32–54.

8 DS Olawuyi, "Climate Justice and Corporate Responsibility: Taking Human Rights Seriously in Climate Actions and Projects", 34 *Journal of Energy & Natural Resources Law* (2016) 27.

operations.[9] These are part of broader theoretical debates and efforts aimed at coordinating the systemic integration of human rights norms into business activities to ensure coherence, coordination and harmonisation.[10] These efforts have assumed greater significance and urgency as the United Nations' 2030 Agenda for Sustainable Development underscores the need for enhanced partnerships – globally, regionally and nationally – as a required step for achieving the Sustainable Development Goals (SDGs), including those on business, human rights and the environment.[11] With a growing international focus on business, human rights and responsible investment, the failure to effectively anticipate, minimise and address ESG concerns may result in significant legal risks for midstream and downstream operators.[12] These legal risks include the "risk of financial, reputational or investment loss, legal liability, or dispute settlement costs to a company or institution that may arise from a defective commercial arrangement or transaction".[13] Such risks may manifest in the form of disruption of projects, suspensions or closures of projects by supervisory bodies, hefty regulatory fines, and director and shareholder liability; and may impact on a company's profitability or ability to maintain licence to operate.[14] There is therefore a strong business case – in terms of cost, reputation and effectiveness – for midstream and downstream operators and other stakeholders to effectively anticipate and manage ESG risks in their operations.

This chapter examines the ESG risk points that are commonly encountered in midstream and downstream oil and gas operations. It discusses the drivers and contours of the growing recognition of ESG risk management in oil and gas operations. It also puts forward ESG risk management strategies that can enable midstream and downstream operators to pursue the efficient, safe, orderly and environmentally responsible development of oil and gas resources. Examples include:

- due diligence strategies for business activities and projects, such as social and environmental impact assessments and human rights impact assessments, which in turn would bolster responsible business management standards; and
- ESG compliance across the entire business value chain.

---

9 See generally R Abate, "Corporate Responsibility and Climate Justice: A Proposal for a Polluter-Financed Relocation Fund for Federally Recognized Tribes Imperiled by Climate Change", 25 *Fordham Environmental Law Review* (2015) 10; also DS Olawuyi, *The Human Rights Based Approach to Carbon Finance* (Cambridge University Press 2018) pp1–25.

10 *Ibid.* See also Mining Working Group at the United Nations, "A Rights-Based Approach to Resource Extraction in the Pursuit of Sustainable Development" (2014) *Advocacy Brief*, miningwg.files. wordpress.com.

11 United Nations, *Transforming Our World: The 2030 Agenda for Sustainable Development*, UNGA Res 70/1 (25 September 2015).

12 DS Olawuyi, "Legal strategies and tools for mitigating legal risks associated with oil and gas investments in Africa" (2015) 39 (3) *OPEC Energy Review*, 247-265, doi: 10.1111/opec.12043; also Reg Fowler, "Corporate social responsibility and joint venture governance – the forgotten issues" (2021) 14 (5) *The Journal of World Energy Law & Business* 297–312.

13 Olawuyi, *ibid.*

14 *Ibid.*

This chapter is organised into the following sections. Section 2 examines the meaning, nature and scope of the ESG concept. Section 3 outlines the ESG risk points in midstream and downstream oil and gas. Section 4 discusses how ESG risk can be managed through risk mitigation and management techniques from strategy to operations to governance. Section 5 presents the conclusions.

2. Meaning, drivers and scope of the ESG concept

'ESG' refers to the wide range of environmental, social and governance factors which, together with financial aspects, must be considered in project planning or decision-making processes in order to minimise legal risks and generate sustainable, long-term financial returns in concert with societal values and stakeholder trust. The environmental pillar emphasises the protection of natural capital (ie, land, air, water, minerals) from degradation and pollution.[15] This includes addressing the impacts which a business enterprise has on the environment – for example, by limiting GHG emissions, reducing the carbon footprint and utilising green supply chains. The social pillar emphasises the need to address social exclusions and human rights violations that may result from economic activities and projects. This includes promoting local content, supplier development, inclusivity, gender justice, corporate social responsibility, infrastructure development, corruption eradication, land justice, and equitable health and fair wages for local labour populations in business operations, among other things.[16] The governance pillar emphasises the need to promote transparency, accountability and full compliance with domestic laws and best practices in business operations. This includes ensuring proactive sustainability disclosure and climate-related reporting that exhibit corporate activities relating to all aspects of ESG management.[17]

The need to integrate these three ESG pillars into investment planning is not new. Ever since the 1972 Stockholm Declaration proclaimed that our natural and man-made environments are essential to our wellbeing and to the enjoyment of our basic human rights – especially the right to life[18] – ESG considerations have become integral to the design, approval, financing and implementation of development activities and projects to minimise adverse human rights outcomes. Virtually all countries now have one or more laws or

15 Organisation for Economic Co-operation and Development (OECD), *ESG Investing and Climate Transition: Market Practices, Issues and Policy Considerations* (OECD, 2021), www.oecd.org/finance/ESG-investing-and-climate- transition-Market-practices-issues-and-policy-considerations.pdf.

16 R Boffo and R Patalano, *ESG Investing: Practices, Progress and Challenges* (OECD, 2020), www.oecd.org/finance/ESG-Investing-Practices-Progress-and-Challenges.pdf. See also Fowler (n 12).

17 Impact Management Project, *Statement of Intent to Work Together Towards Comprehensive Corporate Reporting*. Summary of alignment discussions among leading sustainability and integrated reporting organisations CDP, CDSB, GRI, IIRC and SASB (World Economic Forum and Deloitte, 2020), https://29kjwb3armds2g3gi4lq2sx1-wpengine.netdna-ssl.com/wp-content/uploads/Statement-of-Intent-to-Work-Together-Towards-Comprehensive-Corporate-Reporting.pdf.

18 United Nations Conference on the Human Environment (Stockholm Declaration) UN Doc A/CONF.48/PC.13 (1971), para 1.

sustainable development policies that aim to advance ESG outcomes in the planning and implementation of development activities and projects.[19] The concept of sustainable development – which is historically situated in the 1987 Brundtland Commission Report as "development that meets the needs of the present without compromising the ability of future generations to meet their own needs"[20] – has long been canvassed as encompassing three pillars: economic, environmental and social.[21] Therefore, the need to achieve sound environmental, social and economic outcomes in projects and activities has become an essential component of petroleum law and policy for several decades.[22]

However, the renewed emphasis on ESG risk management has grown in scale and magnitude over the past decade, due to four key drivers.[23] The first is the increasing global recognition of the role of private actors in respecting, protecting and fulfilling human rights in all spheres of their operations.[24] In a globalised economy where influential non-state actors – such as multinational corporations, financial institutions and development agencies – account for a significant portion of domestic economies and trade, the gaps inherent in focusing on state actors alone became increasingly apparent over the past decade.[25] Failure to hold business enterprises to account for adverse human rights impacts of their operations on employees, customers, suppliers and local communities not only shields private actors from responsibility for their actions, but may ultimately stifle the ability of vulnerable communities to obtain redress for adverse human rights impacts.[26] As a result, several resolutions, declarations and expert reports – such as the *Guiding Principles on Business and Human Rights: Implementing the United Nations 'Protect, Respect and Remedy' Framework* (UNGPs) – have emerged, which elaborate that business enterprises have a responsibility to respect, protect and fulfil human rights in their operations and investments.[27] Though not legally binding, the UNGPs make it clear that business enterprises must respect, protect and fulfil human rights and avoid infringing the human rights of others.[28]

---

19 This relationship has been recognised in over 100 constitutions and in several core regional and international human rights instruments. See J May and E Daly (eds), *Encyclopedia of Human Rights and the Environment, Indivisibility, Dignity and Legality* (Edward Elgar Publishing, 2018).

20 World Commission on Environment and Development, *Our Common Future,* https://sustainabledevelopment.un.org/content/documents/5987our-common-future.pdf.

21 DS Olawuyi, *Principles of Nigerian Environmental Law* (Afe Babalola University Press, 2015) pp1–25.

22 *Ibid.*

23 See Olawuyi (n 1).

24 S Deva, *Regulating Corporate Human Rights Violations: Humanizing Business* (Routledge, 2013), pp2–25; also D Weissbrodt and M Kruger, "Human Rights Responsibilities of Businesses as Non-State Actors", in P Alston (ed), *Non-State Actors and Human Rights* (Oxford University Press, 2005) pp315–350.

25 JG Ruggie, *Just Business: Multinational Corporations and Human Rights* (WW Norton & Co, 2013), p1.

26 Olawuyi (n 1); also D Korten, *When Corporations Rule the World* (Berrett-Koehler, 2001).

27 *Guiding Principles on Business and Human Rights: Implementing the United Nations 'Protect, Respect and Remedy' Framework* [UNGPs], www.ohchr.org/documents/publications/guidingprinciplesbusinesshr_en.pdf.

28 *Ibid*, Guiding Principle 11.

A second and related driver is the rise of rights-based approaches to development in all economic sectors, including the oil and gas industry.[29] A wide range of international instruments have increasingly recognised the right to a safe, clean, healthy and sustainable environment as a fundamental right;[30] and have encouraged countries to adopt conservation and pollution reduction policies that protect, respect and fulfil all human rights, including the right to a safe, clean, healthy and sustainable environment.[31] Similarly, at the regional level, the need for transnational corporations and business enterprises to consider, anticipate and prevent human rights implications of extractive projects on the enjoyment of a satisfactory environment was recognised in the African Union's 2012 Resolution on a Human Rights-Based Approach to Natural Resources Governance.[32] Among other things, the 2012 resolution calls on governments to "set up independent monitoring and accountability mechanisms that ensure that human rights are justiciable and extractive industries and investors legally accountable in the country hosting their activities and in the country of legal domicile".[33] The 2012 resolution harmonises and builds on previous efforts by African governments that demand social and environmental safeguards from investors and business enterprises in Africa's extractive industries.[34]

A third driver is the growing effort by countries around the world to address the problem of climate change. With increased manifestation of extreme weather events – such as Cyclone Sitrang in Bangladesh, Cyclone Nalgae in the Philippines and Cyclone Pam in Vanuatu; devastating floods in Nigeria; droughts in South Sudan; and fatal heatwaves across the United States – there is now increased consensus among the scientific community that climate change is real and that the continuous anthropogenic emission of greenhouse gases (GHGs) is a principal cause.[35] As signatories to the Paris Agreement and the United Nations Framework Convention on Climate Change, oil and gas

---

29 United Nations Human Rights Council, *Promotion and Protection of all Human Rights, Civil, Political, Economic, Social and Cultural Rights, including the Right to Development* (A/HRC/48/L 23/Rev 1, adopted on 6 October 2021). See also Resolutions 45/17 of 6 October 2020, 45/30 of 7 October 2020 and 46/7 of 23 March 2021.

30 United Nations Human Rights Special Procedures, *Framework Principles of Human Rights and the Environment* (A/HRC/37/59), http://srenvironment.org/framework-principles.

31 Principles 1 and 2.

32 *Resolution on a Human Rights-Based Approach to Natural Resources Governance*, African Commission on Human and Peoples' Rights, 51st Sess (2012), achpr.org/sessions/51st/resolutions/224.

33 *Ibid.*

34 DS Olawuyi, "Increasing Relevance of Right-Based Approaches to Resource Governance in Africa: Shifting from Regional Aspiration to Local Realization" 11 *McGill International Journal of Sustainable Development Law and Policy* (2015) 113–158.

35 Climate change is an increase in the average temperature of the atmosphere at an abnormal rate caused by the anthropogenic emission of gases, known as GHGs, that trap the sun's heat in the atmosphere. GHGs that contribute to climate change include carbon dioxide, methane, nitrous oxides, water vapour, ozone and high global warming potential gases such as chlorofluorocarbons, hydrofluorocarbons, perfluorocarbons and sulphur hexafluoride. See Intergovernmental Panel on Climate Change (IPCC), *Climate Change 2007*, Fourth Assessment Report, in which the IPCC stated that it is "very likely" that human activity is the main driver of the rise in temperatures since 1950. See DS Olawuyi, *Climate Change Law and Policy in the Middle East and North Africa Region* (Routledge, 2022), pp1–10.

producing countries increasingly recognise the need for business enterprises – including oil and gas operators – to lower current levels of GHG emissions. Several countries have already committed, in their intended nationally determined contributions (INDCs), to contribute to the Paris Agreement's aspirational goal of avoiding 1.5°C warming by investing in climate-smart energy systems – that is, structures and systems that lower GHG emissions and improve the ability to adapt to, and cope with, the risks posed by climate change.[36] Such commitments have seen a rise in regional and national policies that require oil and gas operators to disclose ongoing efforts to reduce GHG emissions and ensure green growth across their entire value chain.[37] For example, the 2007 Arab Ministerial Declaration on Climate Change reflects the regional aspirations of all ministers responsible for environment and climate change in the oil and gas-rich Arab region to include "policies to deal with climate change issues in all sectors within national and regional policies for sustainable development".[38] It calls on all Arab countries to prioritise climate change mitigation and adaptation through cleaner production techniques and environmentally friendly technologies, among other things. Furthermore, the Paris Climate Agreement recognises that parties should, "when taking action to address climate change, respect, promote and consider their respective obligations on human rights".[39] By forging an explicit link between climate action and human rights, the Paris Agreement reinforces the need for countries to ensure that all climate projects and investments within their jurisdictions – including projects conducted by, or in partnership with, private enterprises – integrate ESG considerations.

Furthermore, with the rise of business and human rights norms, business enterprises themselves are increasingly recognising the important roles they can play by adopting cleaner production methods and investing in low-carbon technologies and energy-efficient infrastructure. For example, in 2013 more than 500 businesses under the aegis of the Coalition for Environmentally Responsible Economies (CERES) signed a Climate Declaration that urged US policymakers to adopt "strong climate, clean energy and water policies at the state and federal levels".[40] The coalition also committed to the CERES Principles – a model corporate code of environmental conduct based on the following principles:

- the protection of the biosphere;

36 United Nations Framework Convention on Climate Change, *Paris Agreement under the United Nations Framework Convention on Climate Change, Conference of the Parties Twenty-first Session Paris*, 30 November to 11 December 2015, FCCC/CP/2015/L.9, Articles 2(1), 4, 6, and 7.

37 Olawuyi (n 1).

38 Arab Ministerial Declaration on Climate Change, adopted by the Council of Arab Ministers responsible for the Environment (6 December 2007) E/ESCWA/SDPD/2012/Technical Paper.2.

39 See Preamble, Paris Agreement (n 35).

40 BICEP, *Tackling Climate Change is one of America's Greatest Economic Opportunities of the 21st Century* (2013), www.ceres.org/networks/ceres-policy-network.

- sustainable use of natural resources;
- reduction and disposal of waste;
- energy conservation;
- risk reduction
- safe products and services;
- environmental restoration;
- informing the public;
- management commitments; and
- audits and reports.[41]

Similarly, at the 21st Meeting of the Conference of the Parties to the United Nations Climate Change Conference, held in Paris, several leading business enterprises signed the Paris Pledge for Action, undertaking to "play their part to support the objectives of the Paris Agreement".[42] Moreover, since 2017, an alliance of major oil and gas corporations – including Qatar Petroleum, Exxon Mobil, Total, Shell, BP and ENI, among others – have signed the Guiding Principles on Reducing Methane Emissions Across the Natural Gas Value Chain.[43] As natural gas contains methane – one of the potent GHGs that contribute to climate change – the document acknowledges that "the transition to a low carbon future will be influenced by the extent to which the oil and gas industry reduces its methane emissions".[44] The signatories have undertaken to systematically monitor and reduce methane emissions in their operations, assets and projects. A similar initiative is the Equator Principles, a voluntary set of standards adopted by over 80 commercial banks worldwide to ensure that investments and projects that violate environmental and social goals will not be funded.[45] Likewise, a report issued by the Task Force on Climate-related Financial Disclosures, endorsed by the Financial Stability Board, emphasises the need for companies, banks and investors to transparently monitor and disclose climate-related risks and opportunities across their entire operations.[46] While the foregoing efforts are voluntary and not legally binding, they have played a crucial role in raising awareness of what responsible corporations can do to limit environmental harm and damage that threaten fundamental human rights.

---

41 CERES Principles, www.iisd.org/business/tools/ principles_ceres.aspx.

42 Paris Pledge for Action (2015), www.parispledgeforaction.org.

43 Climate and Clean Air Coalition, *Guiding Principles on Reducing Methane Emissions Across the Natural Gas Value Chain*, www.ccacoalition.org/en/resources/reducing-methane-emissions-across-natural-gas-value-chain-guiding-principles.

44 *Ibid.*

45 *The Equator Principles: A financial industry benchmark for determining, assessing and managing environmental and social risk in project* (June 2013), www.equator-principles.com/resources/equator _principles_III.pdf.

46 Task Force on Climate-related Financial Disclosures, *Recommendations of the Task Force on Climate-related Financial Disclosures* (2017), https://assets.bbhub.io/company/sites/60/2020/10/FINAL-2017-TCFD-Report-11052018.pdf.

Fourth, the role of corporations in limiting ESG risks has assumed greater significance and urgency with the adoption of the United Nations' 2030 Agenda for Sustainable Development.[47] Sustainable Development Goal (SDG) 17 specifically underscores the need for enhanced partnerships by various actors – including civil society organisations and businesses – to actively contribute towards achieving the various SDGs, including those relating to water and sanitation (SDG 6), climate change (SDG 13), sustainable communities (SDG 11) and the preservation of ecosystems and biodiversity (SDG 15), among others. As Ruggie rightly noted, for businesses to fully realise their contribution to sustainable development, they must "put efforts to advance respect for human rights at the heart of the people part of sustainable development".[48] Through corporate accountability and respect for human rights – especially obligations relating to climate change and environmental protection – business enterprises can play prominent roles in advancing sustainable development in many parts of the world. Since the adoption of the SDGs, business enterprises have increasingly used the SDGs to design organisational efforts and policies surrounding sustainability and their possible contributions against all 17 SDGs. For example, Qatar Petroleum's 2018 Sustainability Report specifically identifies the SDGs as "an important reference to frame our sustainability actions and set them in a global context, showing our contribution to this very important international initiative".[49] As Ruggie noted, business enterprises can contribute to the realisation of the SDGs not only by stopping adverse human rights impacts, but also by taking proactive and voluntary efforts to promote human rights in all aspects of their operations.[50] In the context of addressing climate change, important voluntary efforts by business enterprises have been rightly espoused to include four main elements:

- reducing GHGs from enterprises' own activities;
- reducing GHGs from enterprises' products and services;
- considering the GHG emissions of suppliers; and
- proactively disclosing in an accessible manner, including by posting on an enterprise's websites, information about its GHG emissions levels and reduction efforts.[51]

Corporate disclosures and reports must therefore highlight not only steps taken to mitigate environmental risks, but also proactive, positive and

47 United Nations (n 11).

48 JG Ruggie, *Making Globalization Work for All: Achieving the Sustainable Development Goals through Business Respect for Human Rights* (Shift Project, 2016).

49 Qatar Petroleum, *Sustainability Report* (2018), pp28–29, https://qp.com.qa/en/MediaCentre/Lists/QPPublications/Attachments/29/QP%202018%20Sustainability%20Report.pdf.

50 Ruggie (n 48).

51 See Expert Group on Climate Obligations of Enterprises, *The Climate Principles for Enterprises* (Eleven International Publishing, 2018), https://climateprinciplesforenterprises.files.wordpress.com/2017/12/enterprisesprincipleswebpdf.pdf.

transformative steps and actions voluntarily taken to advance each of the 17 SDGs – especially those relating to the environment.

Given these main drivers, the expectation of business enterprises to appropriately investigate, assess and price ESG risks which may arise in the transactional context is no longer an option, but a necessity. In the oil and gas context, understanding ESG risks through a deliberate and thoughtful investment process can help midstream and downstream operators to understand how their activities and operations may result in adverse sustainability outcomes, and how to develop responsive and coherent risk management processes. However, while several of the extant guidelines and declarations recognise corporate accountability for ESG risks, it remains rather unclear how responsible corporations can anticipate, minimise and address ESG risks across the entire value chain of their operations. The next section unpacks ESG risk points that responsible midstream and downstream operators will need to anticipate and address in their operations.

3. ESG risk points in midstream and downstream oil and gas

As indicated in Table 1, midstream and downstream operations increasingly face direct and indirect ESG risks that must be coherently anticipated and managed in investment planning and decision making.

3.1 Direct ESG risks

Direct ESG risks flow from the obligations of operators to proactively anticipate, mitigate and address all sources of environmental pollution, social exclusion and lack of transparency in their activities and projects, especially in the local communities where they operate. Failure to comply with emission reduction, pollution control, local content, corporate disclosure, reporting and other ESG-related standards as stipulated in legislation and industry guidelines may result in significant regulatory fines, penalties and other legal consequences for midstream and downstream operators.

3.2 Indirect ESG risks

Indirect ESG risks relate to associated structural, transitional and disclosure-related uncertainties and risks that may result from ESG standards and obligations, especially considering the ongoing low-carbon energy transition.[52]

(a) Structural risks

Structural risk points include potential disruptions to a company's or third party's business or assets due to the physical impacts of climate change, such as

52 See T Aven and BS Krohn, "A new perspective on how to understand, assess and manage risk and the unforeseen", 121 *Reliability Engineering & System Safety* (2014) 1.

rising sea levels, extreme storms, floods, fires and drought. Apart from climate-induced water scarcity, flooding and fatal heatwaves, climate change could have wide-ranging effects on pipelines, refineries and other physical and associated infrastructure required for midstream and downstream operations.[53] These include:

- the potential failure of facilities;
- reduced life expectancy of buildings; and
- increased operational and maintenance expenditure of electricity, water and aviation infrastructure.[54]

To effectively address the impacts of climate change on critical infrastructure, there is a need for increased investment in climate-smart infrastructure – that is, buildings, structures and systems that reduce GHG emissions and improve society's ability to adapt to, and cope with, the risks posed by climate change.[55] Furthermore, in the transactional context, it is necessary to consider:

- whether the target operates, or whether its raw materials are sourced, in areas that are prone to flooding or at risk of rising sea levels; and
- whether such risks may result in disruptions to infrastructure and supply chains due to climate change and environmental hazards.

(b) Transition risks

Transition risk points relate to new or more stringent ESG standards or requirements that may arise from the ongoing transition to low-carbon energy systems around the world. For example, as more countries and corporations adopt low-carbon transition plans and measures aimed at addressing climate change, midstream and downstream operators will increasingly have to deal with limited access to financing, loss of anticipated revenue, oil price volatility, stringent low carbon technology and efficiency standards, and 'leave it in the ground' obligations – all of which may reduce the prospects and viability of existing projects.[56] In addition, it will be critical to assess the extent of capital required to obtain or maintain ESG compliance. Moreover, the process should be aligned with regard to land and property rights, ethical sourcing of carbon credits and respect for human rights relating to water, environment and food in emission reduction schemes.

---

53 Olawuyi (n 34) 1–10.

54 J Sieber, "Impacts of, and Adaptation Options to, Extreme Weather Events and Climate Change Concerning Thermal Power Plants" 121 *Climatic Change* (2013) 55–66.

55 Olawuyi (n 8).

56 Harro van Asselt, "Governing Fossil Fuel Production in the Age of Climate Disruption: Towards an International Law of 'Leaving It In The Ground'" 9 *Earth System Governance* (2021) 100118.

(c) ***Disclosure risks***

Disclosure risk points relate to requirements for petroleum operators to measure and disclose how their operations advance sustainability and net-zero emission reduction targets, which are increasingly recognised in many countries and supported by a majority of shareholders in dominant energy multinational corporations (eg, ExxonMobil).[57] Disclosure issues focus on how climate-related risks and opportunities are likely to impact on the current and future financial situation of the company. For example, in the transactional context, it will be necessary to assess whether the target has complied with climate change disclosure requirements; and whether, for example, public statements or public disclosures it has issued could potentially be misleading (otherwise known as 'greenwashing' or fraudulent misrepresentation). One such resource in evaluating disclosure risk is the Sustainability Accounting Standards Board (SASB), which in September 2020 announced a shared vision for financial accounting and sustainability disclosures together with four other leading framework and standard-setting organisations: CDP, the Climate Disclosure Standards Board, the Global Reporting Initiative and the International Integrated Reporting Council.[58] This prototype climate-related financial disclosure standard can be applied to climate disclosure; and within this system, the SASB Standards on sustainability reporting could serve as a tool for ESG disclosure for investors and other providers of financial capital.[59]

57 CERES, "ExxonMobil Investors Make History with Majority Vote on Climate Risk Disclosure" (31 May 2017), www.ceres.org/news-center/press-releases/exxonmobil-investors-make-history-majority-vote-climate-risk-disclosure.

58 Value Reporting Foundation, SASB Standards and Other ESG Frameworks, *The Sustainability Reporting Ecosystem*, www.sasb.org/about/sasb-and-other-esg-frameworks/.

59 *Ibid.*

Table 1. Risks and ESG considerations

ESG risks	Key ESG considerations
Direct Direct ESG risks flow from the obligations of operators to comply with all applicable legislation, industry guidelines and codes. These include the need to proactively anticipate, mitigate and redress all sources of environmental pollution, social exclusion and lack of transparency in their activities and projects, especially in local communities where they operate.	• Might the project potentially cause: ◦ flooding; ◦ air and water pollution; ◦ some level of noise in the project construction and operational phase; ◦ mass displacements of people from their homes, traditional lands and forests; ◦ loss of access to drinking water; ◦ loss of arable farmlands; ◦ spillages or explosions; or ◦ the spread of diseases? • Who is likely to be impacted? • Has their free, prior informed consent been obtained prior to the approval and commencement of the project? • Are there programmes in place to promote: ◦ local content; ◦ supplier development; ◦ ethical procurement; ◦ gender justice; ◦ inclusivity; ◦ compliance with labour standards; ◦ tax; ◦ land management; and ◦ the empowerment of local communities, especially indigenous and First Nations? • Are there mechanisms in place to ensure the transparent disclosure of information about the company's assets, liabilities or underlying investment strategy in accordance with legislative requirements?

continued on next page

ESG risks	Key ESG considerations
Indirect Indirect ESG risks flow from associated structural, transitional and disclosure-related uncertainties and risks that may result from ESG standards and obligations, especially in light of the ongoing low-carbon energy transition.	
Structural Disruptions to a company's or third party's business or assets (ie, facilities, infrastructure, land or resources) due to the physical impacts of climate change and environmental hazards, such as rising sea levels, more extreme storms, floods, fires and drought. These include: • the potential failure of facilities; • reduced life expectancy of buildings; and • increased operational and maintenance expenditure of physical and associated infrastructure.	• Does the business operate, or are its raw materials sourced, in areas that are prone to flooding or at risk of rising sea levels? • Which assets may be impacted by climate change and other environmental hazards on physical assets? • Is the physical and associated infrastructure compliant with construction, health, safety, security and environmental codes, including energy efficiency, climate mitigation and adaptation, and net-zero standards?

continued on next page

ESG risks	Key ESG considerations
Transition Ongoing transitions to low-carbon energy systems may result in new standards that may fundamentally change business structures and limit the availability or increase the cost of debt, capital, long-dated securities and insurance; and may result in stranded assets. (For example, sovereign wealth funds (SWFs) in New Zealand, Norway and France have announced plans to divest from high-carbon industries. Norway's SWF has capped coal-related portfolios at 30%.)	• Will the business be required to make significant capital expenditures to obtain or maintain compliance with land use, zoning or other regulations? • Will ongoing or planned low-carbon technologies and projects of the target (eg, renewable energy projects) affect human rights, especially with respect to land and property rights? • Is there a framework for ethical sourcing of carbon credits and respect for human rights relating to water, environment and food in emission reduction schemes? • Are financial and other mechanisms in place to ensure financial resilience and protect the project from transition risks – for example, through insurance or bonds?

Disclosures
 	
Emerging requirements to report on the financial impacts of climate-related risks and opportunities on the business and its shareholders (eg, in May 2017, 62% of shareholders of ExxonMobil voted in favour of climate disclosures). Failure to comply may result in reputational, operational and market risks.
	• How are environment and climate-related risks and opportunities likely to impact on the current and future financial position of the business as reflected in its income statement, cash-flow statement and balance sheet?
	• Has the business complied with climate disclosure requirements or made public statements or disclosures concerning climate change risk that may in any way be considered misleading?
	• Are company reports:
	  ◦ publicly accessible in terms of language translation, reduced technicality and dissemination through internet platforms; and
	  ◦ updated to include timely, recent and relevant information?

Only some of the foregoing risks can be identified and addressed through traditional due diligence and title review processes. This accentuates the need for innovative and proactive risk management approaches that anticipate and minimise a wide range of technical and operational risks in light of the fundamental transformations in the oil and gas sector. The next section discusses how the risk points can be addressed through an integrated planning approach.

4. Addressing the risk points through risk mitigation and management techniques: from strategy to operations to governance

A starting point is for midstream and downstream operators to carefully examine the challenges to integrating ESG considerations into all aspects of their operations. These challenges are varied and include the absence of clear and comprehensive climate change legislation at the national level which would itemise the nature and scope of GHG emission reduction and climate adaptation approaches for operators in key sectors. The absence of up-to-date and coherent operational guidelines on ESG due diligence across a business value chain may further result in ambiguities on the specific steps that project planners and field operators should take to anticipate and address ESG risks. ESG risks are multi-dimensional and quantifying them will require legal, scientific, technological, engineering, procurement, accounting and business analyses. In addition, failure to address capacity and knowledge gaps of key personnel can result in costly ESG risks.

In summary, clearer legislation and unambiguous industry-specific guidelines, combined with more comprehensive technical data on the impacts and risks of non-compliance and increased training and education on ESG considerations, would provide a robust roadmap towards ESG risk management globally. In order for this mapping to take place, there is a need for an internal climate change risk control and management system. Coherent and business-wide operational guidelines on ESGs would establish a multi-stakeholder framework through which all aspects of ESG risks could be identified, elaborated and considered in project design and planning.

Table 2. Risk mitigation and management techniques and ESG considerations

Risk mitigation and management techniques	Key considerations
Material risk identification The wide range of direct and indirect ESG risk exposures of a business operator which must be carefully identified and unpacked in order to effectively mitigate and manage such risks.	• Assess actual and potential ESG impacts through comprehensive environmental social and human rights impact due diligence. • Set risk appetite. • Think creatively about liability scenarios in case of ESG impacts.
Risk control methodology and strategy The need for an integrated, multi-disciplinary and enterprise-wide risk management approach, as opposed to a piecemeal approach, aimed at aligning corporate investment strategy with risk appetite and risk management structure.	• What key departments and personnel are exposed to ESG risks? • Identify key risk control response strategies in case of risk exposure, such as contractual clauses, insurance, dispute resolution, pollution control and infrastructure redesign.
Focal point for risk control To ensure a coordinated response to ESG risks, a focal point that includes wide representation across the business value and supply chain is essential.	• Establish a risk management committee or appoint a focal point responsible for: ◦ risk identification; ◦ dispute resolution; ◦ negotiation; and ◦ expert determination. • Ensure that a feedback mechanism is in place to promote stakeholder engagement throughout the risk control process.

continued on next page

Risk mitigation and management techniques	Key considerations
Information and communication Proactive information disclosure on ESG efforts and plans can promote trust and help an operator to maintain its social licence to operate.	• Communicate how impacts have been anticipated and addressed through proactive ESG disclosures. • Ensure that disclosures are up to date. • Publish and disclose new information. • Facilitate timely access to information at a reasonable cost.
Education and monitoring Capacity development and training for all frontline and other personnel can help to enhance the efficiency of ESG risk mitigation and response.	• Develop tailored training programmes and executive courses on ESG due diligence and risk mitigation methodology in order to keep up to date with new risks. • Monitor and track the effectiveness of all stages of ESG risk anticipation and response to ensure efficiency and compliance.

As shown in Table 2, a step-by-step approach should focus on:

- material risk identification;
- risk control;
- a focal point for risk control;
- information dissemination; and
- monitoring.[60]

4.1 Material risk identification

First is the material risk identification process, which emphasises the need for midstream and downstream operators to carefully examine and aggregate the wide range of direct and indirect ESG risk exposures across their entire value chain in order to effectively mitigate and manage such risks. By elaborating the specific ESG risk exposures, an operator will be better informed to develop holistic and comprehensive risk mitigation strategies and policies. Salient ESG issues can be evaluated through a comprehensive human rights due diligence and impact assessment (HRDD) process.[61] HRDD methodologies identify,

60 See DS Olawuyi, "Corporate Due Diligence in the Era of Climate Change", NNHRR Business and Human Rights Working Group (Asser Institute: Centre for International and European Law, 2020).

prevent, mitigate and account for human rights impacts, including actual and potential impacts, with the end goal being expressive engagement with stakeholders such as employees, community members, human rights defenders, workers in the supply chain and consumers.[62] After identifying actual or potentially adverse ESG risks following a detailed risk assessment, operators will be better placed to understand and set their risk appetites to maximise profitability while minimising avoidable loss.

4.2 Risk control methodology and strategy

Once the risks and exposure levels have been materially identified and unpacked, operators can integrate the findings and act accordingly by devising an integrated, multi-disciplinary and enterprise-wide management approach. A comprehensive, systematic and systemic approach, rather than a piecemeal approach, can ensure that the risk appetite and risk management structure is built into the overall corporate architecture.

Risk control is a comprehensive process that goes beyond traditional corporate social responsibility initiatives.[63] Risk control requires holistic process and product change in order to address ESG risks across the entire business value chain. While process change will include procedural and institutional changes in corporate governance to better anticipate and eliminate ESG risks, product change will include redesigning midstream and downstream operations in order to make them more ESG compliant. This will include making public commitments to invest in technologies, processes and infrastructure that minimise emissions and address all forms of adverse social and governance impacts in midstream and downstream operations.

Furthermore, a wide range of risk allocation and mitigation techniques – including careful contract negotiation, insurance, dispute resolution, ethical sourcing, fair labour and employment standards, pollution control technologies and climate-smart infrastructure redesign, among others – must be carefully considered and integrated into planning prior to the commencement of operations.[64] For example, contractual clauses that allocate ESG risks must be carefully negotiated and incorporated.

4.3 Focal point for risk control mechanism

Third, there is a need to appoint or assign a focal point to identify, collect and report on risks, and to provide instruction to staff on risk management

61 DS Olawuyi, "Energy (and Human Rights) for All: Addressing Human Rights Risks in Energy Access Projects", in R Salter, CG Gonzalez and EK Warner, *Energy Justice: US and International Perspectives* (Edward Elgar Publishing, 2018), pp73–104.

62 *Ibid.*

63 Fowler (n 12).

64 Olawuyi (n 12). See also Emmett J Vaughan and Therese Vaughan, *Fundamentals of Risk and Insurance* (10th edn, John Wiley & Sons, 2007), p2.

strategies and procedures for dispute resolution, negotiation and expert determination. A risk management committee or a dedicated unit can be established to coordinate and monitor ESG risk management across an organisation. Focal points identify, collect and report on risks, and provide instruction to staff on risk management strategies and procedures for dispute resolution, negotiation and expert determination.[65] Furthermore, it is important to ensure that a feedback mechanism is in place that will guarantee stakeholder engagement throughout the risk control process. This ERM system is as applicable to private sector risk control efforts as it is to risk management organisation in national and international governance structures.

4.4 Information and communication

Fourth, proactive and transparent disclosure of ESG mitigation and response plans and efforts is essential to inform the public of the ESG risks associated with downstream and midstream operations and the efforts being taken to eradicate such risks.

Corporate sustainability reporting can provide a means for midstream and downstream operators to respect, protect and fulfil the right to access to information (ATI) – a right that is enshrined in a number of core international human rights instruments.[66] The core elements of ATI include:

- the maximum possible disclosure of project information;
- an obligation to publish and disclose new information;
- the establishment of processes to facilitate timely access to information at a reasonable cost; and
- increased public education and awareness.[67]

For example, through periodic climate reports or sustainability reports that disclose efforts to address ESG risks, members of the public can better understand the big picture in terms of:

- the nature and scope of projects;
- the potential ESG impacts; and
- the efforts taken by the corporation to mitigate those concerns.[68]

To enhance the utility of such reports, it is essential to ensure that they are timely and accurate, and are developed in accessible and simplified language that can be understood by non-experts.

65 United Nations, "Enterprise risk management: approaches and uses in United Nations system organizations", https://undocs.org/pdf?symbol=en/JIU/REP/2020/5, p iv.

66 See Report of the Special Rapporteur, "Promotion and Protection of the Right to Freedom of Opinion and Expression" (28 January 1998) UN Doc E/CN.4/1998/40, para 1.

67 See DS Olawuyi, "Climate Justice and Corporate Responsibility: Taking Human Rights Seriously in Climate Actions and Projects" 34:1 *Journal of Energy & Natural Resources Law* (2016), 27–44.

68 *Ibid.*

4.5 Monitoring

Finally, monitoring can be an important resource in gathering data on performance and the effectiveness of ESG risk anticipation and response. Monitoring tracks the effectiveness of all stages of ESG risk anticipation and response to ensure efficiency and compliance. Additionally, it helps to ensure the aggregation of high-quality and credible data in order to evaluate performance and achieve effective outcomes.

Furthermore, in order to ensure a state of alertness regarding new risks, education – in the form of capacity development and training for all frontline and other personnel – is essential. Specifically, tailored training programmes and executive courses on climate change due diligence and risk mitigation methodology must be integrated and embedded into the business value chain.[69] By training staff to acquire skills, knowledge and attitudes that support more coherent ESG compliance, midstream and downstream operators can strengthen local community relationships and investor trust.

5. Conclusion

The expectation of business enterprises to appropriately investigate, assess, price and manage ESG risks which may arise in the transactional context is no longer an option but a necessity. Midstream and downstream operators can avoid costly legal risk to their operations in terms of financing and reputation by incorporating direct and indirect ESG factors into their investment portfolio evaluations and management procedures. Through interrogatory social and environmental impact assessments and holistic risk management strategies, business enterprises can coherently address the ESG risk points that are commonly encountered in midstream and downstream oil and gas investments.

Furthermore, national authorities can benefit from establishing clear and comprehensive regulatory frameworks that provide clarity on ESG obligations of operators. Even where domestic laws are silent on these issues, the need for ESG due diligence is clear, as non-compliance may result in protracted litigation as well as reputational damage. Adopting sound and responsible operational ESG guidelines, which safeguard environmental and human rights principles, can present robust legal protection across the entire business value chain, enhance social licence to operate and strengthen relationships with host countries, local communities, customers and other stakeholders based on mutual respect, acceptance and trust.

---

69 United Nations Environment Programme, "PSI. Principles for Sustainable Insurance: A global sustainability framework and initiative of the United Nations Environment Programme Finance Initiative", (2012) www.unepfi.org/psi/wp-content/uploads/2012/06/PSI-document.pdf.

Downstream taxation

Rafael Baleroni
Cescon, Barrieu, Flesch & Barreto
Marina Cyrino
Wintershall Dea

1. Introduction

Numerous different categories of taxes are applicable to downstream taxation; they apply to both oil and gas and vary between products. According to the Organisation for Economic Co-operation and Development (OECD), 'taxes' are any "compulsory unrequited payments to the government or to a supranational authority"; they do not include fines, penalties or compulsory loans paid to a government.[1]

The OECD classifies taxes according to the kind of revenue that constitutes the basis for the respective tax calculation. The main groups are:

- taxes on income, profits and capital gains;
- social security contributions;
- taxes on payroll and workforce;
- taxes on property;
- taxes on goods and services; and
- other taxes.[2]

When analysing the downstream oil and gas industry, the main applicable taxes fall within the group of taxes on goods and services. This category encompasses value added taxes and excise taxes.

Taxation is one mechanism through which the externalities associated with carbon emissions can be brought into account. As efforts to charge for emissions gather pace worldwide, carbon-based taxes have been introduced in some countries and are under consideration in others.

This chapter presents the main taxes applicable in the downstream sector, providing examples from the European Union, the United Kingdom and Brazil.

2. Sales taxes, value added taxes and excise taxes

Taxes on goods and services include all taxes and duties levied on extraction,

1 OECD, "The OECD Classification of Taxes and Interpretative Guide", *Revenue Statistics 2020* (OECD, 2021), p319.
2 *Ibid.*

production, transfer, leasing and delivery of goods, sales and provision of services. The following taxes are included in this group:

- multi-stage cumulative taxes;[3]
- general sales taxes;
- value-added taxes;
- excise duties;
- taxes levied on the import and export of goods and services;
- taxes levied on the use of goods and taxes on permission to use goods or to perform certain activities; and
- taxes on the extraction, processing or production of minerals and other products.[4]

Taxes levied on goods and services are also called 'indirect taxes'. 'Direct' taxes are those which are collected from the people and legal entities on which they are imposed (eg, income tax and property tax).

Indirect taxes apply to goods and services and are collected by someone other than the party which "is ostensibly responsible for paying the tax".[5] Although the taxes are passed on to consumers of specific goods, they are usually collected from the wholesaler rather than the consumer. For instance, "excises taxes applicable to gasoline are collected from gasoline wholesalers rather than motorists",[6] even though in practice, the tax value is passed on to motorists in the gasoline price.[7]

Indirect taxes may play a role in tax policy by increasing the cost of luxuries, making the tax system more progressive[8] or even reducing the consumption of certain products that may be harmful to health, such as alcohol and tobacco. Both value-added taxes and excise taxes are considered indirect taxes.

The main taxes on petroleum products and natural gas fall within the

---

3 Multi-stage cumulative taxes are "levied each time a transaction takes place without deduction for taxes paid on inputs. Multi-stage taxes can be combined with elements of value-added or sales taxes". OECD, "The OECD Classification of Taxes and Interpretative Guide", *Revenue Statistics 2020* (OECD, 2021), p329.

4 OECD, "The OECD Classification of Taxes and Interpretative Guide", *Revenue Statistics 2020* (OECD, 2021), p329.

5 Energy Charter Secretariat, *International Pricing Mechanisms for Oil and Gas* (2008), p42.

6 *Ibid.*

7 *Ibid.*

8 In this sense:

> *The fact that the tax structure may be regressive (ie, the rates fall with E) may appear to conflict with the intuitive notion discussed above that efficiency considerations would point to the use of a poll tax and that it is concern for the distribution which leads to the use of commodity taxes. However, when distributional objectives are relevant, indirect taxes play two roles. Firstly, by taxing luxuries at a higher rate they may increase the progressivity of the tax system; secondly, they provide an alternative source of revenue, allowing the regressive poll tax to be reduced or converted into a lump-sum payment. In the latter case, the revenue would be raised in the distortion-minimising way, and the final tax structure would balance the two sets of considerations.*

Cremer, Helmuth, Pierre Pestieau, and Jean-Charles Rochet, "Direct versus Indirect Taxation: The Design of the Tax Structure Revisited", *International Economic Review* 42(3) (2001), 781–99; www.jstor.org/stable/827029, pp65–66.

groups of import taxes, general sales taxes, value-added taxes and excise duties. In general, import taxes are imposed not only as fiscal policy or for revenue generation, but also as a reflection of the country's central power due to their importance as an instrument of macroeconomic policy aimed at the protection of local industry. If the imported product has a nationally produced equivalent, the direct effect of an import tax is to increase the market share of the domestic competitor, which promotes the transfer of income from consumers to local producers.[9]

General sales taxes include:

- all taxes levied at a specific stage of the production chain, such as manufacturing, wholesale or retail; and
- multi-stage cumulative taxes (as distinguished from value added taxes), applicable to each transaction in a cascade effect, with no deductions for the taxes collected at any earlier points in the supply chain.[10]

Value-added tax (VAT) "is a tax upon the net sales of a firm minus an appropriate depreciation charge".[11] This charge may refer to the deduction of the firm's "intermediate purchases on current account and allowable depreciation from its total sales".[12] In some cases – as occurs with Brazilian VAT (charged by the Brazilian states) – the deduction may amount to the VAT collected at the previous point of the supply chain.

Excise taxes are levied "as a product specific unit tax on a predefined range of goods".[13] Usually, as tax policy, they are applied at any stage of production or distribution, at varying rates, on non-essential or luxury goods, alcohol beverages, energy and tobacco.[14]

The points in the oil and gas downstream chain that are usually taxed are:

- imports;
- local sales; and
- processing/refining.

9 In this sense:

> *There remains the need for coordinating domestic excises with import duties. In their desire to impose heavier burdens on luxury consumption, LDCs frequently place higher import duties upon luxury products. At the same time, this measure often goes with a failure to match such duties by corresponding excises on home-produced luxury goods. Thus, luxury tariffs tend to provide protection to domestic substitutes. This is clearly poor policy. If protective tariffs are to be used to permit domestic infant industries to develop, such industries should be chosen according to their development potential and not as a side effect of luxury taxation. The best approach may well be to use largely uniform tariff rates while including luxury imports in the tax base of the domestic excise system.*

Richard A Musgrave and Peggy B Musgrave, *Public Finance in Theory and Practice* (McGraw-Hill, 5th edition, 1989), p601.

10 OECD, *System of National Accounts, 1993 – Glossary* (OECD, 2000), p21.

11 William H Oakland, "The Theory of the Value-Added Tax: I A Comparison of Tax Bases", *National Tax Journal*, vol 20(2) (National Tax Association, 1967), pp119–36, www.jstor.org/stable/41791539, p121.

12 *Ibid*, p121.

13 William H Oakland, "The Theory of the Value Added Tax: I A Comparison of Tax Bases", *National Tax Journal*, 20(2) (National Tax Association, 1967), pp119–36, www.jstor.org/stable/41791539.

14 *Ibid*.

3. Carbon-based taxes

'Externalities' are the costs or benefits imposed on third parties arising from the actions of an individual or legal entity.[15] To try to correct this type of market failure, rules are sought to internalise such costs or benefits by the agent that generated them through its actions. Where there is an externality, the price paid for the consumption of a product does not reflect the cost of production or benefit to society. The internalisation of the cost or benefit of the externality requires that it be included in the commercial relationship between the parties which give rise to the externality.[16]

Ronald Coase was a pioneer in dealing with the issue of externalities. In 1960, the University of Chicago economist conducted a study entitled "The Problem of Social Cost".[17] In the study, Coase sought to analyse the extent to which the private market is effective in dealing with externalities. He concluded that if the economic agents involved can negotiate the allocation of resources based on property rights that are well defined by the state authority, they will be able to agree on the most efficient allocation, thus solving the problem of externalities – provided that there are no transaction costs.[18, 19]

---

15 Robert Cooter and Thomas Ulen, *Law and Economics* (Berkeley Law Books, 6th edition, 2016), p39.

16 In this sense:

> *The reason the market fails in the presence of external costs is that the generator of the externality does not have to pay for harming others, and so exercises too little self-restraint. He or she acts as if the cost of disposing of waste is zero, when, in fact, there are real costs involved, as the people downstream can testify. In a technical sense, the externality generator produces too much output and too much harm because there is a difference between private marginal cost and social marginal cost.*

Ibid.

17 With this work, Coase won the Economics Science Nobel Prize in 1991.

18 Ronald H Coase, "The Problem of Social Cost", *The Journal of Law and Economics*, volume 3 (1960).

19 In the carbon market, there may be some transaction costs, such as search costs, negotiation costs, approval costs, monitoring costs, enforcement costs and insurance costs. In this sense:

> *Search costs will be incurred as investors and hosts seek out partners for mutually advantageous projects. Certain hosts and certain investors may be interested in specific types, sizes, locations, or time horizons of projects, or other characteristics. And more generally, investors and hosts may want to survey the range of alternatives before making a decision. Search costs may be seen in brokers' fees, charges for information services, or the delays incurred while trying to find a suitable partner.*
>
> *Negotiation costs will arise as interested partners work out the details of project design, obligations on each participant, assignment of benefits (such cash or technology payments and GHG abatement credits), and the schedule over which benefits will be paid for multi-year projects. Legal drafting may be needed to spell out contractual terms, and to provide for contingencies. Negotiations will also take time to conclude.*
>
> *Approval costs will be incurred at least when the GHG abatement credits are presented to national or international authorities for recordation. Advance approval of the project may also be required, most likely by the host government, but possibly also by the investor government to meet the terms of its JI program. If the COP of the FCCC decided to require centralised advance approval for each JI project, this would add significantly to approval costs. Approval costs are chiefly likely to be felt in terms of delay and uncertainty, but could also involve out-of-pocket costs involved in generating application information for submission to the approval authority.*
>
> *Monitoring costs will be necessary to ensure that participants are fulfilling their obligations (Is the boiler being converted? Is the forest being protected? Is the payment being made? Is the technology being received in usable form?). Monitoring will also be needed to measure the actual GHG abatement achieved by the project in real time (as opposed to forecast estimates). Thus monitoring costs will largely be in the form of technical expertise, equipment, and operating expenses.*
>
> *Enforcement costs will arise if monitoring reveals departures from the agreed transaction. Enforcement costs may be in the form of litigation or administrative proceedings.*
>
> *Insurance costs will likely be incurred to guard against project failure. If the investor is liable to its government or to the FCCC to demonstrate GHG abatement, the investor will want to safeguard its investment in the JI project. Project failure might occur if, for example, a wildfire destroyed a conserved*

An example of a negative externality is pollution – whether air, water or noise – generated by a certain industry; higher taxation of this industry could be a way to internalise this negative externality.[20] A person who breathes contaminated air, consumes water from a polluted river or finds himself or herself in a noisy environment is not exposed to this pollution of his or her own volition; it is a third party that has created this externality.

The taxation of carbon emissions aims to charge the polluter in order to mitigate this externality. Thus, a carbon tax may be considered as "an instrument of environmental cost internalisation".[21] Such tax is "an excise tax on the producers of raw fossil fuels based on the relative carbon content of those fuels".[22] According to the OECD, however, most countries still apply excise taxes on fuels, rather than explicit carbon taxes.[23]

4. Examples

4.1 European Union

EU member states usually charge import taxes when products originate from countries which are not members of the European Union. For local sales transactions involving oil and gas products, VAT is also applied at all stages of the sale of a specific fuel, thus increasing the value of the goods.

The VAT rate in EU countries is usually around 21%.[24] The downstream supply chain begins with the purchase of feedstock by the refinery, at which point the refinery pays VAT in proportion to the purchase amount, which is transferred to the tax authorities by the feedstock seller. Once the derived products have been refined, a sale is carried out, to which VAT applies once more; the refinery may offset the amount of tax paid on the purchase of feedstock and transfer the balance of the VAT to the tax authorities.

---

forest, if energy technology failed to work, or if the host failed to perform its obligations. Similarly, the host might insure against the risk that it operates the project but the investor fails to pay. Insurance costs might come in many forms, including financial insurance policies, purchases on spot markets, and diversification of projects.

Daniel J Dudek and Jonathan Baert Wiener, *Joint Implementation, Transaction Costs and Climate Change* (OECD, 1996), p20.

20 Mark Seidenfeld, *Microeconomics Predicates to Law and Economics* (Anderson Publishing Co, 1996), p64.

21 OECD, *Glossary of Environment Statistics*, Studies in Methods, Series F, No 67 (United Nations, 1997).

22 *Ibid.*

23 *Only a few countries provide substantial tax-based carbon price signals for non-road emissions. Whereas all but three countries tax road emissions at EUR 30 per tonne of CO2 on average (Figure 3.2, Panel A), only four out of 44 countries do so for non-road emissions. Paradoxically, the four countries are Switzerland, the Netherlands, Denmark, and Norway, which additionally participate in emissions trading systems (OECD, 2018[1]).*

Fuel excise taxes continue to dominate explicit carbon taxes. This holds for all countries in the road sector. In non-road sectors, by contrast, explicit carbon taxes tend to play a relatively more important role. Specifically, in a number of countries – Canada, Chile, Finland, France, Iceland, Ireland, Mexico, Sweden, Switzerland – explicit carbon taxes account for most of the tax-based carbon price signal.

OECD, *Taxing Energy Use 2019: Using Taxes for Climate Action* (OECD, 2019), https://doi.org/10.1787/058ca239-en).

24 OECD, *Tax Database* (OECD, 2021), www.oecd.org/tax/tax-policy/tax-database/.

This mechanism is repeated at the subsequent points of the supply chain until the sale to the end consumer. At the end of the marketing chain, the total value collected as VAT will correspond to 21% of the total value added cumulatively to the product at the various stages and will be borne by the end consumer.

Upstream companies have criticised this tax mechanism, arguing that when they contract services and equipment in the exploratory phase, the transaction will be regarded by the tax system as a final transaction. Upstream companies that do not operate downstream are sometimes unable to recover or deduct VAT that they have paid on historical exploration costs which are not directly attributable to the sales they subsequently make of hydrocarbons that are discovered several years later. The same problem occurs with exports when they are zero rated for VAT, as in this case the exporter is also unable to recover the credit. Countries may apply VAT exemptions to oil and gas refined products. In addition to VAT, European countries may apply excise taxes and carbon taxes.[25]

For instance, France charges VAT on imports from other EU member states, as well as customs duty (common external tariff) and a fee collected by customs by operators from the Professional Committee of Strategic Deployment Stocks.

In addition, excise duties (due on the consumption of certain products and payable on delivery or at the time of customs clearance) are levied as follows:

- internal consumption tax on energy products (TICPE);
- special consumption tax, which is the TICPE equivalent for overseas territories; and
- internal consumption tax on natural gas, which is the TICPE equivalent for natural gas.[26]

Spain also applies VAT on imports of oil and gas, as well as on local transactions; the tax rate is usually 21% (except when oil and gas are placed in a tax warehouse). An excise tax – the hydrocarbons tax – is also applied, with an exemption for imported oil and gas destined for industrial consumption or placed in a tax warehouse. As with custom duties, those taxes are levied on the import of oil and gas from countries outside the European Union and the applicable tariff depends on the types of petroleum products that are imported.[27]

4.2 Brazil

In Brazil, both federal and state taxes apply to imports. The following federal taxes apply:

---

25 OECD (n 23).

26 Thomson Reuters, *Practical Law. Taxes on the import and export of oil and gas* (2021), https://uk.practicallaw.thomsonreuters.com/1-524-3130?transitionType=Default&contextData=(sc.Default)&firstPage=true#:~:text=On%20the%20import%20of%20oil%20and%20gas%3A,placed%20in%20a%20tax%20warehouse.

27 *Ibid.*

- import duty tax, at a rate which varies in accordance with the customs table published in federal regulations;
- federal VAT, comprising two federal social contributions – the Programme of Social Integration (PIS) and the contribution for the financing of social security (COFINS) – with a combined tax rate of 9.25%; and
- a tax termed the 'contribution of intervention in the economic domain' (CIDE), which is levied on the import of oil and its by-products, natural gas and its by-products and ethyl alcohol fuel.

As of October 2021, however, the CIDE rates for most by-products and ethyl alcohol fuel are zero, with the exception of gasoline and diesel, for which the tax rates are set at BRL 100 and BRL 50 per cubic metre, respectively. State VAT (levied on goods, transportation services and communication services) also applies, at a rate which varies from state to state (in most cases, this is 18%).

The same state VAT applies to the sale of petroleum products. PIS and COFINS contributions are also levied by states – not as VAT, but rather in a single-phase manner – on refineries, which can act as a producer or importer, depending on the specific case and the applicable regulations. Once again, the tax rate varies depending on the product. Charging PIS and COFINS at the refinery (rather than at the petrol retail station, for instance) facilitates the collection of taxes on petroleum products; but at the same time, it may create the effect of a higher than intended tax burden if the distributor or petrol station sells the products at a lower price.

As Brazil is a federal republic in which states have autonomous tax power over certain matters – including petroleum products – there are differences in the tax rates applied in the various states. These may be sufficiently relevant to affect decisions on the location of infrastructure: sometimes, tax differences are more relevant than logistical impacts and other economic factors when choosing between alternative locations. While some interstate transactions may face a surcharge with the aim of equalising tax rates and correcting differences that are sufficiently significant to result in the misallocation of resources, these surcharges do not apply to sales of petroleum products.

CIDE may also apply depending on the product. For instance, CIDE-fuels is applied on the sale of:

- gasoline;
- diesel;
- aviation kerosene and other kerosene;
- fuel oil;
- liquefied petroleum gas (LPG), including LPG derived from natural gas and naphtha; and
- fuel ethyl alcohol.

CIDE-fuels is paid by producers, blenders[28] and importers of these liquid fuels. The incidence of CIDE-fuels is single phased. Distributors, retailers, transporters and final consumers are not taxpayers. The final consumer (the *de facto* taxpayer) bears the tax burden of this tax in the fuel purchase price.

CIDE-fuels was originally intended to serve as a regulatory tax, with a double function:

- Its revenues would be ringfenced to cover transportation expenses such as road maintenance and to promote the reduction of fuel consumption; and
- It would be used to absorb and mitigate oil price variations, reducing the tax rate whenever prices increased and increasing the tax rate whenever they decreased.

There have indeed been instances where the CIDE-fuels rate has been reduced to absorb increases in oil prices and avoid inflation, as an example of the regulatory use of indirect taxes in the downstream sector. However, CIDE-fuel revenues have not always been allocated to the funding of transportation expenses in government budgets.[29]

As occurs in EU countries, upon the export of petroleum products, the state VAT credits are converted into costs for the legal entities, since exports are state VAT exempt.

4.3 United Kingdom

The United Kingdom charges VAT at a rate of 20% on the import of petroleum products (with the exception of natural gas) and does not apply customs duties. A reduced VAT rate of 5% applies to domestic heating fuel. VAT is also applied to the domestic sale of petroleum products. For instance, for fuel, VAT applies to domestic fuel bills at a rate of 5%.

A specific excise tax – fuel duty – is levied on fuel and is "included in the price you pay for petrol, diesel and other fuels used in vehicles or for heating".[30] The rate varies according to the product and how it is used. For instance, in October 2021:

- for petrol, diesel, biodiesel and bioethanol, the rate was 57.95 pence per litre;

---

28 Liquid fuel formulators (as defined by the local regulator, the National Petroleum Agency) are legal entities authorised to carry out, in fuel formulation plants:
- the acquisition of streams of liquid hydrocarbons;
- the mechanical mixing of liquid hydrocarbon streams, in order to obtain gasoline and diesel;
- the storage of intermediate streams and formulated fuels; and
- the marketing of gasoline and diesel.

29 There have been judicial discussions challenging the application of this tax given the misapplication of its revenues. However, the Brazilian Supreme Court ruled that the tax remains valid, although budgetary allocations may be challenged in certain situations (ADI 2925, 19 December 2003).

30 UK Government, *Tax on Shopping and Services. Fuel Duty*, www.gov.uk/tax-on-shopping/fuel-duty.

- for LPG, the rate was 31.61 pence per kilogram;
- for natural gas used as fuel in vehicles, such as biogas, the rate was 4.70 pence per kilogram; and
- for fuel oil burned in a furnace or used for heating, the rate was 10.70 pence per litre.[31]

5. Conclusion

Downstream taxation is generally implemented by means of indirect taxes. In all countries analysed in this chapter, VAT is applied. The rates may be summarised as follows:

- European Union: 21%.
- Brazil:
  - 9.25% (federal VAT); and
  - 18% (state VAT).
- United Kingdom:
  - 20% on the import of petroleum products;
  - 5% on domestic heating fuel; and
  - 5% on domestic fuel bills.

Some special taxes also apply in the sector, such as:

- CIDE-fuels in Brazil, applicable at BRL 100 and BRL 50 per cubic metre for gasoline and diesel respectively; and
- fuel duty in the United Kingdom, applicable as follows:
  - for petrol, diesel, biodiesel and bioethanol, 57.95 pence per litre;
  - for LPG, 31.61 pence per kilogram;
  - for natural gas used as fuel in vehicles, such as biogas, 4.70 pence per kilogram; and
  - for fuel oil burned in a furnace or used for heating, 10.70 pence per litre.[32]

As a result of the environmental impact of petroleum products, the taxation of such products often has a regulatory function, whereby the state seeks to internalise into the price the externalities across the wider petroleum chain. Carbon-based taxes are a clear example of this: as the name suggests, they have the regulatory function of reflecting the societal costs of carbon and greenhouse gases.

This notwithstanding, one should not underestimate the typical fiscal purpose of collecting revenues to fund public expenditure. Petroleum products have a fundamental role as energy sources in contemporary society. Most

---

31 *Ibid.*
32 *Ibid.*

importantly, it is typically easy to collect the taxes imposed on them. In the absence of macroeconomic effects on inflation or electoral effects resulting from a public outcry over higher prices, governments are seldom reluctant to impose taxes on petroleum products. Their regulatory function may thus easily be overshadowed by their revenue-generating function.

Antitrust

Paula Camara
Giovani Loss
Mattos Filho

1. Introduction

Unlike sector-specific regulations – such as the framework applicable to oil and gas activities – the main goal of antitrust laws and policy is not to dictate the rules applicable to specific activities, but rather to prevent certain undesired behaviours by agents across all sectors.[1] In other words, the antitrust authorities aim to prevent and punish anti-competitive behaviour – whether in the form of abuse of a dominant position or collusion between competitors. This is also why antitrust intervention in the oil and gas industry is reactive and exceptional.

This chapter summarises:

- antitrust policy and regulation in general (with a special focus on jurisdictions with a high level of activity in the midstream oil and gas sector);
- the main functions and limits of antitrust enforcement in regulated sectors; and
- its applicability to the midstream and downstream oil and gas industry.

2. Antitrust issues in the midstream and downstream oil and gas sector

The oil and gas sector has been subject to antitrust enforcement for more than a century. *Standard Oil Company v United States* 221 US 1 (1911) is considered a landmark case in the history of antitrust scrutiny, due not only to the essential nature of the oil and gas sector, but also to its structural characteristics.

The upstream oil and gas sector involves the extraction of raw materials (crude oil and natural gas). The midstream sector involves transportation and storage services, as well as refining activities. Finally, the downstream sector involves post-production activities, including the marketing and resale of oil products and natural gas to end consumers.

Petroleum refining activities involve a set of chemical processes aimed at transforming crude oil (petroleum) into oil products, such as gasoline, diesel,

1 Carlos Emmanuel Ragazzo, *A Regulação da Concorrência*, January 2013, https://edisciplinas.usp.br/pluginfile.php/174307/mod_resource/content/1/fulltext-2.pdf.

solvent and lubricants. Refining is considered part of the midstream segment of the oil and derivatives production chain, which also includes the transportation of oil products – usually through pipelines or tankers – and their storage at terminals that serve as focal points in the distribution chain. Oil products are normally sold to fuel distributors and petrochemicals companies, which use them to manufacture their finished products (downstream segment).

As shown in Figure 1, the upstream and midstream oil and gas industry is heavily infrastructure based and as such tends to be highly concentrated: market structures have few players and hence less competition. The downstream sector, by contrast, tends to be less concentrated or more fragmented, with a higher number of participants – particularly in relation to fuel marketing/resale activities.

Figure 1. Simplified structure of upstream, midstream and downstream oil activities

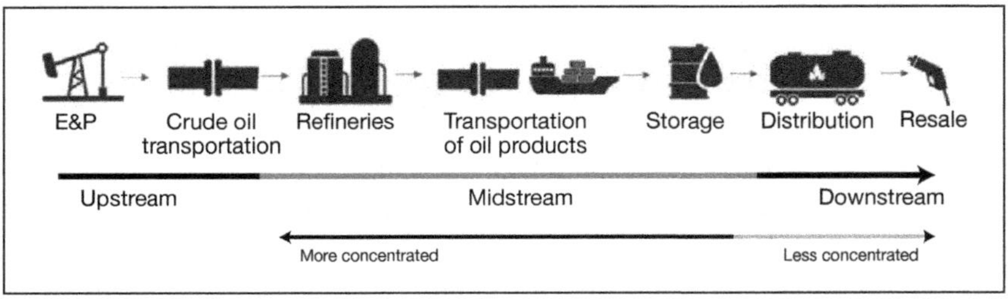

As is explored further below, different antitrust issues tend to arise in different market segments. Abuse of dominance is more common in the more concentrated segments; whereas segments characterised by homogeneous products, price transparency and similar cost structures (eg, fuel marketing and resale) tend to be subject to greater cartel scrutiny. Regardless of the specific characteristics of the markets involved, antitrust enforcement encompasses a range of activities and measures that can be adopted by the competent authorities. Midstream and downstream enterprises must be wary of the potential antitrust issues that may arise in the exercise of their activities.

3. Competition policy overview

One of the main goals of antitrust laws is to promote economic welfare.[2] To this end, antitrust authorities around the globe are commonly vested with both preventive powers – usually exercised through the analysis of mergers that fall

2 Joshua D Wright and Douglas H Ginsburg, *The Goals of Antitrust: Welfare Trumps Choice*, 2013, www.ftc.gov/sites/default/files/documents/public_statements/goals-antitrust-welfare-trumps-choice/130320goalsofantitrustbp4.pdf.

within specific thresholds – and disciplinary powers, allowing them to investigate and punish anti-competitive behaviour. The antitrust authorities also have an educational role, aimed at promoting competition and increasing awareness of antitrust issues.

In general, antitrust enforcement involves the following:

- Abuse of a dominant position: A common concern of antitrust in general is to prevent the abuse of a dominant position. In such cases, the antitrust authorities analyse the extent to which a firm with a dominant position can harm competition and reduce consumer welfare by raising prices, reducing output or preventing the entry of new competitors.[3] This issue has particular relevance in concentrated sectors, such as the midstream and downstream oil and gas industries.
- Collusive agreements: Collusive agreements are horizontal agreements between competitors whose object (or effect) is to restrict competition. This is the case, for instance, of price-fixing arrangements, also known as cartels. Collusive agreements are one of the top priorities of antitrust authorities and are often considered unlawful *per se*, given their high anti-competitive potential. This type of agreement is more likely to arise in sectors whose structural characteristics facilitate the establishment of cartels (eg, few competitors, homogeneous products, similar costs and transparent prices). This is the case, for instance, in the fuel resale segment, which has been subject to intense antitrust scrutiny in many jurisdictions.
- Vertical agreements: These are agreements between players that are active in different levels of the market (eg, oil product suppliers that engage in resale price fixing arrangements with resellers/gas stations). Vertical agreements may be unlawful from an antitrust standpoint to the extent that they can harm competition; however, unlike collusive horizontal agreements, vertical arrangements are not usually considered unlawful *per se*, as they may also result in market efficiency (eg, the elimination of double marginalisation).
- Mergers: The main goal of merger control is to prevent transactions that could present antitrust concerns, such as a significant reduction of competition and/or the creation or strengthening of a dominant position.[4]
- Competition advocacy: This is usually seen as part of the antitrust authorities' educational role. It includes participation in discussions on the rules that apply in regulated sectors, as well as commentary and advice on legislation and regulations issued by other regulatory authorities. As such, it has particular relevance in regulated sectors – such as the midstream and downstream oil and gas industries.

3 Richard Whish, *Competition Law*, Oxford University Press, 2015.
4 See, for instance, Article 88 of Brazilian Federal Law 12,529/2011.

There follows a general overview of antitrust enforcement in the midstream and downstream oil and gas sectors. This highlights the main issues and potential risks that oil and gas players should take into account in terms of antitrust compliance – and, as such, is relevant to most jurisdictions around the globe. Specific comments are made on three key jurisdictions: Brazil, the United States and the European Union.

3.1 Conduct

The antitrust authorities are usually vested with the power to initiate proceedings and investigate and punish anti-competitive behaviour – generally through the imposition of fines.

In Brazil, the Competition Law is enforced by the Administrative Council for Economic Defence (CADE), which has broad powers to initiate proceedings, investigate potential anti-competitive conduct and impose fines. Defendants that are found to have engaged in anti-competitive conduct are subject to fines ranging from 0.1% to 20% of the gross revenues registered by the company, group or conglomerate in the fiscal year prior to commencement of the investigation in the line of business in which the infringement occurred. The law also provides for non-pecuniary sanctions, such as:

- debarment from government procurement procedures for up to five years; and
- publication of the administrative decision in major newspapers.

In Europe, the European Commission is responsible for antitrust enforcement. Article 103 of the Treaty on the Functioning of the European Union empowers the commission to fine companies that are found to have engaged in antitrust infringements. According to Council Regulation 1/2003, fines are based on the gravity and duration of the infringement and must not exceed 10% of the company's turnover.

Finally, in the United States, federal antitrust policy is enforced by both the Federal Trade Commission (FTC) and the US Department of Justice (DOJ) Antitrust Division. The powers of both agencies are complementary and over the years both have developed expertise in specific industries. The oil and gas sector is overseen by the FTC, which has broad powers to initiate and conduct investigations of anti-competitive behaviour in this segment. If the FTC finds that there has been an antitrust violation, it will usually try to secure voluntary compliance by entering into a consent order with the company under investigation. If this is unsuccessful, the FTC can seek injunctive relief in the federal courts and/or file an administrative complaint.[5] US antitrust laws (in

5 More information is available at www.ftc.gov/advice-guidance/competition-guidance/guide-antitrust-laws/enforcers.

particular, the Sherman Act) provide for the imposition of criminal penalties of up to $100 million for corporations and $1 million for individuals, along with up to 10 years in prison.

(a) Unilateral conduct

Antitrust infringements encompass both unilateral and collusive conduct. Unilateral conduct (eg, abuse of dominance or other forms of exclusionary practices) tends to be less threatening to competition than collusive agreements. As such, this type of conduct is usually analysed under a 'rule of reason' approach and may be permitted on the grounds of the so-called 'efficiency defence'. This involves a trade-off analysis between the efficiencies resulting from specific market conduct and its potential anti-competitive effects. In other words, unilateral conduct is not always deemed anti-competitive in most jurisdictions.

This is also the approach adopted by the Brazilian antitrust authority. When analysing the legality of unilateral conduct, CADE reviews the economic rationale of the conduct and balances its positive and negative effects on general market dynamics (not only in relation to specific competitors that may be negatively impacted). Among other things, CADE considers:

- whether the company under investigation has a dominant position in the affected market; and
- whether there are legitimate business reasons for the adoption of such conduct or rather whether such conduct is mainly designed to harm competition in the market.

If the negative effects of such conduct outweigh its efficiencies, the conduct will be deemed anti-competitive by CADE and, as such, will be subject to sanctions. Except for specific cases (eg, those involving resale price maintenance), the burden of proof rests with the plaintiff and/or CADE – that is, the conduct is presumed legal unless proved otherwise.

The European Commission takes a similar approach. According to the commission, a company with a dominant position, when faced with a charge of abuse of dominance/exclusionary practice, may prove that its practice is justified "by demonstrating that its conduct is objectively necessary or by demonstrating that its conduct produces substantial efficiencies which outweigh any anticompetitive effects on consumers". However, the standard of analysis adopted by the commission is stricter. In this sense, depending on the severity of the conduct, the commission may infer its anti-competitive effects[6]

6 See the Directorate-General of Competition Discussion Paper on the application of Article 82 of the EC Treaty to exclusionary abuses (2005): "There may be circumstances where it is not necessary for the Commission to carry out a detailed assessment before concluding that the conduct in question is likely to result in consumer harm. If it appears that the conduct can only raise obstacles to competition and that it creates no efficiencies, its anti-competitive effect may be inferred."

– in which case, the burden of proof shifts to the defendant to demonstrate the justification and/or efficiencies arising from the practice under investigation.

In the United States, the 'rule of reason' approach is also used by the courts to determine most antitrust claims – including those relating to exclusionary practices. In such cases, the burden is on the plaintiff's side to prove that a defendant with market power engaged in exclusionary practices;[7] in simple terms, 'exclusionary conduct' means anti-competitive behaviour aimed at harming existing competitors or preventing new competitors from entering a given market. If the plaintiff meets this burden, the defendant will then have the opportunity to prove any compensatory efficiencies.

Abuse of dominance cases are closely connected to the concept of a dominant position or market power. This is because the anti-competitive potential of exclusionary conduct is dependent on the plaintiff's ability to pose a threat to competition; in other words, conduct by players that do not have a dominant position usually does not (and cannot) have an exclusionary effect.

An economic agent is usually considered dominant when it can individually or jointly change market conditions. In Brazil, it is presumed that a company has a dominant position when it controls 20% or more of a given market.[8] This presumption is not absolute and the 20% threshold may be reviewed on a case-by-case basis, depending on the specific market conditions. The legal test applied by the European Commission is less objective: dominance is found where a certain undertaking has the ability to prevent competition and to behave independently.[9] Finally, in the United States, the courts also analyse market share to determine whether a potentially dominant firm has 'significant and durable market power' (defined as the long-term ability to raise price or exclude competitors); in general, significant and durable market power is usually found in cases where a company (of group of companies) has a share of 50% or more of a given market.

The midstream oil and gas industry – and particularly, activities involving the storage, transportation and production of refined products – has historically been exposed to exclusionary practices, given its structural characteristics (eg, few players, high market shares), as set out in the examples below.

Brazil: CADE has ruled on many cases of abuse of dominance in Brazil throughout the years and is increasingly looking more closely at commercial practices/agreements of companies with a dominant position – including in the midstream and downstream oil and gas industry. Petroleo Brasileiro (Petrobras) – the Brazilian public company that has historically been considered a

---

7 Herbert Hovenkamp, *The Rule of Reason*, 2018, https://scholarship.law.upenn.edu/cgi/viewcontent.cgi?article=2780&context=faculty_scholarship.

8 Article 36, paragraph 2, of Law 12,529/2011.

9 See *United Brands v Commission* (Case 27/76 [1978] ECR 207, [1978], 1 CMLR 429).

monopolist in virtually all segments of the oil and gas chain – has been subject to a number of antitrust investigations involving a series of alleged abuses of dominance in the midstream/downstream oil and gas sector. More recently, Petrobras and CADE settled a series of investigations involving exclusionary conduct in the midstream oil and gas industry and agreed on measures aimed at promoting competition in such segments.

In Cases 08700.002600/2014-30 and 08700.007130/2015-82, Comgás accused Petrobras of engaging in discriminatory treatment in the supply of natural gas to distributors in the state of São Paulo. According to Comgás, Petrobras offered unilateral discounts on gas prices, generating competitive advantages for its subsidiary, Gás Brasiliano Distribuidora SA.

Abegás in turn accused Petrobras of engaging in conduct with anti-competitive effects – specifically:

- arbitrary profit increases;
- abuse of a dominant position; and
- distortion or damage to competition through alleged discriminatory treatment and lack of transparency in relation to its pricing policy and contracting conditions.

In July 2019, Petrobras entered into a settlement agreement with CADE involving both investigations in the national gas market. The main goal of the agreement was to promote competition in segments that had hitherto been dominated by Petrobras. Among other things, Petrobras agreed to:

- sell its equity interests in national gas carriers NTS, TAG and TBG, and its indirect equity interest in gas distribution companies; and
- undertake a series of behavioural commitments aimed at guaranteeing that third parties would have immediate access to the remaining capacities of NTS, TAG and TBG, as well as access to distribution pipelines and to natural gas processing units.

Petrobras also agreed:

- not to contract new volumes of natural gas from third parties or partners (in consortium with other companies); and
- to reduce imports of natural gas from Bolivia and initiate a competitive process for leasing the Baía de Todos os Santos regasification terminal.

In Case 08700.006955/2018-22, CADE initiated an administrative inquiry to investigate Petrobras's abuse of dominant power in the oil refinery market (in 2017, Petrobras was responsible for 98.2% of the total production capacity of oil refinery stations in Brazil).

Petrobras agreed to sell off eight of its 13 operated refineries and their respective transportation assets – namely:

- Refinaria Abreu e Lima;
- Unidade de Industrialização de Xisto;
- Refinaria Landulpho Alves;
- Refinaria Gabriel Passos;
- Refinaria Presidente Getúlio Vargas;
- Refinaria Alberto Pasqualini;
- Refinaria Isaac Sabbá; and
- Lubrificantes e Derivados de Petróleo do Nordeste.

European Union: The oil and gas sector has always been a significant issue for EU member states and, as such, has been subject to a number of actions by local governments and authorities, including attempts to:

- harmonise local laws and regulations across the member states;
- build a single internal market; and
- become independent from the external market.

To this end, the European Commission has also launched a number of exclusionary conduct cases against companies in the oil and gas sector. For example, in Case AT.39316, the European Commission opened a formal investigation against GdF Suez (former Gaz de France SA and Suez SA, which merged in 2008) to examine an alleged abuse of dominant position and restrictive business practices. In particular, the commission believed that GdF Suez had:

- restricted access to its transportation capacity;
- entered into exclusionary import agreements; and
- underinvested in its infrastructure capacity, restricting competition in the downstream gas supply markets.

GdF entered into an agreement with the commission in which it committed to:

- release to third parties the capacity of one of its gas entry pipelines; and
- limit its reservations of capacity of high calorific value gas to less than 50% of the total firm, long-term capacity available in that infrastructure.[10]

In Case AT.39315, the European Commission carried out an investigation into capacity hoarding and strategic underinvestment by ENI in the transmission system, leading to the foreclosure of competitors in the Italian gas supply market. In the commission's view, this conduct could only be explained

10 See the commission's decision on the commitments at https://ec.europa.eu/competition/antitrust/cases/dec_docs/39316/39316_2298_3.pdf.

as an intent to secure profits by limiting gas imports by third parties to Italy – behaviour that negatively affected gas prices.

ENI also entered into an agreement with the commission to:

- divest its share in international gas transmission pipeline companies and in transmission system operators; and
- divest its subsidiaries in Germany and Austria.[11]

United States: The United States also had a history of investigations involving the oil and gas sector. *Standard Oil Co of New Jersey v United States* is often cited as a landmark case in US antitrust history. This was one of the first cases brought under the Sherman Act before the US Supreme Court, which found Standard Oil Co of New Jersey guilty of monopolising the petroleum industry (including oil production, processing, marketing and transportation) through a series of abusive and anti-competitive actions. Standard Oil was ultimately divided into several geographically separate and eventually competing firms.

The midstream and downstream oil and gas sector in the United States has changed significantly since *Standard Oil* was decided. However, the FTC still keeps a close watch out for potential abusive behaviour in this sector, including in the midstream and downstream segments. Examples include the following:

- In 2013, the FTC published a report on activities in the oil and natural gas industries in order to better assess the market and identify potential anti-competitive and anti-consumer practices in the energy sector. The report covered M&A transactions investigated by the FTC in sectors such as:
  - oil pipeline transportation;
  - refineries;
  - refined petroleum product pipelines and terminals;
  - crude oil and petroleum products merchant wholesaling;
  - natural gas liquids; and
  - natural gas exploration, production, transportation, storage and distribution.

The FTC also investigated potentially harmful conduct in the petroleum and natural gas sectors, investigating whether oil producers, refiners, transporters, marketers and physical or financial traders were manipulating prices or providing false information to public agencies.

- A working paper investigating the effects of refinery outages on product prices and investment was released by the FTC in 2014. After analysing both the capacities and the outages of individual refineries, it concluded

11 See the commission's decision on the commitments at https://ec.europa.eu/competition/antitrust/cases/dec_docs/39315/39315_3019_9.pdf.

that outages can have a significant effect on product (eg, gasoline) prices. It also discovered that investment strategies – particularly underinvestment in refining units – were associated with recent outages in those units; although there were other factors that also influenced refiners' decisions to invest in capacity.

- In 2015, the FTC released a study on the evolution of the US refining industry, which concluded that larger refineries were less likely to close and that refineries owned by a corporate group including several refineries were more likely to close. It found that where a multi-refinery group closed a refinery, it was likely to close its smaller refineries. Based on plant-level capacity data from 1947 to 2013, this study found weak evidence that refineries owned by firms with higher market shares were less likely to close. In specifications with more control variables, this relationship was statistically insignificant
- Since 2011, the FTC has released a yearly report on ethanol market concentration together with the US Energy Information Administration. The latest report revealed that while production capacity remained almost the same in 2021, actual production decreased, as did the volume of ethanol exports. The conclusion was that this market is not concentrated and has a high possibility of entry and a low probability of exercise of market power (because of the large number of market participants).

(b) Coordinated conduct: horizontal agreements

In 1776, in *The Wealth of Nations*, Adam Smith stated that "people of the same trade seldom meet together, even for merriment and diversion, but the conversation ends in a conspiracy against the public, or in some contrivance to raise prices". Cartels and other hardcore horizontal agreements to fix prices, divide markets and/or restrict output are often described as the most serious antitrust infringements and one of the top priorities of antitrust enforcement in different jurisdictions. Given the high anti-competitive potential of cartels, they are perhaps the most obvious target of domestic antitrust policies.

For this same reason – unlike the 'rule of reason' approach, which is often adopted by antitrust authorities when analysing unilateral conduct/exclusionary practices – cartels and hardcore horizontal agreements are usually analysed under a '*per se*' analysis, meaning that they will be deemed illegal regardless of the size of the company or the actual effects suffered in the market.

The oil and gas sector has been a key focus of cartel antitrust enforcement – whether due to its structural characteristics (which facilitate the formation of cartels, mainly in downstream segments) or due to the strategic nature of oil and gas in national and international industry policies. Another structural feature that facilitates the formation of cartels in this sector is that oil products tend to have low margins, which is an additional incentive for collusive behaviour.

Brazil: Cartel enforcement has been a top priority for CADE since the first Brazilian competition law entered into force. The oil and gas industry – in particular, the marketing of oil products – has been subject to close antitrust scrutiny in the form of cartel investigations, due mainly to its structural characteristics that facilitate the establishment of cartels (eg, homogeneous products, transparent prices, same cost structure).

Since 1996, CADE has received hundreds of complaints involving the alleged formation of cartels in the downstream oil and gas sector. Most of these were dismissed based on the lack of minimal evidence to justify a formal investigation. In total, CADE has initiated more than 30 administrative procedures, resulting in approximately 15 convictions. To date, the highest fines imposed by CADE in this sector include:

- fines totalling BRL 67 million imposed on gas resellers located in the state of Espírito Santo; and
- fines totalling BRL 156 million imposed on 27 gas resellers, two distributors and 12 employees located in the region of the city of Belo Horizonte.

Table 1 summarises some of the landmark cases involving cartels in the Brazilian downstream sectors. The evolution of Brazilian cartel cases in the gasoline resale market reflects several trends, including:

- the common involvement of trade unions and associations in collusive arrangements in this sector; and
- an increase in both the level of sophistication of CADE's investigation tools and the fines imposed by CADE – including on employees.

Table 1. CADE – cartel cases in downstream markets

Administrative proceeding	Parties involved	Market involved	Fines/penalties
08012.002299/2000-18	Plaintiff: Public Prosecutor's Office of Santa Catarina. Defendants: Florianópolis Trade Union of Retail Trade in Mineral Fuels, as well as several gas stations and their directors.	Gasoline resale in the region of Florianópolis/SC.	Trade union: BRL 400,000. Gas stations/ resale companies: 10% of their respective gross revenues in the year preceding the investigation. Directors: 10% to 15% of the fine attributed to the resale company.
08012.010215/2007-96	Plaintiff: Secretariat of Economic Law. Defendants: Several gas stations in Caxias do Sul/RS	Fuel retail sector in Caxias do Sul/RS.	Service stations: Fines equivalent to 15% to 17% of gross revenues in the year prior to the establishment of the cartel. Service station owners and managers: Fines ranging from 8% to 17% of the fines applied to the respective companies. One owner of a service station without declared billing was fined the equivalent of 160,000 UFIR.[12]

continued on next page

12 The UFIR is a tax index used to calculate debts with the government. Currently, 1 unit of UFIR is equal to approximately BRL 42.

Administrative proceeding	Parties involved	Market involved	Fines/penalties
			The fines varied according to the degree of participation of each person or company in the conduct.
08700.010769.2 014-64	Plaintiff: National Agency of Petroleum, Natural Gas and Biofuels. Defendants: Several gas stations in Belo Horizonte, Betim and Contagem, as well as individuals who acted as employees, partners or administrators of these companies.	Automotive fuel retail and distribution (common gas and ethanol) in Belo Horizonte, Betim and Contagem.	Gas stations: Fines equivalent to 13% to 15% of gross sales, according to their participation in the cartel. Partners and managers: 2% of the fines applied to the respective companies. Employees: 50,000 UFIR.
08012.008847/2 006-17	Plaintiff: Espírito Santo State Prosecutor's Office. Defendants: Several gas stations in Espírito Santo and their partners/ managers.	Fuel retail sector in the metropolitan region of Vitória.	Partners/managers: Fines of 1% to 8% of the fines applied to the respective companies. Gas stations: Information kept confidential by CADE.

Source: Authors based on CADE data.

European Union: As mentioned, antitrust enforcement in the oil and gas sector is one of the European Commission's top priorities, given the sector's strategic importance for all member states. As such, in addition to dominance cases, cartel enforcement has come under close scrutiny from the commission.

For instance, in 2013, the commission carried out inspections at the premises of several players in the crude oil, refined oil and biofuel markets. The inspections were motivated by concerns that the companies were colluding to report distorted prices to a price reporting agency in order to manipulate the published price of oil and biofuel, and were excluding other companies from participating in those price assessments. The following year, the commission also conducted on-site inspections to further investigate alleged collusion on price reporting in the ethanol sector; it did so again in April 2015.

In December 2015, the European Commission opened a formal investigation against Abengoa SA (Spain), Alcogroup SA (Belgium) and Lantmännen ek för (Sweden) and their subsidiaries – all players in the distribution and trading of ethanol – to investigate the manipulation of ethanol benchmark prices. Abengoa SA settled in December 2021 and received a €20 million fine, whereas the other two defendants proceeded with the investigation through the regular cartel procedure. In July 2022, the European Commission informed both groups, through a statement of objections, of its preliminary view that the companies colluded to influence the wholesale price formation mechanism for ethanol in Europe.[13]

United States: Following the end of World War II, the FTC conducted investigations in various industries, including the oil industry. In 1951, amid the beginning of the Cold War, FTC studies of worldwide oil markets provoked a national security debate about the implications for the country if the results were made public. The report found that seven international companies operated through jointly owned subsidiaries and, through this complex web of companies, controlled the oil, refining, cracking and transportation markets. After the report was made public, President Truman ordered the DOJ to set up a grand jury, which investigated 21 companies.[14]

Cartel enforcement in the United States remains one of the key priorities of antitrust enforcement and has received attention from all levels of the US government. For instance, on 17 November 2021, President Joe Biden issued a letter to FTC Chair Lina Khan requesting further investigation of oil and gas prices. The president's letter stated that while prices at the pump seemed to have

---

13 See the European Commission press release at https://ec.europa.eu/commission/presscorner/detail/en/ip_22_4362.

14 Kelly Signs, Bureau of Competition, "FTC Milestones: Cold War chills report on international petroluem cartel", Federal Trade Commission, 17 December 2014, www.ftc.gov/enforcement/competition-matters/2014/ 12/ftc-milestones-cold-war-chills-report-international-petroleum-cartel.

increased, the costs of fuel production were dropping, meaning higher profits for the industry. According to Biden, there was an excessively wide gap between the price of unfinished gasoline and the average price at the pump, in comparison to 2019 (which he highlighted was the last year before the COVID-19 pandemic).[15] In August 2021, Brian Deese, director of the White House National Economic Council, also sent a letter to the FTC to ask it to monitor the gasoline market.[16]

3.2 Merger control

Virtually all of the most important/sophisticated antitrust jurisdictions worldwide have in place a pre-merger control regime, meaning that where certain local thresholds are met, such transactions cannot be implemented without clearance from the antitrust authorities.

This is the so-called 'preventive role' of the antitrust authorities. Mergers that may result in the elimination of competition, create or strengthen a dominant position or result in the domination of the relevant market of goods or services can be rejected altogether by the antitrust authorities or be approved with restrictions – which may include structural remedies (eg, the divestiture of an asset) and/or behavioural commitments.

Each jurisdiction has its own thresholds for determining whether a transaction will be subject to mandatory filing. The thresholds usually include a local effects test and are often based on the revenues registered by the merging entities in a given country.

As such, when engaging in corporate transactions, midstream and downstream oil and gas companies – especially those that are active across several different countries, even if only through exportation – are advised to proceed with a comprehensive analysis of the jurisdictional thresholds of the countries in which they have registered revenues.

Midstream and downstream oil and gas companies must also bear in mind that it is not only mergers and acquisitions that are caught by the merger control rules. Other types of arrangements – many of which are typical in this industry – may also be caught by the merger control rules. These may include consortia, joint ventures and other forms of partnership agreements.

In general, the merger control rules are not sector specific; nor are there exemptions applicable to the oil and gas sector. However, there may be special legislation governing specific aspects of mergers and acquisitions in this highly regulated industry. For instance, in addition to antitrust clearance, the approval of other federal agencies may be required.

---

15 Biden's letter to the Federal Trade Commission can be found at https://int.nyt.com/data/documenttools/ftc-gas-prices/92d93dca9793b8b4/full.pdf.

16 Jennifer Epstein, *Biden urges FTC to probe gasoline market with prices up 50%*, 17 November 2021, www.bloomberg.com/news/articles/2021-11-17/biden-asks-ftc-to-probe-gasoline-market-suggesting-wrongdoing.

Brazil: According to the Competition Law, a transaction is subject to mandatory notification with CADE whenever the following criteria are met:

- The transaction has effects in Brazil;
- The transaction is deemed an 'economic concentration'; and
- The revenues of the groups involved exceed the thresholds provided by law.

In relation to the first point above, the transaction will be considered as having effects in Brazil if:

- it takes place in the Brazilian territory; or
- it takes place abroad, but the target has or will have a direct or indirect presence in Brazil.

In relation to the second point, the following transactions are deemed to be economic concentrations under the Brazilian merger rules:

- the acquisition of control or partial control of a company through the purchase or exchange of stocks, shares, bonds or securities convertible into stocks or assets, whether tangible or intangible, by contract or by any other means;
- the acquisition of 20% or more of the voting or total shares (when there is no overlap or vertical link between the parties involved);
- the acquisition of 5% or more of the voting or total shares (when the parties are either horizontally or vertically related); and
- association agreements, consortia and joint ventures, except if created for the purposes of a tender process launched by the public administration.

In relation to the third point above, the Brazilian merger regime sets forth the following revenue thresholds:

- At least one of the groups involved (seller or buyer) had registered gross revenues in Brazil in excess of BRL 750 million in the year preceding the merger; and
- At least one of the other groups involved has registered gross revenues in Brazil in excess of BRL75 million in the year preceding the merger.

Mergers in the oil and gas are fairly common and CADE analyses an average of 20 cases in the sector annually (including upstream – see Figure 2). Virtually all cases are analysed under CADE's fast-track procedure, which is applicable to cases that do not pose antitrust concerns.

Figure 2. CADE – total merger cases (2017–2021)

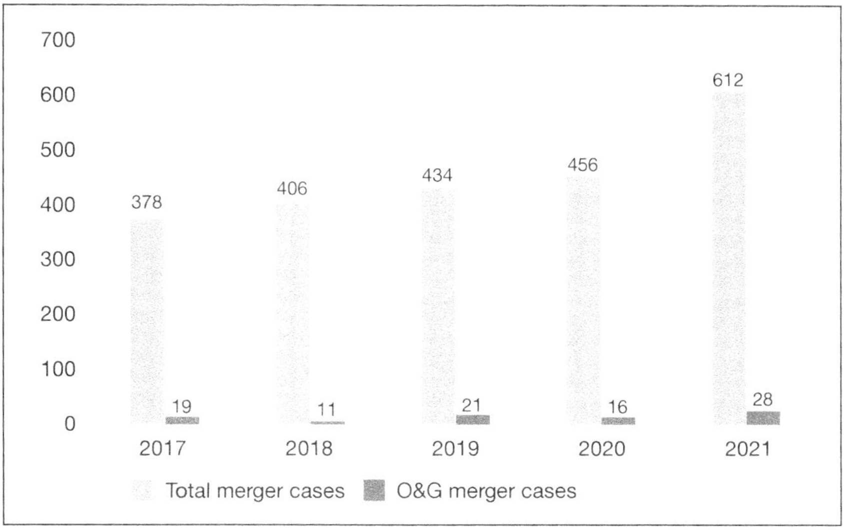

Source: Authors based on CADE data.

European Union: According to the European Commission rules, notification is mandatory for all concentrations that have an EU dimension. The EU system is also suspensory, meaning that such concentrations shall not be closed or implemented until they have been cleared by the commission. According to the EU Merger Regulation, a transaction will only be caught by the EU merger regulation system if it has an 'EU dimension' – meaning that it must meet one of the following alternatives:

- a combined worldwide turnover of all merging firms of over €5 billion; and
- an EU-wide turnover of each of at least two firms of over €250 million;

or

- a worldwide turnover of all merging firms of over €2.5 billion;
- a combined turnover of all merging firms of over €100 million in each of at least three member states;
- a turnover of over €25 million of each of at least two of the firms in each of the above three member states; and
- an EU-wide turnover of each of at least two firms of more than €100 million.[17]

17 See Article 1 of the EU Merger Regulation.

There is an exception for both alternatives: the EU dimension is not met if each of the firms has registered more than two-thirds of its EU turnover within one member state only.

United States: The United States also has in place a pre-merger control regime, established under Section 7A of the Clayton Act (15 United States Code (USC), Section 18a), also known as the Hart-Scott-Rodino Antitrust Improvements Act of 1976. This provides that if the following thresholds are met, the parties to a proposed transaction (including mergers, acquisitions and joint venture and entity formations) cannot implement it before notifying it to the competent authorities (ie, the FTC and the DOJ).

- 'Size of transaction' test: Transactions with a value of $101 million or less[18] are exempted from merger control under the Hart-Scott-Rodino Act (this amount is adjusted on an annual basis).
- 'Size of person' test: Transactions with a value of less than $493.9 million must also meet a 'size of person' test, meaning, basically:
  - on one side, the seller or buyer has annual net sales or total assets of $202 million or more; and
  - on the other side, the seller or buyer has annual net sales or total assets of $20.2 million or more.

4. Antitrust enforcement versus sector-specific regulatory framework

The oil and gas sector is usually highly regulated, given its strategic nature. As such, in addition to antitrust scrutiny (which, as seen above, is not sector specific), oil and gas activities – including in the midstream and downstream sectors – tend to be highly regulated. The roles played by the antitrust authorities and sector-specific regulatory agencies tend to be complementary.

4.1 Brazil

The National Agency of Petroleum, Natural Gas and Biofuels (ANP), established by the Petroleum Act (9478/1997), is the federal entity responsible for the regulation of the oil, natural gas and biofuels industry in Brazil. The ANP reports to the Ministry of Mines and Energy and is a special federal autarchy that implements the national policy for this industry, focusing on ensuring fuel supply and the interests of Brazilian consumers.

The purpose of the ANP is to promote the regulation, contracting and inspection of economic activities in the oil, natural gas and biofuels industry. Its institutional competence is set out in the Petroleum Act Law and regulated by Decree 2455/1998. The ANP's main responsibilities include the following:

---

18 As of 23 February 2022.

- to regulate the performance of geology and geophysical services for oil prospecting;
- to prepare tender protocols and carry out auctions for concessions for exploration, development and production activities, signing the agreements that arise therefrom and monitoring their fulfilment;
- to organise and maintain an inventory of information and technical data relating to the regulated activities of the oil, natural gas and biofuels industry;
- to regulate and authorise activities relating to the national supply of fuels, monitoring them directly or through agreements with other federal, state or local agencies; and
- to regulate and authorise activities relating to the production, import, export, storage, stock, transportation, transfer, distribution, resale and commercialisation of biofuels, as well as to carry out compliance assessments and quality assurance, monitoring them directly or through agreements with other federal, state or local agencies, among others.

Historically, CADE and the ANP have had a longstanding cooperative relationship and have acted together on several merger cases and cartel investigations conducted by CADE.

To consolidate this relationship, CADE and the ANP executed a Technical Cooperation Agreement, valid until 2028, which establishes the rules for interactions and activities between the agencies. The agreement establishes certain obligations between CADE and the ANP, such as the following:

- to exchange information, data, reports, analyses and statistics;
- to share technical opinions and the results of studies and research;
- to organise meetings, workshops and visits;
- to exchange specialists;
- to conduct joint research and studies;
- to organise and promote lectures, conferences, seminars, symposiums, congresses and other events for the training of agency personnel; and
- to jointly develop other projects and specific activities.

These obligations ensure that CADE and the ANP will act together to improve competition in the sector. As per the agreement, the ANP is obliged to provide CADE with companies' pricing policies if:

- it is compelled by CADE to assist in an ongoing investigation; or
- it suspects that any player in the oil and gas sector is acting in breach of competition laws.

In addition to the agreement, in August 2020, CADE and the ANP initiated a working group that aims to:

- analyse the structure of the Brazilian fuel market;
- evaluate the implementation of the measures proposed by CADE to overhaul the fuel sector and the possibility of permanent adoption of the exceptional regulatory measures presented by the ANP; and
- promote competition as an instrument to increase competitiveness and innovation in the Brazilian economy.

More recently, the ANP assisted closely in the review of the acquisition of a 51% stake in gas distributor Gaspetro from state-controlled oil giant Petrobras by Compass Gás e Energia. Although the deal was unconditionally approved by CADE's General Superintendence, the ANP submitted a legal opinion recommending that the transaction be blocked, since it considered that the proposed transaction would adversely affect competition in the natural gas sector. The deal is part of a settlement agreement executed between Petrobras and CADE in 2019, under which the state-controlled oil giant agreed to divest assets in the natural gas market and to adopt several other measures to ensure the increase of competition in the section.

Finally, Law 9847/1999 (Article 10(V)) establishes that market participants found in breach of competition laws due to conduct in the fuel market in Brazil will have their authorisations revoked by the ANP for five years.

4.2 European Union

In the European Union, national governments have control over oil and gas in their territories. Each member state is responsible for assigning to one or more public regulatory authorities the competence to grant authorisations for access to, and the exercise of activities in, the national upstream oil and gas industry and/or to monitor use thereof.

In January 2012, the European Commission established the European Union Offshore Oil and Gas Authorities Group (EUOAG) as a forum for the exchange of information and expertise between national authorities, the European Commission and other stakeholders on all issues relating to major accident prevention and response in offshore oil and gas operations. Member states' authorities are responsible for the regulatory oversight of offshore oil and gas activities. The EUOAG promotes and facilitates the application of best practices and high safety standards in offshore oil and gas operations worldwide. Offshore oil and gas operations are subject to the Directive on Safety of Offshore Oil and Gas Operations (2013/30/EU), which aims to help prevent accidents and ensure a prompt and efficient response should one occur.

4.3 United States

Similarly, in the United States, for onshore oil and gas, each state has its own regulatory agency or agencies that protect the rights of landowners and that regulate the impact of drilling, production, plugging and abandonment, as well as controlling health and safety issues.

There are also additional regulations issued by the federal government relating to hydrocarbon resources that are subject to federal jurisdiction, which are part of federal law and constitutional law and are executed by federal regulatory bodies, such as:

- the Federal Energy Regulatory Commission, which regulates interstate natural gas and petroleum product pipelines;
- the US Department of Energy, which is responsible for instituting and implementing energy policies and authorising entities to import/export natural gas to/from the United States;
- the US Environmental Protection Agency, which is responsible for developing and enforcing environmental regulations; and
- the US Department of Transportation, which is responsible for establishing national policy and setting and enforcing standards for the transportation of energy.

Offshore oil and gas development is independently regulated by US federal law and regulatory bodies, such as:

- the Department of the Interior, which regulates the extraction of oil and gas from federal lands;
- the Bureau of Ocean Energy Management, which manages federal outer continental shelf leasing programmes, conducts resource assessments and licenses seismic surveys;
- the Bureau of Safety and Environmental Enforcement, which regulates all outer continental shelf oil and gas drilling, production and plugging and abandonment; and
- the Office of Natural Resources Revenue, which collects and disburses rents and royalties owed to the government for offshore production.

5. Conclusion

Antitrust policy is applicable across all industries, and the midstream and downstream oil and gas industry is no exception. However, while the different features of antitrust policy explained in this chapter are common to other industries, some specificities of the oil and gas industry must be taken into account by entities active in this sector because, as discussed, different antitrust issues arise in different market structures.

Below is a summary of the main recommendations for midstream and downstream oil and gas companies in order to ensure compliance with (and avoid liability involving) antitrust policies around the globe.

5.1 Merger control

Oil and gas companies may be subject to merger control scrutiny when engaging in corporate transactions such as mergers, acquisitions and even other forms of consortia or partnerships – some of which are particularly common in the midstream sector. The thresholds for mandatory filing often include the revenues registered in the country by the company and/or its economic group, as well as an effects test. As such, midstream and downstream oil and gas companies – especially those active across different countries – are strongly advised to carefully analyse whether their proposed transactions will be subject to mandatory filing with the relevant antitrust authorities prior to engaging in different forms of corporate transactions. Failure to comply with the merger control rules may subject companies to penalties (usually fines).

5.2 Collusive arrangements

Cartel enforcement is often seen as priority in terms of antitrust policy across different jurisdictions and collusive arrangements tend to be heavily punished. As such, oil and gas companies – especially those active in the downstream resale sector, which are commonly considered to have structural characteristics that facilitate cartel behaviour – should have in place clear antitrust compliance guidelines when dealing with competitors to avoid exposure to collusive behaviour and potential antitrust investigation. Special care should be taken when it comes to trade unions and associations – which, as seen above, have historically been involved in cartel cases in the downstream oil and gas market.

5.3 Unilateral conduct

Market power or high levels of market concentration are not deemed illegal in themselves; however, companies with market power or high market shares (which is often the case of oil and gas companies, especially those active in the upstream and midstream sectors) should analyse the legality of their commercial policies from an antitrust perspective (including agreements with clients, suppliers and commercial partners in general), in order to ensure that they do not have the potential to exclude competitors and, as such, are compliant with the antitrust rules.

Third-party access to energy infrastructure

John Paterson
University of Aberdeen

1. Introduction

The essence of third-party access to energy infrastructure is that one party requires access to facilities owned by another in order to introduce its product for onward transport or distribution. Without such access, that party would be left either to construct such facilities itself – which may be inefficient – or to abandon the project altogether on the basis that it is not economically viable. While either of these outcomes might be a matter of indifference to the infrastructure owner, they may be viewed very differently by legislatures and regulators, insofar as they may be contrary to policies aimed at encouraging maximum development of natural resources (in the upstream) or competition (in the downstream). Consequently, what could – all else being equal – be a matter for pure commercial negotiation (with 'no deal' being an entirely possible outcome) is often a matter of considerable interest to legislatures and regulators, which may seek to encourage negotiated access agreements while reserving the power to impose solutions where negotiation fails. In this chapter, the example of the United Kingdom is taken to demonstrate how third-party access operates in the downstream gas market. First, the context within which the issue of third-party access arises – that is, the liberalisation of the gas market – is discussed. Third-party access to gas infrastructure in the United Kingdom is then introduced; while the following sections deal with arrangements where licensed activities and licence-exempt activities respectively are involved. Conclusions are then drawn.

2. Liberalisation of the gas market as the context for third-party access

Third-party access to gas infrastructure assumes that the gas market itself has been liberalised. In a pure state-controlled situation, all relevant infrastructure – from production facilities to the end user – is owned and operated by state-owned enterprises (or indeed a single such entity), meaning that there is an effective monopoly situation. Since the 1980s, gas (and electricity) markets around the world have been liberalised to a greater or lesser extent, with state monopoly providers compelled to unbundle (ie, to separate out production, transportation and supply functions) and to allow new entrants to compete. Crucially for the purposes of this chapter, the need to ensure that new market entrants do not face insurmountable barriers includes the possibility that owners of infrastructure may be compelled to grant them access. The United Kingdom was a pioneer of such liberalisation efforts, with many of its ideas in due course forming the foundation for later European legislation. Indeed, it is this pioneering status that justifies the focus on the United Kingdom in this chapter. Before considering the country's approach to third-party access in greater detail, it will be instructive briefly to understand the history of the United Kingdom's liberalisation process.

This process was by no means straightforward or rapid. At the outset in the early 1980s, the British Gas Corporation (BGC) was a state monopoly with regard to transport and supply, as well as participating in exploration and production and having a monopoly with regard to purchase from other producers. The privatisation process began with the ability of larger consumers to contract directly with producers for supply and an obligation for BGC to carry any such gas.[1] Shortly thereafter, BGC was obliged to sell off its interests in gas production. Formal privatisation followed in 1986 with the formation of British Gas plc (BG);[2] but by that time, no consumers had made use of the powers in the Oil and Gas Enterprise Act 1982. Indeed, it could be argued that the privatisation effort under the Gas Act 1986 was initially flawed insofar as BG remained a single entity and was not required to unbundle its activities, while the regulator had relatively weak powers.[3]

The following years, however, witnessed a concerted effort by regulatory and competition authorities to improve on this situation, requiring:

- publication of contract market prices in 1988;[4]
- reduction of market share in 1991;[5] and
- unbundling of supply from transportation and storage in 1993.[6]

Thereafter, the ability of larger consumers to negotiate with other suppliers was progressively extended until there was full competition by mid-1998.[7] Not all such efforts were initially successful: the government, for all its privatising zeal, rejected the competition authority's recommendation for unbundling. Interestingly, BG itself decided to take this step in 1997, selling its supply business and keeping transportation and storage. The latter functions were then separated from BG's production function to complete the process, and thus to

1 Oil and Gas Enterprise Act 1982, Section 12.
2 Gas Act 1986, Part II.
3 1986 act, Section 31.
4 Monopolies and Mergers Commission, *Gas*, Cmnd 500, (HMSO, 1988).
5 Office of Fair Trading, *The Gas Review* (1991).
6 Monopolies and Mergers Commission, *Gas and British Gas plc*, Cmnd 2314-2317 (HMSO, 1993).
7 1986 act, Section 8B, as inserted by the Competition and Service (Utilities) Act 1992, Section 37.

establish the context within which new market entrants would require access to existing infrastructure to make a reality of the vision of the government and the regulatory authorities for a liberalised market for the supply of gas.[8]

3. Third-party access to gas infrastructure in the United Kingdom

It is first important to clarify which infrastructure is within the scope of the present discussion. Regarding third-party access to gas infrastructure in the United Kingdom, a distinction is drawn between the upstream and the downstream. Arrangements relating to the upstream are entirely separate from those for the downstream. Perhaps reassuringly for present purposes, it has been observed that: "Access to infrastructure tends to be easier onshore ... because there the work to prepare the third-party production to meet infrastructure specification is much cheaper."[9] There is one area where there could be perceived to be an overlap – that is, in relation to a 'gas processing facility', insofar as this term appears in both sets of arrangements. As will be seen further below,[10] however, the crucial consideration in determining which arrangements apply is the purpose for which the gas is being processed, either upstream or downstream.

In relation to the downstream, arrangements for third-party access to gas infrastructure – whether for the processing, transportation or supply of natural gas – differ depending on whether the infrastructure is subject to licence conditions or is licence exempt. Generally speaking, in order to convey gas via pipeline, a licence is required.[11] Such a licence includes an obligation to provide access to third parties. For example, the relevant condition in a transport licence reads: "The licensee must offer access to its system in line with the Act and the Directive. Where access to the system is refused, duly substantiated reasons shall be given."[12] It is possible, however, that an exemption from holding such a licence may have been granted;[13] or that an exemption from the general prohibition on carrying out activities for which a licence is required applies.[14] In either of these cases, in the absence of a relevant licence condition, there was originally no obligation for a so-called 'licence exempt network owner' to provide third-party access – meaning that consumers could not in fact choose from whom they obtained their gas, with consequent negative effects for

8 For a discussion see CW Price, "Competition and regulation in the UK gas industry", *Oxford Review of Economic Policy*, 1997, 13(1), 47–63.

9 Uisdean Vass, "Access to Infrastructure", in Greg Gordon, John Paterson and Emre Usenmez (eds), *UK Oil and Gas Law: Current Practice and Emerging Trends*, (Edinburgh University Press), Vol 1, para 6.11.

10 See text associated with n 28.

11 Gas Act 1986, Section 5.

12 Gas Transporters Licence: Standard Conditions, 1 September 2021, Condition 4F, Access to the System. 'The act' in this condition means the Gas Act 1986 and 'the directive' means Directive 2009/73/EC of the European Parliament and the Council of 13 July 2009 concerning common rules for the internal market in natural gas.

13 By an order granted under the 1986 act, Section 6A, as substituted by the 1995 Act, Section 4.

14 1986 act, Schedule 2A, as inserted by the 1995 act, Section 3(2).

competition. This situation ended following the 2008 judgment of the Court of Justice of the European Union in *Citiworks*.[15] In this case, a third-party electricity supplier wanted to compete with the incumbent supplier at Leipzig Airport. The incumbent benefited from an exemption which meant it did not have to provide third-party access. The court ruled that this contravened the requirement in the Electricity Directive that all distribution systems allow for third-party access so as to enable customer choice. It stated further that for an exemption to be lawful, there would need to be a specific derogation in the directive, which there was not. Although this case was concerned with electricity under the Second Energy Package, it was clear that it would be equally applicable to gas under the Third Energy Package, which came into force on 3 September 2009.[16] As such, the United Kingdom (then still a member of the European Union) took steps to ensure that licence exempt systems would also be open to third-party access.

In the following sections, this chapter considers arrangements for third-party access to downstream gas infrastructure covered by licensed activities and then those arrangements post-*Citiworks* for licence-exempt activities.

4. Arrangements for third-party access in relation to licensed activities

The Gas Act 1986 (as amended) contains, among other things, provisions for third-party access to pipeline systems,[17] storage facilities[18] and liquefied natural gas (LNG) facilities.[19] In the fullness of time, it was realised that there was a gap in these arrangements in respect of gas processing activities. Whereas such facilities were mentioned in upstream arrangements, these were not relevant where access was required for downstream supply. Consequently, new provisions were included in the Gas Act 1995 in order to "fill [the] gap in the present regulatory arrangements and ... complement the existing powers which relate to offshore pipelines".[20] The approach in each case – whether for pipelines, storage, LNG or gas processing – is essentially the same, so it will suffice here to consider one in detail: specifically, the arrangements in relation to gas processing facilities.

A key consideration for any third party seeking access to infrastructure for the onward supply of gas downstream is the ability to have access to gas processing facilities. This matter is dealt with by Section 12 of the Gas Act 1995 (as amended). The owner of any such facility – and specifically, one which

15 *Citiworks AG v Sachsisches Staatsministerium fur Wirtschaft under Arbeit als Landesregulierundsbehorde*, Case C-439/06.
16 See Directive 2009/73/EC concerning common rules for the internal market in natural gas and repealing Directive 2003/55/EC, Articles 32 and 34.
17 1986 Act, Section 19.
18 *Ibid*, Section 19B, as inserted by SI 2000/1937, Regulation 2(2).
19 *Ibid*, Section 19D, as inserted by SI 2000/1937, Regulation 2(2).
20 Earl Ferrers, minister of state, Department of Trade and Industry, the Gas Bill, second reading, House of Lords, *Hansard*, 6 June 1995, Column 1269.

processes gas for a downstream purpose[21] – is obliged to publish at least annually "the main commercial conditions" upon which a third party may acquire the right to have its gas processed.[22] Equally, the owner is obliged to publish any changes to these conditions "as soon as they become effective".[23] In each case, the owner must:

- publish a draft at least two months in advance, notifying third parties of such publication;[24] and
- "take account of any representations received".[25]

The Gas Act 1995 thus essentially assumes that in the first instance, the owner of the gas processing facility and the third party will negotiate commercial terms for access.[26] The statute obliges the third party in this regard to apply to the owner in writing,[27] specifying:

- for how long processing is to be carried out;
- the type of gas (which must at least be similar to that which the facility is intended to process);
- the amount of gas; and
- that "the gas is to be processed for a downstream purpose".[28]

Such application having been made, the parties are then obliged to "negotiate in good faith and endeavour to reach agreement".[29] If they are unable to reach agreement, the third party may apply to the authority (ie, the Gas and Electricity Markets Authority or Ofgem) "for directions which would secure ... the right" sought.[30] Ofgem will not deal with any such application unless it is satisfied that the owner and the third party "have had a reasonable time" to negotiate as per their obligations under the act.[31]

As regards Ofgem's initial response to an application from a third party, three options are laid out in the act:

- Adjourn the application to allow further negotiations between the parties;

---

21 Defined in the 1995 act, Section 12(5A), as substituted by the Energy Act 2011, Section 92(10), to mean gas "processed with a view to its being put into a gas storage facility, an LNG import or export facility, a gas interconnector or a distribution system pipeline".

22 1995 Act, Section 12(1)(a), as amended by the Energy Act 2011, Sections 92(2) and 4(a). Note that 'gas processing facility' is specifically defined in the act as any facility which "(a) carries out gas processing operations; (b) is operated other than by a gas transporter; and (c) is not an LNG import or export facility" (Section 12(6)). Note that 'gas processing operations' are also defined in detail in the same section, but essentially involve purifying, blending, odorising, compressing, removing or separating gas.

23 *Ibid*, Section 12(1)(b).

24 *Ibid*, Sections 12(1ZA)(a) and (b), as inserted by the Energy Act 2011, Section 92(5).

25 *Ibid*, Section 12(1ZB), as inserted by the Energy Act 2011, Section 92(5).

26 *Ibid*, Section 12(1B), as amended by the Energy Act 2011, Sections 92(3) and (6).

27 *Ibid*, Section 12(1C).

28 *Ibid*, Section 12(1D), as amended by the Energy Act 2011, Sections 92(7)(a) and (b).

29 *Ibid*, Section 12(1E).

30 *Ibid*, Section 12(1F), as amended by the Energy Act 2011, Section 92(3).

31 *Ibid*, Section 12(1G), as amended by the Energy Act 2011, Sections 92(3) and (8).

- Consider the application further; or
- Reject the application.[32]

In each case, it must notify the applicant of its decision.[33] If it decides to consider an application further, it must notify the owner, any other person with a right to have gas processed at the facility and the Health and Safety Executive, so that each party may have "an opportunity to be heard about the matter".[34]

Where Ofgem gives directions in response to a third-party application, the act lays out the matters which such directions may specify. First, they may specify the terms on which it considers the owner "should enter into an agreement with" the third party in relation to any of the following purposes:

- securing the applicant's right to have a specified quantity and quality of gas processed for a specified period;
- ensuring that the applicant's exercise of such right is not prevented or impeded;
- regulating the charges; and
- securing "such ancillary or incidental rights" as Ofgem considers necessary, including connection of the third party's pipeline to the processing facility.[35]

Second, directions from Ofgem may specify the amount of money to be paid for such a right (or the means by which such an amount should be determined).[36] Finally, assuming that the third party pays or agrees to pay the sum of money specified, the directions may require the owner of the facility to enter into an agreement with the third party on those terms.[37]

From the point of view of the owner of a gas processing facility, the powers in the hands of Ofgem when approached by a third party following the failure of a negotiation may appear extensive, and perhaps even excessive. It should be borne in mind, after all, that what is envisaged here is a power conferred on Ofgem by Parliament to compel an owner to grant access to its property on terms specified by the authority, notwithstanding that the parties have been unable to negotiate what the owner believes to be commercial terms. The act nevertheless provides some reassurance for processing facility owners insofar as it requires Ofgem to be satisfied that its giving directions "would not prejudice the efficient operation of the facility" or the processing of quantities of gas which the owner or an associate of the owner[38] may reasonably expect, or which another party with a right to have

32 *Ibid*, Section 12(2)(a).
33 *Ibid*, Section 12(2)(b).
34 *Ibid*, Section 12(2)(c).
35 *Ibid*, Section 12(4)(a), as amended by the Energy Act 2011, Section 92(3).
36 *Ibid*, Section 12(4)(b), as amended by the Energy Act 2011, Section 92(3).
37 *Ibid*, Section 12(4)(c).
38 As defined by the Energy Act 2011, Section 91.

gas processed is entitled to require, to be processed.[39] In other words, it might be said that there is an effort to ensure that the legitimate expectations of the infrastructure owner are met – albeit subject to the overarching objective of the legislation to ensure a well-functioning liberalised market.

5. Arrangements for third-party access to license exempt infrastructure

Following *Citiworks*, the UK government consulted on providing third-party access in the context of licence-exempt networks. In its response to that consultation, it stated that it would introduce legislation to bring the country into compliance with relevant EU law.[40] The relevant provisions state that a distribution exemption holder has a duty to provide third-party access to a customer where the following conditions are met:

- "[A] customer owns or occupies premises connected to an exempt distribution system";
- The customer takes gas through that system which is operated or controlled by the exemption holder; and
- The customer has served notice that it wishes to take supply from a third party and provides evidence that one such identified supplier is willing to do so.[41]

Insofar as those network owners had previously enjoyed the advantage of not having to worry about the costs and complications of third-party access, the change in the law clearly raised concerns. To this end, the relevant government department (at that time, the Department of Energy and Climate Change (DECC)) published guidance which sought to reassure all concerned that an appropriate balance was being struck in the process of ensuring compliance with EU law.[42]

The DECC guidance first clarifies the circumstances in which a person may be supplying gas to customers but be exempt from the usual licence conditions or from the new requirements. These may be:

- where the supply is coincidental (ie, part of another service) and thus not covered by the provisions; or
- where the supply is within the scope of the new provisions, but third-party access would require increased capacity that is not technically feasible or "would have a significant and adverse effect impact" on the supplier or any other person.[43]

---

39 1995 act, Section 12(3), as amended by the Energy Act 2011, Section 92(3) and SI 2000/1937, Regulation 2(3), Schedule 3, para 3.

40 The Electricity and Gas (Internal Markets) Regulations 2011, SI 2011/2704.

41 1986 act, Section 6B and Schedule 2AA, as inserted by 2011 Regulations, Regulation 20.

42 DECC, *Guidance: Provision of Third Party Access to Licence Exempt Electricity and Gas Networks*, Revised Version, February 2012.

43 *Ibid*, para 1.5.

As regards the first of these situations, the DECC guidance suggests that a common-sense approach will often be appropriate and will include consideration of factors such as:

- the duration of the relationship between the parties;
- the extent to which gas supply can be "meaningfully separated" from the rest of the service provided; and
- whether separate billing is in place (or possible) for the gas supply element.[44]

Once notice has been served by a customer on a distribution exemption holder, the latter has a relatively short timeframe within which to reply either that:

- it will grant the required third-party access (subject to agreement on the details); or
- it cannot do so for feasibility or adverse effects reasons.[45]

In the case of a positive response, the distribution exemption holder must then provide information on metering and contractual matters to the third-party supplier.[46] In the event of a refusal, it is open to the third party to seek a determination from Ofgem.[47] Having considered the evidence submitted, Ofgem will then determine either that the refusal is appropriate or that access must be given.[48] Once it is clear that an obligation to provide access exists, the distribution exemption holder must grant such access as is required to allow the third party to supply the customer.[49] The legislation goes on to set out what such access may entail in practice.[50] Where a new connection is required, the legislation sets out the duty of the distribution exemption holder in this regard[51] and the conditions under which a connection may be refused (eg, where circumstances exist outside of its control or the connection could involve a danger to the public).[52]

A key consideration in the context of third-party access being granted, of course, is charging for network access. In this regard, the legislation provides that a distribution exemption holder "must not impose a use of system charge unless [Ofgem] has approved the methodology for calculating that charge".[53] This matter is discussed in the DECC guidance; but it is also the subject of more

44 *Ibid*, para 1.9.
45 1986 act, Schedule 2AA, para 1(4).
46 *Ibid*, para 1(6).
47 *Ibid*, para 3(1).
48 *Ibid*, para 3(9).
49 *Ibid*, para 4.
50 *Ibid*, para 4(4).
51 *Ibid*, para 7.
52 *Ibid*, para 8(6).
53 *Ibid*, para 5(1).

specific guidance published by Ofgem, in which the authority stresses that in developing a methodology, the distribution exemption holder must show that it has complied with two principles:

- "[T]he resulting tariffs must be justified by reference to the costs of the distribution network"; and
- "[C]osts must be allocated to individual network users on an objective, justifiable and non-discriminatory basis".[54]

Ofgem goes on to provide a *pro forma* and a worked example to assist distribution exemption holders in the development of a methodology.[55] It stresses that it "will take a proportionate approach to approving the methodologies", recognising that larger entities with greater resources will be expected to provide a higher level of detail than a very small entity with only one or two customers.[56] The Ofgem guidance indicates that a methodology submitted by a distribution exemption holder is "likely to be acceptable" where a number of conditions are met, including where:

- there is "a reasonable and proportionate method of identifying costs";
- there is compliance with the two charging principles mentioned above;
- it is "substantiated with supporting data";
- it explains "how the costs have been allocated between network users"; and
- it "allows parties to understand the basis on which their charges have been calculated".[57]

The Ofgem guidance goes on to detail:

- what further information could be expected from larger distribution exemption holders;[58]
- how network costs should be identified;[59]
- how the *pro forma* should be completed;[60] and
- what would constitute connection costs.[61]

Given the concerns expressed by business in the wake of *Citiworks* and the consequent need for third-party access to be granted, where appropriate, in licence-exempt circumstances, it is interesting to note that the guidance documents are keen to stress that the approach being taken to decisions in this

---

54 Ofgem, *Guidance on third-party access charges for licence exempt gas and electricity distribution networks*, 10 November 2011, para 2.4.
55 *Ibid*, Appendix 2.
56 *Ibid*, p5.
57 *Ibid*, para 2.10.
58 *Ibid*, para 2.11.
59 *Ibid*, paras 2.16-25.
60 *Ibid*, Chapter 3.
61 *Ibid*, Chapter 4.

regard recognises the importance of the market. Thus, for example, the DECC guidance states that:

- it is "not prescribing how stakeholders manage the technical and contractual means of providing third-party access"; and
- "[m]arket participants ... are best placed to determine this".

Equally, the guidance documents stress an approach that is fair to all. Thus, for example, Ofgem is clear that:

- its guidance is "not prescriptive"; and
- "any other reasonable and proportionate methods of identifying network costs and allocating them to customers are likely to be acceptable for the purposes of approval".[62]

In this sense, it may be concluded that the relevant authorities are keen to strike an appropriate balance in ensuring third-party access, recognising the needs of the various stakeholders in the context of the overall obligation to provide such access unless there is good reason not to.

6. Conclusion

As can be seen from the above discussion, third-party access to gas infrastructure is an essential component of a well-functioning liberalised gas market. It involves a degree of complexity in relation to both:

- appropriate identification of the infrastructure involved; and
- the means by which relevant authorities play a role in determining an outcome where commercial negotiations have failed and where there is no good reason for denying access.

As the experience in the United Kingdom has shown, however, this complexity is by no means insurmountable – even if the whole process of liberalisation and of the development of the relevant third-party access arrangements has been lengthy. That said, for countries contemplating similar moves, the experience in jurisdictions such as the United Kingdom can be instructive and hopefully allow for the early identification of potential obstacles – even if there is no suggestion that relevant arrangements could be transplanted wholesale. Nor is it the case that the story of third-party access to gas infrastructure in the United Kingdom is over. The market for natural gas may have been successfully liberalised (even if the events of Winter 2021–22 remind us that resilience in this context is still something to be actively pursued rather than assumed); but in all probability, the energy transition will see the emergence of potentially extensive new gas infrastructure if government plans

62 *Ibid*, p5.

are realised. In this context, the ambitious strategies for carbon capture usage and storage[63] and for hydrogen[64] indicate what sorts of developments in this regard may lie ahead in the coming years. It is to be hoped that the long and often pioneering experience with natural gas will stand the country in good stead to deal with potential practical problems – not least third-party access to relevant infrastructure.

63 Her Majesty's Government, *Clean Growth: The UK Carbon Capture Usage and Storage Deployment Pathway – An Action Plan*, 2018.

64 HM Government, Hydrogen Strategy, August 2021, CP 475, pp41, 43.

About the authors

André Andriw
Founder and CEO, Assentia Consulting
assentiaconsultoria@gmail.com

André Andriw is the founder and CEO of Assentia Consulting, a consultancy firm specialised in business and sustainability advisory in Brazil. He holds a master's degree in international relations from the State University of Campinas, a BA in international relations from the Federal University of Roraima and a second BA in economics from the University of Estácio de Sá. He was president of the Academic Centre of International Relations Bertha Becker and a research intern at Pontifical Catholic University of São Paulo. André is experienced in business diplomacy, market strategy, energy transition policies, regulation and sustainability in industries such as oil and gas, mining and agribusiness.

Elena I Athwal
Research fellow, UNESCO Chair on Environmental Law and Sustainable Development; JD law student, College of Law, Hamad Bin Khalifa University
elat32212@hbku.edu.qa

Elena I Athwal is a JD student at Hamad Bin Khalifa University (HBKU) Law School in Doha, Qatar. She is currently a research fellow of the UNESCO Chair on Environmental Law and Sustainable Development and founder and president of the HBKU Environmental & Energy Law Special Interest Club. She was formerly president of the HBKU Law Society.

Elena holds degrees in international relations and history of the built environment, and has taught and specialised in research on natural gas, energy, environmental law, international law and climate change while based in the United States, France and Qatar. She currently works as a research associate, as well as a communications and editorial assistant for the HBKU Law School. She also volunteers as the Student Liaison from the HBKU Law School, working with Afghan refugees.

Rafael Baleroni
Partner, Cescon, Barrieu, Flesch & Barreto
rafael.baleroni@cesconbarrieu.com.br

Rafael Baleroni is a partner in the infrastructure and project finance department of Brazilian law firm Cescon, Barrieu, Flesch & Barreto, and leads the oil and gas practice. He represents domestic and foreign clients on a wide array of transactions and regulatory matters in the oil and gas, offshore, shipping and maritime, and energy industries. He is recognised as one of Brazil's leading lawyers in oil and gas by different international directories.

He holds a degree in law from *Universidade do Estado do Rio de Janeiro* (UERJ), where he specialised in oil and gas law (merit-based scholarship from the Brazilian Oil Agency); a master of international law degree from UERJ; and an LLM from the University of Chicago. He has authored numerous articles and is a frequent speaker on the topics of oil and gas, project finance, foreign investment and international law.

Paula Camara
Senior associate, Mattos Filho
paula.camara@mattosfilho.com.br

With over 10 years of experience in antitrust matters, Paula Camara represents domestic and international clients in connection with merger cases and cartel investigations. Her practice focuses on complex merger cases. She also advises clients on complex competitive issues and projects in regulated sectors, in particular oil and gas.

Paula holds an LLM from Stanford Law School and is currently a visiting professor at Ibmec, where she teaches antitrust compliance.

Chantal Carriere
Associate, Latham & Watkins LLP
chantal.carriere@lw.com

Chantal Carriere is an associate in the Houston office of Latham & Watkins. Chantal advises clients on energy and infrastructure project development, including liquefied natural gas (LNG), power, biodiesel, upstream oil and gas, pipelines and petrochemical facilities. She serves on the US chapter of the Young Negotiators Group of the Association of International Energy Negotiators (AIEN). Chantal holds law degrees from the University of Calgary and the University of Houston. She is licensed under the Texas State Bar.

Gustavo Castro Ribeiro Ferreira Silva
PhD student, University of São Paulo
guscastroribeiro@usp.br

Gustavo Castro is a PhD student in energy sciences at the University of São Paulo, with an exchange at the *Institut Français du Pétrole* as a visiting student on its petroleum economics and management programme. He has a master's in energy systems planning from the State University of Campinas and a bachelor's degree in petroleum engineering from Santa Cecilia University. He is experienced in research and consultancy in the areas of technology, politics and economics for fossil and renewable energy sources. He has worked as a research fellow in Brazilian foundations and is currently working in the gas market in the advisory and management area.

Marina Cyrino
Senior tax specialist, Wintershall Dea
macyrino@gmail.com

Marina Cyrino is senior tax specialist at Wintershall Dea in Brazil, with extensive experience in leading Brazilian oil and gas law firms. She advises on Brazilian tax consulting, planning and litigation, and on regulatory matters in the Brazilian oil and gas and energy industries.

She holds a law degree from UERJ; an LLM in regulation from *Fundação Getúlio Vargas* (FGV) focused on natural gas; and an LLM in taxation from Northwestern University. She has previously published on the topics of oil and gas taxation and regulation, data protection and regulation.

Carlos Diaz
Associate, White & Case LLP
carlos.diaz@whitecase.com

Carlos Ramon Diaz Sordo is an associate in the firm's Houston office. He recently obtained his

LLM in energy, environment and natural resources from the University of Houston. Before that, Carlos was an associate at White & Case's Mexico City office, where he was actively involved in advising clients bidding for offshore shallow-water and deep-water blocks during the round bidding procedures offered in Mexico. This involved an assessment of the risks and requirements in each type of model contract provided by the Mexican National Hydrocarbons Commission. He is licensed under the Texas State Bar and authorised to practise law in Mexico.

Seyram Dzikunu
Partner, energy and infrastructure, Bentsi-Enchill, Letsa & Ankomah
sdzikunu@belonline.org

Seyram Dzikunu is a partner in the energy and infrastructure department of Bentsi-Enchill, Letsa & Ankomah. She has over 12 years' experience in legal practice. Seyram has extensive experience in corporate and commercial transactions. Her practice focuses on energy and natural resources. She has played a leading role in acting for and advising a range of organisations, from government agencies and multinational corporations to indigenous small-to-medium enterprises, in the power, oil, gas and mining sectors. She has published articles on topics related to energy. She holds an LLM in petroleum law and policy from the University of Dundee, and an LLB and BA from the University of Ghana. She is a member of the Ghana Bar. She has been recommended by the *Legal 500 EMEA 2021* for energy and infrastructure.

Reg Fowler
Senior lawyer and consultant, New Age African Global Energy
fowler1603@gmail.com

Reg Fowler is a senior lawyer and consultant at New Age African Global Energy. He is the co-author of three books on upstream joint operating agreements. He has also written on subjects such as the Northern Sea Route in the Arctic Ocean; joint property in oil and gas joint ventures; the impact of state succession on long-term host government agreements; and human rights due diligence for business. He is presently researching energy transition issues, including carbon market regulation and investment law. He looked after Shell's Kashagan asset until start-up in 2015 and worked in Shell Trading for seven years. He has also worked in Eni and Atlantic Richfield, and has a total of 24 years of in-house experience.

Laura Huomo
Partner, Bird & Bird
laura.huomo@twobirds.com

Laura Huomo heads the Nordic energy practice of Bird & Bird and focuses mainly on Nordic and Baltic energy transactions and regulation. In addition, she has extensive experience in international capital market transactions. She is recognised by international legal directories as one of the leading experts in energy and capital markets in Finland, as well as a recognised practitioner and winner of the Client Choice Award for Energy & Natural Resources in Finland over three consecutive years (2020, 2021 and 2022). Laura is a frequent speaker and has published internationally on topics related to the project financing of energy projects, including her doctoral thesis.

Giovani Loss
Partner, Mattos Filho
giovani.loss@mattosfilho.com.br

Giovani Loss's practice focuses on energy, oil and gas, and in particular on M&A transactions, financing and regulatory issues involving these industries. He was a legal counsel in the Houston office of Fulbright and Jaworski LLP (now Norton Rose Fulbright). He is one of the founding partners of the Brazilian Institute of Energy Law Studies and a former chairman of the Oil & Gas Law Committee of the International Bar Association. He is licensed to practise law in Brazil, New York and England.

Ruchdi Maalouf
COO, KOGAS International
ruchdi.maalouf@kogasinternational.com

Ruchdi Maalouf is a senior commercial executive and lawyer who specialises in LNG. His expertise includes long-term LNG procurement and sales, LNG trading and project development. He currently manages the Singapore-based trading and marketing arm of Korea Gas Corporation (KOGAS), a Korean government entity and the largest LNG end-buyer in the world.

Cea Mittler
Legal counsel
cea.mittler@gmail.com

Cea Mittler is a transformative learner at heart, focusing on maritime shipping's decarbonisation efforts. She holds an LLM in EU energy law from the University of Helsinki and is pursuing an LLM in maritime law combined with coursework within the realm of public policy at the National University of Singapore.

Cea was previously a senior associate at Bird & Bird Attorneys Ltd, tasked with establishing and growing the firm's Finnish Nordic energy practice. Before that, she headed the legal function at the Finnish gas transmission system operator, directing corporate legal affairs while shaping policy connected to the gas transmission business. She has also worked on the Balticconnector pipeline project, the largest EU-funded energy project at the time. She has published articles and spoken on topics related to REPowerEU, future hydrogen regulation and hydrogen marked advancement, LNG, unbundling of gas markets, advancement of energy infrastructure and legal barriers to a circular economy.

Lucas Mota de Lima
Master's student, University of São Paulo; Head of regulation and institutional relations, Energy Platform-EnP
mota.lucaslima@gmail.com

Lucas Mota de Lima is a master's student in energy sciences at the University of São Paulo. He has bachelor's degree in petroleum engineering from the Federal University of Campina Grande, with a 'sandwich' degree in the United States. He was technical adviser for oil and natural gas at the Ministry of Mines and Energy Brazil, where he held senior consulting roles relating to the regulatory structure, institutional nature, technical opinions and bidding rounds in the oil and natural gas sector. He then coordinated the programme for the National Policy for Onshore Oil and Natural Gas. He is currently head of regulation and institutional relations at Energy Platform-EnP.

Cosmos Nike Nwedu
Researcher/lecturer, Federal University Ndufu-Alike Ikwo
cosmosnike.nwedu@gmail.com

Cosmos Nike Nwedu teaches and researches law at the Faculty of Law of the Federal University Ndufu-Alike Ikwo, Nigeria. He received his LLM in climate change and energy law and policy from the Centre for Energy, Petroleum and Mineral Law and Policy (CEPMLP), University of Dundee; his BL from Nigerian Law School, Abuja; and his LLB (Hons) from Ebonyi State University, Nigeria. His research focus brings interdisciplinarity to the interface of climate change and energy law and policy, including oil, gas and renewable energy. He is a member of the Young International Council for Commercial Arbitration; the Young International Arbitration Group; the Energy Institute; the Nigerian Association of Law Teachers; and the Nigerian Bar Association.

Damilola S Olawuyi
Professor of law, Hamad Bin Khalifa University
dolawuyi@hbku.edu.qa

Damilola S Olawuyi is a professor of law and holder of the UNESCO Chair on Environmental Law and Sustainable Development at HBKU Law School in Qatar. He is also chancellor's fellow at the Institute for Oil, Gas, Energy, Environment and Sustainable Development at Afe Babalola University in Nigeria. He is an independent expert on the United Nations Working Group on Business and Human Rights. He formerly served as an independent expert of the African Union's Working Group on Extractive Industries, Environment and Human Rights.

Damilola has published over 100 influential peer-reviewed articles, books and reports on energy finance, sustainable development law and extractive resource governance. He was formerly an international energy lawyer at Norton Rose Fulbright Canada LLP, Calgary, where he served on the firm's global committee on extractive resource investments in Africa. He has lectured on energy and environmental law in over 40 countries worldwide.

A senior advocate of Nigeria, Damilola holds a DPhil in energy and environmental law from the University of Oxford; an LLM from Harvard University; and an LLM from the University of Calgary. He obtained first-class degrees in law from Igbinedion University and from the Nigerian Law School.

John Paterson
Professor of law, University of Aberdeen
j.paterson@abdn.ac.uk

John Paterson is a professor of law at the University of Aberdeen. He has previously been co-director of the Centre for Energy Law; acting head of the School of Law; and university vice-principal for internationalisation. He coordinates Aberdeen's involvement in the North Sea Energy Law Partnership, which – together with the Universities of Copenhagen, Groningen and Oslo – offers an advanced LLM in energy law.

He has been involved in several international energy law projects in research, teaching, training and capacity building; and has provided consultancy to international organisations and expert advice in an international arbitration.

He is series editor (with Julian Webb) of the *Law, Science and Society* series published by Routledge-Cavendish. He co-edits (with Greg Gordon and Emre Usenmez) *Oil and Gas Law in the UK: Current Practice and Emerging Trends*, currently in its third edition, published by Edinburgh University Press.

Eduardo G Pereira
Professor of natural resources and energy law
egp.portugal@gmail.com

Professor Eduardo G Pereira is a worldwide-recognised scholar specialising in natural resources and energy law. He is a founding partner at the International Energy Law Training and Research Company and the International Energy Law Advisory Group. He has been active in the natural resources and energy industry for more than 15 years and is an international expert on oil and gas contracts and regulations. His experience in this area – both academic and practical – is extensive. He has practical experience in over 50 jurisdictions, covering America, Europe, Africa and Asia. He concluded his doctoral thesis on oil and gas joint ventures at the University of Aberdeen and followed this with postdoctoral research at the Oxford Institute for Energy Studies (University of Oxford), the Scandinavian Institute of Maritime Law (University of Oslo) and the Institute of Energy and Environment (University of São Paulo). He holds positions as a full-time, part-time, honorary, adjunct and/or visiting scholar in several leading academic institutions around the world. He is also a managing editor for the Global South Energy and Natural Resources Law Journal and an associate editor of Oil, Gas and Energy Law (OGEL). He is also the author and editor of several leading oil and gas textbooks. Further information about his profile can be found at www.eduardogpereira.com.

Peter Roberts
Principal, Cross Keys Energy
petro@crosskeysenergy.com

Peter Roberts is the principal of Cross Keys Energy, an independent energy consultancy. He is an oil and gas projects lawyer with 30 years of legal and commercial experience, working for oil and gas companies on acquiring, structuring, developing and financing upstream, midstream and downstream petroleum projects and also for governments on oil and gas sector regulatory matters.

He has worked extensively in Asia, Africa, Central and Eastern Europe and South America, and has previously worked in-house and as a partner in several international law firms. He also appears as an expert witness in energy sector disputes.

He is the author of several leading energy sector textbooks; is an honorary lecturer at Dundee University and a visiting professor of law at Austral University in Buenos Aires; and is the editor of the AIEN's *Journal of World Energy Law and Business*.

Chowdhury Ishrak Ahmed Siddiky
Associate professor, University of Asia Pacific
siddiky@uap-bd.edu

Chowdhury Ishrak Ahmed Siddiky has an LLB (Hons) from the University of Kent, United Kingdom and was called to the Bar of England and Wales from the Honourable Society of Middle Temple. He completed his LLM in energy law and policy at the CEPMLP, University of Dundee and his PhD at the same institution. Ishrak has worked as a consultant for various international petroleum companies and has written numerous books and articles in the areas of cross-border pipelines, energy security and energy law. He was also a visiting scholar at Cornell Law School, Ithaca, New York; and is an adjunct associate professor at the University of Asia Pacific, Dhaka, Bangladesh and deputy director of the South Asian Institute of Advanced Legal and Human Rights Studies.

Thomas Kojo Stephens
Senior partner, Stobe Law;
Senior lecturer, University of Ghana School of Law
t.stephens@stobelaw.com; tstephens@ug.edu.gh

Thomas Kojo Stephens obtained his BA in political science and philosophy (Highest Honours) from Emory University, US (Gates scholar), graduating *summa cum laude, phi beta kappa*. He obtained his LLB from the University of Ghana School of Law; his QCL from the Ghana School of Law; and his LLM from Cornell University, United States. He attended the University of Aberdeen (Commonwealth scholar) and obtained a PhD in petroleum law, policy and regulation. He is a senior partner at Stobe Law; a senior lecturer at the University of Ghana School of Law; a jurisdictional author for a number of international publications; an advisory board member of the International Energy Law Advisory Group; and a principal trainer at the International Energy Law Training and Research Center. He was vice-chairman from 2018–2020 of the Public Interest and Accountability Committee, Ghana's statutory body with oversight over petroleum revenue.

Kim Talus
Professor of European energy law, University of Eastern Finland Law School; James McCulloch Chair in Energy Law, Tulane University;
Professor of energy law, University of Helsinki
kim.talus@uef.fi

Kim Talus is professor of European energy law at University of Eastern Finland Law School and the founder and co-director of its Centre for Climate, Energy and Environmental Law. He is also the holder of the James McCulloch Chair in Energy Law at Tulane University and the founding director of the Tulane Center for Energy Law. Additionally, he is a part-time professor of energy law at University of Helsinki.

His extensive experience in research and consultancy has focused on international, comparative and European energy law. He has authored and co-authored more than 190 publications. Kim's work has awarded him many recognitions, including the Willoughby Prize in 2005 for outstanding article published in the *Journal of Energy and Natural Resources Law*. His research has also been recognised by the Court of Justice of the European Union.

He is the editor-in-chief of OGEL and a member of the editorial board for several journals, including the *Journal of World Energy Law and Business* and the *International Journal of Nuclear Law*.

Igor Tostes
Lead counsel, Equinor Brasil
igto@equinor.com

Igor Tostes has worked as a lead counsel in Equinor Brasil since 2021. Before joining Equinor, Igor worked for eight years in the energy department of Mattos Filho Advogados, providing legal support to oil and gas and energy industry clients, and advising on corporate, M&A, financing, contractual and regulatory law issues involving these industries. Igor spent one year at White & Case LLP's Houston office as a member of the Latin American Fellows Program – Energy, Infrastructure, Project and Asset Finance Group. He has been previously seconded as legal counsel to SBM Offshore, Enel Green Power and Rosneft Brasil. Igor holds a law degree from the Fluminense Federal University; a postgraduate degree in corporate law from FGV Rio; a master's degree in regulatory law from FGV Rio; and an LLM from the University of Chicago.

Jose L Valera
Partner, Mayer Brown LLP
jvalera@mayerbrown.com

Jose L Valera is a partner in Mayer Brown LLP's Houston office and a member of the global energy group. He focuses on domestic and international energy transactions and project development, with more than 25 years of legal experience representing oil, gas and electric energy companies throughout the United States, Latin America, Africa, Asia and the Caribbean.

Jose represents clients in a wide range of commercial agreements, including oil and gas exploration and production contracts, investment agreements, production sales, upstream development projects, transportation agreements, mergers and acquisitions, and joint ventures. He also has experience with onshore and marine terminal services agreements for crude oil and petroleum fuels. Jose drafts and negotiates project development agreements for thermal and renewable generation projects, operation and maintenance of power plants, fuel supply, financing, mergers and acquisitions. His LNG practice focuses on LNG liquefaction services, regasification services, development of regasification terminals, and purchase and sale of LNG.

Jose has JDs from the Catholic University of Peru and South Texas College of Law Houston and is a former member of the board of directors of the AIEN.

David Wood
CEO, Sanchez Wood Limited
david.wood@sanchezwood.com

David Wood has developed refinery projects in Brazil, Serbia, Russia, Poland and Bosnia.

He is currently CEO of Sanchez Wood Limited, his own consultancy firm; and CEO of Refinaria Atlântico Sul de Sergipe SA, a proposed 200,000 billion barrels of oil per day oil refinery.

David is a chemical engineer (BSc Hons, University College London) and has qualifications in contract law and banking.

Having worked at Bankers Trust Company (now Deutsche Bank) running the natural resources division for six years, David brings valuable banking and financial structuring experience to energy projects.

With 30 years' experience in general management positions in the oil and gas and banking industries, he has developed businesses and managed complex projects totalling $10 billion.

For the past 30 years, David has worked on developing refinery and related energy projects for diverse companies in Brazil, Morocco, Russia, the United Kingdom, the Philippines, China, Thailand, Poland, Kurdistan and the former Yugoslavia.

About Globe Law and Business

Globe Law and Business was established in 2005. From the very beginning, we set out to create law books that are sufficiently high level to be of real use to the experienced professional, yet still accessible and easy to navigate. Most of our authors are drawn from Magic Circle and other top commercial firms, both in the United Kingdom and internationally.

Our titles are carefully produced, with the utmost attention paid to editorial, design and production processes. We hope this results in high-quality publications that are easy to read and a pleasure to own. Our titles are also available as ebooks, which are compatible with most desktop, laptop and tablet devices. In 2018 we expanded our portfolio to include journals and Special Reports, available both digitally and in hard copy format, and produced to the same high standards as our books.

In 2021, we were very pleased to announce the start of a new chapter for Globe Law and Business following the acquisition of law books under the imprint Ark Publishing. Our law firm management list is now significantly expanded with many well known and loved Ark Publishing titles.

We are also pleased to announce the launch of our online content platform, Globe Law Online. This allows for easy search and networked access across firms. Key collections include the Law Firm Management Collection, Private Client and Energy and the Energy Transition. Email me at sian@globelawandbusiness.com for further details or to arrange a free trial for you or your firm.

Sian O'Neill
Managing director
Globe Law and Business
www.globelawandbusiness.com